NCAER | 1956 2017 QUALITY. RELEVANCE. IMPACT

INDIA POLICY FORUM 2016|17

VOLUME 13

EDITED BY

Shekhar Shah

Barry Bosworth

Karthik Muralidharan

NATIONAL COUNCIL OF APPLIED ECONOMIC RESEARCH

New Delhi

NCAER 60

SAGE

Los Angeles | London | New Delhi

Singapore | Washington DC | Melbourne

First published in 2017 by

SAGE Publications India Pvt Ltd
B1/I-1 Mohan Cooperative Industrial Area
Mathura Road, New Delhi 110 044, India
www.sagepub.in

SAGE Publications Inc
2455 Teller Road
Thousand Oaks, California 91320, USA

SAGE Publications Ltd
1 Oliver's Yard, 55 City Road
London EC1Y 1SP, United Kingdom

SAGE Publications Asia-Pacific Pte Ltd
3 Church Street
#10-04 Samsung Hub
Singapore 049483

Library of Congress Serial Publication Data applied for

Disclaimer: The papers and the associated comments represent the views of the individual authors and do not imply agreement by the Governing Body, officers, or staff of NCAER or by members of the IPF panels.

ISSN: 0973-4805
ISBN: 978-93-528-0000-1 (PB)

Published by Vivek Mehra for SAGE Publications India Pvt Ltd, typeset in 10.5/13 pt Times by Diligent Typesetter India Pvt. Ltd., Delhi, and printed at Avantika Printers, New Delhi.

INDIA POLICY FORUM 2016|17

VOLUME 13

NCAER 1956 2017 QUALITY. RELEVANCE. IMPACT

PURPOSE AND ORGANIZATION

This 13th *India Policy Forum 2016–17 Volume* comprises papers and highlights of the discussions at the India Policy Forum (IPF) held in New Delhi on July 12–13, 2016. The IPF promotes and commissions original economic policy and empirical research on India. It provides a unique combination of intense scholarship and policymaker engagement at the annual IPF Conference for reviewing such research, leading to its eventual publication in this international journal. The IPF commissions both original empirical research and policy-focused expert reviews, the latter themselves based on robust, original research.

The IPF is sponsored and organized by NCAER, the National Council of Applied Economic Research in New Delhi. The IPF started originally in 2004 as a collaborative venture between NCAER and the Brookings Institution in Washington D.C.

An international Research Panel of India-based and overseas scholars with an abiding interest in India supports this initiative through advice, active participation at the IPF Conference, and the search for innovative papers that promise fresh insights. An international Advisory Panel of distinguished economists provides overall guidance. Members of the two IPF panels are listed below.

Papers appear in the annual *IPF Volume* after revisions based on IPF discussants' comments, a lively floor discussion, and the editorial guidance provided by the IPF editors. To allow readers to get a sense of the richness of the conversations that happen at the IPF, discussants' comments are included here as delivered at the IPF, as is a summary of the floor discussion on each paper. The papers and the associated comments represent the views of the individual authors and do not imply agreement by the Governing Body, officers, or staff of NCAER or by members of the IPF panels.

The *Annual IPF Lecture* for 2016 was delivered on July 12th to a packed audience by Dr Arvind Subramanian, Chief Economic Advisor to the Government of India. Subramanian spoke on "India and the Global Economy Post-Brexit." The 2016 IPF Lecture can be viewed on www.ncaer.org.

In recent years the IPF has also featured an IPF Policy Roundtable that allows a timely discussion of policy issues around topics of current policy relevance but where no papers are presented. The 2016 IPF Roundtable focused on "The Challenge of Skilling India for Global Competitiveness". The names of the Roundtable panelists and the moderator can be found at the end of the Editors' Summary.

PARTNERS

NCAER gratefully acknowledges the generous support for IPF 2016 from HDFC Ltd, Reliance Industries Ltd, IDFC Ltd, State Bank of India, Citibank N.A. and SAGE. Their support reflects the deep commitment of the enlightened leadership of these organizations to rigorous, independent, economic policy research that helps promote more informed policy debates and evidence-based policymaking in India.

CORRESPONDENCE

Correspondence about papers in this *IPF Volume* should be addressed directly to the authors (each paper contains the email address(es) of the corresponding author(s)). All author affiliations in the papers are as of the IPF Conference. Unsolicited manuscripts are not accepted for review because the *IPF Volume* is devoted to invited contributions. Feedback on the *IPF Volume* itself may be sent to: The Editor, India Policy Forum, NCAER, 11 Indraprastha Estate, New Delhi 110002, or by email to ipf@ncaer.org. More information on the IPF is available on www.ncaer.org.

THE IPF TEAM

NCAER is responsible for development, planning, organization, and publication for the India Policy Forum. The Editors and IPF Panels are deeply grateful to the following NCAER staff for their dedication and hard work on the 2016 IPF:

Akansha Dubey	*Special Assistant to the Director-General*
Sudesh Bala	*Team Lead and overall coordination*
Anupma Mehta	*Editing*
Jagbir Singh Punia	*Publication*
Sangita Chaudhary	*Team assistance*
P. P. Joshi	*Hospitality and logistics*
Praveen Sachdeva	*Conference production and graphics*

Editors' Summary

The India Policy Forum (IPF) marked its 13th year of publication with its conference in New Delhi on July 12–13, 2016. The primary goal of the IPF is to promote original economic policy and empirical research on India. The annual IPF conference provides a unique combination of intense scholarship and commentary on the research papers commissioned by the IPF and a focus on their policy implications. The revised papers are published in this journal and benefit from a wide international readership. Over the years, interest in India has grown, to the point where there is now much more original research on India appearing in international economic journals. The IPF has also changed, making room for more policy-focused review articles that seek to define the best policy advice based on robust, empirical research. It has also added more roundtable discussions of key policy issues dominating the discussion of Indian economic policymaking and the economy in recent years. This journal edition of the *India Policy Forum* contains the five 2016 IPF conference papers, the comments of the formal paper discussants, and a summary of the floor discussion of each paper.

Exploring the Balance Sheet of the Indian Household

In the economists' models of theoretically well-functioning economies, households efficiently save and borrow to meet their lifetime goals. They are adept at using financial instruments to smooth consumption over the life-cycle and to insure themselves against adverse economic shocks. The balance sheet of the typical household is supposed to reflect these decisions at any given point in time. In reality, however, households may be inhibited from participating in the financial system for a number of reasons, including missing markets for particular instruments, fraud or malfeasance that generates trust gaps between the sellers and buyers of financial products, or high transactions costs that impede access, in particular for relatively poor households.

In this paper, Cristian Badarinza, Vimal Balasubramaniam, and Tarun Ramadorai describe and attempt to explain patterns in Indian households' balance sheets and present an integrated perspective of both their assets and liabilities. They use detailed micro-level data from the All India Debt and Investment Survey (AIDIS 2012) and draw upon a set of representative international household surveys for comparison purposes.

The paper makes four specific contributions: (1) It documents the composition of Indian household assets and liabilities along the life-cycle and across the Indian wealth distribution; (2) It compares these patterns to those of households in a range of advanced countries and China; (3) The authors find several attributes of Indian household finance that are exceptional in the international context and correlate these patterns with demographic characteristics; and (4) They find evidence that even after accounting for household demographic characteristics, considerable residual variation remains, which they connect with institutional factors including state-level variation in inflation uncertainty, financial access as proxied by the density of bank branch networks, and proxies for government-mandated participation in retirement savings plans.

The authors find that the average Indian household holds 77 percent of its total assets in real estate, 7 percent in durable goods, 11 percent in gold, and the remainder 5 percent in financial assets. Non-financial assets account for 95 percent of total assets, slightly more than the corresponding 91 percent for Chinese households. Within the space of non-financial assets, Chinese households, however, hold about 28 percent in durable goods and a negligible fraction in gold (0.4 percent). Compared to Indian and Chinese households, households in advanced economies hold lower fractions of wealth in real estate, retirement assets account for nearly one-fourth of total wealth, and almost all households have some financial assets and durable goods in their asset-mix. In India, only 65 percent of households where the head is younger than 35 years hold any financial assets. The participation rate increases for older households, but a significant part of the population (23 percent) remains outside the formal financial system, even as they approach retirement.

In most countries, real estate holdings (on the asset side) are matched by high proportions of mortgage debt (on the liabilities side). However, despite a high proportion of assets in real estate, mortgage debt in India accounts for only one-fourth of total liabilities. Only 4 percent of Indian households below 35 years of age have a mortgage loan, compared with between 10 percent and 48 percent in other parts of the world. In countries such as the United Kingdom, the authors find a pronounced increase in mortgage loan participation as household heads approach middle-age, and a swift reduction thereafter, while the Indian household participation rate is flat over the life-cycle and mortgages account for increasing shares of liabilities, beyond or close to the retirement age.

The role of other secured debt is similar between Indian and Chinese households and is also well below the levels observed in other countries.

However, Indian households stand out in terms of their heavy reliance on informal (i.e., non-institutional) sources of lending, as reflected by the preponderance of unsecured debt (55 percent of total liabilities) and a non-negligible role of gold loans (4 percent). India is the only country where the share of mortgage loans to total liabilities is lower than the share of unsecured debt across all age cohorts, reflecting the dominance of unsecured credit for all parts of the population.

Even after controlling for demographic characteristics, the authors find substantial residual variation in the ratio of gold to total assets, the ratio of pension funds to total assets, and the incidence of non-institutional lending. They are able to capture a significant amount of this variation using state-level fixed effects, which allows them to condition on any variation in economic and institutional factors at the level of states, potentially permitting inferences (to the extent that causality can be established) about changes to policy that might be of use in promoting better financial health among Indian households.

First, the authors combine the state-level share of gold holdings in total assets with state-level measures of inflation, and find that inflation hedging motives are relevant to explain the lure of gold, but mainly affect the intensive margin within the space of non-financial assets. Second, the puzzling absence of retirement savings becomes even stronger once they account for states where a higher share of the population is employed in the public sector, which suggests that formal retirement savings options seem to be related to labor laws that mandate investments in pension funds. Finally, exploiting state-level variation in the density of bank branches, they find that financial access is negatively associated with the share of non-institutional debt relative to the total level of household liabilities, which lends support to the hypothesis that increasing access to sources of formal debt could affect the behavior of households by facilitating better product choices and substantially decreasing the cost of debt service.

The paper's findings suggest that improving the quality of the Indian household's financial decision making will be a significant determinant of their lifetime outcomes. While the positive effect of financial education is widely documented, this is just a necessary first step, and best thought of as complementary to modern financial product design through nudges and default options. The largest untapped potential may, however, lie in the area of innovations in financial technology. Gaps in the use of financial services by Indian households appear to be opportunities for the future growth of household finance in the country. The challenge that remains is for financial markets to tap into this potential, and for the regulator to ensure that households benefit from fair competition in this emerging area while enjoying consumer protection that has the benefit of all that we know about smart regulation combined with financial technologies that were not available just a few years ago.

Measuring India's Recent GDP Growth

National statistical offices routinely change the base year of their national income accounts from time to time to capture shifts in relative prices and in the structure of the economy. In January 2015, India's Central Statistics Office (CSO) rebased India's national income accounts to 2011–12, also combining it with a shift in methodology to bring it closer to the UN's System of National Accounts 2008. But these changes triggered a storm of questioning and criticism when the new GDP series yielded growth rates widely different from the previous series and at variance with other high frequency macro indicators. To a large extent, the controversy continues to linger. Every new quarterly data release during the first 18 months since the revision appears to have raised fresh questions about the new GDP estimates.

In their paper, R. Nagaraj and T. N. Srinivasan unpack the analytical and data issues underlying the controversy. They first point out the changes made: (a) replacing GDP at factor cost with gross value added (GVA) at basic prices; (b) estimating the output of the private corporate sector (PCS) directly from annual company balance sheet filings with the government, switching thereby from the earlier "establishment" approach to a company approach; (c) using PCS data for estimating manufacturing sector GVA, thereby reducing the role of the Index of Industrial Production (IIP) and Annual Survey of Industries (ASI), the cornerstones of the previous method; (d) estimating output per worker for the non-farm, unorganized sector using in part a Cobb-Douglas production function; (e) transferring unregistered companies with annual accounts ("quasi-corporations") from the unorganized sector to PCS; and (f) replacing gross domestic saving and gross domestic capital formation with gross national saving and gross national investment.

The CSO has justified the new estimates claiming them to be benchmarked against the best international practices, based on newer methods and better datasets, and following UN System of National Accounts 2008 guidelines.

The authors point out that the changes have resulted in: (i) an absolute reduction in GDP by 3.4 percent in the base year 2011–12 as compared to the previous series; (ii) a higher GDP growth rate in 2013–14, with some sectors reporting positive growth rates now compared to their negative growth rates under the old series; (iii) a substantial, 11 percent higher share of PCS in the new GDP series raising it to about 35 percent, with the share of the unorganized or household sector declining by 11 percent to about 45 percent, and the share of the public sector remaining unchanged. Commensurately the private sector's saving and capital formation rates relative to GDP are also much higher in the new series.

The authors' primary concern is that the information accompanying these changes provided by CSO makes it very difficult to decipher whether the changes in GDP composition are the result of moving sub-sectors from one aggregate to the other or the effect of the methodological changes introduced in the new series. They address their concerns in two parts, a concern with the large number of legacy issues that could have been addressed in this major revision, and then a discussion of the changes and their likely impact on the new series.

The Indian national accounts, like many systems worldwide, use a mix of the three methods for estimating output, the production approach, the income approach, and the expenditure approach. This is particularly necessary in India because of its large unorganized sector, whose activities and output are often difficult to measure directly and can only be estimated using ratios derived from sample surveys. The authors feel that the new NAS has passed up an opportunity to address some of the long-standing legacy issues in this regard: (i) the absence of mutually consistent data on income, consumption, saving, and investment in the national accounts; (ii) the need to reconcile inconsistent data on household consumption expenditure between the National Sample Survey and the national income series; (iii) the desirability of publishing India's international trade data in gross and net value added terms to enable much greater understanding of global value chains; and (iv) the need to start nationally representative panel data sets to improve the accuracy of the sample estimates underlying the national accounts.

The paper points out that the controversy around the new series and GDP growth rates principally arises from three areas: measurement problems relating first to the private corporate sector, and second to India's vast unorganized sector, and third from the deflation procedures required to convert nominal values to real values to estimate growth rates. The authors suggest that changes in the estimation of the private corporate sector's output are at the heart of the controversy. Historically, the sector (more precisely, the non-financial private corporate sector) was small, its output coming mostly from a small number of large companies (accounting for most of the paid-up capital of the sector), and therefore easy to measure. These estimates were then scaled-up to the universe of registered companies using so-called blow-up factors.

The authors welcome conceptually the switch in the new series to estimating gross value added for the private corporate sector directly from annual audited company balance sheets required to be filed by all companies registered with the Ministry of Corporate Affairs (MCA). Out of a total of some 1.3 million such registered companies in what is called the MCA-21 database, about 5,24,000 filed their audited returns in 2011–12 and 2012–13 (this number has come down to less than half now). These companies accounted for 85 percent of the paid-up capital of the private corporate sector, so CSO maintained that any error in the blowing-up of estimates for the remaining 15 percent of companies would be marginal.

Despite what appears to be an advance, the authors stress that the use of the MCA-21 database has created problems. First, the database is incomplete and inconsistent, with little knowledge as yet about what fraction of the phenomenal growth in company registrations represents working companies. Whether a company files or not is their decision, so that any estimates based on this data would suffer from unknown self-selection bias. Second, the changing number of filers in the MCA-21 database every year would mean that the scaling up factors will have to change from year to year, though it is not clear if they are being changed.

The old national income series measured the output of the unorganized manufacturing and service sectors indirectly as a product of the point estimates of output per worker and the number of workers employed. In the new series, the unorganized sector's share in GDP has shrunk, the authors suspect, on account of a decline in the output per worker estimated as a weighted sum of the labor inputs of different categories of labor, with weights derived from estimating a nested Cobb-Douglas production function. The reason why the authors and others have found this result surprising is because the accepted view generally has been that the output of the unorganized sector is being under-estimated, but the new series is showing the opposite.

Finally, the authors report the difficulty analysts have had with understanding the measurement of value added at current and constant prices. Indicators reflecting the current situation, such as sales tax revenue in unorganized trade and service tax receipts for some services, are used for deflating current values. While it seems evident that a multiplicity of price indices are being used, there is not much explanation for their choice. This has been further complicated by the divergence since early 2015 between retail inflation measured by the Consumer Price Index moving upwards and the Wholesale Price Index contracting dramatically due to a decline in commodity prices.

The paper recommends conducting a statistical audit of the new series by a credible and independent body of experts. They also recommend that the MCA-21 database and the parameters used for blowing-up sample estimates for the universe of companies should be made available for researchers to verify the new estimates.

Early Childhood Health and Development in India

Despite substantial improvement over the past two decades, the health of India's infants and young children lags behind that of other countries at similar levels of development. Within India, there are substantial differences in health outcomes across states. In this paper, Achyuta Adhvaryu, Prashant Bharadwaj, and Sam Krumholz review and analyze India's experience. They first provide descriptive evidence of how Indian infant and child health outcomes have improved in recent years, as well as detailed evidence of disparities in these outcomes across space. Next, they provide a detailed overview of existing theories and empirical evidence underlying interventions aimed at improving the process of health and human capital formation in early childhood. Finally, they synthesize this existing evidence into recommendations in the Indian policy context.

The descriptive analysis of trends in infant and early childhood health yields two primary results. First, infant and early childhood health indicators in India have improved considerably over the past 30 years. Infant mortality has fallen from 142 deaths per 1,000 live births in 1974 to 39 deaths per 1,000 live births in 2010, while DPT vaccination rates have increased five-fold since 1984. However, when these gains are put in an international context they look less impressive. India's present-day infant mortality rate is still far worse than those of other Asian nations like China and Indonesia, and its improvement in terms of most health indicators is no better than that experienced by most other developing countries during this time period. In sum, there remains room for much improvement.

Second, there is enormous inter-state variation in mortality, vaccination rates, and child math and verbal ability across Indian states. For instance, Kerala has the same infant mortality rate as Mexico (12 deaths per 1,000 live births) while Madhya Pradesh has the same rate as Ethiopia (54 deaths per 1,000 live births). Similarly, while more than 95 percent of 8–10 year olds in Andhra Pradesh can recognize numbers, less than three-quarters of children in the same age group in Bihar have this ability. Additionally, although GDP/capita is a strong predictor of these state-level outcomes, it is not determinative; large differences between states still exist even after controlling for GDP/capita. These findings suggest that state-level policies may have significant impacts on the levels of infant and early childhood health. There may be scope for the more successful states to serve as templates for the under-performing states.

This descriptive evidence suggests that India has substantial room for improvement in child health and development outcomes. Accordingly, the paper next presents an overview of the theoretical and empirical evidence on early childhood health and human capital interventions from the economics and public health literatures. One of the most important theoretical concepts in this area is the idea of dynamic complementarity between existing health and human capital stocks, and subsequent health/human capital investments. Interventions aimed at raising an individual's health and human capital may be differentially effective depending upon an individual's existing level of health or human capital when receiving the investment. A major implication of this theory is that the timing of interventions matters; an early intervention that raises human capital will not only directly raise an individual's human capital, but may also make the individual more receptive to future human capital interventions.

A large number of empirical studies have shown that within a child's first 1,000 days, interventions can be extremely effective at remedying cognitive and nutritional deficits; in contrast, low stocks of health or human capital are much less responsive to investments later in life. As relates to health, these interventions include nutrition supplementation, and effective use of oral rehydration therapy for diarrhea and vaccinations. As relates to cognition, these include psychosocial stimulation and the provision of early childhood pre-school education. Following up samples from large-scale randomized controlled trials, researchers have shown that exposure to these types of interventions yields large long-term gains in addition to remedying short-term deficits. For instance, children in Jamaica exposed to stimulation and nutritional supplementation experienced 12 percent higher earnings later in life (Gertler et al. 2014). Similarly, a high-quality pre-school program for low-income American children had an estimated rate-of-return of 7–10 percent (Heckman et al. 2010).

Yet despite these examples of success, the authors stress that scaling a small-scale program with a proven record of success to the district, state, or national levels in India presents a number of new challenges that raise the probability of failure when the program is implemented at scale. Bureaucrats may fail to deliver the program successfully, either because their incentives are poorly aligned with the program's success, or due to managerial inattention. Beneficiaries may receive misinformation about the program's motives and benefits and refuse to take part. Political cycles may lead to fluctuating intensities of program implementation and follow-up. A large number of studies in the developing world provide examples of low take-up or failed implementation of technologies known to improve health and wellbeing in other contexts (Adhvaryu 2014; Banerjee, Barnhardt, and Duflo 2015; Miller and Mobarak 2014). As a result, they emphasize that designing the way in which an early childhood health or human capital policy is to be implemented is as important as the design of the policy itself.

The authors conclude with three recommendations. First, although focusing on traditional goals like infant mortality and childhood health is important, they believe it is essential that policymakers invest substantial resources in improving cognitive and emotional development in early childhood. Investments made in early childhood in these areas pay large dividends later in life, in many cases comparable or larger than early childhood health interventions.

Second, they argue that the implementation process is as important as the program itself. Policies often fail not because of design flaws but instead because they are not implemented in a way aligned with the goals of beneficiaries. Early childhood interventions should thus be chosen not only on the basis of their proven success, but also on their probability of successful intervention at scale.

Finally, they recommend a greater focus on measurement. This encompasses both empirical (including randomized) evaluations of existing early childhood programs in India such as ASHAs, *anganwadi* centers, and crèche schemes, as well as new surveys to measure existing levels of early childhood cognitive and psychosocial development in a representative way across India. While the authors do use India's only national panel data set that touches on these issues—the NCAER Indian Human Development Survey—they also suggest initiating a nationally representative survey on early childhood development similar to UNICEF's Multiple Indicator Cluster Survey. This new evidence will serve as an important foundation for building and appropriately targeting the early childhood programs necessary for India's children to thrive in the 21st century.

Six Puzzles in the Performance of Indian Agriculture

The agriculture sector in India plays a major role in the livelihoods of the majority of its population and will be critical if India is to adequately address major long-term challenges from food security to natural resource sustainability. Yet, a quarter century after India's historic shift to a more market-oriented economy in 1991, its agriculture sector continues to be buffeted by severe policy distortions. The paper by Shoumitro Chatterjee and Devesh Kapur raises some fundamental and troubling questions about the performance of Indian agriculture by highlighting six major puzzles related to prices, procurement, political economy, trade, productivity, and the near-absence of exit. The authors argue that these puzzles raise important policy issues and are all the more salient when viewed through the lens of a unified framework. By picking on these six puzzles, they hope to spur both more policy research that explains these puzzles and greater political attention to the evidence generated by the research.

The authors first highlight the high and stable spatial price dispersion of wholesale agricultural prices in the decade 2005–14 (others have found the same in retail prices). They document that this empirical finding is robust within states, within crops and even when controlling for quality. This observation is at odds with the Law of One Price, which would predict a decline in price dispersion following massive investments in rural roads and communications (via cell phone penetration) in this period. They find that 37 percent of the variation in log (real) prices is due to time-invariant district specific effects (like local yields), 20 percent is due to location-invariant aggregate time shocks (like global demand), 4 percent can be traced to differences in monthly rainfall across districts, and 39 percent remains unexplained. The residual time and location varying effects could be due to changes in connectivity, crop choice, or the expansion of welfare schemes impacting agriculture. They make a case for investigating the role of local market power of intermediaries in generating this spatial variation in prices.

The second puzzle they highlight relates to India's Minimum Support Price (MSP) policy for its public procurement of grains. While in principle it is a national policy meant to protect the incomes of all farmers, there is substantial variation (both across regions and crops) in its implementation. They show that farmer awareness about the MSP policy, a direct measure of the presence of procurement efforts by the agencies, varies both across states and within states. Expectedly, we also find awareness about the policy to be highly correlated with actual procurement. This geographical variation in procurement not only leaves farmers in certain areas more vulnerable than others, but it also exacerbates inequality. The authors hypothesize that the agencies try to procure at minimum cost and therefore concentrate efforts in high yield regions and find evidence for this. They further conjecture that procurement may be influenced by politicians to selectively channel resources towards their constituencies.

The third puzzle is a political economy one. While farmers' incomes have languished, they have been unable to leverage their sheer numbers into pressuring governments to undertake policies and programs that benefit them as one might expect in a democracy, and indeed as had been the case from the mid-70s to the late-80s. Why has there been so little collective action by farmers to press for more favorable policies and programs? The authors suggest that the growth in identity politics post-Mandal (the 1980 Mandal Commission was the genesis of India's vast affirmative action policies based on caste), and growing political competition at the local level following the passage of the 73rd Amendment to the Indian Constitution, may have led to a fragmentation of farmers' collective interests.

Fourth, they show that India produces excess of, and exports some commodities, which make intensive use of the country's scarce natural resources, especially water and land. This violates one of the central tenets of international trade theory—the Heckscher-Ohlin theorem. They argue that this distortion is being driven by the application of the Minimum Support Price policy to specific crops (paddy, wheat and sugarcane) in specific states. Massive power subsidies complement this distortion. They suggest that a general equilibrium analysis is required to measure the aggregate consequences because removing minimum support prices might adversely affect consumption. It is likely that international trade and free markets will equilibrate demand and supply, but they are concerned that they will also internalize environmental constraints or lead to an even greater rate of ground water depletion.

The large productivity gaps across space, i.e., the productivity level that can be reached conditional on natural endowments, forms their fifth puzzle. Why do these productivity gaps persist? What prevents the diffusion of efficiency/efficacy norms across space? The literature has conjectured that much of this is due to differences in local agriculture production functions, but they find little supporting evidence. Understanding this variation is important not only for improvement of farm incomes but also to understand sustainability issues such as long-run soil health.

Finally, they question why farmers do not exit agriculture. Exit would allow for land consolidation and increases in farm size would in turn allow for more investments and productivity. However, although agricultural incomes remain abysmally low and highly uncertain, and farmers could potentially earn a riskless stream of higher income by selling their land, exit is very low. The authors argue that the opportunity cost of not exiting is low and point to the paucity of other opportunities. The traditional avenue of exit from agriculture, in the course of structural transformation of an economy, has been employment in manufacturing. The implications of the paucity of employment opportunities in non-agriculture sectors highlight inter-sectoral linkages, which needs further research.

An overarching theme of the paper is that it is essential to study these issues in a general equilibrium framework because one policy has the potential of affecting many other margins, which could result in counterproductive outcomes. The issues and mechanisms highlighted in this paper, they argue, should form the core of any such framework.

India's National Rural Employment Guarantee Scheme

Ten years ago, the Mahatma Gandhi National Rural Employment Guarantee Act (MGNREGA)—which entitles every rural household the right to 100 days of minimum-wage employment per year—launched the largest workfare program in the world. The state-level public employment schemes—collectively referred to as National Rural Employment Guarantee Schemes (NREGS)—have received much attention from policymakers, politicians, and academics in India and abroad, and engendered much debate on their implementation and impact. In his paper, Sandip Sukhtankar synthesizes knowledge from the vast array of studies and guides the reader in weighing the evidence on various aspects of the program.

The paper begins with a description of the salient features of MGNREGA, including its main provisions and guidelines laid down by the Act, as well as facts and figures related to program implementation. One feature worth commenting on is the provision for transparency and monitoring, with much of the data being available online and "social audits" to promote accountability. The data tell us that the program is indeed large: in 2013–14, there were 121 million households registered for a job card, 2.2 billion person-days worked, costing about ₹370 billion. The trend in program statistics over its lifetime suggests that expenditure and participation on NREGS rose steadily as it scaled up from 2006 onwards, but both measures have declined somewhat over the last three to four years, possibly due to reduced demand, but also perhaps reduced corruption. In terms of corruption, while it is difficult to nail down precisely a country-wide measure of leakage, the best available evidence suggests that the fiscal losses to the government are in the range of, but smaller than, losses from India's Public Distribution System. From the point of view of the beneficiaries, payment delays and unpredictability may be even more important than any money skimmed off from wages.

The next sections of the paper review the literature on implementation and impacts, yielding four key takeaways. First, there is large heterogeneity in implementation, chiefly across states. One implication of this heterogeneity is that the impact of the program is seen mainly in the better implementing states. Another less appreciated implication is for the interpretation of what 'the program' entails: empirical studies are basically estimating the effects of the program combined with varying implementation quality.

Second, the word 'Guarantee' in the title is a misnomer, as access is rationed. This is true even in the best implementing states, and is true regardless of household income. Unmet demand for work is, however, highest in the poorest states, which seem to lack the administrative capacity to implement the program. There is no relationship between spending per capita or NREGS participation and the rural poverty headcount across states.

Third, while there is a lot of contention regarding the impact of NREGS, there are at least two results that stand out. One, the program seems to have increased rural private sector wages. Two, these higher wages for unskilled manual labor seem to have led to worse educational outcomes for older children. Evidence on other impacts is less comprehensive. In at least one state (Andhra Pradesh), there is some evidence that rural incomes increased. On migration, while it is likely that NREGS reduced short-term distress migration, not much is known about long-term structural transformation. Given the differing data sources, results, and issues with identification, it is difficult to conclude much about the impact of NREGS on civil insurgency or domestic violence.

Fourth, key questions pertaining to overall impacts on rural productivity remain unanswered. For example, little is known about the return on any public assets created, and consequently the labor efficiency impact remains unresolved. Although research on these questions might be difficult, given current standards for causal inference, intensive margin changes as well as improvements in implementation may allow us to make some progress on these subjects.

Two lessons emerge from the experience of doing research on NREGS. The first is to build in early evaluation prior to the rollout of large programs, which the current research environment makes possible. The second is to think harder about how data collection mandates will actually be implemented on the ground.

Sukhtankar concludes with the prospects for the near- and middle-term future of the program. Is NREGS a well-designed program that might perhaps be badly implemented but has scope for improvement, or a fundamentally faulty program that should not be expected to alleviate poverty? The answer to this question necessarily requires conjecture due to the lack of specific evidence, but two streams of thought emerge. The first is that the current state of infrastructure does not necessarily support a large-scale shift to cash transfers, given anticipated logistic and targeting problems. The second is that features of NREGS such as the creation of public assets, if found to be influential, may increase output in the rural economy beyond what might be possible via simple cash transfers.

In the interim, the author suggests that continued tinkering with NREGS implementation may have large benefits, and these modular changes to the program may allow for careful and rigorous evaluation. Ultimately, a balance is needed between central schemes and rules and allowing states to experiment to find local solutions.

The 2016 Annual IPF Lecture and IPF Policy Roundtable

Though not included in this Volume, the 2016 IPF featured *the 2016 Annual IPF Lecture,* delivered by Arvind Subramanian, Chief Economic Advisor to the Government of India, who spoke on "India and the Global Economy Post-Brexit." Subramanian focused on the growing backlash against globalism in the United States and Europe. He perceived it as part of a broader problem in countries that have experienced a marked slowing of economic growth and a widening of the income distribution. He pointed to the increased importance of immigration in Europe and the political pressures that it exerted on the movement toward deeper integration. If the pace of globalization slows in the future, can India succeed with an outwardly oriented policy of promoting exports, or should it emphasize growth of the domestic market? Subramanian did not see the two as being fundamentally in conflict, and called for continued emphasis on an outward-orientated strategy to build formal trade links with Europe.

Also not reported in this volume, another key part of the 2016 IPF was the *IPF Policy Roundtable* on "The Challenge of Skilling India for Global Competitiveness." The Roundtable panelists were Jayant Krishna from the National Skill Development Corporation, John Blomquist of the World Bank, Bornali Bhandari from NCAER, and Karthik Muralidharan from the University of California, San Diego: it was moderated by Shekhar Shah.

Materials on both the IPF 2016 Lecture and Policy Roundtable are available on the NCAER website, www.ncaer.org.

References

Adhvaryu, A. 2014. "Learning, Misallocation, and Technology Adoption: Evidence from New Malaria Therapy in Tanzania," *Review of Economic Studies*, 81(4): 1331–1365.

Banerjee, A., S. Barnhardt, and E. Duflo. 2015. "Movies, Margins and Marketing: Encouraging the Adoption of Iron-Fortified Salt", *NBER Working Paper 21616*, Cambridge, MA: National Bureau of Economic Research.

Gertler, P., J. Heckman, R. Pinto, A. Zanolini, C. Vermeerch, S. M. Chang, and S. Grantham-McGregor. 2014. "Labor Market Returns to an Early Childhood Stimulation Intervention in Jamaica," *Science*, 344(6187): 998–1001.

Heckman, J. J., S. H. Moon, R. Pinto, P. A. Savelyev, and A. Yavitz. 2010. "The Rate of Return to the High Scope Perry Preschool Program," *Journal of Public Economics*, 94(1): 114–128.

Miller, G. and A. M. Mobarak. 2014. "Learning about New Technologies through Social Networks: Experimental Evidence on Non-traditional Stoves in Bangladesh," *Marketing Science*, 34(4): 480–499.

CRISTIAN BADARINZA*
Institute of Real Estate Studies

VIMAL BALASUBRAMANIAM†
Säid Business School and Oxford-Man Institute of Quantitative Finance

TARUN RAMADORAI‡
Imperial College London

The Indian Household Finance Landscape§

ABSTRACT Using the most recent wave of the All India Debt and Investment Survey data, we describe and attempt to explain several important features of Indian household balance sheets. When compared with data on households in a range of developed and emerging economies, Indian households, on average, tend to hold a high fraction of non-financial assets with particularly high relative weights in real estate and gold, hold negligible retirement assets, and rely on non-institutional debt as their primary source of debt. These propensities are also evident along the life cycle, as well as at almost all points in the wealth distribution, and correlated with location (rural versus urban), education, and family composition. Controlling for demographics, substantial state-level variation remains in asset and debt holdings which is related to state-level factors including historical inflation volatility, the share of the population in public sector employment, and the density of bank branch networks. We discuss the potential implications of these results for policy.

Keywords: *Household Finance, Household Balance Sheet, International Comparisons, India, Gold, Indebtedness*

JEL Classification: *G21, N20, R21, R31*

* *cristian.badarinza@nus.edu.sg*

† *vimal.balasubramaniam@sbs.ox.ac.uk*

‡ *t.ramadorai@imperial.ac.uk, corresponding author*

§ The authors are grateful to Suyash Rai and Milan Vaishnav for sharing their state-level inflation dataset, to Hoang Minh Duy and Zhang Yunqi for excellent research assistance, and to Barry Bosworth, Rajnish Mehra, Nirvikar Singh, and conference participants at the 2016 National Council of Applied Economic Research India Policy Forum in New Delhi for comments.

1. Introduction

In theoretically well-functioning economies, agents efficiently save and borrow to meet their lifetime goals and perfectly smooth consumption over their life cycle (see, for example, Campbell 1987; Friedman 1957; Hall 1978). To facilitate any transactions that may be necessary to achieve these goals, the financial system provides instruments such as deposits, bonds, equities, and retirement savings accounts to allow households to accumulate and easily access assets, as well as mortgages, and other secured and unsecured debt instruments to enable borrowing against future income streams or pledged collateral. Optimizing agents resident in these hypothetical economies are adept at using these instruments to achieve their goals and to insure themselves against adverse economic shocks.

In reality, however, economies are far from this utopian ideal. Households may be inhibited from participating in the financial system for a number of reasons, including missing markets for particular financial instruments, fraud or malfeasance that generates trust gaps between the sellers and buyers of financial products, or high transactions costs that impede access, in particular, for relatively poor households. And even when households do participate in financial markets, the complexities of optimization, combined with limits to household cognitive capacity, can generate negative financial outcomes rather than the optimality promised in theory. While such potentially adverse consequences for household welfare are an important issue on their own, it is also worth noting that in models ranging from simple Harrod–Domar formulations (Domar 1946; Harrod 2007 [1939]) to more sophisticated formulations such as Lucas (1988), Romer (1986 and 1989), and Mankiw et al. (1992), household decisions directly affect a country's economic growth, when accumulated savings are transformed into productive investments in physical and human capital (see Deaton 1999 for an excellent survey).[1]

In this paper, we describe and attempt to explain patterns in Indian household balance sheets, using data from the latest wave (2012) of the All India

1. The international evidence suggests that domestic resources are particularly important in this context, as domestic saving and domestic investment rates appear to be highly correlated (Feldstein and Horioka 1980). Empirically, Prasad, Rajan, and Subramanian (2007) present evidence that a reduced reliance on foreign capital is associated with higher growth, which further lends credence to the reliance on domestic savings in emerging economies.

Debt and Investment Survey (AIDIS).[2] By interrogating these data, we hope to glean insights about the extent to which Indian households efficiently participate in financial markets to achieve their lifetime objectives, or may be inhibited in doing so by inadequacies of the supply side, or by a lack of optimizing behavior on the demand side. While we do not explicitly compare household allocations to the prescriptions of a model in this exercise, we provide some benchmarks for evaluation by adopting an international comparative approach (see Badarinza, Campbell, and Ramadorai 2016), comparing the balance sheets of Indian households to those of households in a range of other countries in an attempt to document similarities and differences. Guided by these differences, we construct hypotheses and explore the specific factors driving Indian household decisions using a series of simple empirical tests. We then consider a number of possible policy prescriptions arising from our results.

Our paper makes four specific contributions, which are as follows: (a) we carefully document the composition of Indian household assets and liabilities along the life cycle as well as across the wealth distribution; (b) we compare these patterns to those of households in a range of advanced countries, as well as China, using detailed micro-data from household surveys in these countries; (c) we find several attributes of Indian households that are exceptional in the international context (as we describe below) and correlate these patterns with demographic characteristics; and (d) we find evidence that even after accounting for household demographic characteristics, considerable residual variation remains, which we connect with institutional factors including state-level variation in inflation uncertainty, financial access as proxied by the density of bank branch networks, and proxies for government-mandated participation in retirement savings plans.

We find that the balance sheets of Indian households appear distinct from those in other economies in a number of important respects. Three

2. We use the AIDIS to document patterns in Indian household finance as several committees in India have looked into the nature of aggregate household savings using macroeconomic data available through the National Accounts Statistics and raised concerns about data gaps, measurement challenges, and estimation error (Kaur 2011; Rangarajan 2009), suggesting that the use of micro-data (of which the best publicly available source is AIDIS) will help provide complementary and possibly more accurate evidence. In addition, many important distributional questions can only be addressed using micro-data, especially to document the role of demographic characteristics in household financial decisions (for example, age, education, and wealth).

significant attributes that are unusual in the international context are as follows: (a) Indian households allocate a high share of their wealth to physical assets, and in particular, to gold; (b) a substantial fraction of Indian household debt originates from non-institutional sources, and there is an unusually high reliance (especially in a subset of states) on loans secured with gold; and (c) Indian households have amassed a comparatively low stock of retirement assets.

Of course, some of these features of Indian balance sheets are plausibly explained by broad factors such as the overall state of financial development in the country. For example, American and European households invest significantly more than households in emerging markets in financial assets, partly on account of their significantly higher discretionary and mandatory retirement asset holdings (in both defined benefit and defined contribution schemes).[3] Along the same lines, we find that the ratio of Indian households' physical asset holdings to financial asset holdings is broadly similar to that of Chinese households, with a substantial fraction (about 90 percent) of wealth in both countries held in real estate and other non-financial assets.

However, some of these patterns are difficult to explain by appealing to such macro-factors. For example, household gold holdings in India are exceptionally high when compared to those in China. This issue of excessive gold holdings has been a cause for concern among Indian policymakers for sound reasons. For one, there is the issue that much of Indian gold is imported, with important implications for the current account deficit.

Another important theoretical reason is that models in which savings predict growth connect savings with productive investments, which are more easily mapped to financial savings rather than to stores of value such as gold. One focus of our analysis, therefore, is to attempt to explain this puzzlingly high allocation to non-financial assets, leaving for future work an analysis of asset allocation patterns within the group of financial assets.[4]

While these facts describe the average Indian household's behavior, we also find that there is a great deal of cross-sectional variation in the composition of Indian household balance sheets. This cross-household variation

3. In India, there has been a long-standing problem of encouraging broad participation in pension schemes and incentivizing households not to liquidate retirement savings prior to formal retirement (see, for example, Shah 2006).

4. This is currently an active area of investigation. For example, Campbell, Ramadorai, and Ranish (2014) and Anagol, Balasubramaniam, and Ramadorai (2015 and 2016) explore Indian households' equity portfolio allocations using detailed micro-data, and Anagol and Kim (2012) study the impact of shrouded fees in the mutual funds market.

has a significant correlation with household demographic characteristics. For example, household allocations to physical assets decrease significantly with the level of education, but counterintuitively appear to increase with wealth. Within the set of physical assets, despite the fact that the share of wealth invested in gold falls as wealth rises, this is virtually entirely offset by an increase in the share of real estate in the portfolio, leaving the total physical asset fraction relatively unchanged. However, there is an effect of education, which is associated with an increase in the share of wealth allocated to financial assets and a reduction of borrowing from non-institutional sources. The role of education is a more important explanatory variable for the ratio of non-institutional borrowing to borrowing from more formal sources than the position of the household in the wealth distribution or the age of the household. We also find substantial variation in the composition of household balance sheets that is associated with household location (whether they are in urban or rural areas), and with the number of children in the household, which suggests the role of cultural factors in Indian households' savings and debt decisions.

Even after controlling for demographic characteristics, we find substantial residual variation in the ratio of gold to total assets, the ratio of pension funds to total assets, and the incidence of non-institutional lending. We are able to capture a significant amount of this variation using state-level fixed effects, which is useful, since it allows us to condition on variation in economic and institutional factors at the level of states. This allows us to establish interesting correlations and surmise (though without being able to claim causality in our essentially descriptive analysis) about changes to policy that might be of use in promoting better financial health among Indian households. The fact that regional factors play an important role in explaining the composition of Indian households' balance sheets also raises the possibility that there is intra-India variation in the cultural predisposition of households to make particular allocation decisions.[5]

An article of faith in the popular press is that Indian households hold gold because they perceive it to be an inflation hedge,[6] and we explore the extent to which such hedging motives explain Indian households' propensity to hold gold. It is worth noting that we do not take a stand on whether this perception is indeed accurate, while also noting that the literature has cast

5. For example, we find that gold holdings in southern Indian states are substantial, which accords with casual empiricism about the cultural and religious significance of gold in these regions of the country.

6. See, for example, *Livemint* (2013) and Adappa (2016).

considerable doubt on this view (see, for example, Erb and Harvey 2013; Feldstein 2009). Our empirical specifications use the fact that Indian states, over the period of study, are not a single integrated market for goods given the considerable variation in state-level taxation as well as numerous non-tariff barriers to trade including high transactions costs and the difficulty of establishing supply chains (see, for example, Virmani and Mittal 2006). This means that there is significant cross-sectional variation in historical inflation rates across Indian states. We find that state-level gold holdings ratios are associated with higher experienced inflation volatility, and that the relationship becomes stronger when we condition on households that experienced historical inflation during their working years, in an analysis similar to that of Malmendier and Nagel (2011). We also find that the cross-sectional variation in the impact of inflation volatility on gold holdings is somewhat offset by a corresponding decrease in state-level household allocation to real estate, meaning that the total impact of experienced inflation volatility on the physical asset holdings ratio is flat. This finding suggests that inflation hedging motives may be important for explaining the lure of gold for Indian households, though our results suggest that such motivations appear to mainly affect the intensive margin within the set of physical assets in the household's portfolio.

Our next finding is that household savings for retirement tend to be higher in areas where a higher share of the population is employed in the public sector. Employment in the organized sectors of the economy is governed by labor laws in India that also mandate retirement savings. Since data on the fraction of population engaged in the organized sectors of the economy across Indian states are unknown, we use the share of public sector employment in the economy as a proxy for total organized sector employment. While there are certainly other possible interpretations of this result, we view these findings as suggesting that marginal participation rates in retirement savings observed across different states may be driven by such compulsory participation requirements, suggesting that the international literature on the effectiveness of mandatory pension rules and formal default options on pensions savings outcomes (see Choi et al. 2003) may also be of great relevance in the Indian context.[7]

7. We also note that this finding could be upwardly biased, owing to the fact that private sector employees have access to the option of early withdrawal from the Employees' Provident Fund (EPF) scheme whereas government employees, over the period of study, did not have a prematurity withdrawal option from either the National Pension Scheme (NPS) or the Traditional Civil Servants Pension (TCSP). If so, this potentially strengthens the case for formal default options with no option for early withdrawal prior to plan maturity.

We then turn to the relatively high share of non-institutional debt in Indian household portfolios at the state level. We relate the state-fixed effects for this share, cleaned of household-level demographic variation, to state-level variation in the density of bank branches. We show that financial access as proxied by bank branch density is negatively associated with the share of non-institutional debt in the overall portfolio of household loans. While our specifications do not permit causality to be strictly established, they are consistent with the hypothesis that increasing access to sources of formal debt could affect the behavior of households by facilitating better product choices, substantially decreasing the costs of debt service, and allowing for an improved allocation of resources along the life cycle.

Our work is related to a number of previous papers. A relatively large previous literature using survey data focuses on the credit or liabilities side of the Indian household balance sheet, including household indebtedness, access to formal sources of credit (Burgess, Pande, and Wong 2005; Cole et al. 2013), and alleviating credit constraints (for most recent work using survey data, see Pradhan 2013). A number of authors have done excellent work on household savings using earlier versions of the AIDIS that we use here (see, for example, Divatia 1976; Subramanian and Jayaraj 2006; Vaidyanathan 1993) and have also documented the pattern of a high relative allocation to physical assets. However, the focus of these papers has tended to be on the contribution of household allocation patterns to broad distributional questions, including wealth inequality, in contrast with our focus on household finance, meaning that for the most part, the literature has not attempted to explain the patterns in Indian household balance sheets using demographic characteristics or other factors.[8] Moreover, we also compute estimates from a range of other countries in our paper, in an effort to contrast micro-data on households from these countries with the patterns detected in the AIDIS data. Finally, our work also forms part of the emerging literature on household finance in India, which has thus far tended to focus on and carefully document concerns related to consumer protection in Indian financial markets (Gaurav, Cole, and Tobacman 2011; Halan and Sane 2016; Halan, Sane, and Thomas 2014) and financial inclusion (Sane and Thomas 2015 and 2016).

8. Interestingly, while Subramanian and Jayaraj (2006) focus on wealth inequality across different categories of asset holdings, the paper does not take into account the fact that households choose the fractions of their total savings that they hold in different types of assets.

Our findings lead to a few potentially useful policy prescriptions. The first important finding is that even after controlling for a wide range of household characteristics, experiencing periods of high and volatile inflation, especially when young, is associated with households' propensity to hoard gold. The effect of this experience is considerable, comparable in magnitude to the effect of having children. The long-lasting nature of the impact of such experiences on asset allocation considerably strengthens the case for a strong inflation target to tackle inflation volatility at its source, in addition to strengthening the case for solutions recently put in place such as the RBI's gold monetization and gold bond schemes.

Our second important finding is that there is a strong positive effect of education on Indian households' allocation to financial assets, as well as a strong negative effect on their propensity to take on non-institutional debt, even after controlling for a range of demographic characteristics. This suggests that improving the quality of Indian households' financial decision-making will be a significant determinant of their lifetime outcomes. This could be achieved using a number of policy instruments, including consumer financial regulation and other targeted policy interventions (see Campbell 2016). However, there is clearly also a role for solving demand-side problems. Numerous authors have found a positive effect of financial education (see Lusardi and Mitchell 2009); however, this is just a necessary first step and best thought of as complementary to modern financial product design through nudges (Thaler and Sunstein 2008), peer information (see Beshears et al. 2015), and the design of default options (see Choi et al. 2003).

The largest untapped potential may lie, however, in the area of innovations in financial technology (see Karlan et al. 2016 and Philippon 2016). Gaps in the use of financial services by Indian households, their heavy accumulation of non-financial wealth, and intense reliance on high-cost unsecured debt appear to be opportunities for the future growth of household finance in the country. The challenge that remains is for the financial market to be able to tap into this potential by leveraging technology and for the regulator to ensure that Indian households benefit from fair competition in this emerging area. The remainder of the paper is organized as follows. Section 2 presents the data used in this paper, Section 3 characterizes the composition of Indian households' balance sheets, Section 4 explains the heterogeneity in patterns of allocation using data on household characteristics, Section 5 considers the relationship between state-level factors and residual state-level variation in household balance sheets, and Section 6 concludes.

2. Data

2.1. Macro-data and Micro-data

Before describing the household-level micro-data that we use in our analysis, we note that macroeconomic data estimate gross savings using a residual approach in the construction of the national account statistics and uses assumptions that often generate significant inaccuracies, especially when it pertains to statistics about the household sector. Furthermore, these estimates are often made under severe data constraints.[9] For instance, the total savings in cash on hand for the household sector is determined as a proportion of the total currency in circulation and is currently set at 0.93. This proportion has been used since 1985 to determine the cash on hand with the household sector. The CSO notes in its documentation that, "this proportion is likely to undergo change as soon as more data based on the survey results of the RBI become available."[10] These problems with macroeconomic data are well documented by various high-level committees. Both the sub-group on household sector saving of the Working Group on Savings for the Twelfth Five-Year Plan (2012–13 to 2016–17), Kaur (2011), and the High Level Committee on the Estimation of Savings and Investment set up by the Ministry of Finance (Rangarajan 2009) note that there are weaknesses mainly due to data quality, data gaps, and estimation problems with respect to determining aggregate savings (for the economy as a whole and for the household sector) in India.

9. Direct estimates of household saving and its composition are not available in India as it is a sector comprising not only households but also non-government, non-corporate enterprises of farm business and non-farm business such as sole proprietorships and partnerships, and non-profit institutions. India does not have income–expenditure surveys that normally form the basis of analysis for savings and investments, and such surveys are not conducted for all these components of the household sector in India. Household financial savings are calculated as the sum of annual increase in financial assets net of increase in financial liabilities. The financial savings of households are estimated as residuals from the flow of funds accounts, compiled by the Reserve Bank of India. The Central Statistical Organisation (CSO) estimates household investment in physical capital (using another residual method) and this is defined as physical savings. Net addition to fixed assets include: investment in fixed assets of construction and machinery, equipment, and change in stocks. The residual approach for physical investments proceeds as follows: The CSO estimates total physical capital formation and then deducts estimates of public and private corporate sector investments from the total. The remainder is considered physical savings.

10. See http://goo.gl/bByvID, accessed June 7, 2016.

This does mean that for one of the main issues that we consider, the ratio of physical to total assets (which we term the "non-financial ratio" in the remainder of this paper), macroeconomic and household data show different patterns. Having said this, the broad patterns are similar across the two sources.[11] Broadly speaking, India's aggregate savings rate is comparable to that of emerging economies such as Indonesia, Thailand, and South Korea and substantially higher than in most developed countries.[12] While the aggregate gross savings rate in the economy has been growing in the long historical context (see Mohan and Kapur 2015, for example), over the past several decades, this rate has levelled off at about 20 percent of GDP. When these savings are decomposed into those in physical assets (such as gold and real estate), as opposed to those in financial assets (in claims such as deposits, debt, and equity), a striking feature of the data is that Indian households have greatly favored physical over financial assets. To be more specific, in 2011–12, nearly 70 percent of aggregate annual household savings flowed into physical assets.[13] The ratio of physical to financial asset holdings (the sum total of historical accumulated savings) for the average household are much higher, reflecting the fact that this allocation of savings flow to physical assets is a long-standing issue.

The implications of this phenomenon are non-trivial. In every period, households allocate limited resources to different saving vehicles, some of which are non-productive and solely serve as a store of value (for example, gold). However, both the households' current income and welfare, as well as the productive capacity of the economy are determined by the accumulated stock of wealth, for example, the aggregate stock of household capital available for productive purposes. The current economic situation of Indian households, as reflected by their wealth holdings, is the product of decades of individual decisions taken within a wider macroeconomic

11. The differences in computing the non-financial ratio using micro and macro-data sources are similar to the discrepancy between per capita consumption expenditure estimated using National Accounts Statistics and the National Sample Survey (NSS) in India. For instance, see Ravallion (2003), Srinivasan (2000), and Sen (2000). Sundaram and Tendulkar (2002) seek to explain the discrepancy by looking into the consumption basket measured in micro surveys and document the differences with the macroeconomic data.

12. World Bank data on the saving rate in economies ranks India at 37th out of 164 economies in 2014. See http://goo.gl/scp5tP. However, this aggregate saving rate is much lower than that of China whose saving as a percentage of GDP stands at 50 percent (ranked 9th).

13. In 2013, press reports highlighted that the rise in the share of physical savings seemed to have stalled. For instance, see http://goo.gl/C7tkAg and http://goo.gl/crivp2. However, the levels of these shares are still significant.

context and strongly influenced by social norms and personal experiences. This paper proposes a disaggregated micro-level view of both wealth and liabilities that enables us to map the Indian household finance landscape and to understand the underlying factors that determine product choice and allocation decisions.

2.2. AIDIS Data

Our main data source for this study is the NSS's AIDIS that records asset holdings as of June 2012 for households in India.[14] AIDIS is a decennial survey conducted by the National Sample Survey Office (NSSO) since 1971, with a roughly 0.01 percent sample of the Indian population, through a multi-stage design that is adopted in all NSS data collection exercises.[15] We observe demographic information such as the gender of the head of the household, age, education level, the number of children, the household sector (rural/urban), and the location of residence (state–region–district). To exclude the possibility that outliers drive our results, we drop observations for which the household head is younger than 24 years of age.

Over and above demographic and household characteristics, on the asset side of the household balance sheet, this survey records information on land holdings, buildings, and other constructions owned, livestock and poultry, transport equipment, farm equipment, non-farm business equipment, financial assets such as shares and debentures, bank deposits, insurance, pensions and other financial assets, amounts receivable for services rendered, and gold holdings. While other surveys such as the India Human Development Survey (IHDS) contain information about participation or ownership of different asset types, to the best of our knowledge, AIDIS is the only data source that provides explicit valuation of all assets held by households in great detail.

Some of the assets in AIDIS are valued not merely by asking respondents what the value of the asset is, but by government records of these assets. For instance, to assess the value of land, AIDIS records land acquired prior

14. Liabilities of the household were recorded in June 2012 and June 2013 depending on the visit during which this information was recorded.

15. A stratified multi-stage design has a First Stage Unit (FSU), consisting of the census villages (as of the 2001 Census) in rural areas, and Urban Frame Survey (UFS) blocks in urban areas (as of the 2007–12 list). Further, within these FSUs, the "Ultimate Stage Units" (USUs) are households. Should any of the FSUs be large, an additional intermediate stage of sampling using sub-blocks (hamlet groups in case of rural areas) is used. For more details, we refer to the NSS (2012) Handbook on Survey Design and Definitions available upon request from the authors or directly from the Ministry of Statistics and Programme Implementation, Government of India.

to the survey year on a guideline basis: these are valuations obtained from *patwaris* (village government accountants) for rural areas and the registrar's office (where land transactions are registered) in urban areas. It is important to note that these valuations are, in general, the lower bound of the value of these asset holdings, as the market prices of land are almost always higher, and the registered prices of land transactions are often understated to avoid paying stamp duty and state government taxes. For buildings, a similar approach is adopted and floor area prices are computed using government registration records. Residential building values exclude the value of the land on which the building is constructed and are thus not inclusive of the value of land recorded separately. For all other asset valuations, the value as stated by the respondent for the household is recorded.

For our purpose, we classify financial assets to include shares and debentures, all types of deposits, saving schemes, annuity schemes, provident fund, pension fund, NPS, other contributory funds, and payments receivable by the household. Likewise, non-financial assets include real estate assets (including land and buildings), durable assets and equipment (including livestock and poultry, transport equipment, agricultural machinery, non-farm business equipment),[16] and finally holdings of gold/bullion.[17] The survey also provides the sampling weight of each observation. The empirical measure of interest is the non-financial ratio and its sub-components, that is, the fraction of total assets that are held in non-financial, physical form, and in categories such as real estate and gold. Although this is the best source of data on the asset composition of households in India, there are some important limitations to keep in mind while interpreting the data. For example, the valuations of real estate and buildings are likely to be understated by official sources across the distribution and not just for one or the other household.[18] As reiterated in Jayadev, Motiram, and Vakulabharanam (2007) and Brandolini et al.

16. Business assets are included at market value and no residual value is attached to goodwill and other non-tangible equity.

17. Although the survey collects information on gold and bullion, and classifies them as "financial" assets, our rationale behind this classification is also based on the liquidity in the asset market to which each asset belongs. Gold in India is physically held and not traded frequently.

18. The extent to which asset holdings in land, buildings, and gold are understated is difficult to assess for lack of alternate and better sources of information on such asset holdings. Having said that, Subramaniam and Jayaraj (2006) document that it is likely that some households (especially in the upper tail of the wealth distribution) understate their real estate holdings for fear of being reported for potential tax implications.

(2004), unless conscious efforts are made to oversample the wealthy, the extent of financialization of wealth will be misrepresented.[19]

Turning to liabilities, all types of personal liabilities are captured as amounts outstanding in June 2012. There are two broad categories of loans: secured and unsecured. Secured loans cover the following collateral types: surety security or guarantees by third party, crops, immovable property, gold/bullion/ornaments, shares of companies, government securities, insurance policies, and agricultural commodities. For each loan, we also know the type of the originating agency, which allows us to classify debt holdings as institutional (originated by government agencies, cooperative societies, banks, insurance companies, bank-linked self-help groups, non-bank financial companies) and non-institutional (originated by landlords, agricultural and professional moneylenders, input suppliers, relatives and friends, doctors, lawyers, and other professionals).

2.3. International Micro-data

We construct analogous measures for other countries for international comparison. We use the China Household Finance Survey (CHFS; 2012); the Household, Income and Labour Dynamics in Australia (HILDA) Survey (2010); the UK Wealth and Assets Survey (WAS; 2012); the Eurosystem's Household Finance and Consumption Survey (HFCS; 2010) for Germany; and the US Survey of Consumer Finances (SCF; 2010).[20] It is important to note that different surveys cover different asset categories and with different degrees of precision. To ensure comparability across countries and consistency with the structure of the Indian dataset, we pool asset categories with similar features.

One notable difference between India, China, and the remaining countries concerns holdings of private retirement savings in defined-contribution accounts. In the US, the UK, Australia, and Germany, such products have been robust fixtures of financial markets for decades. Most of the population relies at least partially on such private products to finance consumption in retirement, and respective household surveys adequately account for this observation. On the contrary, defined-contribution savings accounts are only held by a small part of the population both in China and India.

19. Income levels are not adequately captured by the survey. We use the age of the household head and their highest completed education level as proxy measures to capture the evolution of income along the life cycle and the distribution of income across households.

20. The US SCF was the first to capture detailed categorization of household balance sheets on a large scale and for representative cross-sections of the population. In this study, we report results based on the 2010 wave, which is the closest point in time to ensure comparability with the Indian micro-level data.

2.4. India: State-level Data

The state-level inflation data for this study is drawn from the Labour Bureau and uses the consumer price index (CPI) (Agricultural Workers [AW]) inflation as representative for all sampled households.[21] The correlation between CPI (AW) and CPI (Industrial Workers [IW]) is high at 0.92 for the period during which the data is available. Since CPI (AW) is available for a longer time period to capture volatility experience, we use CPI (AW) for analysis. Finally, we measure financial access by using the Branch Banking Statistics of the RBI, in particular its Table 3, "State/Union Territory-wise Number of Branches of Scheduled Commercial Banks and Average Population per Bank Branch."

3. International Comparative Approach

3.1. The Structure of the Household Balance Sheet

We begin by comparing the average allocations of household assets across different countries in Panel A of Figure 1. In India, the average household holds 77 percent of its total assets in real estate (which includes residential buildings, buildings used for farm and non-farm activities, constructions such as recreational facilities, and rural and urban land), 7 percent in other durable goods (such as transportation vehicles, livestock and poultry, agricultural machinery, and non-farm business equipment), 11 percent in gold, and the residual 5 percent in financial assets (such as deposits and savings accounts, publicly traded shares, mutual funds, life insurance, and retirement accounts). Non-financial assets, therefore, account for 95 percent of the household balance sheet, which is only slightly higher than the corresponding 91 percent for Chinese households. However, the average Chinese household has a relatively lower share of real estate wealth (62 percent), a higher share of durable assets (28 percent), and negligible amounts of gold (0.4 percent). Furthermore, household allocation choices are very different in India and China when compared with more advanced economies. On average, holdings of real estate account for low fractions of wealth in countries such as the US (44 percent) and particularly Germany (37 percent). Instead, retirement assets account for relatively large shares of wealth in Australia (23 percent) and the UK (25 percent).

Panel B of Figure 1 presents the value-weighted average allocations of household assets across countries. Value-weighted quantities are calculated

21. We thank Suyash Rai and Milan Vaishnav for providing us with the cleaned monthly CPI (AW) series for each state by taking the average of all centers available in each state.

FIGURE 1. Allocation of Household Wealth

In this figure, we compare the average allocations of household assets across countries. The data sources are the AIDIS (2012 wave), the Eurosystem's Household Finance and Consumption Survey (HFCS), the US SCF (2010 wave), the CHFS (2012 wave), the Australian HILDA (2010 wave), and the UK WAS (2012 wave). For consistency, in the CHFS, we classify business loans that originated with banks as secured loans and informal private loans as unsecured. In Panel A, we compute averages across households using population weights, as indicated in each survey. Additionally, in Panel B, we present the value-weighted averages across households.

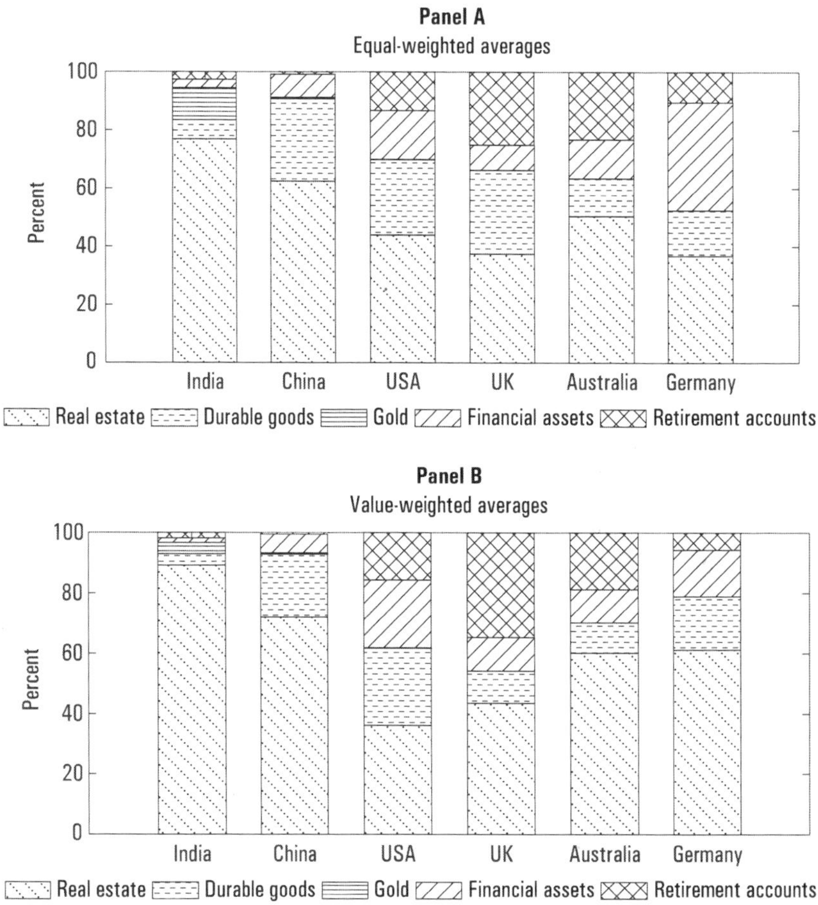

by summing up the different types of assets across all surveyed households, appropriately weighted to ensure that the result is representative for the entire population. The resulting ratios of financial and non-financial assets relative to the sum total of household wealth, therefore, reflect the aggregate composition of asset holdings for the country as a whole. They are, however, unrepresentative of the way in which the total wealth of the country is distributed among the population. That being said, the resulting pattern is quite similar to the equally weighted average allocations and suggests that Indian and Chinese households are heavily skewed toward real estate assets in their wealth composition, in contrast with the greater prevalence of financial assets in developed economies. The overall value-weighted non-financial assets ratio (the sum of real estate, durable goods, and gold holdings relative to total assets) is highest in India (96.6 percent) and only slightly lower in China (93.3 percent). At the other extreme, non-financial assets account for only 54.2 percent of total household wealth in the UK. Despite high rates of home ownership, which are also partially stimulated by government intervention (such as in the US), the overall role of real estate remains lower in advanced economies.

Households in advanced economies hold slightly more financial assets than their Indian counterparts, but perhaps more importantly, they accumulate sizeable amounts of funds in retirement accounts over the course of their lifetimes. The German case illustrates the substitution effect between public and private pension systems particularly well. Since the retirement system is mostly based on state-sponsored defined-benefit pensions, households in Germany only save small amounts in private retirement accounts and instead decide to invest larger amounts in financial assets such as sight deposits, government bonds, publicly traded shares, and mutual funds.

Turning to the liabilities side of the household balance sheet, in most countries, real estate holdings are financed through secured debt (that is, mortgages). Panel A of Figure 2 reports the average allocation of liabilities across all households that carry a positive amount of debt at the date of the survey. Mirroring the dominance of real estate as the dominant component of wealth, we find that mortgage loans are the largest liability of households in China, the US, the UK, and Australia. In these countries, the average household's mortgage holdings account for close to 60 percent of their total debt exposure. Germany is an exception to this rule (the share of mortgage debt is 44 percent), which is not surprising, given the low home ownership rate and the relative preference for renting over owning in the German population.

India stands out in a number of ways. Despite the prominent role of non-financial assets in the household balance sheet, mortgage loans account for only a small part of total liabilities (23 percent), and the role of other secured debt (such as vehicle loans and instalment credit for durable goods) is well below the levels observed in other countries, except China. Instead, most debt is unsecured (55 percent), which as we will see, also reflects the predominant reliance of Indian households on informal sources of lending. We also document a non-negligible role for gold loans (4 percent), which

FIGURE 2. Allocation of Household Liabilities

In this figure, we compare the average allocations of household liabilities across countries. We restrict the samples to observations for which total liabilities are positive. The data sources are the AIDIS (2012 wave), the Eurosystem's HFCS, the US SCF (2010 wave), the CHFS (2012 wave), the Australian HILDA (2010 wave), and the UK WAS (2012 wave). For consistency, in the CHFS, we classify business loans originated with banks as secured loans and informal private loans as unsecured. In Panel A, we compute averages across households using population weights, as indicated in each survey. Additionally, in Panel B, we present the value-weighted averages across households.

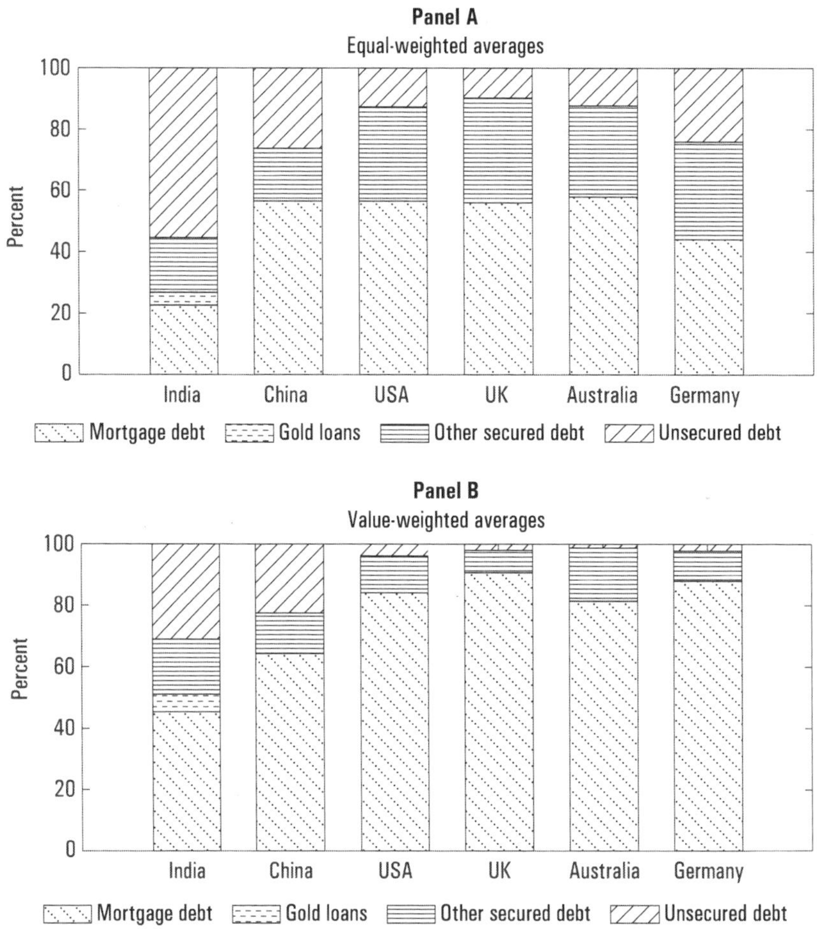

are a unique feature of the Indian market and absent from other countries. These conclusions are also apparent when averages are computed by value weighting (see Panel B of Figure 2), which suggests that for India and China, unsecured debt and gold loans also matter in the aggregate. Quantitatively, the two categories of loans account for 23 percent of total debt in China and 35 percent in India, while they play a negligible role in the financial systems of developed countries (except in the US, where households rely relatively more on credit card debt for daily expenses and purchases of long-lived consumer goods).

These patterns mask a significant heterogeneity of decisions along the life cycle and across the wealth distribution. We next analyze this aspect of the data.

3.2. Decisions along the Life Cycle

Figure 3 reports the fractions of households that participate in asset and debt markets, by age of the household head. Panel A of the figure suggests that in developed countries, almost all households have positive amounts of financial assets and durable goods. In contrast, in India, only 65 percent of households where the head is younger than 35 years hold any financial assets. The participation rate increases to 77 percent for more mature households, but remains well below the one observed in developed countries, where close to all households own at least one bank account and use formal financial products as the preferred means of saving. In China, the pattern is reversed: young cohorts are more likely to hold financial assets, even relative to their Indian counterparts, but the participation rate decreases to 52 percent for older households and retirees. This reflects the very limited access to formal banking for large parts of the Chinese population, in particular in rural areas (see Gan et al. 2012).

In both China and India, the rate of participation in land and housing assets is 78 percent for the lowest age cohort, and increases to 95 percent for people close to retirement. More mature households are generally more likely to own real estate in all countries, but the upward-sloping life cycle profiles are much more pronounced in Australia, the UK and the US, where only 40–50 percent of young households own any land or housing. Germany is also an extreme case in this regard. The participation rate of households with heads below 35 years of age is as low as 19 percent and only reaches 67 percent for middle-aged cohorts.

Similar to the retirement asset puzzle that was widely documented in the US (and unlike in countries such as the UK, Australia, Germany, and even China), Indian households do not appear to reduce their holdings of real estate as they pass retirement age. This is probably the consequence of the prevalence of multi-generational households, in which land and residential properties constitute a significant share of bequests.

While these variations in behavior may seem striking, we note that home ownership can potentially have very different meanings in India and China relative to the other countries that we consider. Land is scarce and construction activity is expensive in developed countries, which leads to a natural threshold in terms of the type of buildings that can serve as residential property. In India and China, the urbanization rate is much lower, rental markets are virtually absent, and agricultural work is widely prevalent. People are, therefore, more likely to have legal or quasi-legal ownership status over the dwelling used as accommodation, such as a family farm, shop-house, workshop, or warehouse, either within or outside the village/town.

Panel B of Figure 3 shows clear trends in credit market participation rates for developed countries because down payment requirements and relatively large house prices prevent households from taking mortgage loans early in life, the participation profiles are upward sloping for age cohorts below 50 years; as they approach retirement age, property loans are paid off and the extent of home equity extraction is on aggregate too low to offset this pattern. For example, in the UK, the participation rate rises from 48 percent for the youngest cohort to 62 percent in middle age and decreases to 6 percent after retirement. This pattern is slightly less pronounced in the US and China, albeit probably for different reasons. The home ownership rate is high in the US even for older cohorts, and the mortgage loan remains the primary financing vehicle for house purchase. In China, the urbanization process has accelerated during recent years and house prices have been rising strongly, which makes it more difficult for younger households to amass enough savings to meet down payment requirements.

The case of India is quite different from all other countries, primarily because of a very significant difference in magnitudes. First, only 4 percent of Indian households with heads below 35 years of age have a mortgage loan, which is lower relative to their counterparts in developed countries (between 10 percent and 48 percent) and China (27 percent). Second, the participation trend is positive across life cycle groups, suggesting significant development potential in the market, once borrowing constraints are relaxed for young and middle-aged households. Third, the participation rate of old households and retirees is comparable to the ones prevalent in Australia and the UK. This suggests relatively higher financial burdens toward the end of life, probably reflecting intergenerational transfers. The same striking difference obtains when looking at other types of secured debt. Indian and Chinese households seem generally much less likely to use debt finance for durable assets such as transportation vehicles, which is very different from the behavior of people in developed countries, especially at young

FIGURE 3. Participation in Asset and Debt Markets along the Life Cycle

This figure reports the shares of the population that holds positive amounts of different assets and debt classes. The data sources are the AIDIS (2012 wave), the Eurosystem's HFCS (2010 wave), the US SCF (2010 wave), the CHFS (2012 wave), the Australian HILDA (2010 wave), and the UK WAS (2012 wave). For consistency, in the CHFS we classify business loans originated with banks as secured loans and informal private loans as unsecured. We compute averages across households using population weights, as indicated in each survey.

Panel A

The assets side of the household balance sheet

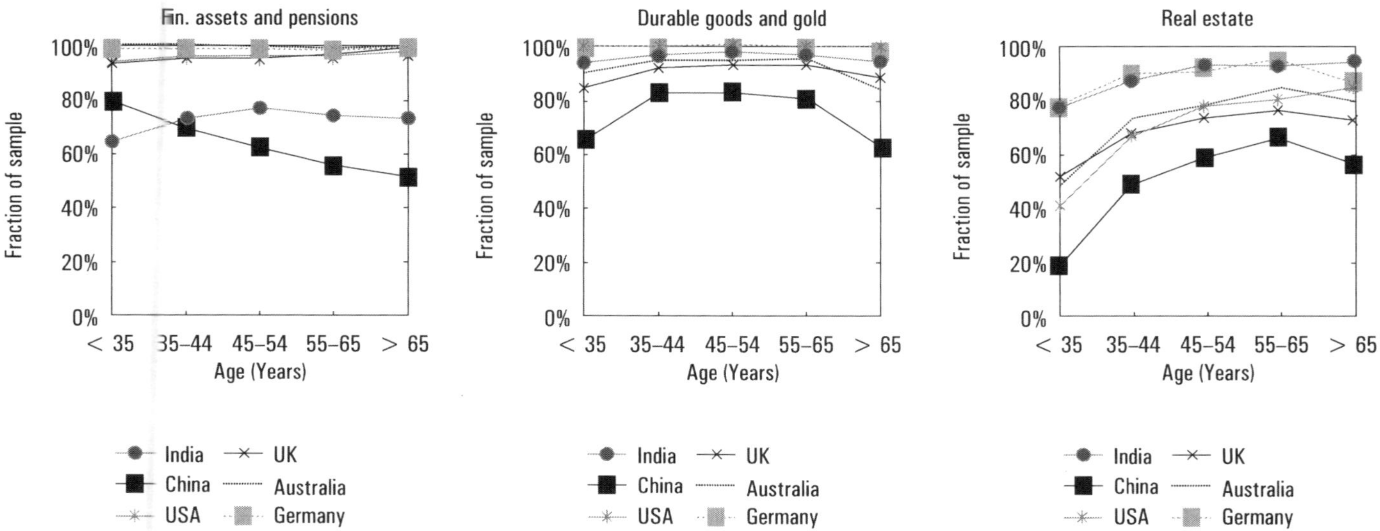

Panel B

The liabilities side of the household balance sheet

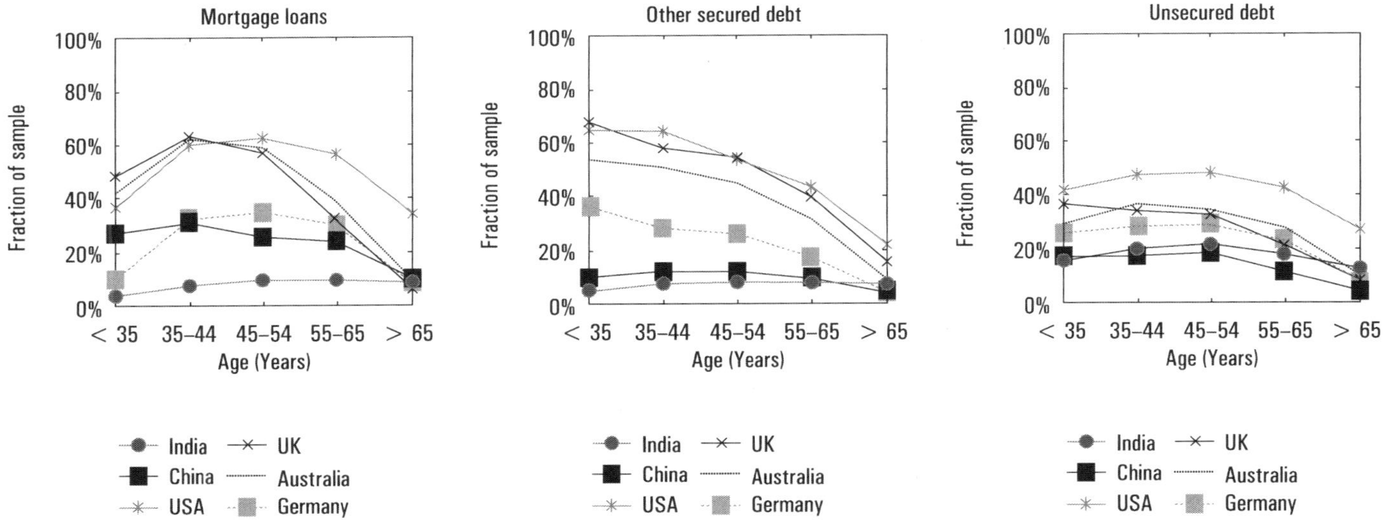

ages. Finally, the use of unsecured debt is also atypical in India and China. In particular, in these countries, young households are more likely to have unsecured debt, unlike in the other countries where instruments such as credit cards, overdraft facilities, and other instalment loans are equally likely to be used by all age groups.

In Figure 4, we turn to analyzing the actual role played by different asset and debt categories in the overall structure of the household balance sheet. Panel A of the figure shows that households of all ages in both India and China have low savings in the form of both financial assets and retirement accounts. For the average household in these countries, financial assets account for between 3.6 percent and 13.3 percent of total asset holdings. In contrast with the more advanced economies, a large fraction of the wealth of young households in India and China is in the form of durable goods and gold (33 percent in China and 25 percent in India), and most of their wealth, as they approach retirement, is comprised of land and housing (65 percent in China and 84 percent in India).

In Panel B of Figure 4, we show that for households in developed countries, the share of mortgage debt relative to total liabilities follows a hump-shaped pattern along the life cycle. This observation is not surprising, given that very young and very old households have lower access to the market and may use alternative financing vehicles such as secured leasing arrangements and instalment loans. In China, the pattern is reversed, mostly reflecting the high rates of home ownership in retirement. India is exceptional in this context—it is the only country in which the share of mortgage loans relative to total liabilities is lower than the share of unsecured debt across all age cohorts. Moreover, unlike in other countries, in India, mortgages account for an increasing share of total liabilities as people approach retirement age.

3.3. Decisions across the Wealth Distribution

In Figure 5, we study participation rates for groups of households sorted in increasing order of their holdings of gross assets, with each group representing 20 percent of the sample. Panel A of the figure confirms the significant variation in magnitudes between participation rates across countries. In Australia, the UK, the US, and Germany, the use of financial instruments is pervasive across all parts of the population. In India, only 55 percent of the poorest and 90 percent of the richest households hold financial assets. Similarly, in China, 40 percent of the poor and 88 percent of the rich participate.

As regards non-financial assets, one particular finding stands out. At the bottom end of the wealth distribution, 60 percent of Indian and Chinese households have ownership over land or buildings, while in Germany,

FIGURE 4. Allocation of Household Assets and Liabilities Along the Life Cycle

This figure reports the average shares of different assets and debt classes, relative to total household wealth and total household liabilities, respectively. The data sources are the AIDIS (2012 wave), the Eurosystem's HFCS (2010 wave), the US SCF (2010 wave), the CHFS (2012 wave), the Australian HILDA (2010 wave), and the UK WAS (2012 wave). For consistency, in the CHFS, we classify business loans originated with banks as secured loans and informal private loans as unsecured. We compute averages across households using population weights, as indicated in each survey.

Panel A

The assets side of the household balance sheet

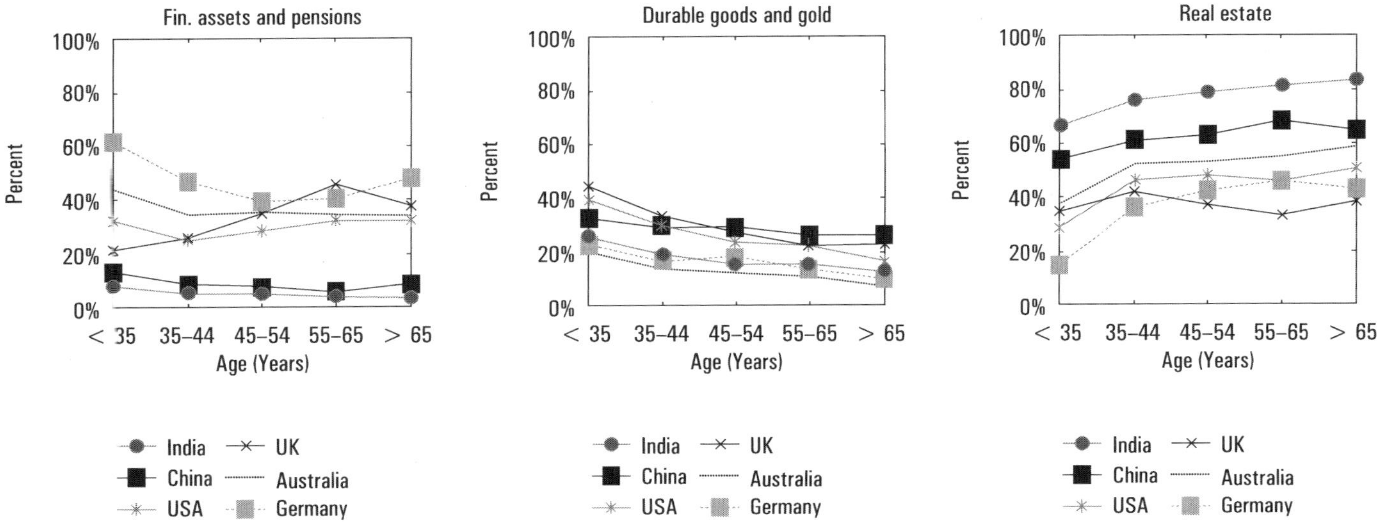

(Figure 4 Continued)

(Figure 4 Continued)

Panel B

The liabilities side of the household balance sheet

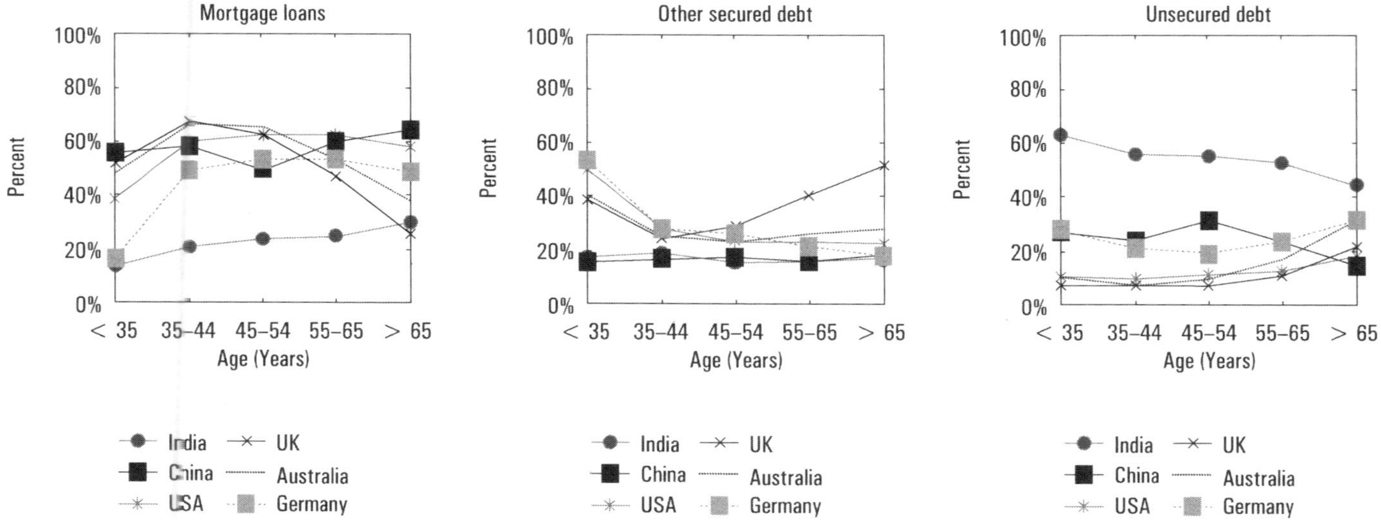

the UK, and Australia, this number is less than 1 percent. Even in the US, it rises to only around 5 percent. At least part of this observation can be attributed to the very different nature of what is considered and recorded as ownership of real estate across these countries.

The average value of the main residence in the bottom quintile group of Indian households is equal to ₹22,000, which is significantly lower than the lowest percentile of the value of the main residence in Germany (₹15 lakh) or the US (₹3.7 lakh). That having been said, our results show that almost all of the overall difference in the allocation of household wealth between India, China, and the other developed countries is driven by households in the lowest two quintile groups of the wealth distribution, that is, the 40 percent of people with the lowest amounts of gross assets.

Turning to the liabilities side in Panel B of Figure 5, we note a pronounced substitution effect within the pool of available secured debt products across all developed countries. Relatively poorer households in the credit market tilt toward loans secured with assets such as vehicles or long-term consumer goods (between 35 percent and 53 percent). In contrast, richer households are much more likely to participate in the market for mortgage loans (between 45 percent and 68 percent), which is also reflected in their higher rate of home ownership. However in India, very few households have mortgage loans outstanding and it is only for the very rich that the rate of mortgage indebtedness rises significantly (18 percent), albeit remaining much lower than that in developed countries.

In Figure 6, we look at the assets and liabilities of households relative to their total amounts of wealth and total debt exposure, respectively. Panel A of the figure shows that despite more than half of Indian and Chinese households participating in financial markets, the actual amounts of financial assets and pensions account for a negligible portion of their total balance sheet (between 11.8 percent for the poor and 3.7 percent for the rich in India, and between 11.7 percent for the poor and 6.8 percent for the rich in China). Instead, we observe a pronounced substitution effect between durable goods, gold, and real estate. Poor households own more of the former two assets, and as they grow richer, they appear to move away from these assets and toward real estate. This pattern is partially consistent with the behavior of households in the UK, the US, Germany, and Australia, though in these countries, as households grow richer, they also tend to move toward financial and away from non-financial assets.

Panel B of Figure 6 reports the average allocation of liabilities across different forms of credit, for households that participate in the credit market, that is, those with positive amounts of debt. The debt allocation pattern

FIGURE 5. Participation in Asset and Debt Markets Across the Wealth Distribution

This figure reports the shares of the population that holds positive amounts of different assets and debt classes. The data sources are the AIDIS (2012 wave), the Eurosystem's HFCS (2010 wave), the US SCF (2010 wave), the CHFS (2012 wave), the Australian HILDA (2010 wave), and the UK WAS (2012 wave). For consistency, in the CHFS, we classify business loans that originated with banks as secured loans and informal private loans as unsecured. We compute averages across households using population weights, as indicated in each survey.

Panel A

The assets side of the household balance sheet

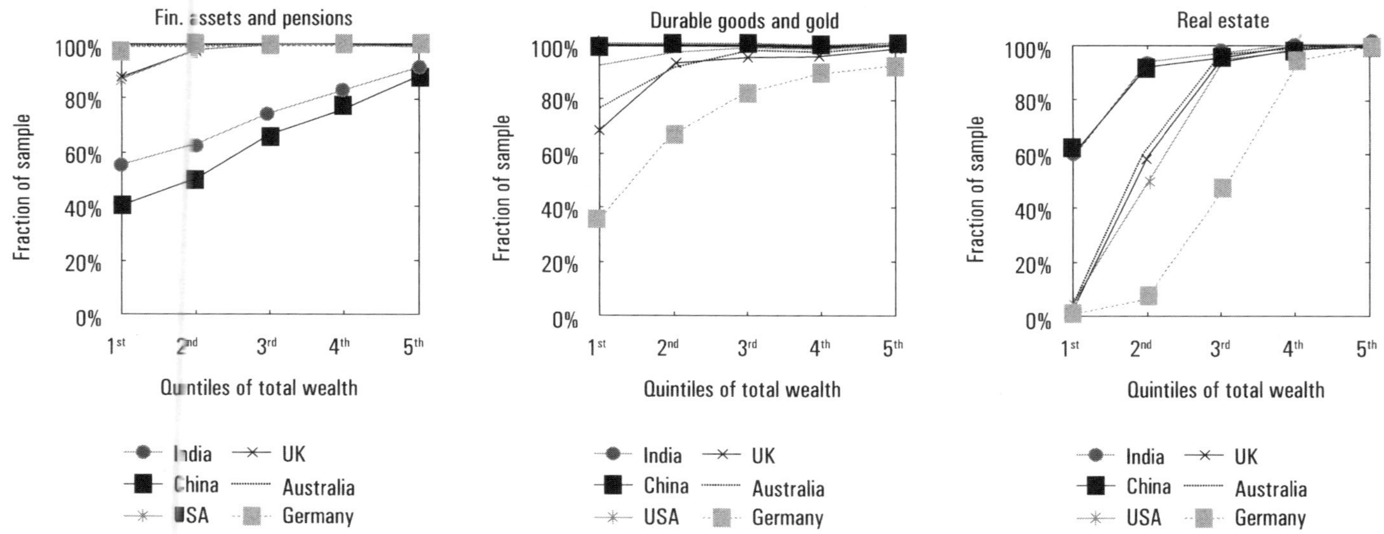

Panel B

The liabilities side of the household balance sheet

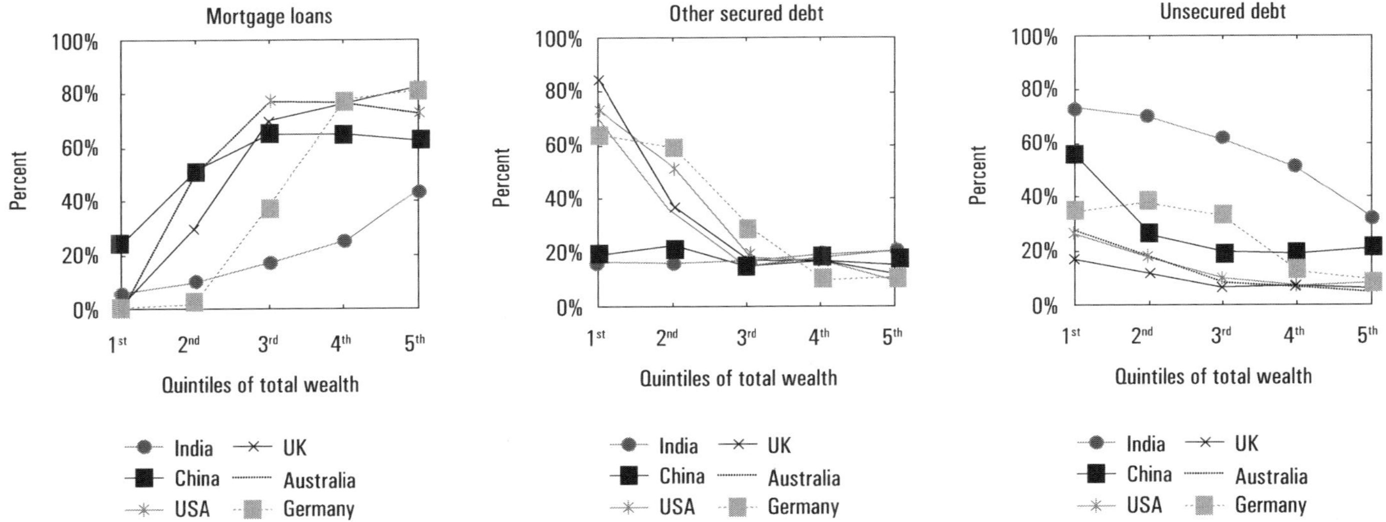

FIGURE 6. Allocation of Household Assets and Liabilities Across the Wealth Distribution

This figure reports the average shares of different assets and debt classes, relative to total household wealth and total household liabilities, respectively. The data sources are the AIDIS (2012 wave), the Eurosystem's HFCS (2010 wave), the US SCF (2010 wave), the CHFS (2012 wave), the Australian HILDA (2010 wave), and the UK WAS (2012 wave). For consistency, in the CHFS, we classify business loans originated with banks as secured loans and informal private loans as unsecured. We compute averages across households using population weights, as indicated in each survey.

Panel A

The assets side of the household balance sheet

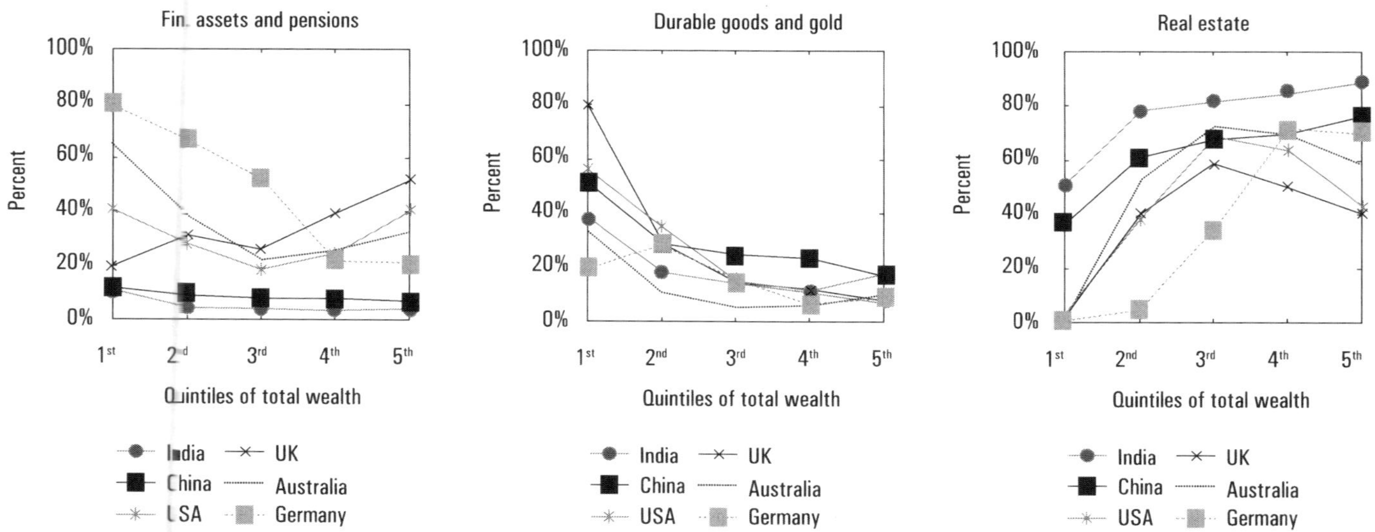

Panel B

The liabilities side of the household balance sheet

of the average Indian household stands out in a number of ways, even in contrast with the pattern observed in China. First, the role of mortgage credit is relatively low in India and not just at the very bottom of the wealth distribution. The relative share of mortgage debt in total liabilities remains lower in India than in China across all parts of the population, with the gap narrowing only at the very top. Second, in developed countries, secured debt backed by vehicles and consumer goods seems to be the preferred alternative to mortgage debt. This is very different in India, where unsecured debt accounts for close to two-thirds of the total liabilities for the very poor and one-third for the rich. In China, the patterns are similar in nature, that is, households also hold relatively high amounts of unsecured debt, but the variation across the population goes in the opposite direction from India, that is, there is a slight decrease of mortgage indebtedness among the rich.

4. Assets and Liabilities of Indian Households

4.1. Summary Statistics

Figure 7 reports the performance of alternative asset classes in India over the decade prior to 2012. While most households have experienced large (nominal) appreciation of their real estate holdings, we note that the housing market is also highly illiquid. Particularly in rural areas and for farmers or holders of private family businesses, only a very small part of these returns have actually been realized during the period. Moreover, the evidence on the relative risk-adjusted performance of financial assets versus gold is inconclusive at best, and the benefits of diversification rather than over-investment in a single asset class are theoretically (and empirically) clear. The fact that there is negligible participation in financial products with exposure to the stock market suggests that there is significant potential for large improvements in the welfare of households.

We now focus on the micro-data from the AIDIS to understand Indian wealth allocation across the asset space in more detail. Panel A of Table 1 presents summary statistics on the asset composition held by Indian households. The value-weighted average household owns 96.6 percent of all assets in physical form, 90 percent of which are in real estate and housing assets. The next few columns present the distribution of each of the variables in columns from the 1st to the 99th percentile and document the wide variation in the composition of asset holdings by Indian households. At the median, households own about ₹1,350 of financial assets (which include bank deposits and small savings) and nearly 15 times more (₹20,000) in gold. Holdings of financial assets vary from

FIGURE 7. Nominal Portfolio Returns for Alternative Asset Classes

This figure reports the average cumulative returns for types of assets that are available as savings instruments for Indian households. Residential real estate returns data is computed as in Campbell, Ramadorai, and Ranish (2014); data on gold, certificate of deposits (>1 year tenure), and publicly traded stocks are obtained from the Handbook of Statistics on the Indian Economy from the Reserve Bank of India. Livestock returns are computed as the equally weighted average of returns across all livestock markets in India for cows, sheep, buffaloes, and goats, and the data is obtained from the Ministry of Agriculture and Farmers Welfare's price portal (http://agmarknet.nic.in/index_old.html).

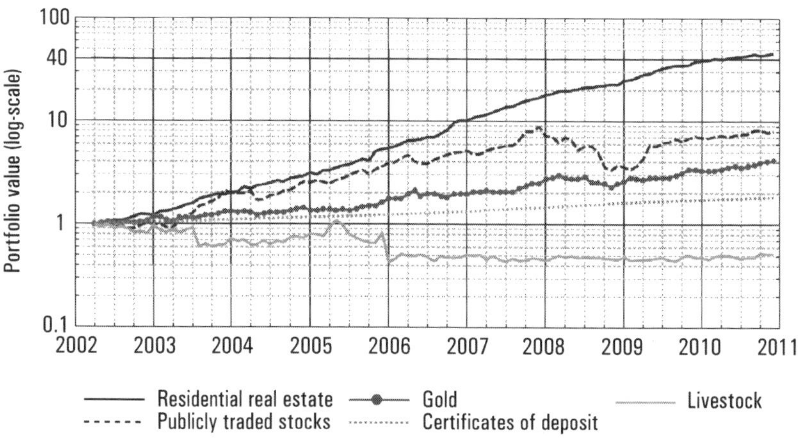

₹0 to over ₹10 million. Household financial assets, even at the maximum, only comprise 55 percent of total assets. On average (and across the distribution), Indian households mostly favor physical (non-financial) assets. Moreover, two important patterns emerge, namely, that Indian households hold a substantial fraction of wealth in gold and that retirement assets are nearly absent across the distribution. Even at the upper end of the distribution, the fraction of wealth held in retirement assets only just reaches the extent of wealth held in gold, and the combined total fraction of wealth in financial assets and retirement accounts is merely 4 percent of the wealth in real estate.

Panel B of Table 1 presents stylized facts about the liabilities side of the household balance sheet. Of the household debt, 67 percent is backed by some form of collateral, and a large proportion of secured loans are mortgage loans. Although unsecured loans form the remainder of the liabilities of a typical household, an important observation is that nearly half of Indian household liabilities are in the form of debt from non-institutional sources. Even at the top end of the distribution, one-fourth of total debt is from non-institutional sources, including that sourced from moneylenders and similar

TABLE 1. All India Debt and Investment Survey, 2012: Summary Statistics

This table reports summary statistics for each asset and debt category on the Indian households' balance sheets. In each row of the table, we report the mean, median, and selected percentile values, characterizing separately the distribution of each asset and debt category across the population.

Panel A

The assets side of the household balance sheet (₹)

					Percentiles			
	Mean	*1st*	*10th*	*25th*	*50th*	*75th*	*90th*	*99th*
Financial assets	24,681	0	0	0	1,350	8,000	34,000	400,000
Retirement accounts	28,317	0	0	0	0	1,300	43,050	552,000
Non-financial assets	1,528,232	1,200	59,700	172,550	478,300	1,277,131	3,197,200	14,700,000
Real estate	1,411,279	0	0	130,000	407,000	1,149,855	2,960,000	14,000,000
Durable goods	58,660	0	0	1,050	11,680	42,150	108,500	767,400
Gold/bullion	58,292	0	0	4,000	20,000	60,000	150,000	550,000
Total assets	1,581,228	4,000	67,954	183,000	501,880	1,330,200	3,320,700	15,000,000

Panel B

The liabilities side of the household balance sheet (₹)

					Percentiles			
	Mean	*1st*	*10th*	*25th*	*50th*	*75th*	*90th*	*99th*
Secured loans	120,845	0	0	0	0	63,557	264,700	1,989,981
Mortgage loans	86,631	0	0	0	0	11,000	138,375	1,800,000
Gold loans	10,817	0	0	0	0	0	1,650	259,900
Other secured loans	23,397	0	0	0	0	0	33,411	486,259
Unsecured loans	59,308	0	0	0	11,250	50,000	137,500	613,218
Total debt	180,153	2,000	9,203	20,000	51,614	147,000	378,000	2,220,950
Non-institutional debt	49,108	0	0	0	8,000	48,000	128,000	539,260

Source: AIDIS (2012).

sources, where interest rates are far higher than from institutional sources such as scheduled commercial banks.[22]

Alongside these patterns in the share of assets and liabilities in different vehicles of savings and debt, we observe important differences along the life cycle and across the wealth distribution. Panel A of Figure 8 presents the variation along the life cycle, and Panel B of the figure presents the variation across the wealth distribution for three elements of the average Indian household balance sheet: gold (Column 1), retirement accounts (Column 2), and non-institutional debt (Column 3). The share of total assets in gold is highest at 20 percent for households whose heads are under 35 years of age and diminishes to about half at ages above 65. Similarly, the poorest households hold more gold than the richest, and the difference between the wealthiest and poorest households is large. The near absence of savings in retirement accounts for all parts of the population is also prominent. Finally, the share of non-institutional debt to total debt diminishes from 58 percent for households with head under 35 years of age to 38 percent for households with head over 65 years of age. The non-institutional debt share is 25 percent of total debt for the wealthiest households, suggesting that non-institutional sources play a prominent role across all wealth categories in India.

The patterns uncovered along the life cycle and across the wealth distribution are important because they suggest two distinct features that affect the economic welfare of households in India. Since retirement savings are minimal, households, regardless of how wealthy they are, do not have a steady source of financial savings to smooth consumption after retirement. At the same time, with a large fraction of non-institutional debt, Indian households are exposed to an intergenerational bequest not just of assets, but also of debt.[23]

4.2. Regional Variation

Table 2 presents the average share of wealth in each asset type and share of debt across product types for Indian states. While a (poor) state like Bihar has households with barely any financial assets, cities/Union Territories[24] such as Chandigarh have the highest levels of financialization of the household balance sheet. Households in Tamil Nadu hold, on average, about 28 percent

22. This pattern has been documented extensively in the Indian policy discourse. For instance, see Kochar (1997) and more recently Banerjee et al. (2015).

23. The average life expectancy of an adult in India is 65. Non-institutional sources of debt primarily comprise loans from moneylenders, friends, and family where limited liability may not apply.

24. Union Territories in India, unlike the states, are ruled directly by the Central Government and are federal territories that have no elected sub-national governments of their own.

FIGURE 8. Wea th and Debt Allocation of Indian Households

This figure reports the ave age shares of different assets and debt classes, relative to total household wealth and total household liabilities, respectively. The source of the data is the 2012 wave of the AIDIS. e report equal-weighted averages, using population weights as indicated in AIDIS.

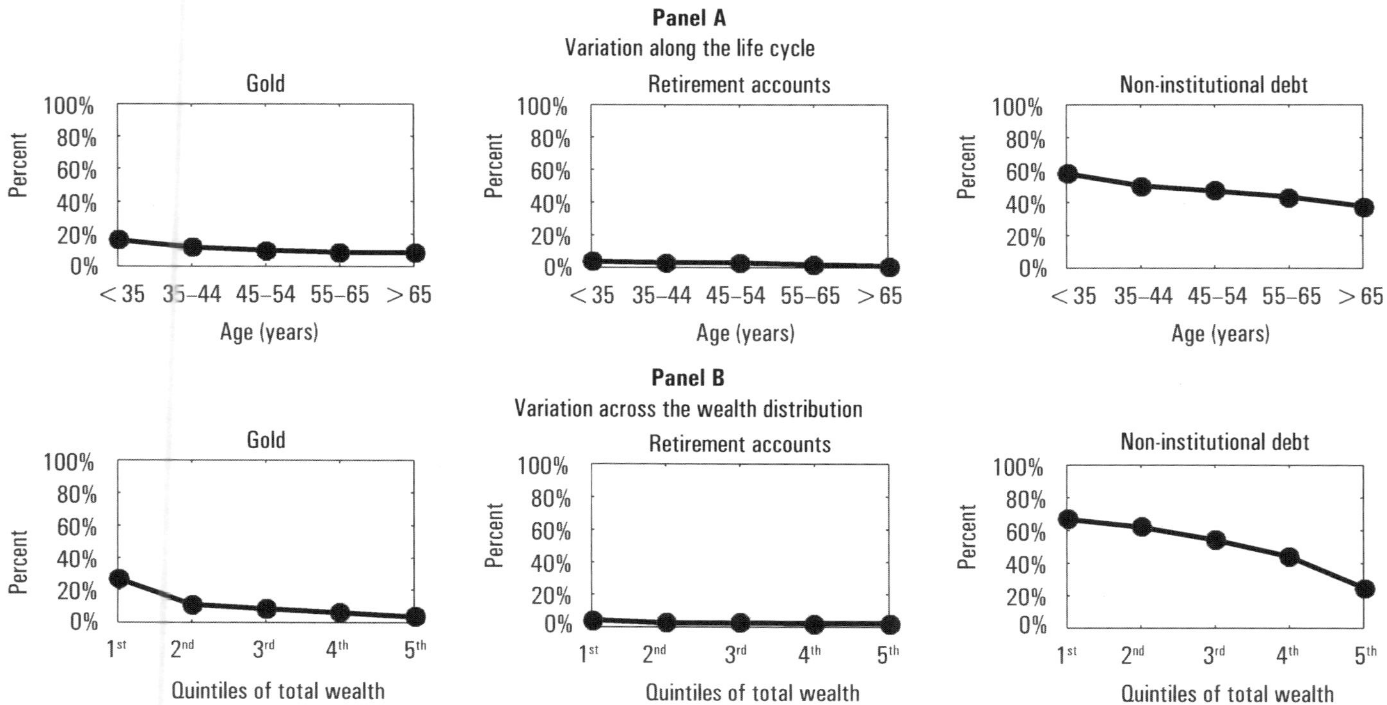

TABLE 2. Regional Variation in Household Balance Sheets

This table presents the average share of wealth in each asset type across Indian states (in rows) presented in the increasing order of the financial assets ratio.

	Portfolio Allocation Across Asset Categories				*Allocation of Debt Across Product Types*			
	Real Estate	*Gold*	*Financial Assets*	*Retirement Accounts*	*Mortgage Loans*	*Gold Loans*	*Unsecured Loans*	*Non-institutional Debt*
Bihar	90.5%	2.7%	1.0%	0.5%	8.2%	0.3%	81.9%	82.2%
Rajasthan	79.4%	9.5%	1.4%	1.7%	21.3%	1.0%	70.2%	68.7%
Nagaland	82.6%	1.6%	1.5%	7.3%	8.0%	0.0%	30.8%	40.3%
Manipur	84.0%	5.1%	1.6%	2.8%	3.1%	14.2%	30.4%	77.7%
Uttar Pradesh	85.4%	5.6%	1.8%	1.5%	27.3%	1.3%	63.0%	59.2%
Madhya Pradesh	82.2%	7.4%	1.9%	1.7%	30.4%	1.0%	60.0%	53.6%
Telangana	70.5%	17.5%	2.0%	2.4%	11.3%	2.9%	73.0%	55.8%
Odisha	78.9%	10.0%	2.1%	2.0%	26.9%	2.3%	59.1%	47.1%
Gujarat	72.5%	13.7%	2.1%	3.5%	38.0%	2.8%	38.2%	39.9%
Uttarakhand	78.7%	10.0%	2.2%	2.2%	18.8%	0.0%	67.6%	45.4%
Lakshadweep	80.4%	11.2%	2.5%	3.1%	9.7%	9.3%	66.7%	24.2%
Jharkhand	85.6%	4.4%	2.5%	1.9%	12.9%	0.2%	79.7%	62.8%
Chhattisgarh	81.7%	6.8%	2.7%	1.1%	14.7%	0.2%	65.2%	54.3%
Kerala	78.9%	13.1%	2.8%	1.8%	38.3%	17.2%	31.6%	20.0%
Jammu & Kashmir	84.2%	4.7%	2.9%	3.1%	10.1%	0.0%	62.2%	56.3%
Tripura	76.5%	10.0%	3.0%	3.8%	3.8%	0.2%	72.7%	44.7%
Maharashtra	76.6%	10.4%	3.1%	3.6%	47.0%	1.4%	36.0%	27.9%
Tamil Nadu	59.4%	28.3%	3.1%	3.2%	11.3%	41.3%	37.9%	42.1%
Punjab	81.6%	4.9%	3.1%	4.5%	25.7%	2.1%	57.4%	57.7%
Haryana	81.1%	5.9%	3.4%	3.0%	27.8%	0.0%	53.2%	48.1%
Goa	60.0%	20.2%	3.7%	6.0%	18.1%	3.5%	19.0%	8.0%
Andhra Pradesh	62.8%	21.6%	3.8%	3.1%	9.5%	9.5%	55.3%	48.9%

(Table 2 Continued)

(Table 2 Continued)

	Portfolio Allocation Across Asset Categories				Allocation of Debt Across Product Types			
	Real Estate	*Gold*	*Financial Assets*	*Retirement Accounts*	*Mortgage Loans*	*Gold Loans*	*Unsecured Loans*	*Non-institutional Debt*
West Bengal	81.2%	6.7%	4.0%	3.3%	16.7%	2.8%	69.5%	47.4%
Meghalaya	80.7%	3.0%	4.3%	3.5%	2.3%	0.2%	74.0%	24.7%
Mizoram	79.6%	1.2%	5.0%	5.7%	40.7%	0.0%	34.0%	17.2%
Karnataka	67.1%	16.1%	5.0%	4.4%	24.8%	3.4%	53.8%	49.2%
Assam	76.1%	6.6%	5.3%	2.6%	15.8%	1.2%	62.9%	48.0%
Andaman & Nicobar	42.5%	23.5%	6.3%	18.1%	6.4%	13.1%	66.4%	36.2%
Himachal Pradesh	71.8%	13.6%	6.8%	3.5%	35.6%	0.0%	42.4%	35.1%
Puducherry	56.9%	25.7%	7.2%	4.5%	3.4%	50.1%	33.3%	40.2%
Arunachal Pradesh	63.3%	5.1%	8.3%	5.0%	18.1%	1.3%	33.3%	45.7%
Chandigarh	57.0%	10.2%	8.3%	14.1%	47.1%	0.0%	23.0%	9.5%
Delhi	54.9%	17.4%	9.8%	6.2%	15.6%	0.4%	63.9%	46.6%
Dadra & Nagar Haveli	62.8%	6.5%	10.5%	12.4%	52.7%	2.4%	34.6%	31.3%
Sikkim	55.6%	14.6%	11.6%	10.3%	27.0%	0.0%	48.2%	17.8%
Daman & Diu	48.0%	24.4%	11.8%	10.8%	5.0%	0.0%	69.1%	66.9%

Source: AIDIS (2012).

of assets in gold (and bullion), followed closely by Andhra Pradesh (at 22 percent)—these high gold holdings in southern Indian states suggest that strong cultural factors may be at play in these cross-state patterns. Across states, we observe much more variation within the non-financial ratio, that is, between real estate and gold.

Similarly, large differences can be observed in patterns of debt allocation across states in India. While poor states such as Bihar have nearly 82 percent of their loans as unsecured debt and almost the same magnitude from non-institutional sources, states such as Goa have only 19 percent of their debt in unsecured loans and 8 percent of debt from non-institutional sources. States such as Tamil Nadu that own a high fraction of their assets in gold also have more than 40 percent of their total debt in gold loans. However, asset ownership shares do not necessarily translate into similar debt allocation patterns. For instance, households in Andhra Pradesh, one of the states with the highest average allocations of total assets to gold, only hold 9.5 percent of total debt in gold loans.

So far, we observe a few broad features of Indian household balance sheets. Differences exist at the household level along the life cycle and across the wealth distribution. At the same time, we also observe that the average household in different states of India exhibits strong differences, suggesting patterns potentially associated with regional characteristics. In the next sections, we explore this heterogeneity more formally in a multiple regression set-up and then use this setting to study the role of regional characteristics that potentially explain the regional variation observed in household balance sheet decisions.

4.3. Explaining the Heterogeneity of Household Balance Sheets

The framework of interest is given by a cross-sectional regression at the household level, across all Indian states. We estimate the following empirical specification:

$$f_{i,k} = \alpha + \mu_k + \beta X_{i,k} + \varepsilon_{i,k}$$

where $f_{i,k}$ are wealth shares of different asset types of household i in state k, μ_k are the state-fixed effects, and $X_{i,k}$ are dummy variables capturing wealth and age quintiles, education groups, rural and urban residency, and number of children. Table 3 presents the regression results where $f_{i,k}$ is the non-financial ratio, real estate ratio, and gold ratio across three adjacent columns.

The non-financial ratio is a declining function of education. Relative to the group of households with illiterate heads (or ones with below primary school

TABLE 3. Explaining Heterogeneity in Wealth Allocation across Indian Households

This table reports estimated β coefficients from the following estimated specification:

$$f_{i,k} = \alpha + \mu_k + \beta X_{i,k} + \varepsilon_{i,k},$$

where $f_{i,k}$ are wealth shares of household i in state k, and $X_{i,k}$ are dummy variables capturing wealth and age quintiles, education groups, rural versus urban residence, and number of children. We use household-level data from the 2012 wave of the Indian AIDIS and inflation data from the Labour Bureau, Government of India. *, **, and *** denote statistical significance at the 10 percent, 5 percent, and 1 percent levels, respectively.

		Real Estate	*Gold*	*Financial Assets*	*Retirement Accounts*
Total Assets	< 136,000	–	–	–	–
	136,000 to 344,560	0.253***	–0.143***	–0.049***	–0.011***
	344,560 to 7 lakh	0.324***	–0.186***	–0.056***	–0.016***
	7 lakh to 17 lakh	0.388***	–0.224***	–0.063***	–0.024***
	> 17 lakh	0.495***	–0.279***	–0.079***	–0.044***
Age	24 to 34 years	–	–	–	–
	35 to 44 years	0.020**	–0.012***	–0.005	0.000
	45 to 54 years	0.013	–0.011**	–0.003	0.002
	55 to 65 years	0.021*	–0.011***	–0.002	–0.006***
	> 65 years	0.038***	–0.012*	–0.002	–0.013***
Education	Illiterate/Below Primary School	–	–	–	–
	Primary and Middle School	–0.042***	0.023***	0.009***	0.004***
	Secondary School	–0.080***	0.039***	0.017***	0.010***
	Diploma	–0.130***	0.051***	0.026***	0.030***
	Graduate and Post-graduate	–0.194***	0.045***	0.043***	0.067***
Region Type	Rural	–	–	–	–
	Urban	–0.137***	0.065***	0.029***	0.033***
Children	0	–	–	–	–
	1	–0.028***	0.030***	–0.014***	–0.004
	> 1	–0.020**	0.027***	–0.017***	–0.008*
Constant term		0.603***	0.206***	0.068***	0.030***
State-fixed effects		Yes	Yes	Yes	Yes
No. of obs.		107,947	107,947	107,947	107,947
Adjusted R^2		0.42	0.33	0.13	0.10

education), having earned a diploma is associated with a 13 percentage points lower real estate assets share. For graduate and post-graduate household heads, the difference is even more substantial, reaching 19.4 percentage points. In contrast, investments in gold are an increasing, though non-monotonic function of education, even after controlling for total asset holdings.

Compared to households with less than ₹136,000 in total assets, we observe a very large increase in the non-financial ratio at the highest ends of the wealth distribution. While the overall increase in non-financial ratio is noteworthy, the rise in the fraction of real estate (land and buildings) owned by rich households (a nearly 50 percentage point increase) is offset by the decline in the role of gold (a drop of 28 percentage points relative to households with less than ₹136,000). To the extent that the wealth distribution is representative of rich households in India, this suggests that the financialization of the asset side of the household balance sheet is meager, even among the rich. Urban households hold 3 percentage points more financial assets than their rural counterparts. However, urban households notably also carry 6.5 percentage points more gold on their balance sheets. One possible explanation for the decline in real estate holdings for urban households is that the relative costs of these assets may be higher; another is that there is a greater prevalence of rental contracts in such locations, precluding the need to own a housing asset.

The non-financial ratio does not exhibit much variation across the life cycle. At different segments of the age distribution, there is no significant difference in the non-financial ratio or the real estate ratio, except for the highest end of the age distribution where households tend to reduce their gold holdings (by a small margin of 1 percentage point) and increase land and housing holdings (by 3.8 percentage points). Put differently, the real estate holdings appear to become a slightly higher fraction on the household balance sheet as households age, perhaps on account of liquid assets being drawn down as they approach and pass the point of retirement. As a function of the number of children in the household, gold holdings increase relative to households with no children and then decrease marginally.

Turning to the liabilities side, family composition seems to be less relevant in determining household choice among alternative products (see Table 4). Instead, education continues to play an important role, in particular with regard to the relative contributions of non-institutional debt and gold loans. Households with at least one member with graduate or post-graduate education have 15.1 percent more mortgage debt relative to the poorly educated group and a 28.7 percent lower share of non-institutional debt.

After controlling for household characteristics, the extent of variation across states remains large. Figure 9 suggests that the maximum (average) real

TABLE 4. Explaining Heterogeneity in Credit Product Choice across Indian Households

This table reports estimated β coefficients from the following estimated specification:

$$f_{i,k} = \alpha + \mu_k + \beta X_{i,k} + \varepsilon_{i,k,}$$

where $f_{i,k}$ are wealth shares of household i in state k, and $X_{i,k}$ are dummy variables capturing wealth and age quintiles, education groups, rural versus urban residence, and number of children. We use household-level data from the 2012 wave of the Indian AIDIS and inflation data from the Labour Bureau, Government of India. *, **, and *** denote statistical significance at the 10 percent, 5 percent, and 1 percent levels, respectively.

		Mortgage Loans	*Gold Loans*	*Unsecured Debt*	*Non-institutional Debt*
Total Assets	< 136,000	–	–	–	–
	136,000 to 344,560	0.028	0.011	–0.035	–0.044
	344,560 to 7 lakh	0.085***	0.023	–0.097***	–0.100***
	7 lakh to 17 lakh	0.153***	0.017	–0.182***	–0.184***
	> 17 lakh	0.299***	–0.005	–0.307***	–0.297***
Age	24 to 34 years	–	–	–	–
	35 to 44 years	0.027**	–0.023**	–0.023	–0.035*
	45 to 54 years	0.027***	–0.033**	–0.009	–0.051***
	55 to 65 years	0.038***	–0.021	–0.039*	–0.100***
	> 65 years	0.069***	–0.005	–0.085***	–0.132***
Education	Illiterate/Below Primary School	–	–	–	–
	Primary and Middle School	0.025**	0.015	–0.061***	–0.060***
	Secondary School	0.037***	0.008	–0.060***	–0.090***
	Diploma	0.049***	0.015	–0.108***	–0.157***
	Graduate and Post-graduate	0.151***	–0.017**	–0.206***	–0.287***
Region Type	Rural	–	–	–	–
	Urban	–0.036*	0.002	0.035*	0.010
Children	0	–	–	–	–
	1	0.001	0.001	–0.024	–0.009
	> 1	–0.025***	0.008	–0.014	–0.012
Constant term		0.253***	0.015	0.654***	0.636***
State-fixed effects		Yes	Yes	Yes	Yes
No. of obs.		45,292	45,292	45,292	45,292
Adjusted R^2		0.18	0.26	0.18	0.20

estate ratio unexplained by household characteristics is in the state of Bihar and the least in the Andaman and Nicobar Islands. Similarly, the maximum unexplained gold ratio is in the state of Tamil Nadu and least in the state of Mizoram. Figure 10 suggests that the highest unexplained retirement accounts ratio is in the Andaman and Nicobar Islands and the lowest in the state of Bihar. The state with the highest unexplained ratio of non-institutional debt is Manipur and the one with the lowest is Goa. This variation is important, as

FIGURE 9. Residual Variation of Real Estate and Gold Ratios across Indian States

This figure reports estimated μ_k coefficients from the following specification:

$$f_{i,k} = \alpha + \mu_k + \beta X_{i,k} + \varepsilon_{i,k},$$

where $f_{i,k}$ are wealth shares of household i in state k, and $X_{i,k}$ are dummy variables capturing wealth and age quintiles, education groups, rural versus urban residence, and number of children. The indicator variable for the state of Maharashtra is omitted from the regressions, which implies that this state is taken as a reference. We use household-level data from the 2012 wave of the Indian AIDIS.

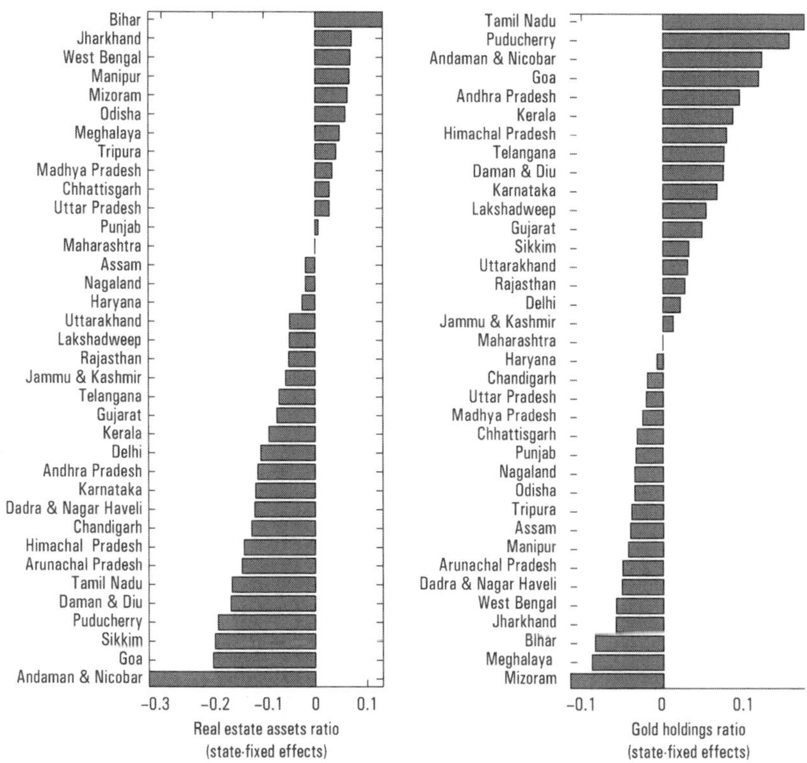

FIGURE 10. Residual Variation of Retirement Accounts and Non-institutional Debt Ratios across Indian States

This figure reports estimated μ_k coefficients from the following specification:

$$f_{i,k} = \alpha + \mu_k + \beta X_{i,k} + \varepsilon_{i,k},$$

where $f_{i,k}$ are wealth and liability shares of household i in state k, and $X_{i,k}$ are dummy variables capturing wealth and age quintiles, education groups, rural versus urban residence, and number of children. The indicator variable for the state of Maharashtra is omitted from the regressions, which implies that this state is taken as a reference. We use household-level data from the 2012 wave of the Indian AIDIS.

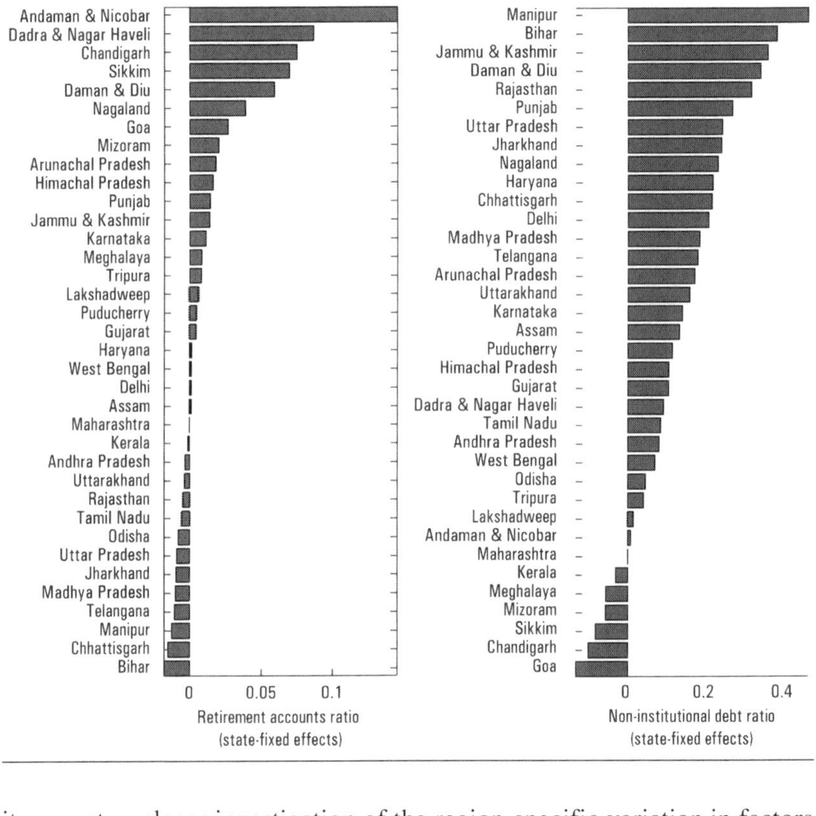

it suggests a closer investigation of the region-specific variation in factors that determine household asset and liability choices.

5. Explaining Residual Cross-state Variation

We now turn to explaining the residual cross-state variation in the composition of household balance sheets, cleaned of household demographic characteristics. We focus on three specific attributes of Indian household balance sheets, namely the high allocation to gold, the low fraction of retirement assets, and the high incidence of non-institutional debt. In each case, we employ features of the institutional and economic environment which vary at the state level, in an attempt to better understand potential levers of policy to enable better household financial outcomes.

5.1. Inflation Uncertainty and Wealth Allocation

In terms of household welfare, the theoretical benefits of participating in formal financial markets are well documented (see, for example, Campbell 2006; Karlan and Morduch 2009). While the optimal split between physical and financial assets involves complex life cycle portfolio choice calculations, most models struggle to explain the observed Indian household's average allocation to physical assets, and in particular, to gold, as an optimal portfolio allocation given the liquidity benefits of financial assets in addition to basic diversification arguments.

The permanent income hypothesis counterfactually predicts a low savings rate for fast-growing countries like India, since households expecting higher income in the future should borrow against future income.[25] To explain the data, an intriguing possibility that has been raised is that high-growth countries might exhibit high savings rates and low indebtedness for precautionary motives, for example, to hedge against expected adverse shocks to future income (see Chamon and Prasad 2010 for evidence in China of this channel), as well as likely binding borrowing constraints. We are motivated by this hedging argument and by the repeated assertions in the popular press that Indian households hold gold because they perceive it to be an inflation hedge. We, therefore, check how the extent of inflation uncertainty experienced by households in different regions in India affects their allocation decisions.

To identify this effect, we use the fact that India does not have a unified market for goods and the state-level markets are deeply segmented, meaning that a regional demand or supply shock is almost always not arbitraged. This means that we can use realized inflation, which differs across Indian states, to attempt to explain the state-level variation in physical asset holdings, under the assumption that households' lived experience of inflation is a strong predictor of their inflation hedging motivations.

25. In contrast, most standard life cycle models such as Modigliani (1986) would predict an increasing savings rate accompanying high levels of growth using standard age-compositional arguments (that is, households that are saving in middle age are more highly weighted than ageing households that are dissaving in retirement), but given the lack of a wide prevalence of formal retirement savings schemes in most emerging economies, this explanation is somewhat less appealing for such economies.

How do inflation and inflation uncertainty affect wealth allocations in India? We study this by reporting the correlation between household wealth shares and inflation developments across states. We obtain the state-specific wealth share as fixed effects (μ_k) from Section 4, after having controlled for an array of household-level characteristics. For 15 of the Indian states, state-wise inflation experience can be computed on the basis of reported inflation data collected from centers across India, which is also used to compute the national inflation series. We proxy inflation uncertainty using the in-sample standard deviation of the CPI (AW) between 2003 and 2012. Figure 11 presents the relationship between inflation experience and the non-financial ratio and its sub-components.

While the relationship between inflation and total non-financial ratio is flat, the relationship between inflation volatility and the real estate ratio, and inflation volatility and the gold ratio are strongly (and statistically significantly) decreasing and increasing, respectively. Within the set of non-financial assets that households could choose from, these correlations suggest that there is a substitution effect between real estate and gold that can be explained by the extent of inflation uncertainty in different regions of India.

Our explanation of the result is that if financial assets are not easily available/accessible or if demand-side frictions cause investors to eschew them, investors seek alternative savings vehicles.[26] Since very few households invest internationally, and there are regulatory restrictions to how much money can be invested abroad, the set of viable alternatives is restricted to the space of non-financial, physical assets.[27] In the space of non-financial assets, gold may be seen as an inflation hedge.

At the same time, the relationship between inflation uncertainty and real estate suggests that people with high experienced inflation volatility avoid real estate. Several potential channels of explanation exist. Most plausibly, real estate has lower liquidity when compared with gold, and if liquidity needs are correlated with inflation volatility, gold better serves the purpose than real estate. Gold as a non-financial asset also has additional properties that are not provided for by real estate, such as a high collateral value and physical verifiability (as opposed to the great many challenges inherent in property verification in India). Yet another possibility has to do with the

26. Most recently, an RBI-appointed committee on financial inclusion concluded that "despite improved financial access, usage remains low, underscoring the need to better leverage technology to facilitate usage" (Mohanty 2015).

27. Caballero and Krishnamurthy (2009) show that these have real macroeconomic consequences in terms of the global imbalances in savings.

FIGURE 11. Relationship between Inflation Uncertainty and Wealth Allocation in India

This figure reports the correlation between household wealth shares and inflation developments across Indian states. We obtain state-specific wealth shares as fixed effects μk from the following estimated specification:

$$f_{i,k} = \mu_k + \beta X_{i,k} + \varepsilon_{i,k}$$

where $f_{i,k}$ are wealth shares of household i in state k, and $X_{i,k}$ are dummy variables capturing wealth and age quintiles, education groups, rural versus urban residence, and number of children. The sample contains 15 states for which we are able to match household-level information from the AIDIS and historical regional consumer price indexes: Maharashtra, Andhra Pradesh, Karnataka, Rajasthan, Gujarat, Uttar Pradesh, West Bengal, Bihar, Madhya Pradesh, Odisha, Tamil Nadu, Assam, Kerala, Punjab, and Jammu & Kashmir. We use household-level data from the 2012 wave of the Indian AIDIS. Inflation volatility is calculated as the in-sample standard deviation of the consumer price index between 2003 and 2012. Inflation data is sourced from the Labour Bureau, Government of India.

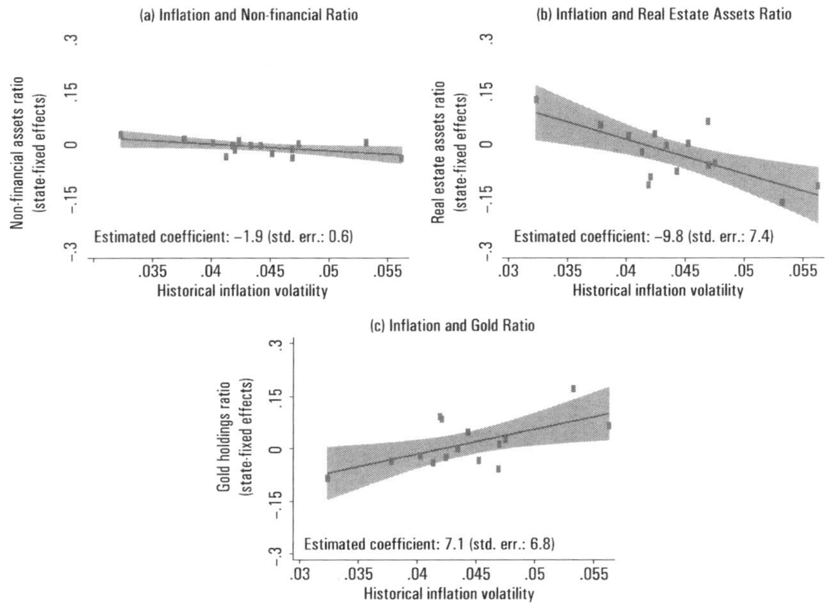

financing mechanism for real estate investments. It may be that the prevalence of adjustable rate mortgages in India makes mortgage-financed real estate a more risky proposition in an environment of high inflation volatility, especially if households face a current income affordability constraint (see Campbell and Cocco 2003).

For a deeper understanding of these phenomena, and in the spirit of Malmendier and Nagel (2011), we go on to run a regression in which we explicitly consider the role of experienced inflation at the age of 25 (Table 5), under the assumption that experiences earlier in one's working life have stronger effects on future financial decision-making. We find that the magnitude of the estimated effect is large: a shift from the mean to the top inflation observed in the sample is associated with an increase of 1.4 percent in the gold ratio. In terms of benchmarking, the size of the effect amounts to about half the contribution of having a child in the household. This suggests that inflation remains important in shaping household decisions on the intensive margin, beyond other more deep-seated household preferences that are related to social norms in India.

5.2. Public Sector Employment and Retirement Accounts

We turn our attention to retirement savings as a share of total assets in the balance sheets of Indian households. Although the share of retirement savings is low, households in the highest wealth quintile do have some retirement savings, and the average amount of savings varies across different Indian

TABLE 5. The Role of Inflation Experiences

This table reports estimated γ coefficients from the following specification:

$$f_{i,k} = \alpha + \mu_k + \beta X_{i,k} + \gamma \Pi^{25}_{i,k} + \varepsilon_{i,k},$$

where $f_{i,k}$ are wealth shares of household i in state k, and $X_{i,k}$ are dummy variables capturing wealth and age quintiles, education groups, rural versus urban residence, and number of children. $\Pi_{i,k}$ is inflation in state k during the year in which the head of household i was 25 years of age. We normalize the inflation level by subtracting the in-sample mean and dividing by the standard deviation. We use household-level data from the 2012 wave of the Indian AIDIS and inflation data from the Labour Bureau, Government of India. *, **, and *** denote statistical significance at the 10 percent, 5 percent, and 1 percent levels, respectively.

	Non-financial Ratio	*Real Estate Ratio*	*Gold Ratio*
Inflation experience when young	0.001	−0.000	0.002**
State-fixed effects	Yes	Yes	Yes
Demographic characteristics	Yes	Yes	Yes
No. of obs.	78,486	78,486	78,486
Adjusted R^2	0.18	0.41	0.33

states even after controlling for demographic characteristics. We explore the extent to which these differences can be explained by policy-induced, compulsory retirement programs such as the NPS and EPF contributions. If they are, this suggests the potential relevance of mandating participation in retirement savings programs in which investments are locked away for a long period of time.[28]

Employment in the organized sectors of the Indian economy is governed by labor laws that also mandate retirement savings. Since data on the fraction of population engaged in the organized sectors of the economy across Indian states are unknown, in this section, we proxy for this fraction by the share of state residents that are in public sector employment in each state. The AIDIS indicates the type of organization in which the household head is employed. We use this information to compute an estimated fraction of each state's population that is employed by a government organization or a public sector enterprise. We note that this is a noisy proxy for the channel that we attempt to identify and also note that it is difficult to establish causality using this approach.

Nevertheless, Figure 12 shows that the variation in state-level share of assets in retirement accounts is explained by the share of public sector employment in these states. However, a large share of the residual variation remains unexplained by public sector employment as it may be a relatively poor proxy for organized employment in India. Overall, we view this finding as suggesting that households in India may be driven by the immediacy of their economic needs and may not place enough importance on long-term financial savings for retirement. To the extent that such behavior can be countered by compulsory participation programs, a means to counter the lack of retirement savings exist and should be considered seriously.

5.3. Financial Access and Non-institutional Lending

Financial market imperfections such as information asymmetries, transactions costs, and contract enforcement costs are particularly binding on households that lack collateral, credit histories, and networks (Levine 2005). To the extent that formal financial penetration is low, households have little choice but to borrow from traditional and other non-institutional sources such as friends and family, and moneylenders. Non-institutional sources of credit can be costly to households in a variety of ways. For one, interest rates

28. Policies surrounding retirement saving have been seen from the prism of self-control and disparities emanating out of socio-economic characteristics. See, for instance, Laibson et al. (1998) and Sunden and Surette (1998).

FIGURE 12. Relationship between Public Sector Employment and Retirement Accounts Ratios in India

This figure reports the correlation between household shares of retirement accounts and the share of households employed by the public sector across Indian states. We obtain state-specific shares as fixed effects μ_k from the following estimated specification:

$$f_{i,k} = \mu_k + \beta X_{i,k} + \varepsilon_{i,k},$$

where $f_{i,k}$ is the retirement accounts share of household i in state k, and $X_{i,k}$ are dummy variables capturing wealth and age quintiles, education groups, rural versus urban residence, and number of children. We use household-level data from the 2012 wave of the Indian AIDIS.

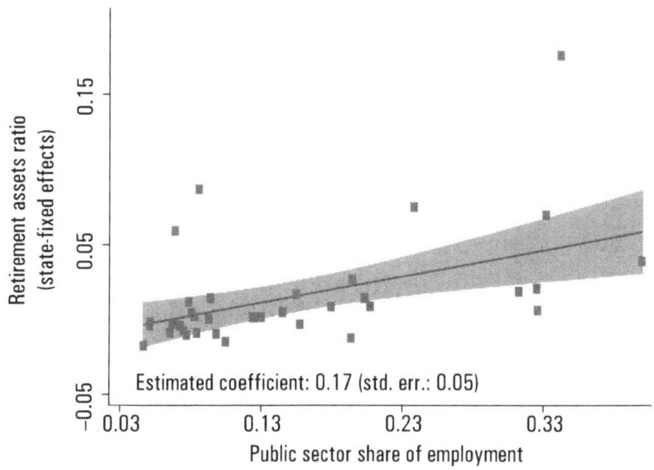

can be higher, especially when extended by moneylenders. Another issue is that credit from such sources is often not bound by limited liability or other legal protections that govern formal credit contracts between borrowers and lenders. This, in turn, could have serious implications for how risk sharing occurs intergenerationally, as younger generations may be called upon to fulfil the credit obligations of older generations, especially when such debt is not backed by collateral.

Our principal focus is on whether the residual variation in non-institutional debt ratios across Indian states is correlated with the extent to which institutional sources of credit are available to households. Burgess, Pande, and Wong (2005) provide some evidence on how directed bank lending requirements, which presuppose the existence of a bank branch in a local area, have increased credit uptake from institutional sources. If the correlation between residual variation in non-institutional debt and institutional penetration—measured as the log density of bank branches

FIGURE 13. Relationship between Bank Presence and Non-institutional Lending in India

This figure reports the correlation between household shares of non-institutional liabilities and the density of bank branches across Indian states. We obtain state-specific shares as fixed effects μ_k from the following estimated specification:

$$f_{i,k} = \mu_k + \beta X_{i,k} + \varepsilon_{i,k},$$

where $f_{i,k}$ is the non-institutional debt share of household i in state k, and $X_{i,k}$ are dummy variables capturing wealth and age quintiles, education groups, rural versus urban residence, and number of children. We use household-level data from the 2012 wave of the Indian AIDIS. The density of bank branches is obtained from the RBI.

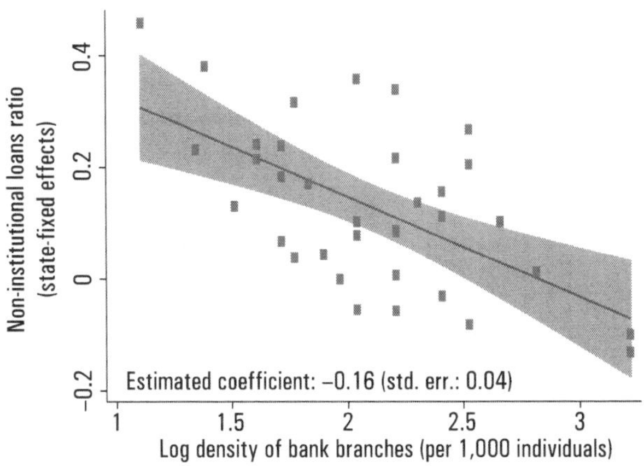

per 1,000 individuals in a state—is negative, it could suggest that access to institutional credit might help to explain variations across states in non-institutional debt.

Figure 13 presents the relationship between bank presence and non-institutional lending in India. We find a negative relationship between bank branch penetration, which we associate with supply-side variation in institutional debt and the fraction of non-institutional debt that households take on. Of course, this analysis is descriptive rather than causal, and this raises the possibility that high penetration of bank branches in certain states could be caused by the fraction of non-institutional debt on household balance sheets—or both could be caused by a common source. Nonetheless, the relationship between these two variables does raise the possibility that the high levels of non-institutional debt that we observe may not be the result of an active choice by Indian households to avoid institutional sources, but rather, could reflect the lack of a menu of options for households to alleviate credit constraints.

6. Conclusion

This paper describes the allocation of Indian household wealth and liabilities, and compares these allocations with those observed in other countries, using the most recent wave of the AIDIS (2012) household survey, in combination with international micro-data on household balance sheets. We document the dominant role of non-financial assets in the balance sheets of Indian households, particularly of gold holdings and residential real estate, both land and buildings. Other important features of the typical Indian household balance sheet include the lack of investment in retirement accounts, the very low participation rate in mortgage loans, and the heavy reliance on non-institutional debt.

The structure of household balance sheets varies significantly between rural and urban areas, by household characteristics (such as the age and education of the household head and the number of children), and by wealth. Controlling for these determinants, we find substantial residual heterogeneity across Indian states.

We attempt to explain this residual heterogeneity in the balance sheets of Indian households. For one, we exploit the state-level history of inflation developments and highlight the role of personal experiences of variable inflation in shaping the reliance of Indian households on non-financial assets. Our results suggest that a part of this demand could be attributed to the perceived role of gold as an inflation hedge. We also show that public sector employment (where retirement savings plans are compulsory) at the state level is related to the variation in state-level retirement savings in household balance sheets after controlling for demographic characteristics, suggesting the potential importance of mandating retirement savings. Finally, using variation in the density of bank branches across Indian states, we find that states with high bank branch penetration also exhibit a lower reliance on non-institutional sources of debt. While these correlations clearly cannot be interpreted as causal, they do highlight potentially important links that might hold the clue for future policy interventions and certainly suggest the need for more detailed research in this area.

In terms of specific directions for future policy, we suggest that there is a continuing need for policy to alleviate the dependence on physical savings such as gold. In particular, our results on the long-lasting correlation between inflation experiences and asset allocation strengthens the case for a strong inflation target to tackle inflation volatility, in addition to solutions recently put in place such as the RBI's gold monetization and gold bond schemes.

Second, improving the quality of financial decision-making by Indian households holds the promise of significant improvements in their welfare. Education is correlated with increases in household allocation to financial assets and is associated with a shift toward lower cost institutional sources of debt. This suggests that further investment in education, and in particular financial education, could generate gains on this margin as well as the more obvious ones.

Positive outcomes could also be achieved using a number of other policy instruments, including consumer financial regulation. However, our results suggest that great benefit may lie in specifically targeting the households' demand-side problems. These include modern financial product design through nudges, peer information, and default options.

The largest untapped potential may, however, lie in the area of innovations in financial technology that help solve demand-side issues (see Karlan et al. 2016 and Philippon 2016). Gaps in the use of financial services by Indian households, their heavy accumulation of non-financial wealth, and intense reliance on high-cost unsecured debt are also potential opportunities for the future growth of household finance in the country. The challenge that remains is for the financial market to be able to tap into this potential by leveraging technology and for the regulator to ensure that Indian households benefit from fair competition in this emerging area. Carefully designing a regulatory regime for financial technology that will help to alleviate the obvious shortcomings in Indian household finance, while enabling competition and controlling risks to Indian households, will be an important policy imperative going forward.

References

Adappa, Rajeshwari. 2016. "Why Gold Won't Lose Its Allure," *DNA India*, October 28, http://www.dnaindia.com/money/report-why-gold-won-t-lose-its-allure-2268125 (accessed May 10, 2017).

Anagol, Santosh and Hugh Hoikwang Kim. 2012. "The Impact of Shrouded Fees: Evidence from a Natural Experiment in the Indian Mutual Funds Market," *The American Economic Review*, 102(1): 576–593.

Anagol, Santosh, Vimal Balasubramaniam, and Tarun Ramadorai. 2015. *The Effects of Experience on Investor Behavior: Evidence from India's IPO Lotteries*, https://papers.ssrn.com/sol3/papers.cfm?abstract_id=2568748 (accessed May 10, 2017).

———. 2016. *Endowment Effects in the Field: Evidence from India's IPO Lotteries*, https://papers.ssrn.com/sol3/papers.cfm?abstract_id=2702555 (accessed May 10, 2017).

Badarinza, Cristian, John Y. Campbell, and Tarun Ramadorai. 2016. "International Comparative Household Finance," *Annual Review of Economics*, 8(1): 111–144.

Banerjee, Abhijit, Esther Duflo, Rachel Glennerster, and Cynthia Kinnan. 2015. "The Miracle of Microfinance? Evidence from a Randomized Evaluation," *American Economic Journal: Applied Economics*, 7(1): 22–53.

Beshears, John, James J. Choi, David Laibson, Brigitte C. Madrian, and Katherine L. Milkman. 2015. "The Effect of Providing Peer Information on Retirement Savings Decisions," *The Journal of Finance*, 70(3): 1161–1201.

Brandolini, Andrea, Luigi Cannari, Giovanni D'Alessio, and Ivan Faiella. 2004. "Household Wealth Distribution in Italy in the 1990s," *Temi di discussione, Economic Working Paper No. 530*. Rome: Economic Research Department, Bank of Italy.

Burgess, Robin, Rohini Pande, and Grace Wong. 2005. "Banking for the Poor: Evidence from India," *Journal of the European Economic Association*, 3(2–3): 268–278.

Caballero, Ricardo J. and Arvind Krishnamurthy. 2009. "Global Imbalances and Financial Fragility," *American Economic Review*, May, 99(2): 584–588.

Campbell, John Y. 1987. "Does Saving Anticipate Declining Labor Income? An Alternative Test of the Permanent Income Hypothesis," *Econometrica*, 55(6): 1249–1273.

———. 2006. "Household Finance," *The Journal of Finance*, 61(4): 1553–1604.

———. 2016. "Richard T. Ely Lecture: Restoring Rational Choice: The Challenge of Consumer Financial Regulation," *The American Economic Review*, 106(5): 1–30.

Campbell, John Y. and J.F. Cocco. 2003. "Household Risk Management and Optimal Mortgage Choice," *The Quarterly Journal of Economics*, 118(4): 1449–1494.

Campbell, John Y., Tarun Ramadorai, and Benjamin Ranish. 2014. "Getting Better or Feeling Better? How Equity Investors Respond to Investment Experience," *NBER Working Paper No. 20,000*. Cambridge, MA: National Bureau of Economic Research.

Chamon, Marcos D. and Eswar S. Prasad. 2010. "Why Are Saving Rates of Urban Households in China Rising?" *American Economic Journal: Macroeconomics*, 2(1): 93–130.

Choi, James J., David Laibson, Brigitte C. Madrian, and Andrew Metrick. 2003. "Optimal Defaults," *The American Economic Review,* 93(2): 180–185.

Cole, Shawn, Xavier Gin'e, Jeremy Tobacman, Petia Topalova, Robert Townsend, and James Vickery. 2013. "Barriers to Household Risk Management: Evidence from India," *American Economic Journal: Applied Economics*, 5(1): 104–135.

Deaton, Angus. 1999. "Saving and Growth," in Klaus Schmidt-Hebbel and Luis Servén (eds.), *The Economics of Saving and Growth: Theory, Evidence, and Implications for Policy*, pp. 33–70. Cambridge: Cambridge University Press.

Divatia, V.V. 1976. "Inequalities in Asset Distribution of Rural Households," *Reserve Bank of India Staff Occasional Papers*, 1(1): 1–45.

Domar, Evsey D. 1946. "Capital Expansion, Rate of Growth, and Employment," *Econometrica*, 14(2): 137–147.

Erb, Claude B. and Campbell R. Harvey. 2013. "The Golden Dilemma," *Financial Analysts Journal*, 69(4): 10–42.

Feldstein, Martin. December 25, 2009. "Is Gold a Good Hedge?" *Project Syndicate*.

Feldstein, Martin and Charles Horioka. 1980. "Domestic Savings and International Capital Flows," *The Economic Journal,* 90(358): 314–329.

Friedman, Milton. 1957. "The Permanent Income Hypothesis," in Milton Friedman (ed.), *A Theory of the Consumption Function*, pp. 20–37. Princeton: Princeton University Press.

Gan, Li, Zhichao Yin, Nan Jia, Shu Xu, Shuang Ma, and Lu Zheng. 2012. *Data You Need to Know about China: Research Report of China Household Finance Survey*. Berlin: Springer Science and Business Media.

Gaurav, Sarthak, Shawn Cole, and Jeremy Tobacman. 2011. "Marketing Complex Financial Products in Emerging Markets: Evidence from Rainfall Insurance in India," *Journal of Marketing Research*, 48(SPL): S150–S162.

Halan, Monica and Renuka Sane. 2016. "Misled and Mis-sold: Financial Misbehaviour in Retail Banks?" *Working Paper No. 174*, NIPFP Working Paper Series. New Delhi: National Institute of Public Finance and Policy.

Halan, Monika, Renuka Sane, and Susan Thomas. 2014. "The Case of the Missing Billions: Estimating Losses to Customers due to Mis-sold Life Insurance Policies," *Journal of Economic Policy Reform*, 17(4): 285–302.

Hall, Robert E. 1978. "Stochastic Implications of the Life-cycle—Permanent Income Hypothesis: Theory and Evidence," *Journal of Political Economy*, 86(6): 971–87.

Harrod, Roy F. 2007 [1939]. "An Essay in Dynamic Theory," *The Economic Journal*, 49(193): 14–33.

Jayadev, Arjun, Sripad Motiram, and Vamsi Vakulabharanam. 2007. "Patterns of Wealth Disparities in India during the Liberalisation Era," *Economic and Political Weekly*, 42(38): 3853–3863.

Karlan, Dean and Jonathan Morduch. 2009. "Access to Finance", in Dani Rodrik and Mark Rosenzweig (eds.), *Handbook of Development Economics*, Volume 5. New York: North-Holland.

Karlan, Dean, Jake Kendall, Rebecca Mann, Rohini Pande, Tavneet Suri, and Jonathan Zinman. 2016. "Research and Impacts of Digital Financial Services," *NBER Working Paper No. 22633*. Cambridge, MA: National Bureau of Economic Research.

Kaur, Balbir. 2011. *Report of Sub-Committee on Household Sector Savings*. New Delhi: Planning Commission of India.

Kochar, Anjini. 1997. "An Empirical Investigation of Rationing Constraints in Rural Credit Markets in India," *Journal of Development Economics*, 53(2): 339–371.

Laibson, David I., Andrea Repetto, Jeremy Tobacman, Robert E. Hall, William G. Gale, and George A. Akerlof. 1998. "Self-control and Saving for Retirement," *Brookings Papers on Economic Activity*, 1998(1): 91–196.

Levine, Ross. 2005. "Finance and Growth: Theory and Evidence," in Philippe Aghion and Steven Durlauf (ed.), *Handbook of Economic Growth*, pp. 865–934, Edition 1, Volume 1, Chapter 12. Amsterdam: Elsevier.

Livemint. 2013. "Gold Is Last Man Standing as Rupee Fuels Inflation", August 26, http://www.livemint.com/Money/3QBZkkAgHKeOiIFDdbha7J/Gold-is-last-man-standing-as-rupee-fuels-inflation.html#comments_box (accessed May 1, 2017).

Lucas, Robert E. 1988. "On the Mechanics of Economic Development," *Journal of Monetary Economics,* 22(1): 3–42.

Lusardi, Annamaria and Olivia S. Mitchell. 2009. "How Ordinary Consumers Make Complex Economic Decisions: Financial Literacy and Retirement Readiness," *NBER Working Paper No. 15350*. Cambridge, MA: National Bureau of Economic Research.

Malmendier, Ulrike and Stefan Nagel. 2011. "Depression Babies: Do Macro Economic Experiences Affect Risk Taking?" *Quarterly Journal of Economics*, 126(1): 373–416.

Mankiw, Gregory N., David Romer, and David N. Weil. 1992. "A Contribution to the Empirics of Economic Growth," *Quarterly Journal of Economics*, 107(2): 407–437.

Modigliani, Franco. 1986. "Life-cycle, Individual Thrift, and the Wealth of Nations," *The American Economic Review*, 76(3): 297–313.

Mohan, Rakesh and Muneesh Kapur. 2015. "Pressing the Indian Growth Accelerator: Policy Imperatives," *WP/15/53, IMF Working Paper*. Washington, DC: International Monetary Fund.

Mohanty, Deepak. 2015. *Report of the Committee on Medium-term Path on Financial Inclusion*. New Delhi: Reserve Bank of India.

Philippon, Thomas. 2016. "The FinTech Opportunity," *NBER Working Paper No. 22476*, NBER Working Paper Series. Cambridge, MA: National Bureau of Economic Research.

Pradhan, Narayan Chandra. 2013. "Persistence of Informal Credit in Rural India: Evidence from All-India debt and Investment Survey and Beyond," *WPS (DEPR): 5 (2013)*, RBI Working Paper Series. New Delhi: Reserve Bank of India.

Prasad, Eswar S., Raghuram G. Rajan, and Arvind Subramanian. 2007. "Foreign Capital and Economic Growth," *NBER Working Paper 13619*, NBER Working Paper Series. Cambridge, MA: National Bureau of Economic Research.

Rangarajan, C. 2009. *Report of the High Level Committee on Savings and Investment*. New Delhi: Ministry of Finance, Government of India.

Ravallion, Martin. 2003. "Measuring Aggregate Welfare in Developing Countries: How Well Do National Accounts and Surveys Agree?" *Review of Economics and Statistics*, 85(3): 645–652.

Romer, Paul M. 1986. "Increasing Returns and Long-run Growth," *The Journal of Political Economy*, 94(5): 1002–1037.

———. 1989. "Human Capital and Growth: Theory and Evidence," *NBER Working Paper No. 3173*. Cambridge, MA: National Bureau of Economic Research.

Sane, Renuka and Susan Thomas. 2015. "In Search of Inclusion: Informal Sector Participation in a Voluntary, Defined Contribution Pension System," *The Journal of Development Studies*, 51(10): 1409–1424.

Sane, Renuka and Susan Thomas. 2016. "From Participation to Repurchase: Low-income Households and Micro-insurance," Technical Report. Mumbai: Indira Gandhi Institute of Development Research.

Sen, Abhijit. 2000. "Estimates of Consumer Expenditure and Its Distribution: Statistical Priorities after NSS 55th Round," *Economic and Political Weekly*, 35(51): 4499–4518.

Shah, Ajay. 2006. "Indian Pension Reform: A Sustainable and Scalable Approach," in David A. Kelly, Ramkishan S. Rajan and Gillian H.L. Goh (eds.), *Managing Globalization: Lessons from China and India*, Ch. 7, pp. 167–218. New York: World Scientific.

Srinivasan, T.N. 2000, June. "Growth, Poverty Reduction and Inequality." Paper presented at the European Annual World Bank Conference on Development Economics, Paris, June.

Subramanian, S. and D. Jayaraj. 2006. "The Distribution of Household Wealth in India," *Research Paper No. 2006/116*, UNU-WIDER. Tokyo: United Nations University.

Sundaram, K. and Suresh D. Tendulkar. 2002. "Recent Debates on Database for Measurement of Poverty in India: Some Fresh Evidence." Paper presented at Workshop on Poverty, organized by the Indian Planning Commission and the World Bank, Delhi, January 11–12.

Sunden, Annika E. and Brian J. Surette. 1998. "Gender Differences in the Allocation of Assets in Retirement Savings Plans," *The American Economic Review*, 88(2): 207–211.

Thaler, Richard H. and Cass R. Sunstein. 2008. *Nudge: Improving Decisions about Health, Wealth, and Happiness*. New Haven, CT: Yale University Press.

Vaidyanathan, A. 1993. "Asset Holdings and Consumption of Rural Households in India: A Study of Spatial and Temporal Variations," in *Agricultural Development Policy: Adjustments and Reorientation*. New Delhi and Oxford: Indian Society of Agricultural Economics.

Virmani, Arvind and Surabhi Mittal. 2006. "Domestic Market Integration," *Working Paper No. 183*. New Delhi: Indian Council for Research on International Economic Relations.

Comments and Discussion*

Rajnish Mehra[δ]
Arizona State University, NBER, and NCAER

Introduction

When I concluded my discussion of this paper at the IPF, I noted that this was "... a thought provoking, unique paper ... [but it] is still a work in progress. I look forward to a more detailed parsing of its implications for financial theory." In the current version, the authors have substantially revised it, incorporating the comments of both the discussants and the participants. I view the revised version as complementary to the excellent paper, "Sources of Growth in the Indian Economy" by Bosworth, Collins, and Virmani (2006). It is likely to become a definitive reference on Indian household finance.

To briefly summarize the paper, the authors use the latest wave (2012) of the All India Debt and Investment Survey (AIDIS) to characterize and provide a snapshot of the asset holdings of Indian households. They also construct similar measures for other countries—China, Australia, the UK, Germany, and the US—to facilitate international comparisons.

In the first part of the paper, the authors highlight two observations:

a) As compared to households in developed countries, households in India and China hold a substantially higher fraction of non-financial assets in their portfolios.
b) Household portfolios in India hold a relatively higher fraction of gold bullion than in any other developed or developing country.

* To preserve the sense of the discussions at the India Policy Forum (IPF), these discussants' comments reflect the views expressed at the IPF and do not necessarily take into account revisions to the conference version of the paper in response to these and other comments in preparing the final, revised version published in this volume. The original conference version of the paper is available at www.ncaer.org.

δ I am thankful to Ravi Bansal, John Donaldson, Chaitanya Mehra, and Edward Prescott for several stimulating discussions and comments.

In the second part of the paper, they focus on two questions:

a) Why are the portfolio allocations of Indian and Chinese households different from households in developed markets?
b) Do the portfolio allocations of Indian households differ by region, age, education, and family characteristics?

Assets and Liabilities of Indian Households

The strength and the major contribution of the paper is its comprehensive documentation of data in Section 4. Table 1 summarizes the assets and liabilities of Indian households using a number of statistics, Panels A and B in Figure 8 illustrate the variation along the life cycle and wealth distribution, while Table 2 documents the regional variation in household balance sheets. The authors are careful in pointing out the limitations of their dataset.[1] A striking feature of the data in Table 1 is the extreme skewness in the distribution of assets and liabilities. It reinforces the conclusions of a Credit Suisse report (Credit Suisse Research Institute 2014) that in 2014, the top 1 percent of the Indian population owned 49 percent of the country's total wealth and the top decile 74 percent. Further, the bottom 50 percent owned 4.5 percent, and the bottom 80 percent owned 16.6 percent of the wealth.

Given this highly skewed wealth distribution, the value-weighted asset holdings represent the holdings of the top decile, rather than the holdings of an average household.[2] The mean and median household allocations are very different.

The reader should be cautioned that the data presented is a cross-sectional snapshot of the composition of household savings. It is one (invaluable) observation of a stochastic process characterizing the evolution of different types of asset holdings. The Indian economy is in transition and this process is unlikely to be ergodic—ensemble averages and averages over time are likely to be quite different. It would be unwise to use this one observation for either policy prescriptions or to evaluate portfolio allocations.

1. Given the data limitations, it would have been comforting had the authors done a robustness check on the micro-data using the macro-data in the National Accounts and reported the findings.

2. In the Indian context, this is a meaningless concept. Unfortunately, the authors extensively use the potentially misleading phrase "average household." For example, on page 14 they state, "In India, the average household holds 77 percent of its total assets in real estate."

To elaborate, at a point in time, all assets must be held. The aggregate portfolio holdings simply reflect the value-weighted average of the available assets in the economy. While an individual investor or a group of investors may allocate assets taking prices as given, in the aggregate, at a point in time, the aggregate holdings simply reflect the assets available in the economy. Aggregate household net worth mimics the economy-wide fluctuation in asset valuation. As the relative market value of different asset classes changes over time, this will be reflected as changes in aggregate portfolio weights, even without active portfolio rebalancing.

For example, had this analysis been done in the 1990s, the holdings of debt and equity assets would have been negligible. Thus, rather than being suggestive of long-term portfolio decisions of Indian households, the results reported in the paper may simply reflect the degree of financial development in India.

As Figure 1 below illustrates, it is only very recently that financial markets in India amounted to any significant fraction of GDP, so it should not come as a surprise that this is mirrored in the balance sheets of the households.

In contrast, in developed economies, financial assets are a substantially larger multiple of GDP. In the US, for example, they have averaged about 250 percent of GDP over the past 25 years. See Figure 2 below.

FIGURE 1. Evolution of the Financial Sector in India: 1990–2011

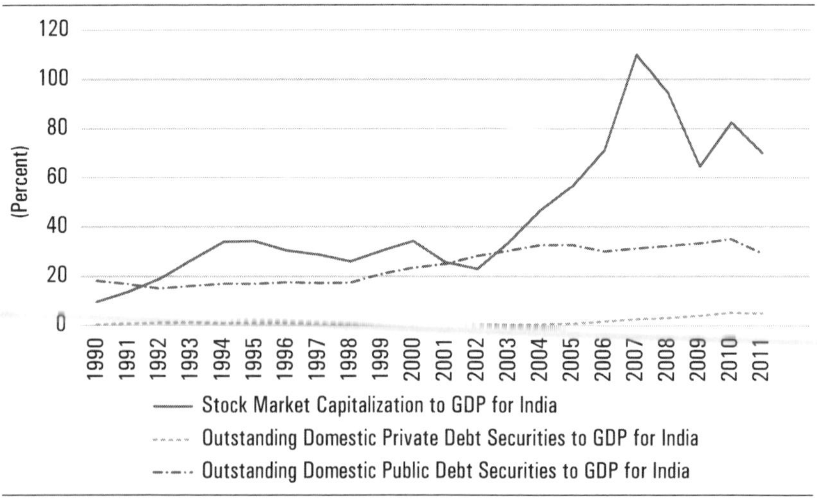

Source: 2015 research.stloiusfed.org

FIGURE 2. Evolution of the Financial Sector in the United States: 1990–2011

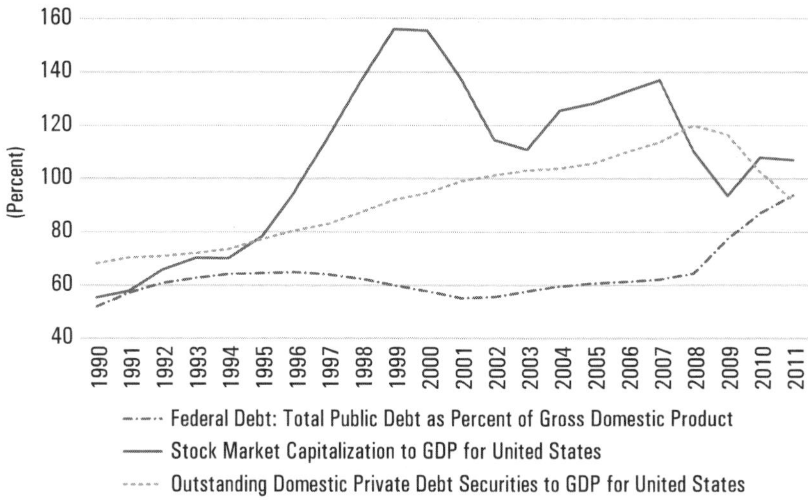

Source: 2015 research.stlouisfed.org

Household Borrowing and Lending

For every borrower, there must be a lender. In equilibrium, the total amount lent by households (D_L) is equal to the total amount borrowed by households, (D_B) plus Government debt (D_G)[3] since household lending (D_L) is a subset of financial assets held by households (FA_H). It follows that $FA_H > D_B$. However, in Table 1, the mean financial assets are listed as ₹24,681 while the mean household debt (D_B) is listed as ₹120,845. This needs to be clarified.

Life Cycle Effects

I find the lack of any significant life cycle effects in Figure 8 in the paper to be somewhat anomalous. Historically, the static one-period mean–variance model has been the basis of portfolio advice. In this setting, the appropriate objective is end-of-period wealth maximization, and the only risk management tool that needs to be employed is diversification. However, recent advances in portfolio theory suggest that this objective may be inappropriate. As the correlation of asset returns with wage income changes over the life

3. Corporate debt in India is insignificant. However, since households own corporations, corporate borrowings show up as both assets and liabilities of households and hence nets out.

cycle, this is likely to lead to significant differences in portfolio allocations over the life cycle.[4]

Allocations may also differ due to differing objectives over the life cycle, such as wealth accumulation (while young) versus wealth preservation (nearing retirement) and different preferences for bequests. In the absence of a bequest motive, the optimal strategy for a household is to buy a life annuity rather than maximize wealth at retirement. In a recent paper, Mehra, Piguillem, and Prescott (2011) show that even with a 2 percent lower rate of return, it is welfare-enhancing for households that derive little or no utility from bequests to invest in annuities, to insure against outliving their savings.

Cross-country Comparisons

While it is illuminating to document portfolio allocations of households in China, Australia, the UK, Germany and the US, these statistics add little to the key message of the paper, especially since the authors provide no justification for their selection.[5] Do these countries represent a benchmark or ideal that Indian households should mimic? If so, why? The paper is silent on this issue.

Angus Deaton (1990) starts his paper, "Saving in Developing Countries: Theory and Evidence" with the sentence, "I can think of four good reasons for studying savings in developing countries separately from saving behavior in developed countries." I think the same applies to the composition of savings, especially since portfolio allocations in developed countries are likely to be drawn from a stationary distribution along a balanced growth path.[6]

There is another, orthogonal observation that questions the relevance of these cross-country comparisons. Portfolio allocations across households vary considerably with the wealth level. For the US, this is illustrated in Figure 3 below. Given the extreme skewness in wealth distribution in India, is it appropriate to compare the "averages" in India with average portfolio holdings in countries where the wealth distribution is less skewed? If indeed a comparison must be made, a more appropriate comparison set would be the holdings of the ultrarich in various countries (see Ravina, Viceira, and Walter 2016).

4. See, for example, Constantinides, Donaldson, and Mehra (2002) or Davis and Mehra (2001).

5. Why not look at household portfolios in economies in transition such as Taiwan, Korea, Indonesia, Malaysia, Thailand, Brazil, or Argentina?

6. See my earlier comment.

FIGURE 3. **Snapshot of Asset Portfolios of US Households in the 2007 US Survey of Consumer Finances**

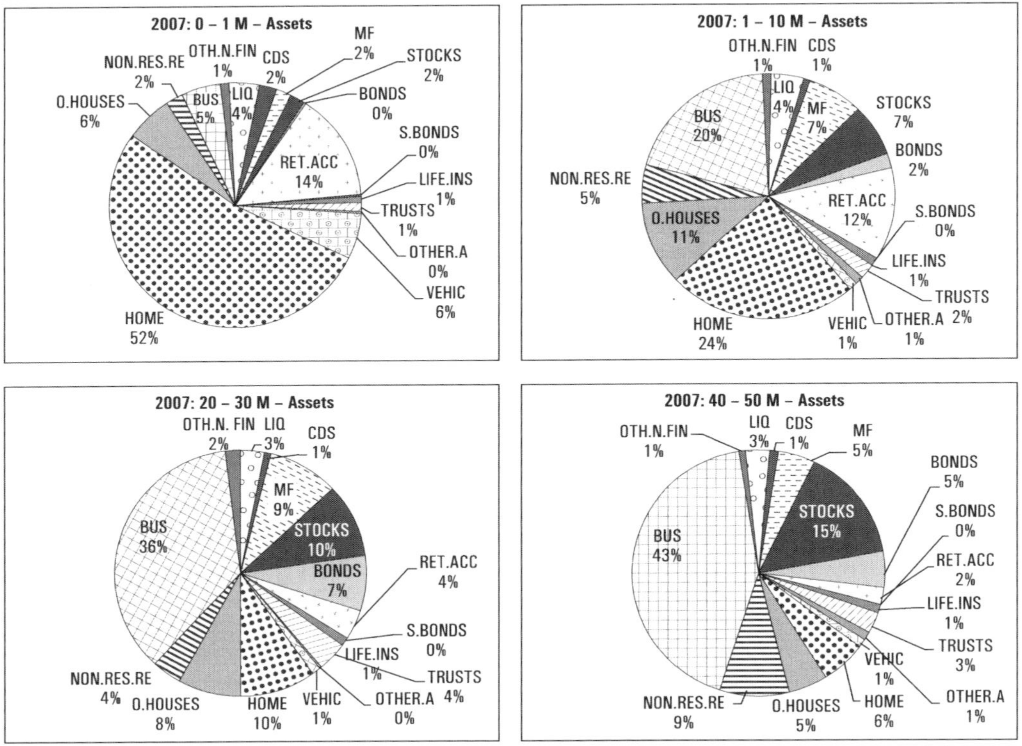

Notes: OTH.N.FIN = Other misc. non-financial assets. LIQ = All types of transaction accounts (cash holdings). CDS = certificates of deposits. MF = mutual funds. STOCKS = directly held stocks. BONDS = directly held bonds. RET.ACC = retirement accounts. S.BONDS = savings bonds. LIFE.INS = cash value of whole life insurance. TRUSTS = other managed assets. OTHER.A = other miscellaneous financial assets. VEHIC = vehicles. HOME = primary residence(s). O.HOUSES = residential houses excluding primary residence(s). NON.RES.RE = net equity in non-residential real estate. BUS = businesses.

Holding Gold: An Optimal Response to Expropriation?

India has a history of "expropriation"[7] going back to at least the Mughal era (Eraly 2007). Examples in the post-Independence era include bank nationalization, land reforms, the abolition of "privy purses," and the recent demonetization. Holding gold may be a cultural norm that developed as an optimal response to expropriation.

The travelogues of Jean-Baptiste Tavernier and François Bernier provide a detailed description of life in the Mughal court. The Mughals employed the "Mansabdari System." A feature of this system was that the property and title of a *mansabdar* was confiscated after his death. His widow and children had to start life from scratch. This practice led to perverse incentives, and *mansabdar*s became experts in the art of concealing wealth, largely in the form of gold and precious stones.

Until the mid-1990s, the only viable financial asset that could be used for savings by the vast majority of Indians was that of bank time deposits. As Figure 7 in the paper clearly illustrates, the nominal returns on these deposits were dominated by returns on gold. So it should come as no surprise that gold features prominently in Indian household portfolios.[8]

Gold holdings in India are less of an anomaly if one recognizes that internationally too, households indirectly hold gold in the form of exchange-traded funds (ETFs) and other financial assets backed by physical gold. Although the paper characterizes gold as a non-financial asset, it could easily be characterized as a financial asset. I conjecture that substantial gold holdings in the portfolios of households in developed countries are probably classified as financial assets whereas the holdings of Indian households are classified as non-financial assets.

Prescription for Growth

The authors seem to imply that a change in the composition of the portfolio of savings will lead to a higher growth rate,[9] specifically, reducing the holdings of gold and increasing the holdings of financial assets. However, this cannot be addressed without a model linking investment and growth. Perhaps the authors have in mind a Harrod–Domar model of the type $g_y = i_y/k_y$ where g_y is the growth rate of output y, i_y the investment as fraction of output (equal to the savings rate s), and k_y the capital output ratio. If the capital output ratio is

7. This is not a value judgment but a documentation of facts.

8. The low correlation with equity returns further enhances its appeal.

9. See their discussion in Section 1.

"assumed to be constant," then presumably increasing "productive" investment by reducing gold holdings in household portfolios will increase the growth rate. A key feature of "neoclassical" growth models (Cass 1966; Koopmans 1965; Solow 1956) is that the steady state growth rate of an economy is independent of the savings rate and largely dependent on the growth rate of total factor productivity. From the perspective of neoclassical economic theory, gold is a "consumption good," like jewelry. A shift out of gold would represent an increase in the Indian equilibrium savings as a fraction of GDP; however, the long-run growth in output per worker will not increase, without improvements in the growth rate of total factor productivity. These improvements are more likely to occur via technological improvements and the modernization of Indian labor laws than through "portfolio rebalancing."

Another complicating factor is that India is transitioning toward an open economy regime. In open economies, as is well known, there is no direct link between domestic savings and investment as investments can be financed by capital inflows.

I think that this and other policy recommendations are best addressed in the context of well-specified models. Perhaps the authors should pursue them in a subsequent paper.

References

Bosworth, Barry, Susan M. Collins, and Arvind Virmani. 2006. "Sources of Growth in the Indian Economy," *India Policy Forum*, 3: 1–69.

Cass, David. 1966. "Optimum Growth in an Aggregative Model of Capital Accumulation: A Turnpike Theorem," *Econometrica*, 34(4): 833–850.

Constantinides, George M., John B. Donaldson, and Rajnish Mehra. 2002. "Junior Can't Borrow: A New Perspective on the Equity Premium Puzzle," *Quarterly Journal of Economics,* 118(1): 269–296.

Credit Suisse Research Institute. 2014. *Global Wealth Data Handbook*. Zurich: Credit Suisse AG.

Davis, Steven J. and Rajnish Mehra. 2001. "Stocks and Bonds in the Portfolio Life-Cycle," *Financial Times*, June 4.

Deaton, Angus S. 1990. "Saving in Developing Countries: Theory and Review," Proceedings of the World Bank Annual Conference on Development Economics 1989, *The World Bank Economic Review*, Washington, D.C.

Eraly, Abraham. 2007. *The Mughal World: Life in India's Last Golden Age*. London: Orion Publishing.

Koopmans, Tjalling C. 1965. "On the Concept of Optimal Economic Growth," *Pontif. Acad. Sc. Scripta Varia*, 28: 225–300.

Mehra, Rajnish, Facundo Piguillem, and Edward C Prescott. 2011, March. "Costly Financial Intermediation in Neoclassical Growth Theory," *Quantitative Economics*, 2(1): 1–36.

Ravina, Enrichetta, Luis Viceira, and Ingo Walter. 2016. "The Portfolios and Financial Decisions of High Net Worth US Households," *Working Paper*, New York: Columbia Business School, Columbia University.

Solow, Robert M. 1956. "A Contribution to the Theory of Economic Growth," *The Quarterly Journal of Economics*, 70(1): 65–94.

Nirvikar Singh
University of California, Santa Barbara, and NCAER

This is an important paper for the obvious reason that savings and investment are critical for economic growth. The current version of the paper is considerably expanded from the draft presented at the IPF in July 2016, and I will take both versions into account in my comments. A major and welcome new analysis compared to the earlier version is the inclusion of the liabilities side of household balance sheets, which has also led to a change in the name of the original paper, which referred only to the "savings landscape."

The well-known phenomenon of "home bias" means that domestic savings are vital for growth: foreign savings are a relatively small source of funds for investment. Furthermore, household savings comprise 70–80 percent of domestic savings in India. It is important to understand where these savings go. In particular, the answer to this question has implications for whether and how savings are channeled into productive investment. The current paper, by considering the liabilities side of household balance sheets, also gives a sense of whether and how Indian households can access others' savings, whether for household investment or for consumption smoothing and risk management (in conjunction with the savings side). Indeed, high savings rates in fast-growing countries have been explained by precautionary motives, and this motivates the authors' exploration of the Indian propensity to hold a relatively high fraction of savings in gold as a possible inflation hedge.

On the macroeconomic front, there has been prior work on the relationship of household savings to growth in India. For example, Samantaraya and Patra (2014) find that

> ... in the long run, one percentage increase in GDP leads to 2.56 percent increase in household savings, while one percentage increase in age dependency, raises household

savings by close to one-fifth percentage point. Similarly, one percentage increase in interest rate and inflation reduces household savings by 0.07 percent each.

These results are somewhat contrary to a precautionary motive for savings, but they do not tell us anything about the composition of savings. This is something that the current paper focuses on, in examining savings in gold. Other macroeconomic data tallies the split between physical and financial assets for household savings in India. Physical savings, in property as well as gold, have tended to dominate, but there has been a long-run trend toward increased financial savings (for example, Goyal 2015). On the other hand, there was at least a temporary reversal of this trend in 2011–13 (Kant 2014, Chart 1) associated with higher inflation.

The current paper uses detailed household level data from June 2012, from National Sample Survey Office's (NSSO's) AIDIS, with over 100,000 households sampled, and this allows for a much more in-depth analysis of patterns of household saving and borrowing, not just across different types of saving and borrowing but also across different types of households and different parts of India. This has not been attempted before and is impossible to achieve with aggregate data at the national or state level. Of course, the cost of this is that the analysis is cross-sectional only, so one cannot say anything about changes over time in the patterns analyzed here.

The paper begins with an extensive comparison of India to several other countries. For me, the main takeaways from this section are that India and China have similar levels of non-financial household assets, but differing patterns. Chinese households hold higher proportions of assets in durable goods and less in gold and real estate, though they have more mortgage debt. Indian households also stand out in having a high proportion of unsecured debt. Broadly, India and China both differ from the four advanced countries considered (the US, the UK, Australia, and Germany), reflecting their lower financial development.

The authors go on to compare India to other countries along the life cycle and across the wealth distribution. In India, lower proportions of younger households hold financial assets, in contrast to China. India is atypical in several other respects: Indian households do not reduce real estate holdings as they cross retirement age, there is no drop-off in mortgage loan participation at these ages, and unsecured debt is more significant in all age groups. Similar differences are reflected in comparisons across the wealth distribution. Another noteworthy feature of the Indian data is a "near absence of savings in retirement accounts." Overall, the differences in India seem to reflect its relative poverty (even compared to China), its underdeveloped financial markets, and perhaps its family structures as well.[10] The lack of financial development is also illustrated by the authors' presentation of aggregate data on returns to different asset classes: they suggest that there is an indication of under-participation in financial products connected to the stock market and inefficient diversification. This is a reasonable suggestion, though it is conjectural, as they acknowledge.

The paper then documents regional variations in household balance sheets. There is considerable variation across states and Union Territories in the proportions of financial assets and in patterns of holdings of non-financial assets. State-level income and urbanization are both relevant for explaining these variations, but unspecified cultural factors may also matter, especially for gold holdings. Cross-section regressions to explain heterogeneity in wealth allocation and credit choice across households yield a variety of results on patterns, some not that different from those observed with the univariate tabulations presented earlier in the paper.[11] It would have been helpful to include some interaction terms in the regressions. As specified in the paper, they assume, for example, that education effects are the same for different ages and wealth levels, and for rural and urban households. The estimations do not allow one to answer reasonable questions such as the following:

- Is the age variation in asset holding and borrowing patterns the same for rural and urban households?
- Are the education effects the same for younger and older households?
- Does education matter in the same way for the wealthy as for the less well-off for their asset holding and borrowing patterns?[12]

10. In the earlier version of the paper, the authors did not have the comparisons across countries, but included information on variation by education, family size, and whether urban or rural. For example, more educated households, urban households, and those with no children tended to hold higher proportions of financial assets. These relationships are explored in greater detail in the regression analysis, discussed later.

11. Some of these are not in the revised version. The revised version also adds retirement accounts on the asset side in the regressions in Table 3, but does not appear to discuss the results for this variable in the text accompanying the table.

12. One issue, for which there is no real solution, is that the authors refer to the top wealth category as the "rich" and "very rich." In fact, wealth over ₹1.7 million is not rich by the standards of many politicians and industrialists. These people are likely not included in the sample. Even for those included in the sample, under-reporting is likely to be very severe at this upper end. Furthermore, the wealthy may hold assets in trusts, corporations, societies, and so on, off the household balance sheet. All these factors must temper the conclusions that the authors reach about patterns of financialization and other asset holdings.

Another useful modification to the regressions would have been to use the middle category for wealth, age, and education as the omitted category—this would have made it easier to see the significance in differences across categories. For example, for real estate (Table 3 in the paper), the coefficients on the wealth categories are all positive and significant relative to the poorest households. Omitting the middle wealth level would have allowed one to see directly whether the adjacent wealth level categories had significantly different coefficients.

The authors present state-fixed effects from the regressions in Figures 9 and 10 of the paper. These fixed effects vary considerably across the states and Union Territories, and there is no obvious pattern to the differences in magnitudes.[13] The labeling of the figures and the discussion are a bit inaccurate, since they refer to residual or unexplained variation. Since these are fixed effects and not the actual residuals, the discussion is potentially misleading, although one can infer what the authors are referring to with appropriate corrections in the wording.[14] Finally, the authors do not provide information on the assumptions they made with respect to the properties of the error terms, in particular, whether they allowed for clustered standard errors.

Some of the most striking results of the paper are with respect to gold holdings and inflation experience. Using simple regressions of state-fixed effects on a measure of historical inflation volatility, as well as the previous household-level regressions with an inflation experience measure added in, the authors show that experiences of higher past inflation volatility or of higher past levels of inflation are associated with higher proportions of gold holdings. Other assets show negative or insignificant relationships, suggesting that gold is indeed viewed as an inflation hedge by Indian households. These regressions might have benefited from additional state-level controls, such as state domestic product per capita, or degree of urbanization. Although in the state-level regressions, there are relatively few degrees of freedom, this is not a problem in the household-level regressions.

13. The authors could also have explored possible geographical patterns, or correlations across fixed effects from different regressions, to get a sense of whether some economically interesting and identifiable phenomena are lurking behind the fixed effects.

14. The same problem of wording occurs in Section 5, which refers to residual cross-state variation. Of course, at the state level, household residuals should average out, and one can think of state-fixed effects as "residuals" in that they are unexplained, but the issue is partly with the statistical properties being assumed. For example, one could have assumed random effects at the state level and tested between the two specifications.

Another interesting exercise performed by the authors is to relate state-level fixed effects derived from a household-level regression to state-level public sector employment shares. The simple regression yields a positive and significant coefficient, although the authors acknowledge that the explanatory power is low. They note that organized sector employment as a whole should matter, and they offer some conjectures about households' inability or lack of recognition of long-term financial needs. As the authors acknowledge, this is a large and complex topic, and even in developed countries, there is evidence of myopia or other absences of full rationality in long-term financial planning. Hence, the results in the paper can be seen as merely an initial exploration.

Another very useful analysis provided by the paper is to consider the impact of the supply of formal finance.[15] In particular, they regress the state-fixed effects estimated from a household-level regression of the share of non-institutional liabilities on the state-level density of bank branches and find a negative relationship. The authors are careful not to ascribe causality, but again point out that the results bear further investigation.[16]

While this paper represents a pioneering empirical analysis, deals with an extraordinary amount of data from multiple sources, and has a rich set of empirical results, I think it would have been useful to consider additional data. It seems the authors did take my earlier suggestion and incorporated data on bank branches, but there is also data on credit–deposit ratios[17] and other economic data that could have been used. While the household survey is a cross-section for a single year (and it is unclear whether that year was "typical" or not), household balance sheets are the result of accumulated decisions over many years. Just as the authors used past inflation data to test for the impacts of inflation experiences on patterns of asset holdings, other variables from the past could have been used, either in state-level regressions or as state-level controls in the household regressions. I realize that this would have lengthened an already substantial paper and added considerable effort, but it is something to be kept in mind for the future.

The importance of examining trends in the data, wherever possible, is highlighted in the context of the authors' concluding section, which ventures into discussion of several policy options with respect to the demand and supply of financial services. To some extent, the recommendations in the

15. This analysis, and the previous one, are important additions to the first draft of the paper.

16. In this and the previous analysis, the authors do not report R-squareds, so the precise explanatory power of the regression remains unclear.

17. See, for example, Singh et al. (2014).

paper are generic and innocuous (for example, "investment in education, and in particular financial education"), but going beyond these to specifics, and prioritizing and designing policy interventions, will require much more detailed analysis of all the data we have. Policymaking also has to consider the functioning of India's existing institutions for financial intermediation, in terms of factors such as internal organization, competition, and systemic risk. All that being said, this paper can really be a seminal one for a relatively neglected aspect of India's financial policymaking, and is likely to take on that role.

References

Goyal, Malini. 2015, December 6. "Why Indians Are Shifting from Physical to Financial Assets, and Why This Bodes Well for Economy, *ET Bureau*, http://articles.economictimes.indiatimes.com/2015-12-06/news/68809288_1_financial-savings-real-estate-sector-gold-demand (accessed May 15, 2017).

Kant, Krishna. 2014, May 31. "Households Put Two-thirds of Their Savings in Houses, Gold," *Business Standard*, http://www.business-standard.com/article/economy-policy/households-put-two-thirds-of-their-savings-in-houses-gold-114053001457_1.html (accessed May 15, 2017).

Samantaraya, Amaresh and Suresh Kumar Patra. 2014. "Determinants of Household Savings in India: An Empirical Analysis Using ARDL Approach," *Economics Research International*, http://dx.doi.org/10.1155/2014/454675 (accessed May 15, 2017).

Singh, Nirvikar, Jake Kendall, R.K. Jain, and Jai Chander. 2014. "Regional Inequality in India in the 1990s: A District-level View," *Economic and Political Weekly*, 49 (15): 71–76.

General Discussion

Barry Bosworth (chair) pointed out that in the US, surveys to identify the savings of the rich end up missing a huge proportion of their wealth. These US surveys used the same representative sampling approach as the Indian All India Debt and Investment Survey (AIDIS) did. He was surprised, therefore, that the Indian survey was assumed to have captured the savings of the wealthy. It would be important to validate this with some other control measure or total. Second, he pointed to the confusion between using "saving" and "savings" interchangeably in this paper. He noted that the simple rule followed in years past was that "saving" always referred to the flow and "savings" to the stock. He suggested that the confusion could be avoided by using the word "wealth" for savings to measure the stock of savings.

T. N. Srinivasan noted that the RBI aggregate data on household saving was a residual from the national accounts after deducting corporate saving from the total. He was concerned about comparing that aggregate data with information from the National Sample Survey (NSS) of individual households. He asked for greater clarity in the paper on whether the NSS survey represented a steady state or a point on a transition path and whether causality was implied or not. This would need a closer link to economic theory. Without that he felt it was unclear what one learns from the paper, particularly relating to policy.

Andreas Bauer commended the paper's focus on the quality of asset holdings. He noted the low share of financial assets in the total assets holdings across the income spectrum and suggested that while limited access might be a reasonable explanation for low-income households, tax avoidance would be the right explanation for upper income households.

Dilip Mookherjee suggested that the distinction between productive and non-productive assets might be of greater importance than financial versus non-financial savings. Real estate is one of the most important assets for Indian households. If the definition of real estate includes agricultural land, then the relevant measure might be the distinction between agricultural and non-agricultural investments, but it is not clear from the paper how real estate is measured. Even for capital assets, previous research by Larry Summers and others has stressed the differences in the rates of return between investments in building and in equipment, and their different impacts.

Mookherjee also emphasized that one of the most important assets for poor households is children and their relationship to old age security. This is tied to the demographic transition. There is earlier research, such as by Jeff Williamson for 19th-century UK, which associates increased household saving rates with declines in fertility and the migration of sons to the US. Mookherjee also pointed to evidence from China where the one-child policy has had a strong impact on saving rates. He suggested that fertility and migration may be important factors in determining household saving. The paper could be confusing the impact of education on saving with that of fertility and migration. He reinforced Nirvikar Singh's comments about caution in drawing policy conclusions.

Surjit Bhalla expressed some surprise that low-income households were investing in financial assets, as opposed to gold. He suggested looking at this much more closely. He expressed surprise on the small estimated value of the effect of inflation on saving.

Suman Bery, picking up on an earlier comment made by T. N. Srinivasan, remarked that in considering the allocation of assets when liabilities are in a sense pre-ordained, it would be helpful to have some sense of the behavioral model underlying the analysis of the AIDIS data. He also noted that while there may be a legal distinction between financial and non-financial assets that considers gold as the latter, for the purposes of monetary policy, gold is better seen as a financial asset.

Taking up Dilip Mookherjee's point on the importance of real estate, Devesh Kapur asked if the definition of wealth included farm animals like cattle, which are extremely important assets for rural farming households.

R. NAGARAJ*
Indira Gandhi Institute of Development Research

T.N. SRINIVASAN†
Yale University

Measuring India's GDP Growth: Unpacking the Analytics and Data Issues behind a Controversy That Has Refused to Go Away‡

ABSTRACT The Indian Central Statistics Office's (CSO's) new series of National Accounts Statistics (NAS) with 2011–12 as the base year—and incorporating methodological changes drawn—from the UN System of National Accounts (SNA)—has been criticized for reporting annual gross domestic product (GDP) growth rates widely different from the older series, and being at variance with other available macroeconomic indicators. Critics have raised many analytical and empirical issues that in their view were not adequately addressed by CSO and which could have caused the discrepancy in growth rates. However, CSO has claimed the new series to be a distinct improvement since it uses new, large, data sources and incorporates advances in methodology. Taking stock of this debate, the paper makes an overall assessment of the new NAS and offers recommendations for going forward.

Keywords: *National Income, National Accounts Statistics, India, GDP Growth, Base Year, Consumption, Saving, Investment, SNA 2008, MCA 21, CSO*

JEL Classification: *E01, E02*

* *nag@igidr.ac.in*
† *t.srinivasan@yale.edu*
‡ **Acknowledgments**: We are indebted to the Editors, Barry Bosworth and Shekhar Shah, for their immense patience with us and for their constructive suggestions and to Shekhar Shah for helping pull the paper into its final shape. We are also grateful to the anonymous referees for their comments on the first draft of the paper, to Bishwanath Goldar and Pronab Sen, our designated discussants at the IPF 2016, and to members of the audience for their helpful responses to our presentations. The usual disclaimer applies.

1. Introduction

In January 2015, the Government of India's Central Statistics Office (CSO) introduced a new series of National Accounts Statistics (NAS) with base year 2011–12, replacing the earlier series with base year 2004–05 (CSO 2015a).[1] This is a routine matter for the CSO—as with the statistical offices of most countries—to change the base year of the NAS periodically to account for structural changes in the economy and in relative prices and to replace older survey data with newer surveys that better capture current economic activity.[2] This time around, the revision also had another objective: to update to the extent possible the underlying methodology of NAS to the most recent international guidelines, namely the UN System of National Accounts 2008 (SNA 2008).[3]

In changing the methodology and data sources for the new series, the CSO said:

> Besides shifting the base year from 2004–05 to 2011–12, this series incorporates latest available data from surveys, censuses, new economic activities, expansion of coverage of activities and improvement in procedures, and to the extent possible, the latest recommendations of System of National Accounts (SNA) 2008 in the compilation of national accounts. (CSO 2015b, Foreword)

CSO held a "Data User Conference" in 2015 on the new series, and slides of the presentation at this conference (CSO 2015c) have been in circulation, though not officially as a CSO paper. In addition, there has been extensive discussion in the media, as well as in professional journals by

1. See the website of the Ministry of Statistics and Programme Implementation (MOSPI) http://mospi.gov.in/publication/documents-report-sub-committee-national-income-0 for a number of reports of the government's Sub-committee on National Income and background studies relating to the new series. A good reference for the previous revision of the NAS to base year 2004–05 done in 2010 is available in CSO (2010).

2. Professor P. C. Mahalanobis, chairman of the First National Income Committee, was instrumental in the founding of CSO. He also founded the National Sample Survey (NSS) in the Indian Statistical Institute at Kolkata, later transferred to the central government and called the National Sample Survey Organization. The preliminary and final reports of this Committee set the standards, not necessarily thereafter followed by the CSO, for compilation and publication of the National Income Accounts in India.

3. For a brief exposition of SNA 2008, and a factual account of the main changes in the new NAS, see EPW Research Foundation (2015). SNA 2008 was prepared under the auspices of the Inter-Secretariat Working Group on National Accounts, comprising the European Community, the International Monetary Fund, the Organization for Economic Development and Cooperation, United Nations, and the World Bank.

experts on national accounts, including, importantly, in the *Economic and Political Weekly*. Critically reviewing and summarizing this large and diverse literature is beyond the scope of this paper. What we do instead is to draw on this literature selectively while including all the important CSO publications in our assessment of the new NAS series and the major controversies surrounding it.

Section 2 of CSO (2015b), entitled "Guiding Principles for the New Series," lists the three major components influencing the present revision exercise as:

> (i) revision of base year to a most recent year (for meaningful analysis of structural changes in the economy in real terms); (ii) complete review of the existing database and methodology employed in the estimation of various macroeconomic aggregates, including the choice of alternative databases on individual subjects; and (iii) to the extent feasible, implementing the international guidelines on the compilation of national accounts, the System of National Accounts, 2008.... (CSO 2015b, p. 3).

The first two components are almost routinely undertaken during any revision of the base year. Whether or not the second component was in fact a "complete" review will depend on the extent of structural changes in the Indian economy that must be incorporated, the new data that had become available since the previous base year, and the time and resources CSO devoted to the task.

The structure of the paper is as follows. Section 2 describes the main changes made in the new series, and compares them to the old series, particularly those that are at the heart of the ongoing debate. Before coming to the current debate, it is important to point out that there have been many, long-standing methodological issues that have beset the Indian NAS, which, strictly speaking, does not follow the global SNA templates. Only some of these long-standing issues were addressed in the recent revision. We believe that many of these issues warrant flagging in any methodological review of the NAS. Section 3, therefore, describes the legacy issues relating to the methodologies followed in the revised series.

Section 4 describes the principal methodological changes made in the revision that seem to have affected the rates of output growth and how they might relate to the structure of the economy. While the methodological changes in the new series are substantive and extensive, this review will focus on the main issues that have come up for scrutiny in the public debate and not address all the changes made. To keep the main strands of ideas and evidence easily understandable, a lot of detail is relegated to footnotes and appendices. Section 5 explores our individual concerns on the problems confronting the old and new NAS series. Section 6 concludes by making several recommendations.

2. Changes in the New National Account Statistics

For India, with its overwhelming majority of the labor force unorganized and informal (as measured by the NSS in its quinquennial employment and unemployment surveys [EUS]), and with the uneven quality of economic data used in the estimation of the NAS, a base year revision is usually an occasion to improve methodologies, bring in newer and better databases, and address long recognized infirmities in the national accounts.[4] Until the latest revision, the rebasing has usually led to a marginal rise in the absolute size of the aggregate measures as economic activities get better represented. However, their annual growth rates invariably did not change—implying that though the absolute size of the economy may have altered slightly in the new base year, its rate of growth had remained the same.

The recent revision has been different. The absolute size of India's gross value added (GVA) at current basic prices in the 2011–12 base year was marginally "smaller" by 2.1 percent compared to the earlier gross domestic product (GDP) estimates at current factor costs, and there was a significant change in the growth rates for the subsequent years. For instance, India's annual economic growth rate for 2013–14 at constant base prices according to the new series was 6.2 percent, compared to 4.8 percent at constant factor cost according to the old series (Figure 1). Further, the manufacturing sector GVA's growth rate in real terms for the same year changed from –0.7 percent to +5.3 percent. Furthermore, the revised estimates did not seem consistent with other macroeconomic indicators such as corporate earnings or credit growth (Figures 2a and 2b).

Similarly, rates of domestic saving and investment as a percentage of gross domestic disposable income were also much higher in the new series

4. The definitions of the terms "organized" and "unorganized," "establishment," and "enterprise" depend on data sources, such as the population and economic censuses, follow-up enterprise surveys and, of course, the NSS Employment and Unemployment Surveys. The comparability of data across sources and over time cannot be taken for granted since the definitions of the concepts used in the surveys also seem to vary across surveys.

FIGURE 1. Disaggregated GDP Growth Rates for 2013–14

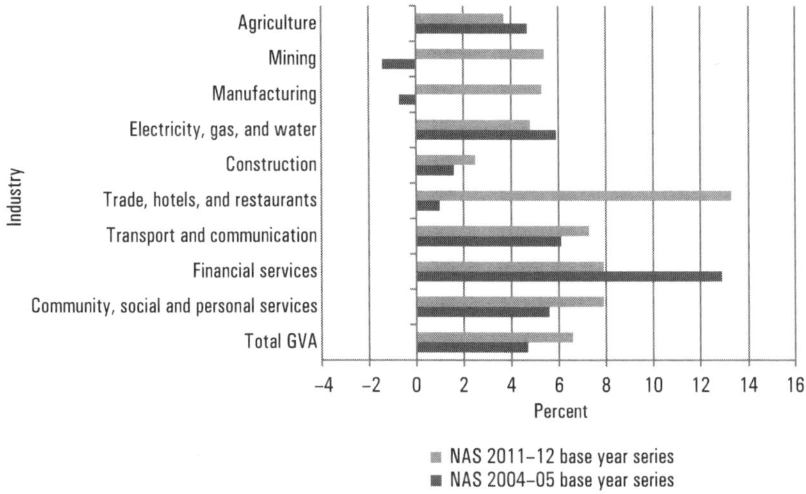

Source: CSO (2014, 2015b).

FIGURE 2a. Bank Credit to GDP Ratio, 2009–15

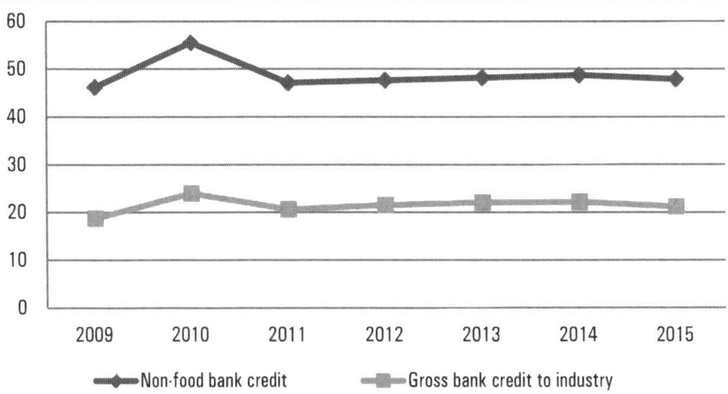

Source: www.rbi.org.in.

as compared to the same rates relative to GDP at current market prices from the old series (Table 1).

In January 2016, following its regular calendar of NAS press notes, CSO released the "First Revised Estimates" (FRE) of the new series, in which even the base year estimates had changed, thus causing more uncertainty

FIGURE 2b. Growth in Bank Credit, 2010–15

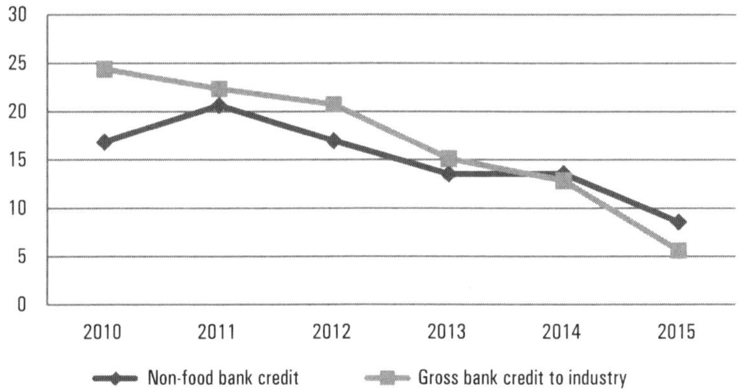

Source: www.rbi.org.in.

TABLE 1. Saving and Investment Ratios and Growth Rates, 2010–11 to 2013–14

	Growth Rate of GDS (%)		*Growth Rate of GCF (%)*		*Saving/GNDI (%)*		*GCF/GNDI (%)*	
Year	*2004–05 Series*	*2011–12 Series*	*2004–05 Series*	*2011–12 Series*	*2004–05 Series*	*2011–12 Series*	*2004–05 Series*	*2011–12 Series*
2010–11					6.7		12.8	
2011–12	6.2		–8.5		6.4	9.4	10.1	13.3
2012–13	8.3	16.6	1.3	14.7	6.1	9.7	9.2	13.5
2013–14		23.7		6.2		10.6		12.6

Source: CSO (2014, 2015b).

according to some (CSO 2016b; Rajakumar and Shetty 2016). For instance, the FRE showed domestic output size (GVA at current basic prices) in the base year 2011–12 lower than in the old series (GDP at factor cost at current prices) by 3.4 percent (compared to 2.3 percent as estimated in 2015). Thus, for example, for 2013–14, we have three sets of GDP growth rate estimates with considerable differences between them (Figure 3).

Over the past 20 months, critics of the methodologies and databases used in the revised estimates have questioned the credibility of the new NAS.[5] Their critiques have led to skepticism about the new GDP estimates among the media, policymakers, international investors, and economic analysts.

5. Srinivasan (2003) notes that many of these criticisms had been discussed, though by no means resolved, by the 2001 Rangarajan National Statistical Commission (MOSPI 2001).

FIGURE 3. Growth Rates in 2013–14

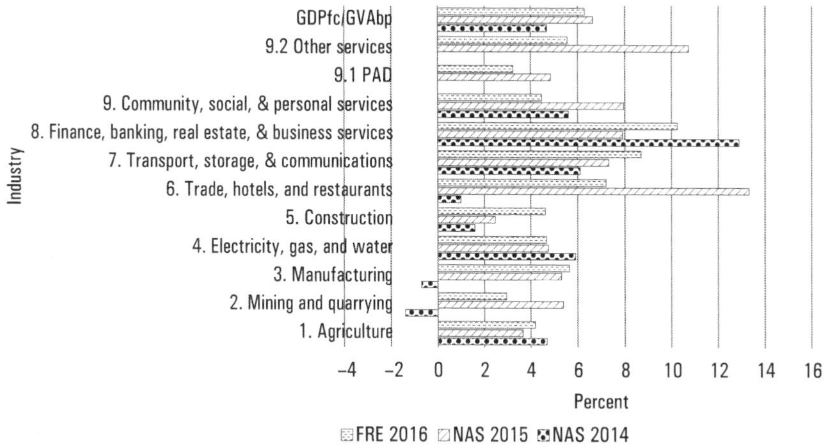

Source: CSO (2014, 2015b, 2016b).

The growth rate estimates for 2013–14 are FRE 2016 = first revised estimate of GVA at basic prices (*GVAbp*) released in 2016; NAS 2015 = new series GVAbp with base 2011–12 released in 2015; NAS 2014 = original GDP series at factor cost (*GDPfc*) with base 2004–05 released in 2014.

However, CSO and other statistics officials have repeatedly responded to these criticisms by asserting that the NAS revision is benchmarked against the best international practices and has used larger and improved datasets, hence the estimates are technically better and therefore more credible. But the debate has refused to go away, and the doubts seem to get reinforced with every release of the new estimates.[6]

2.1. Changes in the Sectoral Composition of Domestic Output

To begin with, it is useful to list the principal changes in the domestic output estimates at current prices in the new series. The main changes are the following:

1. The industrial (also referred to in this paper as sectoral) composition of domestic output has changed somewhat: the industrial sector's size at market prices has swelled by about 5 percent of GDP in the new series, with a corresponding decline in the tertiary sector's size and the share of agriculture remaining broadly the same (Table 2).

6. For instance, in first week of June 2016, just ahead of the IPF Conference, there were two op-ed columns critical of the new estimates, which showed that the high and rising growth rate is made up of unexplainable "discrepancies" and accounted for nearly half of the incremental output growth in the January–March 2016 quarter.

TABLE 2. Sectoral/Industrial Composition of GDP at Factor Cost (Old Series) and GVA at Basic Prices (New Series), Base Year 2011–12

Sector/Industry Percentages	*GDPfc (%), Old Series*	*GVA bp (%) New Series (2016 Rev.)*
1. Agriculture, forestry, and fishing	17.9	18.5
2. Mining and quarrying	2.7	3.2
3. Manufacturing	14.7	17.4
4. Electricity, gas, water supply, and other utility services	1.6	2.3
5. Construction	8.2	9.6
6. Trade, repair, hotels, and restaurants	**17.4**	**10.9**
7. Transport, storage, communication, and services related to broadcasting	7.3	6.5
8. Financial, real estate, and professional services	16.5	18.9
9. Public administration, defense, and other services	**13.8**	**12.7**
10. Total %age	100.0	100.0
GDP at fc and GVA at bp (₹ crore)	8,391,691	8,106,656

Source: CSO (2014, 2015b).

2. Table 2 shows the industrial distribution of GDP at current market prices for the base year 2011–12, as per the new (revised estimates of January 2016) and the old (2004–05) series. It shows that the shares of manufacturing and the financial sector have expanded, while those of trade, hotels, and restaurants, and of community, social, and public services have declined.

2.2. Changes in the Institutional Composition of GDP

There have been important shifts in the institutional composition of GDP (Figure 4). The new series uses the corporate form of organization in four out of six institutional sectors. The two excluded are general government and the household sector. This change could have implications for the measurement of output in many activities, as discussed below.

2.3. Changes in the Organizational Units of Measurement

In the old series, a factory or a plant was the unit of record. In any plant, activities could include the production of goods and services, the latter including the management of the plant (and possibly also of other plants of the same owner) and auditing, and accounting services for that plant (and possibly for other plants owned by the same owner). Therefore, unless the owner owned only one plant, the traditional statements of assets and liabilities, and of income and expenditure for the plant would have been meaningless in the old series.

FIGURE 4. Institutional Composition of GDP in Old and New NAS Series, for 2011–12 (Percent)

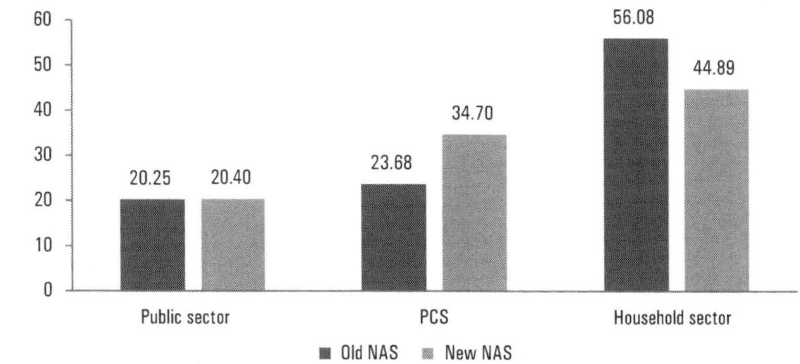

Source: CSO (2014, 2015b).

In the new series, outside of agriculture and the public sector, an enterprise rather than a factory is now the organizational unit of measurement used for recording output and other data. Value addition in all its activities is, in principle, captured in the enterprise's or company's balance sheet. Table 3a lists the institutional framework of the old NAS and the framework adopted in the new 2011–12 base year NAS. Table 3b presents comparative data for the new and old NAS, using the new NAS classification in Table 3a. In the old series, the organized sector consisted of the overlapping categories of (a) the public sector, (b) the private corporate sector (PCS), and (c) factory manufacturing and recognized educational and medical institutions, accounting for 40–45 percent of GDP.

Table 3b shows that public sector's share in GDP in the new series has remained the same as in the old series, though there has been some reshuffling within the public sector in the new series: "Administrative

TABLE 3a. Institutional Framework of NAS 2004-05 and NAS 2011–12

Old Series (Base Year 2004–05)	*New Series (Base Year 2011–12)*
1. Public Sector	1. Public Non-financial Corporations
1.1 Administrative Departments	2. Private Non-financial Corporations
1.2 Departmental Enterprises	3. Public Financial Corporations
1.3 Non-departmental Enterprises	4. Private Financial Corporations
2. Private Sector	5. General Government
2.1 PCS	6. Household Sector, including NPISHs
2.2 Household Sector, including NPISHs	

Source: CSO (2015c).

TABLE 3b GDP Shares, 2011–12

Old Series (Base Year 2004–05)	*GDP Share (%)*	*New Series (Base year 2011–12)*	*GDP Share (%)*
I. Organized Sector	43.9	**I. Organized Sector**	55.1
1. Public Sector	20.3	*1. Public Sector*	20.4
(i) Administrative Departments		(i) General Government	9.7
(ii) Departmental Enterprises		(ii) Public Non-financial Corporations	2.1
(iii) Non-departmental Financial Enterprises		(iii) Public Financial Corporations	8.6
2. PCS	23.7	*2. PCS*	34.7
3. Factory Manufacturing		(a) Private Financial Corporations	
		(b) Private Non-financial Corporations	
4. Recognized Educational and Medical Institutions			
II. Unorganized Sector	56.1	**II. Household Sector**	44.9

Source: CSO (2015c).

departments" in the old series have now become "General government," which, in principle, includes local administration as well. "Departmental enterprises" and "Non-departmental and non-financial non-enterprises" are now put under the subheading "Public non-financial corporations." "Non-departmental financial enterprises" are now placed under a separate subheading called "Public financial corporations."

Within PCS, the scope of the non-financial private corporate sector (NF-PCS) has expanded significantly with the inclusion of quasi corporations (QCs), defined as noncorporate entities that appear to maintain accounts like the corporate sector, now shifted from the household sector (more about this below). As a result, the size of PCS has gone up by 11 percentage points of GDP, with a corresponding reduction in the size of the household sector. As is widely known, PCS consists of NF-PCS and financial PCS (F-PCS). In the new NAS, the larger size of PCS seems to be on account of NF-PCS, while the F-PCS' size has remained the same.

Correspondingly, the GVA of the household sector has contracted. There could, however, be another possible reason for the shrinkage of the household sector: the methodology for estimating GDP in the nonagricultural household sector has changed (CSO 2015e; more about this in Section 4).

2.4. Changes in the Estimation of Manufacturing Output

A lot of the debate on the new NAS has centered around the manufacturing sector.[7] The manufacturing sector has traditionally been measured in two parts. First, the registered sector, consisting of all factories registered under the Factories Act—that is, factories employing 10 or more workers using power (or 20 or more workers without power)—accounting for about two-thirds of manufacturing sector output and employing about 20 percent of manufacturing employment. The Annual Survey of Industries (ASI) is the principal database to capture the output of registered manufacturing. ASI, in turn, consists of two parts: an annual census of all registered factories employing 50 or more workers using power (or 100 or more workers without power) and a sample survey of smaller registered factories, with roughly one-third of such factories surveyed each year.

Second, the rest of the manufacturing sector—small workshops and household enterprises employing less than 10 workers with power (or 20 workers without power) and called unregistered or unorganized

7. For details of the debate on the manufacturing sector output estimation, see Goldar (2015) and Nagaraj (2015c).

manufacturing—has had its value added estimated "indirectly" via periodic NSS sample surveys.

The list of factories used for canvassing the ASI is incomplete and often out of date due to the widespread and growing evasion of registration under the Factories Act, especially by smaller factories (Nagaraj 2002). Further, there is a problem of nonresponse by factories that do not comply with the law to submit their production information under the ASI.

The foregoing method of measuring manufacturing output has many shortcomings: first, there is about a two-year lag in getting ASI results, during which the Index of Industrial Production (IIP) was used for estimating manufacturing sector GVA. Second, the IIP's quality has been deteriorating over time, adversely affecting the quality of value added estimates in manufacturing. Third, the estimation of the unorganized manufacturing sector's output was widely considered unsatisfactory, as the value added per worker (VAPW) parameter that was being used tended to get outdated, leading to the underestimation of its output.

The new NAS series has largely done away with the ASI, replacing it with corporate sector data called the Ministry of Corporate Affairs (MCA) 21 database and accounting for nearly two-thirds of manufacturing value added (Tables 4a and 4b). As mentioned earlier, partnership and proprietary firms in unregistered manufacturing that use books of accounts (as per the NSS survey data) are now defined as QCs and shifted to PCS. Their growth rate is taken to be the same as that of the manufacturing sector in PCS in the new series.

2.5. Shrinkage of the Household Sector[8]

As shown earlier, for 2011–12, the household sector's share of GDP has fallen from 54 percent in the old series to 43 percent in the new series mainly for two reasons: first, QCs have been moved to PCS, and second,

TABLE 4a. Data Sources Used for Estimating GVA in Manufacturing

Series	*Year 1 (Advance & Provisional)*	*Year 2 (1st Revised Estimate)*	*Year 3 (2nd Revised Estimate)*
Old 2004–05 Base Year Series	IIP	IIP	ASI
New 2011–12 Base Year Series	IIP + Advance Filing of Corporate Accounts	IIP + MCA 21	MCA 21 + Non-corporate ASI

Source: http://mospi.nic.in/Mospi_New/upload/Understanding_New_GDP.pdf, p. 3.

8. See Section 3.2 also.

TABLE 4b. Institutional Composition of the Manufacturing Sector

	2013–14		2014–15	
Sectors	*Percent Share*	*Growth*	*Percent Share*	*Growth*
Public Sector, including Public Sector Enterprises	7.9	(NDCU= 6.3, DCU=1.7)‡	8.4	12**
PCS	65.2	7.9§	66.0	8.0@
ASI (Non-corporate) and Household	26.9	0.7*	25.6	1.9*
	100.0	(IIP Growth= (–0.8)	100.0	

Source: http://mospi.nic.in/Mospi_New/upload/Understanding_New_GDP.pdf, page 3; CSO (2014, 2015b).
* Growth is derived from relevant two-digit CCs. Hence growth is not the same as total IIP growth.
§ derived from the MCA 21 database.
@ derived from the RBI sample study and BSE database.
** derived from past trends.
‡ derived from the analysis of accounts of PSUs and government budget.

output per worker in many activities has contracted on account of the change in methodology. In the old series, the unregistered sector's output was estimated "indirectly" as a product of (a) output per worker (as estimated using NSS sample surveys of employment and unemployment) and (b) the number of workers employed in the activity.[9] The new NAS estimates of output per worker are obtained using a Cobb–Douglas (CD) production function. This latter method categorizes workers with varying productivities into (a) wage workers, (b) self-employed workers, and (c) helpers.

9. The CSO explains this process as follows:

> 2.2 At present, the estimates of value added and related macroeconomic aggregates for a number of economic activities carried out in the unorganized segment of the economy are compiled using an indirect method called the Labor Input Method (LIM). In this method, first the labor input (LI) is compiled as the sum of workers, either on the principal status or on the subsidiary status (including the work on subsidiary status of principal status workers), at detailed activity level known as "compilation categories" (CCs).
>
> 2.3 The CCs are determined by regrouping the economic activities at 3, 4, and 5 digit level described in the National Industrial Classification (NIC), which, in turn, follows the International Standards Industrial Classification (ISIC) of All Economic Activities of the United Nations. As per the recommendations of the Advisory Committee, the same CCs of 1999–2000 series based on NIC 1998 were used for the current series (2004–05 –100) because of marginal changes in NIC 2004.
>
> 2.4 The benchmark GVA estimates of the unorganized manufacturing and services sectors are then prepared for the CCs for the base year of national accounts series using the estimated labor input (LI) engaged and the VAPW in the activity.
>
> 2.5 The base year estimates are projected to subsequent years ... (CSO 2015d, p. 3).

2.6. Gross Saving and Capital Formation Estimates

The new series has published a gross national saving and capital formation series, in place of a gross domestic saving (GDS) and capital formation series, signifying the growing role of the external sector in the economy. Thus, in place of the concepts of GDP, GDS, and gross domestic investment, the corresponding gross national product concepts are used. The relevant income concept includes net factor income and transfers from abroad. Further, for the first time, saving is reported more meaningfully in an economic sense as a proportion of gross national disposable income (GNDI), rather than the earlier measure of a gross saving to GDP ratio. Similarly, expenditure on valuables, which was once treated as consumption expenditure, was separately recorded in the old series as one of the assets in the standard table on "Gross Capital Formation by Institutions and Asset Class," but without indicating which institution owned it and their ownership shares (Rajakumar, Sawant, and Shetty 2015; Srinivasan 2014).[10] In the new series, the entire ownership of valuables has been assigned to the household sector. But CSO has not indicated how the household sector finances this investment, thereby making a consistent, consolidated account of the national capital and finance accounts difficult to estimate (more about this in Section 3).

2.7. The Treatment of Quasi Corporations

QCs are defined in the SNA 2008 as "an unincorporated enterprise that has sufficient information to compile a complete set of accounts as if it were a separate corporation and whose de facto relationship to its owner is that of a corporation to its shareholders" (as quoted in Subba Rao 2015). As per CSO, QCs include (CSO 2015c, p. 6):

1. Unincorporated enterprises covered in ASI
2. Unincorporated enterprises of manufacturing that are not covered in ASI but maintain accounts
3. Cooperatives providing non-financial services
4. Unincorporated enterprises providing non-financial services and maintaining accounts
5. Unorganized financial enterprises.

10. T. N. Srinivasan (2014) has discussed the issue of "valuables" in his unpublished note shared with RBI and CSO officials, and it is available from the author.

The above list implies that QCs include financial enterprises as well.[11] QCs account for 8 percent of GVA in the new series.[12] There is no comparable estimate available for the old series, so there is little basis to make a comparison. However, the absolute size of this QC component seems very large.[13] Moreover, QCs are assumed to grow at the same rate as PCS, though CSO does not provide any supporting evidence for it.

3. Legacy Issues[14]

3.1. Approaches to the Measurement of Gross Domestic Product

The task of putting together the NAS in an emerging market country such as India is a continuing activity. As the economy develops, it has to respond, as it must, to the dynamics of development at home and abroad, opportunities from a shifting global technology frontier, and from demographic changes, and more methodologically, to advances in economic and statistical theories, economic measurement and econometrics, and computational capabilities and techniques. This being the case, at any point in time, there will invariably be a legacy of unfinished tasks and known, but yet to be availed, opportunities, and importantly, anticipated opportunities likely to be available in the near future. This makes any description of legacy issues difficult, imprecise, uncertain, and subjective, if not entirely arbitrary. Also some of the tasks described in this section as unfinished legacy are as relevant for the new series of NAS as they would have been for the old series. For this reason,

11. Two tables in CSO (2015b) provide data on institutional-cum-industrial classification of output. Table 2 on page 19 gives data on "GVA for non-financial PCS excluding quasi corporate sector in 2011–12;" Annexure I on page A-1 gives data on "GVA at basic prices for the year 2011–12 by industry and institutional sector." The difference in the estimates for PCS between the two tables is on account of QCs. This is the evidence to show that in the official statistics, QCs are defined as part of NF-PCS. But the information given in the text above shows that unorganized financial enterprises are also included in QCs. Therefore, the arguments we raised in Nagaraj (2015d) and in our rejoinder to CSO (Nagaraj 2015e) merit attention. We gratefully owe this clarification to Rymond Zhong.

12. This is estimated using the industry by institutions GVA table in Annexure–I, page A-1, and GVA for NF-PCS excluding QCs from Table 2, page 19 (CSO 2015b).

13. This hunch is based on the following reason. As a large part of QCs is unregistered manufacturing, which accounts for about 4–5 percent of GDP, QCs in services are likely to have much smaller VA per worker. Further, following the methodological reasoning in "Mystery of Private Corporate Saving," Subba Rao (2015) suggests that QC size is perhaps overstated in the new NAS.

14. This section largely reflects T. N. Srinivasan's views.

the boundary between this section on legacy problems and Section 5 on the agenda for the future is unavoidably blurred.

The three independent approaches for estimating GDP and related aggregates are: (a) the production or product approach in which GVA by units of production of goods and services in the economy is aggregated; (b) the income approach in which the income accruing to domestic primary factor owners for their supply of factors of production such as land, labor, and capital is aggregated; and (c) the expenditure approach in which government and resident private sector expenditures on consumption, gross capital formation (GCF), and foreigners' expenditures on exports net of imports are aggregated. If we ignore for simplicity the complications arising from direct and indirect taxes, except for measurement errors, the three approaches should lead to the same estimate of GDP. CSO (2016) gives a good account of these measurement approaches. Syrquin's (2016) review of Coyle (2014) is a good source for the intellectual history of the GDP concept.

Strictly speaking, even in advanced countries, the product-, income-, and expenditure-based estimates are not independently derived, and some mixture of the three is used. In the Indian NAS, the mixture is so extensive that it is better called a mishmash, or a confused mixture of the three, that is, in large part, attributable to the persistence of a large unorganized sector in GDP as well as in employment. Yet from Table 6.1 of CSO (2015b), which lists items/sectors for which either a production or income approach is being used, even with the changes in methodology and data sources in the new series, no significant dent seems to have been made in this mishmash legacy.

3.2. Absence of Mutually Consistent Data on Income, Consumption, Saving, and Investment in the NAS

The household sector in the NAS (in the old as well as the new series) includes households as defined in the household consumption expenditure surveys (CES) of the NSS, that is, by the conventional "kitchen" definition: a household consists of all those who usually eat out of the same kitchen. It also includes unincorporated enterprises and partnerships. Not only in the CES but in almost all household surveys of the NSS, such as the EUS, the conventional "kitchen" definition for households is used.

In the CES, data only on consumption (quantities and values) are collected from the sampled households. Data on household income and their sources are not collected, both for valid analytical reasons as well as keeping in mind the results of sampling experiments in early rounds of the NSS on the reliability of income data. So the NSS does not collect data from households on their income from their factor supplies. Moreover, the NSS EUS show that a significant number of labor force participants from conventional households are self-employed, so that their income is a mixture of operating surpluses from their production activity in agricultural, cottage, or village industry in which they are self-employed, and wage income from their supply of labor.

Without data on household income, clearly household saving cannot be derived from the CES. In fact, only limited use is made in the NAS (old and new) of the commodity pattern of consumption expenditure from the CES, and instead Table 3 commodity-flow approach is used.[15] Importantly, the asset composition of GCF is derived by using the commodity-flow method. Also, some of the durables purchased by households could be dual use, in that their services could be consumed as well as used as intermediate inputs in home production and/or other income-earning activities. Data on household purchases of financial instruments are not available in the CES. This means that consistent data on income, saving, and investment, and its financing by households, as conventionally defined, are not available from the CES. The NSS had experimented with collecting income, consumption, saving, and investment data in a mutually consistent manner through an integrated schedule in a few early rounds. In fact, the 2001 Rangarajan National Statistical Commission had recommended that NSS should resume canvassing this data again.[16] Whether in response or otherwise, the NSS in its Survey on the Status of Agricultural Households in Rural India in the 70th NSS Round in 2014 collected data on incomes, their principal sources, expenditures on consumption, and productive investment. Whether such a survey will be extended to urban areas and continued is not known.

It is worth recognizing that the legacy of not having data collected from direct responses of households on a mutually consistent basis on consumption, saving, and investment necessarily means the NAS estimates of PFCE,

15. Private final consumption expenditure (PFCE) in the NAS is based on a commodity-flow approach, with ratios where relevant for quantities retained for own consumption and retail prices worked out from the NSS Consumer Expenditure Surveys. This approach covers the consumption of primary goods, manufactured products, other products, and services. For extensive details on the methodology and indicators used, see CSO (2015b, 176–81).

16. For a critique of the Report of the Rangarajan Commission, see Srinivasan (2003). In his comments as a formal discussant for this paper at the 2016 IPF, Pronab Sen said that CSO, following the Rangarajan Commission's suggestion, had tried the integrated schedule of income, consumption, savings, and investment, but the results were again not satisfactory. It would be very useful for CSO to prepare a briefing note on the pilot and the unsatisfactory results that were obtained.

capital formation, and its financing are all based on indirect sources. The issue is discussed in more detail in Section 5.

3.3. Outsourcing, Fragmentation of Production, Regional, and Global Value Chains

Although strictly speaking this is not a legacy issue, newer forms of production could have significant implication for the new NAS series. With the WTO's GATS agreement on services trade in 2001, service activities that used to be done within a manufacturing company are being outsourced to specialized service companies within a country or in a foreign country, so that the value that used to be added by service employees of the manufacturing company is now being outsourced to service companies. This process, originally described by Jagdish Bhagwati, is now very extensive, leading to growing international trade in components and parts and in what is called process trade, in which goods are shipped back and forth among countries for completion of all processes before the goods are ready. Although the quantitative significance for India of the growth of global value chains over the last two decades is not known, what is known is that India is a latecomer in its participation in such chains. Such an analysis should begin as soon as possible. Unfortunately, the MCA 21 database is fairly recent and makes a reliable retrospective analysis difficult. However, as a start, CSO should begin publishing India's international trade data in gross and net value added terms.

3.4. Error Estimates for Sectoral and Aggregate Value Added

The first and final reports of the First National Income Committee, chaired by the late Professor P. C. Mahalanobis, provided approximate error estimates for aggregate and sectoral value added. Although these were not sampling errors in a statistical sense, they were very informative. The CSO does not provide similar error estimates, so that it is impossible to tell whether NAS estimates are now less error prone after more than six decades. On the principle of better late than never, CSO should start publishing error estimates as soon as possible.

3.5. Panel Data

Although CSO collects and publishes several time series, almost all of them are cross sections, with some repeated over time. There are many issues for which panel data are essential for drawing valid inferences. The econometric theory and tools for panel data analysis, including panel cointegration techniques, are well developed. It is time that CSO introduces panel features in its time series, which would also help considerably in the correct estimation of the NAS.

4. The Ongoing Debate[17]

This section deals with the methodological changes made in the new NAS series and the main debates surrounding the new estimates that ensued. It focuses on the private corporate and household sectors, whose estimates have undergone the most significant changes. For the sake of convenience, the term "GDP" denotes GVA at basic prices in the new series and GDP at factor cost in the old series.

4.1. The Private Corporate Sector

Historically, due to poor enforcement of the law, only a small fraction of registered companies filed their audited balance sheets with the Registrar of Companies (Nagaraj 2015d).[18] However, as all large companies (that is, with high paid-up capital [PUC]) mostly filed their balance sheets, and PCS was then a small part of the economy, RBI's small sample of companies with high PUC was deemed adequate to capture the PCS' saving and capital formation.[19] RBI sample estimates were then "blown up" to the universe of registered companies—using PUC as the parameter—to get estimates for PCS.

However, with the phenomenal growth in company registrations during the last three decades, and with the majority of them not complying with the statutory requirement to file a return, the foregoing method has become unreliable as there is no record of the universe of "working" companies. The 2001 National Statistical Commission Report had clearly stated this fact and recommended conducting a census of working companies at least once in a decade to ascertain the universe of working companies. To quote the report:

> There are more than five lakh (500,000) companies registered in the Registrar of Companies, but the actual number of companies that are operating is not known. This situation seriously affects the reliability of various estimates. An exercise conducted in

17. This section largely reflects R. Nagaraj's views.

18. See the quotation from the National Statistical Commission report below in the text.

19. This is a case of using information from a regulatory filing by companies to estimate saving and capital formation in PCS.

March 1999 indicated that about 47 per cent of the registered companies filed their balance sheets for the year 1997–98 with the Registrar of Companies. (MOSPI 2001, 22)

During the last decade, GDP growth accelerated to 7–8 percent per year mainly on account of the services sector. Disaggregating the growth shows that GDP in the PCS was the source of rapid growth. Inquiring into the possible overestimation of services output growth, Nagaraj (2009) had found a substantial rise in the share of PCS in GDP using estimates derived indirectly from the NAS. Comparing these estimates with those obtained using Centre for Monitoring Indian Economy Pvt. Ltd (CMIE)'s Prowess database, we had shown that there seems to be a systematic overestimation of PCS output in GDP (Figure 5). For instance, for 2005–06 the share of PCS in GDP as per NAS was about 18 percent, whereas it was just about 8 percent based on the CMIE data. Even assuming that the CMIE data underestimates the size of the PCS since it ignores small private limited companies, the gap between the two estimates is so wide that it clearly points to overestimation in the NAS.[20]

In about 2006, MCA initiated an effort to encourage companies to file their financial returns electronically and created a web portal where companies could e-file their returns. After considerable efforts, including incentives and threats of de-registration, the e-filing of returns peaked at over 500,000

FIGURE 5. Size of Corporate Sector as Percent of GDP

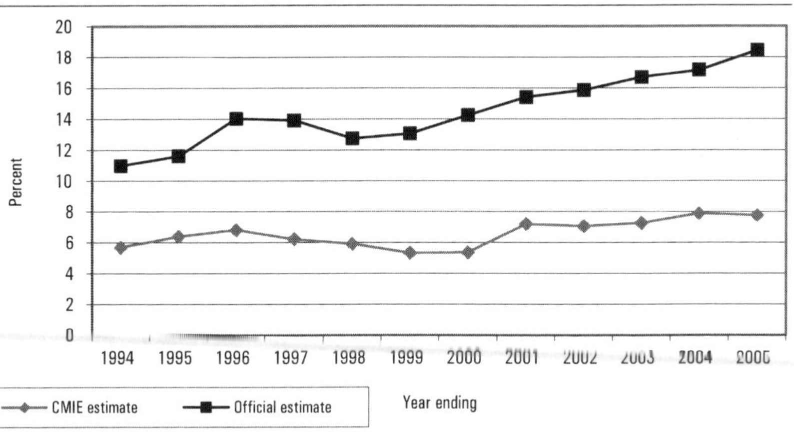

Source: CSO (2014, 2015b).

20. Estimates based on CMIE data use audited balance sheet data; therefore they should not be underestimates for companies in the database.

companies during 2011–12 and 2012–13, out of a total of over 900,000 registered companies. In other words, in spite of its best efforts, the regulatory authority could at best get little over one-half of registered companies to comply with the mandatory requirement. With the phenomenal growth in company registration in the last two decades, a growing proportion of the newer companies seem to be bogus/fictitious, thus seriously eroding credibility and validity problems with the MCA 21 database (Nagaraj 2015d).

CSO's decision to use the MCA 21 database to directly estimate national income aggregates for NF-PCS for the new NAS series was widely welcomed at that time. The new NAS showed that the PCS accounted for about 35 percent of GDP in 2011–12, significantly larger than its previous, indirectly estimated size. The growth rate of the PCS also turned out to be higher. And since a large part of manufacturing firms belonged to the PCS, manufacturing's share in GDP also increased. Both changes led to skepticism about the veracity of the new estimates and have been at the center of the debate between the CSO and the NAS-user community.

There are two methodological changes introduced by CSO that are key to the debate, as revealed when the reliability of the PCS estimates has been questioned (Nagaraj 2015a, 2015b). These are, first, the "blow-up" factor, and second, the inconsistency between the aggregated and the disaggregated cost data that seem to have yielded widely differing GVA estimates.

Put simply, since the number of companies for which accounts are available varies from year to year, the "blowing-up" or "scaling-up" factor changes correspondingly, thus greatly affecting the final estimates. To illustrate, for the years 2011–12 and 2012–13, the MCA 21 database consisted of about 500,000 companies. Estimates based on the PUC of these companies were "blown up" to about 900,000 "active companies." However, for 2013–14, the number of companies in the MCA database submitting their financials plummeted to about 300,000. When the estimates based on the PUC of 300,000 companies were blown up to 900,000 companies, the overall population estimates seem to have been overestimated (compared to the previous year), thereby also raising the estimated growth rates.

Another factor that seems to affect the sample estimates for the companies for which data are available is that the cost data obtained from the MCA database seems incomplete and inconsistent, which seems to lead to differing estimates when disaggregated data is used, compared to when aggregated data are used. To quote CSO:

> [T]he output as per database was restricted to the total revenue reported [which led to smaller estimates]. However at the time of preparing the final report, it was felt that the

individual components under total revenue would reveal the real picture of the economy in a better way. Hence the restriction was removed and output as per database was estimated using the individual components under total revenue in the database. (CSO 2015d, 87)

The debate on the reliability of the PCS estimates draws attention again to the lack of accurate estimates of the number of working companies, a factor that was highlighted in the 2001 Rangarajan Commission Report. We really do not know how many of the nearly one million companies registered with the MCA actually produce goods and services on a reasonably regular basis. Describing the size and structure of PCS, Nagaraj (2015d) argued that a majority of the companies could be bogus, fictitious, or shell companies that exist only on paper. They may not be able to produce socially useful output and may simply serve the interests of their owners in camouflaging their true operations.

If the foregoing arguments and evidence have some value, then there is a serious need to re-examine the blowing-up or scaling-up procedure. Further, given the inconsistencies in the MCA database, there is a need for a thorough review of the database and a cleanup before it is used to estimate the NAS. Moreover, the MCA 21 database needs to be made public for anyone to verify the official estimates.

4.2. The Household Sector

As mentioned earlier, until the recent revision, the unorganized sector's output was estimated indirectly as a product of the VAPW, obtained from nationwide sample surveys and the number of workers employed in each industry. There is a long and widely held perception that the unorganized sector's output is invariably under-reported or escapes large-scale official surveys, given the predominance of traditional or non-formal modes of production. The 2001 National Statistical Commission endorsed such a view. It said:

Estimate of gross value added (GVA) per worker as per the FuS [follow-up enterprise surveys] is used for the purpose of GDP calculation. Sometimes there are perceptions from the data users that the FuS estimate of GVA per worker does not reflect the reality (see Annex 5.17) for the estimates of GVA per worker as per the NSS 51st Round for 1994–95 and the Special Enterprise Survey for 1998–99. *In fact, the perception is that the same is quite often under-estimated.* Reluctance on the part of the enterprises to supply correct and complete information in the surveys is one of the reasons for likely under-reporting of receipts and GVA. This reluctance might be due to various reasons, such as apprehension that the information supplied may be utilised for taxation purposes (emphasis added). (MOSPI 2001, para. 5.2.23)

The unorganized sector, by definition, consists of innumerable small, traditional, at times irregular, labor-intensive, and household enterprises, often representing nonmarket or premodern forms of production bordering on survival strategies of the disguised unemployed. The majority of such enterprises often do not (or cannot) maintain modern double entry book keeping, or they cannot do so given the informal, irregular nature of their production, and the low levels of literacy of self-employed workers. Even granting that some small enterprises do maintain financial accounts, these tend not to be kept separate from their personal or family accounts and therefore cannot be used for estimating value added and the profit and loss of such enterprises. The Indian unorganized sector largely consists of subsistence activities, as opposed to modern or capitalist enterprises with a clear separation of individual and family ownership from the legal entity of the company.

Ignoring these well-received views and the above-mentioned conceptual problems, the new NAS has assumed that the older methodology overestimated output per worker since it did not distinguish between different kinds of labor. The subcommittee that looked into the matter made the following critical comments on the older methodology. To quote the report:

> The Labour Input Method, however, suffers from inherent problems. Firstly, while compiling GVAPW [gross value added per worker] ..., it is assumed that there is equal contribution from all categories of workers engaged in an economic activity i.e., the contribution of an employer, a wage-employee (regular or casual), or a family worker, is taken to be equal. Second issue is in projecting the LI [labour input] for subsequent years ... The CAGR [compound average growth rate] concept based on past two rounds of EUS [employment unemployment surveys] being used to project the LI ends up overestimating the LI for most of the compilation categories, especially in the scenario where there is a drop in the LI over the next two consecutive surveys (EUS). (CSO 2015a, 6)

To overcome the problem, the new NAS estimated labor productivity of different categories of workers using a nested CD production function, as discussed in Section 3 of the paper (for details see Nagaraj 2016). This has resulted in a contraction of LIs in the unorganized sector in the new NAS compared to the old series (Figure 6).

As shown in Annex 1 of this paper, this production function methodology used for estimation is arguable. There is a need to justify the specific functional form chosen to estimate effective LI and how its results are superior to alternative estimates.

As Nagaraj (2016) has shown, there is an inconsistency between the LIM, which has contracted the contribution of self-employed labor and the large

FIGURE 6. Comparison of Labor Input and Effective Labor Input in Unorganized Manufacturing

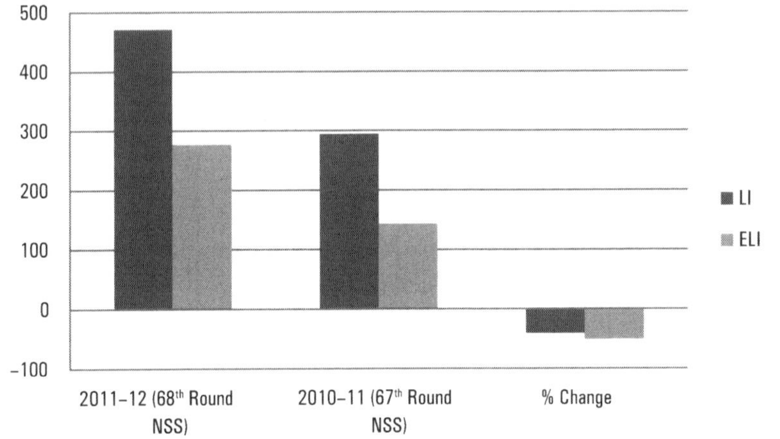

Source: CSO (2014, 2015b).

size of mixed income in the data on income distribution by factors in the unorganized sector. If the contribution of self-employed or owner–workers is really a fraction of that of a wage worker, how is it that the share of mixed income accounts for over 70 percent of all factor incomes in the unorganized sector (Figure 7)?[21] We therefore have reason to suspect that the new methodology for estimating LI has "underestimated" the contribution of this sector to domestic output.

5. Exploring the Issues

5.1. Comments by T. N. Srinivasan

We noted in our Introduction that the new NAS series introduced and used a major new data source—the MCA 21 database—and also updated the NAS methodology in several ways, including, importantly, conforming to the most recent international template, the UN SNA 2008. Moreover, the base year of the new series was shifted from 2004–05 to 2011–12, the concept of factor cost of the old series was replaced by a base price concept, and

21. Since inputs other than labor are miniscule in this sector, it is very unlikely that wage workers' share in mixed income is over 70 percent of the total factor income.

FIGURE 7. Factor Income in Organized and Unorganized Sectors in 2011–12

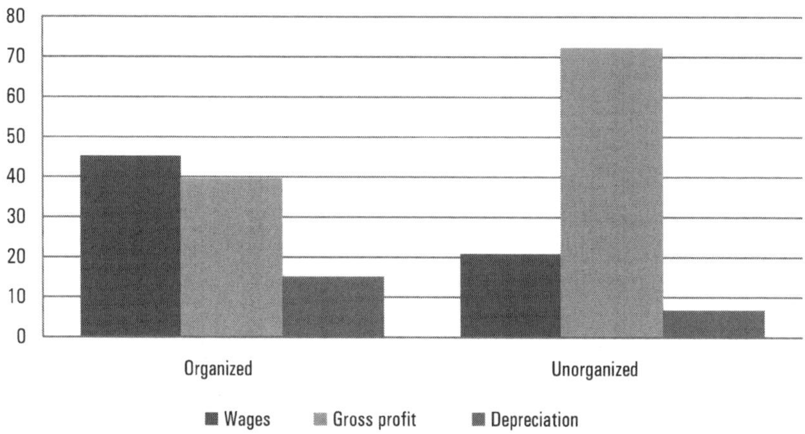

Source: CSO (2014, 2015b).

the word "GDP" was restricted to GVA at market prices. Also, there were changes in deflation procedures and in the price indices used in arriving at constant price values of GDP and its components. Furthermore, in conformity with SNA 2008, the organizational unit for data collection was shifted to an enterprise, and away from the concept of an establishment, and there were some shifts of activities across industries and also across institutional sectors in GVA.

With the methodological changes and the new data sources being introduced simultaneously, some of them for the first time, it is understandable that the new NAS data—particularly of the new series at its introduction in January 2015 and after its scheduled first revision in January 2016—surprised most analysts, presumably relative to their expectations of relatively modest changes in GDP, its components, and in growth projections, following previous base revisions. This has led to considerable skepticism around the new GDP estimates among the media, policy makers, international investors, and economic analysts.

This section offers some additional comments on the handling of the new source data from the MCA 21 data.

5.1.1. Use of MCA 21 Data and the "Bluw-Up" Factor: The problem of Self-selection

A country's GDP and its components cover the whole economy. Estimating them often involves the analogue of the standard inductive statistical inference of estimating population values from sample values. Consider the simple problem of estimating the population of a district of N villages. If we take a simple random sample of n villages out of N with replacement and the total population of the sample villages is p, then the unbiased estimate of the population of the district is $(N/n) \times p$. The value p of the population of n sample villages is "blown up" by (N/n) to arrive at the total population of the villages.

Chapter VIII of the MCA's annual report 2013, entitled "Financial Aggregates of Corporate Sector," in paragraph 8.1 says, "As of 31-03-2013, the MCA repository had information for almost 13.02 lakh companies that have been registered in India." As is to be expected, CSO (2015c) devotes many slides to MCA 21. The one entitled "MCA data" mentions in brief its two e-platforms, namely 23 AC/ACA and XBRL, and lists the legal provisions by which companies are required to file their returns. An important slide with the title "Use of MCA 21 data" mentions:

> CSO estimates in 2011–12 series [New Series] for 2011–12 and 2012–13 prepared based on the analysis 5.24 lakh non-financial private companies who [*sic*] constituted approximately 85 percent of total PUC of active non-financial corporate sector as provided by MCA.
>
> For default companies, the estimates are blown up by a scaler [*sic*] factor determined based on PUC [paid up capital] of reporting companies/PUC of all active companies.
>
> For 2013–14, industry-wise estimated parameters are moved using the growth rate as observed for the 3.08 lakh common companies between 2012–13 and 2013–14. (CSO 2015c)

From the above, though it is not explicit, it is evident that 5.24 lakh companies were presumably active and submitted returns in 2012–13, from which estimates for both the years 2011–12 and 2012–13 were prepared. In analogy with the above population example, "n" is the equivalent of the PUC of the 5.24 lakh active companies that reported in 2012–13, and "N" is the PUC of all active companies, whether they reported or not, and the blow-up factor N/n is 1/0.85 or 1.15. Applying this factor to the 5.24 lakh active companies that filed, the total number of companies including those that did not file would be around 5.8 lakhs.

On the other hand, if indeed there are 13.04 lakh companies in the MCA repository, and not just 5.24 lakhs that filed, using the 85 percent share of the 5.24 lakh companies in the total PUC of all registered companies for deriving the blow-up factor, it must be the case that the companies out of the 13.04 lakh that did not file, namely, 7.8 lakhs, with only 15 percent share in the total PUC of all registered companies, must be, on an average, small with low values of PUC.[22]

However, as T.C.A. Anant, the chief statistician of India and secretary, MOSPI, said in an interview with Ishan Bakshi of *Business Standard* on April 4, 2016:

> Even with the MCA data you do not get reports of all active companies that are participating. So ... you make an estimate for the ones whose accounts are as yet awaited. The practice in national accounts has been [to] make an estimate for the whole [of all participating companies]. So you blow up or make some adjustment for the whole. (Bakshi 2016)

While Dr Anant's arguments seem logical, there is a serious statistical problem in applying the procedure, and the blow-up factor such as the one used in estimating the population of a district, to the MCA data. In the case of choosing a village in the sample for estimating the district population, the choice is random and is made by the statistician, with the village authorities playing no role. On the other hand, whether a company files in time, or files at all, is the company's decision. The MCA data are reported by companies that are self-selected. Furthermore, the 3.08 lakh companies that were common to both 2012–13 and 2013–14 are also self-selected from those that filed in 2012–13 choosing to file also in 2013–14. Any blow-up factor that does not model self-selection, and appropriately allows for it, will lead to inconsistent and biased estimates, with unknown size and direction of bias. In particular, one cannot rule out the possibility that a company's decision to report or not might depend on the contents of the report were one to be submitted.

The implication of the self-selection of companies in the MCA 21 database is that ceteris paribus comparisons of the values of GDP and its components for 2011–12 in the new series—based on data from self-selected companies from MCA 21—with the corresponding values for the same year from the old series, would be vitiated by the self-selection bias of the new series. This is likely to be of particular relevance for comparisons of total GDP, its industrial composition, the relative shares in GDP of the household, and PCSs when such comparisons are made without adjusting for the self-selection bias of MCA 21-based estimates. Moreover, there is the fact

22. Press reports quoted the Revenue Secretary to the Government of India in April 2017 saying that "There are 15 lakh registered companies ... as many as 8–9 lakh are not filing returns with the Corporate Affairs Ministry." See http://www.financialexpress.com/economy/8-9-lakh-registered-companies-not-filing-returns-says-hasmukh-adhia/646840/.

that the composition of the household and PCSs are not the same in the old and new series—QCs have been shifted from the household sector in the old series to private corporations in the new series—so that there is a "non ceteris paribus" factor as well in the comparisons.

5.1.2. Measurement of Labor Input and Labor Income: Production Functions

For the unorganized manufacturing and service sectors,[23] which are part of the household sector of NAS, the new series uses the concept of an "effective LI" by defining it as a weighted sum of the LIs of owners, hired labor, and helpers, using as weights their marginal productivities in value added terms in the base year relative to that of hired labor. It is to be noted that by this definition, different categories of labor are perfect substitutes for each other in production, a rather restrictive and avoidable assumption. The weights of the labor categories are derived by estimating nested CD production functions for the base year for each of the relevant estimation categories/sectors.

As of May end 2017, the parameters of the estimated production functions, and in particular, the data used for non-LIs, such as capital and land, have not been released. Nor is there any information available on whether any robustness checks on the empirical results were done. However, an unnumbered slide in CSO (2015c) lists, for eight categories of non-financial service sectors, what it calls conversion factors for converting a unit of owner and helper labor into equivalent units of hired labor. These are the production function parameters. It turns out that except in education and other services, where more than one

23. The distinction between organized and unorganized sectors, though economically important, plays only a minor role in NAS. In the annual publication of NAS, the unorganized sector is explicitly mentioned only as contributing a part of industrial value added from unregistered manufacturing.

Conversations and exchanges at various fora organized by CSO with their officers, supplemented by CSO (2015b), suggest that:

In the old series, the unorganized sector consisted of the household sector (unorganized sector not maintaining accounts), unorganized enterprises maintaining accounts, and nonprofit institutions serving households (NPISHs). This was nothing but a residual, negative list of sectors not included in the public sector or the PCS.

In the new series, all unincorporated enterprises that do not maintain accounts and NPISHs are classified as part of the household sector. Unorganized enterprises maintaining accounts are classified as QCs and included in PCS.

As noted earlier, it appears that NSS consumption expenditure has been used extensively in the new series for deriving implicit prices (ex-farm price) and also to work out new ratios for use in estimating PFCE. Benchmark estimates for the household sector for the survey year are obtained from NSS surveys and are used to project relevant estimates for both enterprises maintaining accounts (QCs) and not maintaining accounts (household sector). The estimates for QCs are not published separately.

unit of an owner's labor is equivalent to a unit of labor of a hired worker, in all the other 14 cases of activity by labor type, less than one unit of owner's or helper's labor is equivalent to that of a unit of labor of a hired worker. It is unclear whether production functions were estimated for compilation categories or sectors other than the eight sectors.

For some CCs, for example, trade and repair services, "where it was felt that the productivity of different categories of labor may not have a significant impact on GVA, especially in the unorganized segment, the labor input (LI) method was used" (CSO 2015b, 10). In this case, all workers were, in effect, deemed to be equally productive. Clearly, whether significant marginal productivity differences exist across categories of workers or not is an empirical issue, given technology, that is, the production function, and quantities of other inputs. This being the case, there is no reason why a production function was not estimated for all relevant CCs/sectors in the base year, letting the data determine whether or not significant productivity differences exist. Comparing the average VAPW in the old series, in which all workers were assumed to be equally productive, with the weighted average productivity of a workforce composed of workers with differing productivities without correcting for selection bias, is inappropriate.

The annexures 2.3.1–2.3.4 of CSO (2015b) list compiling categories by their method of LI measurement. The effective LIM is used in 34 categories of unincorporated manufacturing in 2.3.1 and 13 categories of unincorporated non-financial services in 2.3.3; a modified effective LI is used in 11 categories of unincorporated non-financial services in 2.3.4; and finally, a simple LI is used in 9 categories of unincorporated non-financial services in 2.3.2. For each of the 57 CCs, a production function could have been estimated, with the parameter values determining the weighting of the three categories of labor, instead of an ex ante specification of the LIM to be used, as in Annexures 2.3.1–2.3.4.

Beyond these problems, there are also technical issues relating to the particular production function used by CSO, and whether differences in the marginal productivities of different types of labor, while statistically significant in individual sectors, cancel out in the aggregate. Appendix 1 discusses these issues.

5.1.3. Measurement of Value Added at Current and Constant Prices: Choice of Price Indices and Deflation Procedures

For extrapolating value added in years succeeding the base year for each CC in the unorganized non-financial services sector, some indicators reflecting the current situation—such as sales tax revenue in the case of unorganized trade and service tax receipts for some services (CSO 2015c)—are used in the new series. Annex 2.5 of CSO (2015c) lists the indicators used for each of 37 CCs, with Annex 2.5.1, listing indicators for value added at current prices, and Annex 2.5.2 listing indicators for value added at constant prices.

The rationale for the choice of indicators is not set forth. For example, in the CC "Maintenance and repair of motor vehicles and motor cycles," the indicator listed in Annex 2.5.2 for extrapolating value added at constant prices is, plausibly, "Motor Vehicles Sales Growth." The corresponding indicator for extrapolating value added at current prices in Annex 2.5.1 is "Motor Vehicles Sales Growth × WPI." Thus, the index for extrapolating value added at constant prices is unaffected by choice of a price index for deflating the value added at current prices, such as WPI, which in turn has nothing to do with the repair and maintenance of motor vehicles and motor cycles, or for that matter any service.

The lack of rationale for the choice of price deflators is equally striking in the case of CCs 7–11 relating to "land transport of passengers and freight." The indicator for current price value added in Annexure 2.5.1 is "growth in registered vehicles × consumer price index (CPI) (transport and communication)." For constant price value added, the index is "growth in registered vehicles!" Again there is no reason to expect CPI (transport and communication) to have anything to do with value added in land transport of passengers and freight. Replacing CPI (transport and communication) with any arbitrary price index would change value added at current prices without affecting constant price value added.

Value added at constant prices of different sectors and in the aggregate are important indicators of real growth. Section 6 of CSO (2015b) is devoted to a summary of the estimation procedures for compilation of national accounts in the new series. Table 6.1, entitled "Gross Value Added (GVA) at Basic Prices," lists products and services in its rows by sectors. Columns 3 and 4 describe the method of estimation of GVA at current and constant prices. Again, it is evident that a multiplicity of price indices is being used without much of an explanation of the rationale of their choice. Defining and measuring real value added has attracted the attention of economists. Appendix 2 of this paper is devoted to a brief discussion of the issues. Other issues relating to price indexes, including the absence of a regular procedure for incorporating new goods as they come on the market, rather than waiting for the next base year revision to do so, are also discussed in Appendix 2.

5.1.4. Institutional Sectors

In the new series, there are six "institutional" sectors comprising private sector financial and non-financial corporations, their two public sector counterparts, general government, and a heterogeneous sector misleadingly called the "household sector," which in effect consists of all CCs of the economy other than those included in the four corporate institutions and general government.

In the old series with base 2004–05, the "household sector" included what are called "QCs." In the new series, QCs have been included under private non-financial corporations. No evidence on changes in their structure and inherent characteristics warranting the shift is offered. It seems to have been done for no reason except that the corporate form of organization is emphasized in SNA 2008. Thus, the so-called "household sector" in the new NAS includes much more than conventional households consisting of individuals eating from the same kitchen. It includes entities such as NPISHs and privately owned partnerships and other noncorporate financial and non-financial entities. In fact, much of unorganized and unregistered manufacturing, including enterprises either with no employees other than its owner, or with the owner and an unpaid family member as employees, is now part of the household sector.

In my view, the statistical implications of the interdependence between the measurement errors and biases in estimating household incomes, consumption and investment, and in estimating corresponding statistics for the other five sectors have not been carefully analyzed. We refer to this issue, and to its treatment in CSO (2012), in Appendix 2. For example, investment in fixed capital assets such as equipment, etc., and in stocks in the aggregate and by public and PCSs is estimated by the commodity-flow method, while the funds available for financing the investment from domestic saving and net capital inflow from abroad are estimated by a flow-of-funds method. The CSO doctrine holds that the data on flow of funds are more reliable than the data on commodity flows, so that the discrepancy between the two is treated as statistical errors of omission, commission, and measurement. It is to be stressed that this is only a doctrine, albeit plausible. We are not aware of any study providing theoretical or empirical support for it.

Another aspect of the residual nature of the household sector is that its GCF is derived as the residual after subtracting from the aggregate GCF (estimated by the commodity-flow method) the directly estimated GCF of the public and PCSs. It is not only a part of the household sector's aggregate GCF by definition but is also a part of the sector's GDS: it is for this reason that it is called "direct household saving in the form of physical assets," which includes valuables.

Since no information is available to distribute the aggregate discrepancy, for example, between estimated GCF by the commodity-flow method and the funds from domestic and foreign saving available for financing it (as estimated by the flow-of-funds method), the assumptions one makes about the joint probability distribution of the aggregate discrepancy and its distribution among the five sectors implies a probability density of the discrepancy for the residual household sector. Interestingly, investment in "valuables" was shown in the table showing capital formation by asset categories for the old 2004–05 series but with no attribution as to which institutions financed the whole or part of it. In the new series, the investment in valuables is assumed to be done and financed by households. However, the saving and capital formation by all the six institutional sectors do not appear to be depicted in a consistent fashion to reflect this assumption in the consolidated investment and financing accounts of the country (Srinivasan 2014).

5.1.5. Private Final Consumption Expenditure: CES and NAS

An issue that has attracted attention from the late 1950s is the growing excess of NAS-based estimates of PFCE of households over that of the consumer expenditure surveys of the NSS. As mentioned earlier, the aggregate and commodity patterns of expenditure from the CES play only a limited role in the estimation of their corresponding values in the NAS. The volume edited by Angus Deaton and Valerie Kozel (2005) includes several papers going back to the late 1950s on the issue, in particular, the careful analysis and conclusion of Minhas ([1988] 2005). Minhas found that

> The independent data set (NAS), it would seem fair to conclude, is far short of the touchstone of quality expected of an independent validator dataset. A number of its components are based on such weak evidence and unverified assumptions as to seriously diminish its value in a cross validation exercise, On the other hand, the NSS estimates of expenditure on such minor vices such as tobacco and intoxicants, and consumer durables and modern consumer services are of doubtful reliability. Nevertheless, despite these difficulties, which have to be overcome in both data sets, an overwhelming proportion of household consumer expenditure data of the NSS and independent private consumption estimates of the NAS do get cross validation. (Minhas [1988] 2005, p. 91).

Deaton and Kozel, writing in 2005, concluded, and we agree with them more than a decade later, that

> [T]he Minhas paper should be compulsory reading for anyone concerned with the issue of national accounts, particularly anyone who does not understand the complexities and

approximations involved in the construction of the former. Minhas' chapter lays out the issues that have dominated the contemporary debate, the differential definition and coverage of NAS and NSS consumption, differences in timing, and the heavy reliance in national accounting practice on various rates and ratios that link the observable but irrelevant quantities to relevant but unobservable ones. (2005, p. 5).

Indeed, our experience in the course of writing this paper suggests that difficulties in NAS and NSS datasets that Minhas cautioned that needed to be overcome still remain. In my view, overcoming them and generating data whose reliability would no longer be in doubt should have been of greater priority than the rush to incorporate SNA 2008.

5.1.6. Revalidation of the Industry Classification of Companies in MCA 21

Paragraph 23 and the Annexure to CSO (2016) mention changes in both levels and growth estimates of GVA that follow from the use of latest available data from various (unnamed) sources and the consequent revalidation of the classification of companies in the MCA 21 dataset. Since new data become available every year, the revalidation exercise has to be an ongoing process. Furthermore, companies that have filed annual returns for some time may choose not to file in some years and never come back or may come back after a lapse of time. It is not clear whether the filed statements give any clues to a company's decision to stop filing or to resume filing. It would be of great help if CSO would publish and show how relevant NAS estimates were extracted from the annual statements and the procedures followed for that purpose and in the revalidation exercise.

5.1.7. Conclusions

The substantial changes in the new NAS are basically two: the use of a new data source, namely, MCA 21, and the production function methodology for estimating LIs. In principle, both would have been indeed appropriate and sensible had they been done right. It is very unfortunate that CSO has not acknowledged that not strictly enforcing the mandatory filing of their annual balance sheets by companies would lead to a selection bias in the NAS of unknown size and direction. Abandoning the new series and returning to the old series, which by no means is free of problems, however, would be inappropriate. In my view, whatever legal remedies—along with incentives and punishments—are needed to achieve full compliance with the filing mandate should be adopted as soon as possible. In the meantime, statisticians in government and the private sector should acknowledge that the new NAS series suffers from biases and pursue the needed technical and statistical work for estimating NAS while correcting the estimates for possible selection bias.

5.2. Comments by R. Nagaraj

Professor Srinivasan's views on self-selection bias in the MCA database and the previously used RBI sample of companies are well known, and these have also been acknowledged by the 2001 National Statistical Commission.

It is hard to deny the problems of selection bias. But we are faced with a bigger problem of not even knowing the universe of working companies to draw a suitable sample. We have argued that in the absence of knowing the universe of working companies, the methods used by the new NAS to obtain estimates for the universe of companies in the new series have accentuated the problems already present in the old series rather than solving them. The solution adopted by the NAS revision seems worse than the disease, as discussed in Section 4.

The only way to take the debate forward and hopefully resolve it, as we have jointly recommended, is by making public the MCA data and the NAS methodology for using that data so that other users can independently verify the official estimates.

We have described in Section 2 how shifting QCs from the household sector in the old series to PCS in the new series, and assuming them to grow at the same rate as corporate firms, has affected the structure of GDP. In Section 4, we have explained how the methodological changes (and their shortcomings) could have affected size and growth rates of the PCS. For details we have referred to Nagaraj (2015d).

I agree with Professor Srinivasan that the legacy issues are very important. But they perhaps cannot explain the observed discrepancies in the growth rates, the changes with every revision even in the base year, and changes in the structure of GDP in the new series compared to the old series. These are the outcomes directly of the changed methodologies and databases used.

To say that the methodological changes are appropriate, but their implementation is wrong seems as correct as saying that "Indian planning was perfect but its implementation was wrong." I have questioned both the methodological changes introduced and their implementation, whereas Professor Srinivasan seems to focus only on the latter. Either way, the issues can be best resolved by a thorough and independent investigation of the entire process as well as by giving researchers full access to the MCA database.

6. The Way Forward

The 2011–12 revision of the Indian national accounts has greatly altered the size and composition of domestic output in the following manner:

1. The absolute size of domestic output in the 2011–12 base year is smaller by 3.4 percent, compared to the old series.
2. Industry's share in GDP has expanded by about 5 percentage points, and the share of services or tertiary sector contracted proportionately, with the agriculture sector share remaining the same.
3. In terms of institutional composition, PCS' share has expanded by about 11 percentage points, and the household or unorganized sector's share has declined proportionately, with the public sector's share remaining the same.

If these compositional changes represented actual adjustments of the economy's sub-sectors without any change in methodology, then there would be no issue. However, these are apparently the result of changes made in the methodologies and databases used in preparing the new NAS. As many of the changes seem questionable, the compositional changes in domestic output in turn become questionable, and as a result the new NAS estimates have been contested widely.

Analytically, the new NAS conceives India, except for the household sector and general government, as a corporate economy with the dominant, unorganized sector sheltering most of the labor force, the bulk of whom are self-employed or unpaid family labor. In the old series, the economy was first divided into the organized and the unorganized sectors, and then the organized sector was divided into the public sector and the PCS. The new NAS has narrowed the distinction between the organized and the unorganized sectors; the primary distinction now is between the corporate and the noncorporate sectors, and the secondary distinction is between the financial and the non-financial sectors within each ownership category.

The methodological changes made in the new NAS are widespread, affecting the estimates for all sectors except the public sector and for agriculture and allied activities. This is so because the institutional composition of NAS has changed significantly, together with the methods of estimation and the databases used for the purpose. The institutional sectors have not changed, but their composition in terms of enterprises has.

The most significant change in the new NAS—as the CSO admits—is the direct estimation of the macroeconomic aggregates for the PCS using the statutory filing of financial returns by corporate firms. Previously, only the saving and investment of the PCS were estimated using the RBI sample of large firms (with high PUC), value added in PCS could only be indirectly obtained—and was not reported officially—as a residual within the organized sector.

The PCS is now expanded to include QCs (defined in SNA 2008 as "an unincorporated enterprise that has sufficient information to compile a complete set of accounts as if it were a separate corporation and whose de facto relationship to its owner is that of a corporation to its shareholders," having moved them from the unorganized sector. This expansion of the domain of the PCS and the use of the newer database has enlarged the share of PCS in GDP (with a corresponding contraction in the size of the unorganized and the household sector).

Another reason for the contraction of the unorganized sector is change in the methodology for estimating output per worker, which has been reduced sharply (under the view that the older series overestimated output per worker).

As this sectoral shuffling is analytically questionable, and the new methodologies are widely debated, the new macro aggregates have also become deeply contested. Furthermore, as the FRE (released in January 2016) have even altered the base year (2011–12) estimates, which, to the best of our knowledge and going by past practice, never change during the life of the series, they have cast further doubt on the veracity of the new NAS.

Our conclusions and suggestions for the way forward are as follows:

1. What has the new GDP series really accomplished? Our view is that the legacy issues remain, and a host of new problems have been added that may have rendered the new GDP estimates even more unreliable.
2. So what should be done? In our view:
   i. We need a statistical audit of the new NAS, drawing upon the best expertise from everywhere.
   ii. The principal problem centers around the use of the MCA 21 database. In our view, since the MCA data are based on the responses of self-selected companies (not the entire population mandated to respond), and, as is well known, uncorrected self-selection can lead to biased estimates of unknown magnitude and sign, efforts must be made to address this problem. Making the MCA 21 data public will allow independent experts to begin to find solutions and test them with peers and policy makers.

iii. Other changes, such as the adoption of the move from factor cost to basic prices, and a new base year, are less controversial. But the CSO needs to make progress in other areas, such as improved price deflators and validation of its new procedure for extrapolating output of the unorganized sectors on the basis of the effective LIM.

We are all for updating the NAS to the latest global templates. However, their adoption for a specific country must be made to reflect the country's context and its experience.

References

Arrow, Kenneth J. 1974. "Measurement of Real Value Added," in Paul David and Melvin Reder (eds.), *Nations and Households in Economic Growth: Essays in Honor of Moses Abramovitz*, pp. 3–20. New York, NY: Academic Press.

Bakshi, Ishan. 2016. "Growth Rates in FY05-FY11 Will Be Lower under the New GDP Series: T. C. A. Anant, Interview with Secretary, MOSPI." *Business Standard*, http://www.business-standard.com/article/economy-policy/growth-rates-in-fy05-fy11-will-be-lower-under-the-new-gdp-series-t-c-a-anant-116040400042_1.html (accessed May 1, 2017).

Central Statistical Office (CSO). 2010. *New Series of National Accounts Statistics (Base Year 2004–05)*. New Delhi: Central Statistical Office, http://mospiold.nic.in/Mospi_New/upload/brochure_%202004-05.pdf (accessed May 1, 2017).

———. 2012. *National Accounts Statistics: Sources and Methods*. New Delhi: Central Statistical Office.

———. 2014. *National Accounts Statistics*. New Delhi: Ministry of Statistics and Programme Implementation.

———. 2015a. *New Series of Estimates of National Income, Consumption Expenditure. Saving and Capital Formation for the Years 2011–12 to 2013–14*. Press Note, January 30. New Delhi: Central Statistical Office.

———. 2015b. *Changes in Methodology and Data Sources in the New Series of National Accounts, Base Year 2011–12*, June. New Delhi: Central Statistical Office.

———. 2015c, April 13. Presentation made to *Data Users' Conference on New Series of National Accounts with Base Year 2011–12*. New Delhi: National Accounts Division, Ministry of Statistics and Programme Implementation

———. 2015d. "No Room for Doubts on New GDP Numbers," *Economic and Political Weekly*, 50(16): 86–89.

———. 2015e, February 27. *Report of the Sub-committee on Unorganised Manufacturing and Services Sectors for Compilation of National Accounts*

Statistics with Base-Year 2011–12. New Delhi: Ministry of Statistics and Programme Implementation, Government of India.

———. 2016a. *Consumer Price Index*. New Delhi: Ministry of Statistics and Programme Implementation, http://mospi-nic-in/Mospi/upload_cpi_pr_12may16th.pdf (accessed May 26, 2017).

———. 2016b, January 29. *First Revised Estimates of National Income, Consumption Expenditure, Saving and Capital Formation 2014–15*. Press Note. New Delhi: Central Statistical Office.

Coyle, Diana. 2014. *GDP: A Brief but Affectionate History*. Princeton, NJ: Princeton University Press.

Deaton, Angus and Valerie Kozel. 2005. *The Great Indian Poverty Debate*. New Delhi: Macmillan Publishers.

Diewert, Erwin and Alice Nakamura. 2002. *The Measurement of Aggregate Total Factor Productivity Growth*, http://economics.ubc.ca/files/2013/06/pdf_paper_erwin-diewert-02-05-measurement-aggregate.pdf (accessed May 1, 2017).

———. 2003. "Index Numbers, Concepts, Measures and Decomposition of Productivity Growth," *Journal of Productivity Analysis*, 19(2–3): 127–59.

EPW Research Foundation. 2015. "New Series of National Accounts: A Review," *Economic and Political Weekly*, 50(7): 74–78.

Goldar, Bishwanath. 2015. "Growth in Gross Value Added of Indian Manufacturing: 2011–12 Series vs. 2004–05 Series," *Economic and Political Weekly*, 50(21): 10–13.

Kumar, Ashish and G.M. Boopathy. 2013. *National Price Indices and Inflation During 2012*, http://mospiold.nic.in/Mospi_New/upload/price_stat_8mar13.pdf (accessed March 31, 2017).

Minhas, B.S. 1962, April. "The Homohypallagic Production Function, Factor Intensity Reversals and the Heckscher–Ohlin Theorem," *Journal of Political Economy*, 70(2): 138–146.

———. (1988) 2005. "Validation of Large Scale Sample Survey Data: Case of NSS Household Consumption Expenditure," *Sankhya Series B*, 50(Supp): 1–61.

Ministry of Corporate Affairs. 2013. "Financial Aggregates of Corporate Sector," *Chapter VIII: 57th Annual Report on the Working and Administration of the Companies Act, 1956, Year ending 31-03-2013*, http://www.mca.gov.in/Ministry/pdf/57AR_English.pdf (accessed May 26, 2017).

Ministry of Industry. 2010. *WPI Compilation Manual*. New Delhi: Ministry of Industry, http://easindustry-nic-in/WPI_Manual.pdf (accessed May 26, 2016).

Ministry of Statistics and Programme Implementation. 2001, September 5. *Report of the National Statistical Commission*. Dr C. Rangarajan (Chair), http://www.mospi.gov.in/report-dr-rangarajan-commission (accessed May 15, 2017).

Nagaraj, R. (2002). "Performance of India's Manufacturing Sector in the 1990s: Some Tentative Findings," in Shuji Uchikawa (ed.), *Economic Reforms and Industrial Structure in India*, pp. 13–28. New Delhi: Manohar.

———. 2009. "Is Services Sector Output Overestimated? An Inquiry," *Economic and Political Weekly*, 44(5): 40–45.

Nagaraj, R. 2015a. "Seeds of Doubts on New GDP Numbers: Private Corporate Sector Overestimated?" *Economic and Political Weekly*, 50(13): 14–17.

———. 2015b. "Seeds of Doubt Remain: A Reply to CSO's Rejoinder," *Economic and Political Weekly*, 50(18): 64–66.

———. 2015c. "Growth in GVA in Indian Manufacturing," *Economic and Political Weekly*, 50(24): 117–120.

———. 2015d. "Size and Structure of India's Private Corporate Sector: Implications for the New GDP Series," *Economic and Political Weekly*, 50(45): 41–47.

———. 2015e. "Reply to PIB's Rejoinder," *Economic and Political Weekly*, 50(51): 87–88.

———. 2016. "Unorganised Sector in the New GDP Series: Why Has It Shrunk?" *Economic and Political Weekly*, 51(14): 24–27.

Rajakumar, Dennis J. and S.L. Shetty. 2016. "Continuous Revisions Cast Doubts on the GDP Advanced Estimates," *Economic and Political Weekly*, 51(10): 70–74.

Rajakumar, Dennis J., Vijayata B. Sawant, and Anita B Shetty. 2015. "New Estimates of Saving and Capital Formation," *Economic and Political Weekly*, 50(12): 64–66.

Sims, Christopher. 1969. "A Theoretical Basis for Double-deflation of Value Added," *Review of Economics and Statistics*, 51: 470–471, November.

Srinivasan, T. N. 2003. "India's Statistical System: Critiquing the Report of the National Statistical Commission," *Economic and Political Weekly*, 38(4): 303–306.

———. 2008a. "Price Indices and Inflation Rates," *Economic and Political Weekly*, 43(26–27): 217–223.

———. 2008b. "Some Aspects of Price Indices, Inflation Rates and the Services Sector in National Accounts Statistic," in N. Jayaram and R. S. Deshpande (eds.), *Footprints of Development and Change: Essays in memory of Professor V.K.R.V. Rao*, pp. 417–474. New Delhi: Academic Foundation.

———. 2014. *Valuables in Gross Capital Formation: A Puzzle*. Unpublished and Privately Circulated.

Subba Rao, K.G.K. 2015. "Mystery of Private Corporate Saving," *Economic and Political Weekly*, 50(22): 158–162.

Syrquin, Moshe. 2016. "A Review Essay on GDP: A Brief but Affectionate History by Diane Coyle," *Journal of Economic Literature*, 54(2): 537–588.

Appendix 1. Some Technical Issues Relating to Production Functions for Estimating Value Added

CSO (2015b) points out that:

> [I]n the Labour Input Method (LI Method), as was being used in earlier series, while compiling Gross Value Added Per Worker (GVAPWI) from the Enterprise Survey, it is assumed that there is equal contribution from all categories of workers engaged in an

economic activity, i.e. the productivity of an employer, a casual wage worker, or a family worker is equal. The new method addresses differential labour productivity by assigning weights to the different categories of workers engaged in an economic activity based on their productivity. The weights were compiled using data on establishments covered in the NSS 67th Round on Unincorporated Enterprises (ES). A nested Cobb–Douglas Function has been used for computing the weights for different categories of workers. (Para 2.18)

Thus, the total LI in person days is a weighted average of the person days of LIs of the three types, with the weight of a person day of labor of each type expressed in equivalent person days of hired labor. It should be noted that instead of treating different categories of labor as different inputs, CSO is assuming that they are perfect substitutes for each other so that total LI is a weighted sum of the inputs of different categories of labor.

The production function in natural logarithms estimated by CSO is:

$$Log\,Y = Log\,A + \beta\,Log\,K + \alpha\,Log\left[L_2 + \delta_1 L_1 + \delta_2 L_3\right] + \gamma S + \varepsilon \qquad \text{(I)}$$

Where

Y is GVA

K is the capital input

L_1 is the LI of owner (in person days per year)

L_2 is the LI of hired worker (formal and informal, in person days per year)

L_3 is the LI of helper (in person days per year)

S is a dummy variable with rural = 0, urban = 1

ε is the random error term

There are many implicit assumptions in this formulation of the production function. First, value added by assumption is the difference between the value of goods and services produced by an enterprise—valued at the "prices they fetch" in the market (the enterprise is assumed to be a price taker in the markets for all goods and services it produces and sells)—and the value of non-primary factor inputs (that is, intermediate or material inputs it uses in production)—again valued at the "prices it pays" for them (the enterprise is assumed to be a price taker in its markets for factor and nonfactor inputs). Since the production function is being estimated over several periods, the question arises whether GVA is being computed at current or constant prices. Also, since GVA is the difference between the value of outputs and the value of material inputs, if it is to be computed at constant prices should the difference be deflated by the single price index, or should the value of outputs be deflated by an output price index and value of material inputs by an input price index? We discuss the price deflation issues in Appendix 2, assuming here that Y is the real value added obtained through some deflation procedure.

Unlike a commodity or service for which there is a natural unit of measurement and an associated price per unit there is no natural unit of measurement with an associated price per unit for value added. In a classic paper, entitled "Measurement of Real Value Added," Kenneth Arrow (1974) addressed this issue in the context of an enterprise with a single output X which was produced with a vector F of n primary factors as well as a vector M of m material inputs using a production function

$$G(F, M) = G(F_1, F_2, F_n, M_1, M_2, M_m) \tag{1}$$

Arrow's analysis, which we reproduce here, proceeded under the assumptions that G is homogeneous of degree (that is, the technology of production has constant returns to scale) and is separable in primary factors and material inputs, so that it can be written as

$$G = H\left[J\left(F_1.....F_n\right), N\left(M_1.....M_m\right)\right] \tag{2}$$

Where without loss of generality G, H, and N can be chosen to be homogenous of degree 1.

In (2), J can be interpreted as a value added production function in primary factors and given that it is homogeneous of degree 1, its unit isoquant describes the technology of production function in full.

$$[(F_1.....F_n) \geq 0 \mid (\mathrm{H}(F_1.....F_n) \equiv 1)] \tag{3}$$

Similarly, N can be interpreted as a production function for an aggregator of intermediate inputs. Once again given that N is homogeneous of degree 1, its unit isoquant describes the technology of aggregation of intermediate inputs in full.

$$[(M_1.....M_m) \geq 0 \mid (\mathrm{N}(M_1.....M_m) \equiv 1)] \tag{4}$$

So far we have been discussing purely technological aspects. Bringing in economics, and using output as the numeraire for measuring prices (so that its price per unit of output $P^x \equiv 1$). Let the unit primary factor prices be

P_1^F ..... P_n^F and the unit material input prices be P_1^M ..... P_n^M, then the cost of producing a unit of output X will be

$$=\sum_{i=1}^{n} P_i^F F_i + \sum_{j=1}^{m} P_j^M M_j \tag{5}$$

$$\text{Subject to } H\left[J\left(F_1.....F_n\right), N\left(M_1.....M_m\right)\right] \geq 1 \tag{6}$$

Assuming J and N to be quasi-concave, the first-order conditions for minimization of unit cost (5) will be

$$\frac{\delta H}{\delta J}\frac{\delta J}{\delta F_i} \geq P_i^F \text{ with equality if } F_i > 0, \forall i \tag{7}$$

$$\frac{\delta H}{\delta N}\frac{\delta M}{\delta M_j} \geq P_j^M \text{ with equality if } M_j > 0, \forall j \tag{8}$$

where in the left-hand side of (7) we denote the product of the partial derivative of H with respect to its argument J and the partial derivative of J with respect to its ith argument $F_{i.}$ Analogously the left-hand side of (8) we denote the product of the partial derivative of H with respect to its argument N and the partial derivative of N with respect to its jth argument M_j.

Multiplying by F_i both sides of (6) for each I and each sides of (7) by M_j for each j and noting that J and N are homogeneous of degree 1 we get

$$J\left(F_1.....F_n\right) = \sum P \frac{F}{i} \frac{\delta J}{\delta F_i} \tag{9}$$

$$N\left(M_1.....M_n\right) = \sum P \frac{M}{j} \frac{\delta N}{\delta M_j} \tag{10}$$

$$\text{and } \frac{dH}{dJ}J + \frac{dH}{dN}N = H\left(J, N\right) = 1 \tag{11}$$

We can interpret (9)–(11) as follows: At the unit cost minimizing levels of F_i^* and M_j^*, the "quantity" of real value added produced is $J(F_1^*, \ldots F_n^*)$

and its "price" per unit is $\frac{\delta H}{\delta J}$ at $(F_1^*, \ldots F_n^*, M_1^*, \ldots M_m^*)$, and the quantity of aggregate intermediate inputs is $N(M_1^*, \ldots M_m^*)$ and its price is $\frac{\delta H}{\delta J}$ at $(F_1^*, \ldots F_n^*, M_1^*, \ldots M_m^*)$. Equation (11) says that just 1 unit of output and no more is being produced, that (6) is an equality, which is an implication of the efficiency of input use in production.

These results could be generalized to homothetic production functions, etc. Also one could consider enterprises producing more than one output by viewing X not as a scalar measure of the physical output of a single good or service, but as a vector $(X_1, \ldots X_q)$ of physical outputs of Q goods and services. As long as the appropriately defined production possibility set is convex, most of the above results will hold. We will not pursue this here.

Coming back to the new series, the nested CD production function can be formally viewed as a special case of Arrow's more general formulation above. It starts with an estimate of value added Y for a sector as the difference between value of output and the value of material inputs M at basic prices and expresses it as a multiplicative function of a function of primary factors of capital and three types of labor, a sectoral dummy, and a random measurement error term. Thus, taking antilogs of (I), this function is

$$AK^{\beta}\left[L_2 + \delta_1 L_1 + \delta_2 L_3\right]^{\alpha} S^{\alpha} e^{\varepsilon}$$

One can understand the choice of the CD functional form for the production function for estimating value added from the perspective of computational convenience—for example—that the observed share of wages in the cost of output under pure competition would equal the exponent of labor in the CD function, etc. However, given CSO's presumed access to up-to-date computation methods and software, there is no reason for the CSO not to estimate other production functions to check whether they explain the data better.

At the very least, CSO could have estimated the Constant Elasticity of Substitution (CES) Production functions, originally worked out in the doctoral thesis at Stanford of the late B. S. Minhas of the Indian Statistical Institute and a former member of the Planning Commission. The CD function with its elasticity substitution equaling 1 is a special case of the CES function, which allows an elasticity from 0 (corresponding to a fixed coefficient, that is, a Leontief production function with L-shaped isoquants) to infinity (perfect substitution, with linear isoquants). Moreover, instead of linearly aggregating the three types of labor by weighting them by their marginal productivity, in estimating CES there would have been no need to aggregate at all by treating the types of labor, along with capital as producing real value added through a CES production function.

In our specification of a separable production function for a single output through *H*(*J*, *N*), each of the aggregates of value added *J* and of material inputs *M* could be modeled as CES aggregates, with *H* itself being a CES function of *J* and *M*. The generalization to several final outputs could be accomplished by viewing the enterprise's technology as one that enables it to produce a CES index of several final outputs from primary factors and material inputs.

Appendix 2: Price Deflators

In any national income system, the evaluation of aggregates such as GVA, GDP, GCF, private and government final consumption expenditure, and gross national income at current and constant prices, and their components and offshoots, is an important task. By definition, the constant price or "real" version of any aggregate is its version at current prices deflated by some price deflator or price index. It is, therefore, important to assess how the price indexes are put together, their strengths and weaknesses, and their ongoing improvements. Furthermore, inflation, and policies to keep it from becoming sustained and excessive, requires an appropriate index for measuring inflation. Srinivasan (2008a, 2008b) discusses many aspects of price indices available as of 2008. Kumar and Boopathy (2013) update the factual details in the Srinivasan paper. We would like to emphasize a few issues here.

First, GVA at current basic prices is the difference between the value of aggregate gross output of goods and services and the value of intermediate or material inputs used in production. In general, there is no physical unit and price for value added, so how does one deflate GVA at current prices? Do we deflate with a single deflator for GVA or use at least two deflators, deflating the value of gross output by an output price deflator and the value of material inputs by an input price deflator, with the resulting difference between the two deflated values as Real GVA? Christopher Sims (1969) has provided a theoretical justification for double deflation.

However, in practice, CSO mostly uses single deflator, except for few sectors. The latest NAS manual published in 2012 on sources and methods of NAS applies to the old series with base 2004–05 (CSO 2012). In its Chapter 3 on net factor income from the rest of the world, it says "estimates at constant (2004–05) prices have been prepared using single deflation method by adopting(sic) implicit price deflators of service sector on the current price estimate of net factor income from abroad" (CSO 2012, para 3.5). However, for the agricultural sector Chapter 9, para 9.68 says, "For estimation of value added at constant prices, the double deflation method is used…."

A single deflator for value added has to balance its role as a deflator for the current price value of gross output and its role as a deflator for the current price value of material/intermediate inputs. CSO (2015b) unfortunately does not even attempt to explain its particular choice of single deflators in the new series.

Turning to price indices, there have been many improvements in the compilation and dissemination of price indices since Srinivasan (2008a). The numbers of villages and towns from which price quotes are collected have increased substantially. Commodity coverage has increased as well. However, two important issues relating to the wholesale price index (WPI) have not been addressed yet: to introduce services into the index and to convert WPI, which is neither a producer price index (PPI), nor a CPI, into a proper PPI. Both these issues were especially emphasized on the terms of reference of the Abhijit Sen Committee, established in 2003, that prepared the shift of the base year of WPI from 1993–94 to 2004–05. The committee submitted its report in 2008, and the base year change was implemented from April 2010. But the committee left the two issues to be addressed the next time the WPI was revised (Ministry of Industry [MOI] 2010).

The news about the CPI is better. The base year of the National Rural, Urban, and Combined CPI, for example, was changed to 2012=100 from its prior base of 2010, along with other improvements, according to the May 12, 2016 press release from CSO/MOSPI (CSO 2016a).

Srinivasan (2008a, 2008b), taking his cue from the report of the Boskin Commission in the United States, argued that by not incorporating the availability of new goods and improvements in the quality of existing goods in a systematic and analytically appropriate way, we could be overstating estimated inflation rates. In India, while new goods and new versions of existing goods do enter the price indices during a base year change, there is no systematic procedure for the introduction of new goods and new versions of existing goods as they become available.

The approach of Divisia in putting together continuous, time differentiable price and quantity indices, their use in the measurement of value added and total factor productivity, and its growth is worth exploring, but is not discussed here for the sake of brevity. Diewert and Nakamura (2002, 2003) discuss it in detail.

Comments and Discussion*

B. N. Goldar
Institute of Economic Growth

I think I should begin by saying that in my comments I shall try to highlight some of the issues raised in the paper, and I shall offer some suggestions on how the paper can be improved.

The paper contains a comprehensive discussion on the methodology of the new national accounts series, pointing out several weaknesses of the methodology and accordingly making recommendations. This is a valuable and welcome contribution to the literature. What are the main conclusions of the paper? On the question whether it is really worthwhile pursing the new national accounts series, as it is at present, the authors say no. They point out a number of changes that are needed, and take the position that methodological changes should be made after a statistical audit. The paper suggests that the principal problem lies in the use of the MCA data.

Why is there a problem with the MCA 21 data? The paper holds that there is an estimation problem caused by a process of self-selection: many more well-performing companies are likely to be reporting than poorly performing ones. There are people who feel that the use of MCA 21 data is a major step forward for the new national accounts series, but the authors suggest that this is its worst feature. In my view, the paper should have given greater attention to what needs to be done rather than merely finding fault. As an academic paper, a more balanced view, had it been taken, would have also highlighted the improvements made in the new series.

This leads me to ask, can the criticism in the paper be made more useful and insightful? I feel there are places in the paper where this could have been done. Consider, for example, the case of trade. The growth rate in gross value added (GVA) in trade, repairs, hotels, and restaurants in the new series was 11 percent in 2012, as against 4 percent in the earlier series.

* To preserve the sense of the discussions at the India Policy Forum (IPF), these discussants' comments reflect the views expressed at the IPF and do not necessarily take into account revisions to the conference version of the paper in response to these and other comments in preparing the final, revised version published in this volume. The original conference version of the paper is available at www.ncaer.org.

For 2013, the growth rate was 7.2 percent, as against 1 percent earlier. So, clearly the growth rate in GVA in trade in the new series is quite high as compared to the earlier series.

Trade in India is mostly in the unorganized sector. Therefore, what is happening is that there is a benchmark estimate of value added in the base year that is being grown over time. In the new series, sales tax revenue is being used for this benchmarking purpose. The paper could have examined and contrasted the indicator used earlier with sale tax revenue that is being used now to grow the base year value added estimate. The question is: Is the new indicator better or worse than what was being used earlier? In my opinion, it is probably better, but this is a topic that the paper could have very usefully discussed. Is the high growth rate of GVA in trade that we are finding in the new series caused essentially by the change in the indicator? If so, it would have been very useful for the paper to have examined the indicator in depth and highlighted the limitations of using it.

At several places in the paper, the comment has been made that the size of the unorganized sector has gone down in the new national accounts as compared to the earlier series, but there is really no basis for saying so. Actually, with the data available, nobody can say if the size of the unorganized sector has declined in the new series. There are no publicly available data to meaningfully compare GVA of the unorganized sector in the new series with that in the old series. Let us look at this example of the estimate of GVA in unorganized manufacturing for 2011.

As also reported in the paper, the 2011–12 GVA estimate for manufacturing in the old series for the registered portion, which is organized, was ₹886 thousand crore (₹8.86 trillion), whereas for the unorganized portion it was ₹351 thousand crore (₹3.51 trillion). The classification changed in the new series. Now, it is ₹1,089 thousand crore (₹10.89 trillion) for the corporate sector and ₹180 thousand crore (₹1.8 trillion) for the household sector. Out of the unorganized manufacturing sector, units that maintain accounts, referred to as quasi-corporations, have been shifted out to the corporate sector. The remaining unorganized manufacturing is the household manufacturing sector. Hence, if one compares the figures, 351 and 180, and infers that the estimate of GVA in unorganized manufacturing has gone down in the new series, that is incorrect. To get a comparable estimate, we have to split the GVA of the quasi-corporate segment of manufacturing into both organized sector enterprises and unorganized sector enterprises. In order to have comparable numbers, we have to get the GVA of the unorganized component of the quasi-corporate sector and add that to the GVA of the household sector of manufacturing. However, this computation can be done only by the National Accounts Division of the CSO since academic researchers do not have access to the required data.

There is a need to recognize that there were certain problems in the earlier national accounts series, which have now been addressed. One problem with the 2004–05 series was that the use of the Index of Industrial Production (IIP) for computing growth in manufacturing GDP had often caused an under-estimation for the most current year, which used to get corrected a year or so later when Annual Survey of Industries data become available. The paper notes that for 2013, the growth rate in manufacturing GVA was negative in the earlier series and became positive 6 percent in the new series. Why did this happen? When the growth rate was initially computed, for example, for 2011, it was based on the IIP and was 2.7 percent. However, when the more reliable ASI data became available, manufacturing GVA was revised upward to 7.4 percent. Similarly, for 2013, the growth rate in manufacturing on the basis of the IIP went up from a negative rate to positive 6 percent when more reliable ASI data become available. The initial under-estimation of manufacturing GVA growth and the correction later has been a persistent problem in the previous national accounts series, which has now been solved. I thought this improvement might have got greater recognition in the paper.

The MCA 21 database has come under a lot of criticism in the paper, which considers this to be the biggest problem in the new national accounts series. The use of the MCA database really is a major change. Earlier, the estimates for GVA for services were being made from a small sample, maybe 1,000 companies or 1,500 companies. Now the estimate of the services sector GVA is being made from maybe 300,000 companies, that is, the number of companies being considered is huge. Let me explain the problem as perceived by the authors. The problem is that at present, a blow-up factor is being used based on paid-up capital. There are companies for which we have data, while there are other companies which are known to be active but for which we do not have the data. Therefore, a blow-up factor is being used to get an estimate of GVA for the active companies for which we do not have data. The authors have suggested the use of some sort of modeling for correcting the self-selection process. This is a valid point. The fact that there is self-selection means that the blow-up factor is not correct. The important question is how the modeling is to be done. One suggestion is to utilize income tax data. It is a useful suggestion, but is there a statistical method by which the correction for self-selection can be done?

I feel that the problem relating to the MCA data has been somewhat exaggerated. How serious is the problem? If we assume that in the current MCA data the companies that are reporting account for 85 percent of the GVA of all active companies, then most of the GVA is actually being covered. As regards the issue of using a blow-up factor of 1.15, one can argue that there are companies which are not reporting, and the reason for this is that they are not performing well. So, this blow-up factor should not be 1.15, but lower. At worst, what should it be? Suppose companies that are not reporting have zero GVA, then the blow up factor should be equal to one. But if we assume that some companies with positive GVA are also not reporting, then maybe a blow-up factor of 1.1 or 1.08 should be used.

The question is: Will that make such a big difference to the GVA numbers, and the bigger issue is, why should that affect the growth rate, if the blow-up factor is not 1.15 but 1.08? Suppose it is 1.08 in year 1, 1.08 in year 2, and 1.09 in year 3. This can affect the level of the GVA estimate, but how can it affect the growth rate? This is a real issue because most of the criticism of the new National Accounts series stems from the relatively higher growth rate being reported in the new series. But, why should the use of the blow-up factor cause a high growth rate and, in fact, why should it affect the growth rate at all? A related question the paper should discuss is: Why should the self-selection process in the MCA data always lead to an overestimation of the growth rate?

One important difference that has emerged in the new series is a shift from the establishment concept to the enterprise concept. Earlier, the manufacturing GVA estimate was based on establishment level data, and now the manufacturing GVA estimate is based on enterprise level data. The current method of computing GVA in manufacturing, which is based on company data, also needs to take into account the fact that a manufacturing enterprise may also have establishments providing services. This point has been noted by the CSO. Trade carried out by manufacturing companies, which has now become a part of manufacturing GVA, was earlier covered under trade. That is the reason why the relative share of manufacturing in the national accounts has gone up in the new series, because now a part of the services activity is also getting counted under manufacturing.

Most of the discussion in the paper concerns the years up to 2014–15. But, if we look at 2015–16, we find that the manufacturing growth rate, which was earlier about 5 to 6 percent, suddenly jumped to 9 percent. Is that possible? If we look at IIP growth, then the jump in the manufacturing growth rate does not seem credible. But, what about credit growth? This aspect has been discussed in the paper. If we study real credit growth, that is, credit flow deflated by the wholesale price index excluding crude oil and petroleum products, we find that in 2015–16 credit growth suddenly went up. One can then argue that as the credit growth rate was high, the industrial growth rate should also have been high, since it is commonly held that credit growth and industrial growth are connected.

Finally, there are two points regarding the estimation of the production function for estimating marginal products of different categories of workers in the unorganized sector. The authors have suggested that the nested Constant Elasticity of Substitution (CES) function should be used instead of the nested Cobb–Douglas function. This will, however, be difficult to estimate, as it will involve a nonlinear combination of many parameters. This does not mean that it cannot be done, but perhaps it could be done for checking the robustness of the estimates obtained by using the nested Cobb–Douglas function. The second suggestion in the paper is to deflate value added and capital for estimation of the production function. But, when regressions are being done separately for each National Sample Survey (NSS) round, why would we have to deflate? It is not clear to me that deflation is necessary here.

Pronab Sen

International Growth Centre, India

When I got the paper, I was really quite excited. I thought I would learn something new. A lot of what is in the paper is of course known. T. N. Srinivasan has been saying for quite some time that the long-standing legacy issues must be addressed, and they really have been around, no question about that.

The real issue that I feel should exercise us is: How do we look at the national income accounts? Do we look at them as a statistical product, or do we look at them, as the nomenclature suggests, as a system of accounts? If it is the latter, then you really need to start from where all accounting starts, which is that there are well-established conventions and procedures that are laid down and agreed to, so that there is a commonality of approach. That is precisely what the national accounts are. The national accounts, in terms of the economics of a nation, have been pretty well known for a long time, but they are today a codified document, and it is the UN System of National Accounts (SNA) that lays down not merely the principles underlying the accounts but also the procedures with which these accounts are to be calculated under various scenarios.

All countries that are signatories are expected to follow the SNA. Now, the question was raised, why are we jumping to SNA 2008? The short answer is: we are not. Today, if you look around the world, there are three SNAs that coexist. You have the 1968 SNA, the 1993 SNA, and the 2008 SNA. Around 60–65 percent of countries continue to be in the 1960s, they did not or could not move to the 1993. Most other countries, with the exception of a handful of developed countries, are at 1993 and incidentally so are we. Not only are we at the 1993 SNA, but of the 1993 SNA we have actually incorporated only about 75 percent of the recommendations. We still have not been able to incorporate 25 percent of the 1993 SNA recommendations simply because we do not have the data. The biggest chunk of what is missing is that we do not have the ability to produce a balance sheet of the country. So, what we produce, in terms of the sequence of accounts, is essentially what in accounting would be called the profit and loss account. So, where does the SNA 2008 come in? Where the SNA 2008 does come in is in a few recommendations that change definitions, and nothing more than that, and these as signatories we are all expected to do.

Given that this is an accounting framework driven by conventions, what does it mean to say that the national accounts should be audited? The question is, audited by whom? Audited by statisticians or audited by national accounts experts? If it is the latter, because we are talking about conventions, then they have already been audited. The Central Statistics Office (CSO) has a central team which has audited and found the accounts to be consistent with the approved principles and procedures. The IMF has come in and has given the accounts a clean bill of health, end of the matter. They are the custodians of the accounting standards, and we have all agreed to that. Now, there can be and are differences of opinion, and that is something I will come to, and something that would have been useful for the paper to have talked about, because in my opinion that is where the fundamental issues are.

Where are really the problems? There has been a lot of talk about GDP shares shifting around, growth rates shifting around. All that is fine, if that is what the data is saying, that is what you get. But what is in the data that is really different has been discussed briefly in the paper, too briefly, and even then it really does not touch upon the fundamentals. The real issue is the following. What this particular revision of the national accounts has done is that it has moved a whole bunch of sectors from following a physical output approach to measurement to a value approach. Think of the Annual Survey of Industries (ASI). The ASI is one of the most comprehensive datasets. You can not only directly measure value added from that, but you can also measure the volume of output. The Ministry of Corporate Affairs (MCA) database, on the other hand, is pure values—there is nothing physical anywhere in the MCA database.

We talked about trade. Earlier, the way we were measuring the growth of the trade sector was to use the output of traded goods, not services, but traded goods. Now we are measuring it by the sales tax, which is a value added tax, so again we are measuring values.

The real question that we need to ask is: If we are shifting from measuring physical output to measuring values, how should we do the deflation, and are we doing it appropriately? The short answer is: No, we are not doing it appropriately. But the longer answer is that we are not sure about the type of deflation we should do. There is talk in the paper about single deflation and double deflation. But this raises the question, and this is an issue that the IMF also brought up in their audit of the revised series, whether we are clear about what the two approaches mean. Think of what we do, and we have been doing since the accounts began—I am surprised Professor Srinivasan did not point this out as a legacy issue—we have been doing single deflation all along, and we continue to do so. The question to ask is: While doing single deflation for the new series, are we making matters worse than they were before? There is actually a very strong case to be made for saying yes, we may be making matters worse. Earlier, at least for a whole bunch of sectors, we had physical indicators, and today when we have moved to values, a wrong deflation approach is making matters worse. That is a legitimate criticism. But as economists, we really need to ask ourselves what double deflation means. This is something I have been searching for in the literature. And I have never found a suitable explanation.

But think of it in the following manner. As the paper rightly says, there are three ways to measure GDP: the production approach, the income approach, and the expenditure approach. Presumably, we should use different deflators for each approach. Or, should we not? At the end of the day, it is the funds flow that matters. These three approaches should equate in nominal terms, then what do we mean by real income? As a consumer or as a spender, real income means what it buys for me in terms of consumer goods or investment goods. But, for a producer, what does double deflation mean? Mechanically, I take the product price and deflate the output value, and I take the input price and deflate the input values, and whatever I get as a residual, I say it is real value added. But when I say real, what is that animal? Why should it necessarily equal real GDP measured from the expenditure side?

Unless as economists we are very clear about how we should deflate nominal values, we will be tying ourselves into knots. The paper does ask this question, and it is, I think, the appropriate question to ask in the Indian context, where, as in most countries of the world, the dominant approach to measuring GDP has been the production approach. Both the income approach (which is irrelevant for India since we do not measure incomes directly) and the expenditure approach have straightforward deflators for arriving at real income. So, when we think about the issue of deflation and what we mean by real GDP, we have to think about appropriate deflators for the production approach. Asking this question, however, raises a whole bunch of even more fundamental questions, which I had hoped the paper would go into, but did not.

General Discussion

Rohini Somanathan said she found the discussion very useful and hoped that at least in manufacturing it may be possible through iteration to eventually resolve the two datasets. She suggested that it may be possible to match the MCA 21 returns of firms with their Annual Survey of Industries (ASI) data, which has been available at the plant level for a long time without identifiers and which the firms may also be willing to provide. If we can have access to both sets of data, we could iteratively match firms up until we got a reasonable fit, and this would then help resolve the differences between the two datasets and what they were telling us about manufacturing growth. She noted that the National Accounts Statistics (NAS) is both a system of accounts and a powerful tool to measure growth and change in the structure of the economy, and there was a strong need to understand why the same manufacturing sector appeared to be behaving in very different ways as measured by the old NAS series and the new one.

Surjit Bhalla suggested that it would be very useful for this paper, or a new paper, to document and analyze the academic criticism of the new NAS series, as distinguished from the critiques of investment bankers or the media. Second, Bhalla suggested that base revisions in GDP series do result in anomalies, and we should not get too exercised about few percentage point differences. He recalled that previous base revisions had also thrown up differences between the old and the new series, differences possibly much bigger than what the current revision was showing. He particularly recalled the base revision of 1993–94 where the change may have been as much as 25 percent. Third, Bhalla noted the genuine improvements in things like measuring wholesale and retail trade, which has moved from an archaic approach to one based on the analysis of sales tax data. He maintained that 75 percent of GDP remains unchanged between the old and the new series, with only wholesale and retail trade and manufacturing doing a switch in terms of shares. On the faster GDP growth shown by the new series, he agreed with Goldar's comments on how rapid "real" credit growth during this period could very well explain the acceleration.

T. N. Srinivasan noted that the Rangarajan Committee had recommended CSO's doing an integrated household survey including measuring consumption, saving, and productive investment. This has not yet been done on a full NSS round. Another important task for CSO to do was to put together a credible list of firms and enterprises based on the Economic Census, a follow-up enterprise survey from which to draw samples. This has also not been done. He felt that these were fundamental issues that need addressing, but instead the CSO has made some marginal changes that should have had lower priority.

R. Nagaraj, referring to their paper, pointed to the discussion of credit growth as a ratio of GDP and showing it to be flat or declining, and not growing. He agreed with Rohini Somanathan's suggestion to map the MCA 21 data on to the ASI data over the past few years to understand what was going on. He noted the problems with the IIP data, which had not been updated since 2004–05 as the base year. After revision, IIP and ASI move together in unison for 4 to 5 years, and then the IIP base becomes out of date and they start diverging. He finally turned to the fragilities of the MCA data. Even the data for the companies which were reporting had problems, and it would appear that CSO had not done the preparatory work required to make the data fully useable.

Vijay Joshi pointed out that as a consumer of the data what was troubling was that the rapid GDP growth suggested by the new series was not matching up with other high frequency data. How does one explain a vigorously growing economy at 7 percent per year and a negative growth rate of non-oil imports?

Sudipto Mundle also found the discussion very useful, but was also troubled by how polarized it was. This made it difficult to figure out a way forward out of the controversy around the new GDP series. To the authors, he asked the question of why growth rates should be affected so much even if we assume all the problems with the new series that have been highlighted are present, since they would affect both the base year and a measurement year. From Goldar and Sen, the discussants, he wanted to know if it would be possible to get the back numbers for the new series so that the comparisons between the old and the new series could be gone into greater detail. This would help greatly in reducing the apprehensions around the new series, particularly the disconnect with the high frequency economic data that Vijay Joshi had also referred to. Finally, Mundle wanted to know if the sharp divergence between WPI inflation, which had fallen dramatically as of July 2017 and had actually turned negative, and CPI inflation, which was higher and had continued to remain positive, meant that the share of domestic trade was going up sharply in recent years.

T. N. Srinivasan noted that their paper did deal with the divergence between WPI and CPI, and he was himself concerned about the impact of this divergence on the GDP deflator. He felt that issues such as this deserved much more attention than simply introducing the MCA 21 database. R. Nagaraj noted that with the number of companies submitting data in the MCA database jumping around from year to year, the blow-up factor also had to change from year to year. So the levels would be differentially affected from year to year, and it is not as simple as saying that even if there are errors in calculating levels, those errors would apply to all years and hence growth would not be affected. Growth will be affected if the methodology is affecting levels differently in different years. He also supported the concern voiced by Vijay Joshi about the disconnect between the faster growth shown by the new series and other data such as the import numbers.

Bishwanath Goldar acknowledged that the point made in the paper emphasizing the need to address the problem of self-selection in the MCA database was very appropriate. But he said that it was not clear what econometric technique should be deployed to obtain the adjustment for self-selection bias. He also felt that ultimately any adjustment would manifest itself in a smaller or larger blow-up factor, and the adjustment would be unlikely to fluctuate much from year to year and would not, therefore, make a big difference on growth. Similarly, even assuming that the MCA database had a lot of errors, it was difficult to believe that these errors would consistently only push up the growth rate every year, as seems to have happened with the GDP growth higher for four years under the new series. What is instead more credible is that there has been genuine growth. The other point he noted was that not all manufacturing firms were registered under the ASI. However, it is very likely that these firms would be covered by the Companies Act and would therefore have data in the MCA database. So there are problems with the ASI numbers as well, and it would not be fair to say that ASI was always more accurate and represented the real picture, and MCA 21 did not. Both have problems.

Pronab Sen responded to the concern expressed by Vijay Joshi about how to square the higher growth numbers with other macro-data that were not showing the same vibrancy. He noted that the ASI data consistently showed that for the longest time in Indian manufacturing the ratio of gross value added (GVA) to the gross value of output was stagnating at around 16 percent up to about 2004. Thereafter, during 2004–11, it went up marginally from 16 to just over 18 percent, and between 2011–12 and 2014–15, it went up further from 18 to 22.5 percent. The overall measure of value added in the economy is arrived at by multiplying this ratio by the gross value of output. This particular ratio going up by roughly 5 percentage points a year over the last 3 to 4 years, and with manufacturing growth hanging at around 7.5 to 8 percent, suggests that manufacturing turnover is growing at about 2 to 2.5 percent. Imports are really related to the volume of output and not necessarily value added. So value added is going up much faster than the gross value of output. A similar situation had also occurred during 1998–2002, after which the ratio had stabilized. He suggested that economists need to analyze why this measure of production efficiency has improved dramatically in the last four years, which would then also explain why the growth of value added appears to be faster than some of the other macro-variables.

ACHYUTA ADHVARYU*
University of Michigan, Ross School of Business

PRASHANT BHARADWAJ†
University of California, San Diego

SAM KRUMHOLZ‡
University of California, San Diego

Early Childhood Health and Development in India: A Review of the Evidence and Recommendations for the Future

ABSTRACT This paper documents temporal trends and interstate and intrastate disparities in child health and cognitive ability in India, and reviews the theoretical and empirical literature on policy interventions that may help ameliorate these gaps. We show that despite rapid improvements in early childhood health across much of India over the past three decades, many areas still experience persistently high rates of infant mortality, low rates of child immunization, and low levels of child academic achievement. We outline a series of interventions with a strong theoretical and empirical evidence base for improving physical and cognitive development of young children in these areas, including improved nutrition and sanitation, parental stimulation, and caretaker focus on cognitive and emotional development of the child. We then describe various challenges that must be overcome before these interventions can be carried out successfully, as other market failures and issues of state capacity are often present. We conclude by recommending that as India scales up programs aimed at early childhood health and development, it must (a) collect extensive data to understand where programs should be deployed in order to maximize their impact and (b) perform rigorous program evaluations to ensure that interventions which have been shown to work in more favorable settings are also successful in the Indian context.

Keywords: *Child Health and Development, India, Policy*

JEL Classification: *I1, O*

* *achyuta.adhvaryu@gmail.com*
† *pjags1@gmail.com*
‡ *skrumhol@ad.ucsd.edu*

1. Introduction

Children's experiences in utero and in early life can have large, long-lasting impacts that translate into health and economic well-being in adulthood (Almond and Currie 2011; Currie and Vogl 2013; Heckman 2006, 2007). Microeffects have also been shown to extend to the macrolevel, for example, in robust international associations between health in early life and economic indicators such as GDP per capita (Weil 2014). These findings suggest that policies that bolster the survival and development of infants and young children have more than just an ethical imperative: when implemented well, they generate large economic returns. Still, despite the growing academic consensus, policy makers in low-income countries have been slow to shift their focus to this issue, resulting in insufficient funding and regulatory oversight for programs that improve the welfare of young children (Britto, Engle, and Super 2013).

With regard to child health, India's story over the past decade has largely been one of success in reducing infant mortality and encouraging healthy growth through immunization and supplementation. Infant mortality has fallen from 66 deaths per 1,000 live births in 2000 to 39 deaths per 1,000 live births in 2014, and DPT immunization rates have increased from 58 percent to 83 percent during the same time period.

Yet progress has been uneven. Both the level and the rate of improvement of child health in India remain widely unequal. Infant mortality rates (IMRs) in Uttar Pradesh and Madhya Pradesh are more than four times those of Kerala, while the gap between the most and least vaccinated states is more than 40 percentage points. Even within states, there exist stark disparities. IMRs of children born in rural areas are more than 1.5 times those of their urban counterparts. Similarly, the difference between the most and least vaccinated districts "within" states is almost always greater than 30 percentage points.

Of course, greater economic development should help improve many of these outcomes. Figure 1 shows state-level infant mortality and immunization rates as a function of (log) state income per capita. There is a clear relationship between the level of economic development and infant mortality and immunization rates. However, almost equally striking is the amount of variation in performance among states with similar levels of income. This variation suggests that, at least for intermediate stages of growth, economic development is not a panacea; there is an important role for government programs and policies to improve early childhood outcomes (and by extension later-life outcomes) among its citizens.

FIGURE 1. State Infant Mortality and Vaccination Rates as a Function of Log GDP/Capita

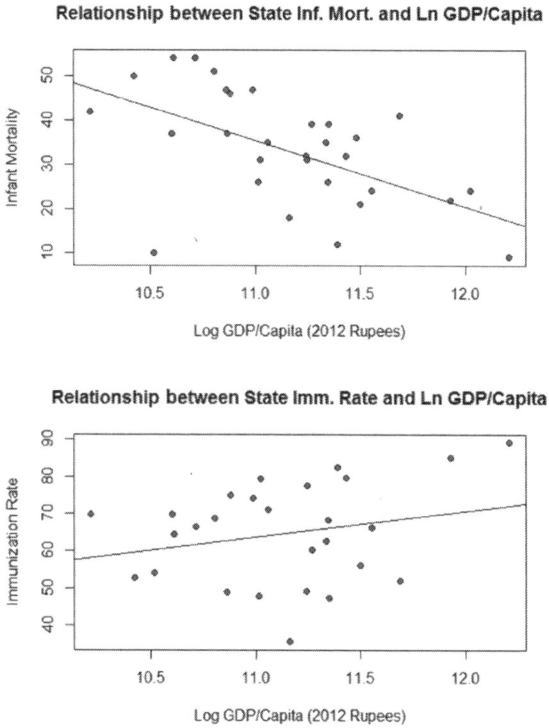

Source: Infant mortality data from the 2013 Indian Census State Sample Registration Statistical Report.

These statistics pose a natural question: How can governments help to remediate disadvantage and reduce the inequalities of early childhood that translate to wide gaps in achievement and well-being in adulthood? With regard to health, the best tools for fighting these inequalities are well known: access to vital micro and macronutrients, immunization from life-threatening diseases, access to clean water and local sanitation, and prevention and rapid treatment of infectious diseases. These tools must be combined with strategies that prioritize the so-called "last mile"—getting effective interventions to the (often disenfranchised) populations that need them most but get them at rather high marginal costs. This is where the most work is still needed, to stimulate consumer demand and bolster the incentives of local agents to provide high-quality health and nutrition services.

While the survival and health of young children is paramount, cognitive and non-cognitive skills (which are not perfectly correlated with child health) are often more strongly associated with economic outcomes in adulthood.[1] In this regard, the picture in India is fuzzier. While there is some nationally representative evidence on spatial patterns of cognitive development in later childhood in India (ages 5 and up), the country is lacking a comprehensive data source for skill and capability development at early ages (below age 3, for instance). These data are important to assess where the geographic disparities in skill deficits at early ages are most important.

The importance of addressing under-investment in early childhood development was highlighted by a recent series in *The Lancet*. The authors suggest that 53 percent of the under-five-year olds in South Asia are at risk of "not reaching their development potential" (Black et al. 2016). To combat these deficits, governments must employ a rapid scaling-up of interventions focused on "nurturing care," or "a stable environment that is sensitive to children's health and nutritional needs, with protection from threats, opportunities for early learning, and interactions that are responsive, emotionally supportive, and developmentally stimulating" (Britto et al. 2016). Nutrition and health interventions are affordable starting points to implement these policies more broadly (Richter et al. 2016).

In recent years, the Indian government has spearheaded early childhood education initiatives, guided by the emphasis given to this topic in the Eleventh Five Year Plan (2007–12) and subsequently by the Right of Children to Free and Compulsory Education Act in 2009. These commitments from the central government—along with several high-profile initiatives to support them—establish a set of national priorities related to early childhood development. Such initiatives include the delivery of preschool education through the Integrated Child Development Services (ICDS); community-based child development support through Accredited Social Health Activists (ASHAs); and the Rajiv Gandhi National Crèche Scheme (RGNCS).

These programs have the potential to become vital components of a holistic set of national policies that promote early childhood development. In this paper, we highlight three critiques of the status quo and point to potential solutions that have proven successful in other contexts (covered in detail in Section 4). The critiques are as follows. First, policy implementation, which is largely administered by individual states in India, has thus far been inadequate. Second, empirically sound evaluation of pilot

1. Of course, these correlations are conditional on survival. More work is necessary to determine what part, if any, of these correlations comes from selection bias.

initiatives is needed to identify the highest return policy levers and weed out low-return programs. Third, even successful pilots may flounder when brought to scale; this problem may be particularly salient given India's complex political and institutional environment. We thus emphasize the need for proper monitoring and evaluation of at-scale initiatives through purposeful investment in data gathering and analysis, while also adjusting program implementation to take into account provider incentives and stimulation of public demand.

The remainder of the paper is organized as follows. Section 2 provides some background on the current status of and recent trends in child health and development in India, with special attention given to the inequality in these measures across Indian states (and between districts within states). Section 3 describes a theoretical framework for health and skill formation in childhood, through which we identify key elements of good policy making for the early advancement of children. Section 4 reviews the relevant literature in public health and economics for successful interventions aimed at reducing inequities in child health and early skill development, discusses the potential scalability of these interventions in the Indian context, and recommends next steps for public policy. Section 5 concludes the paper.

2. The State of Child Health in India

In this section, we use data from several large, nationally representative surveys to characterize both the current state of early childhood health in India and variation in these outcomes by gender, urbanity, and state. There are three key findings. First, Indian infant mortality and immunization rates have improved considerably since 1980. By 2013, the Indian IMR had dropped to one-third of its 1980 level and DPT immunization rates increased from 16 percent in 1984 to 83 percent in 2013. However, there is substantial heterogeneity across and within Indian states in both immunization and infant mortality. For instance, in 2013, IMRs in Kerala were similar to those of Mexico, while IMRs in Madhya Pradesh were slightly higher than Ethiopia's. Additionally, all states have severe rural-to-urban disparities in infant mortality but much smaller gaps in immunization rates. Finally, there is also large variability in childhood cognitive outcomes across states: while 99 percent of 8 to 11 year olds in Kerala can recognize letters, the same is true for only 76 percent of 8 to 11 year olds in Uttar Pradesh. The following sub-sections describe these findings in greater detail.

2.1. Measurement of Early Childhood Health Outcomes

We study changes over time and differences across space in Indian early childhood health outcomes and Indian early childhood health investments. To summarize early childhood health outcomes, we use infant mortality, which has several advantages as a measure of early childhood health. First, saving the lives of young children is an inherently important policy outcome. Second, IMRs can be objectively measured through surveys (vital registration records from hospitals, for example, would not be as representative for this purpose since many deaths do not occur in hospitals). Third, IMRs are at least moderately correlated with many other early childhood health outcomes of interest. Fourth, IMRs are widely measured across the developing and developed world, allowing for the Indian experience to be placed in an international context.

As a proxy for early childhood health investments, we use the percentage of 12 to 23 month olds receiving all appropriate DPT, measles, polio, and BCG (tuberculosis) vaccinations. Immunization rates were chosen because they are easily and objectively measured (most survey enumerators examine an individual's immunization card); they are highly correlated with other outcomes of interest; and they provide large payoffs in terms of reduced mortality, improved later-life health, and human capital accumulation. While it would be beneficial to have data on other forms of household-based investments such as time spent playing (stimulation), providing a varied diet to the child etc., such data is not available to us.

Table 1 shows the pair-wise correlations between state-level IMRs, full vaccination rates, percentage of institutional births, percentage of mothers receiving an antenatal checkup, percentage of children receiving Vitamin A supplementation, and percentage of children experiencing stunting (less than –2 standard deviations below average height-for-age). The correlations for stunting are for a subset of 19 states with sufficient data. Infant mortality is moderately correlated with all major outcomes of interest in the expected direction, although no correlations are significant. Vaccination rates are highly and significantly correlated with all other measures of child investment and improved maternal/neonatal care.

All the 2013 data on state and district immunization rates were collected from the District Level Household and Facility Survey IV (DLHS) and the Annual Health Survey (AHS) 2012–13 state reports. The 2013 data on infant mortality was collected from the Indian Census Sample Registration System 2013 Statistical Report. All 1993 data on infant mortality and immunizations were collected from the 1992–93 Demographic Health

TABLE 1. State-level Correlations between Key Outcomes of Interest

	Infant Mortality	*% Fully Vaccinated*	*% Institutional Deliveries*	*% Antenatal Check-up*	*% Receiving Vitamin A*	*% Stunting*
Infant mortality	1					
% fully vaccinated	–.1537	**1**				
% institutional deliveries	–.2555	**.4096****	1			
% antenatal check-up	.1728	**.6583*****	.6243***	1		
% receiving vitamin A	–.2778	**.5436*****	.7107***	.6346***	1	
% stunting	.29	**–.4216***	–.7843***	–.5662***	–.7462***	1

Source: 2012 India Human Development Survey (IHDS).

Note: $^{*}p < .1$, $^{**}p < .05$, $^{***}p < .001$

Survey (DHS). The DHS and DLHS are large, nationally representative surveys of Indian population health with an emphasis on reproductive and early childhood outcomes.

Finally, as a proxy for child cognitive development, we use a rudimentary reading, writing, and math test given to children aged 8 through 11 in the 2012 India Human Development Survey (IHDS), India's only national panel dataset collected by the National Council of Applied Economic Research (NCAER). Despite the amount of attention paid to early childhood physical health interventions and measurement, there has not been a commensurate focus on early childhood cognitive and socio-emotional outcomes. This gap in knowledge is important: A large number of studies from across the developed and developing worlds have shown that cognitive and non-cognitive developmental outcomes are closely linked with adult labor market productivity. Indeed, the wide disparities found in this study based on a much cruder measure of child cognitive development suggest that much more work in this area is needed.

2.2. Aggregate Trends in Indian Early Childhood Health

Indian early childhood health care and health outcomes have improved markedly over the past 30 to 40 years. Figure 2 shows trends in Indian infant mortality and Indian immunization rates relative to other large developing countries using data collected by the World Bank. Infant mortality has fallen from 142 deaths per 1,000 live births in 1974 to 39 deaths per 1,000 live births in 2014. Similarly, the proportion of children receiving the DPT immunization has increased from 16 percent in 1984 to 84 percent by 2014. However, despite these advances, Indian IMRs remain more than three times those of China and 1.7 times those of Indonesia, leaving considerable room for improvement.

Figure 3 shows the current ratio of rural-to-urban Indian IMRs and immunization across Indian states. As pictured, there are stark disparities in IMRs between rural and urban areas: the rural IMR is 25–75 percent greater than the urban rate in most Indian states and more than double the urban rate in a small number of states in the northeast. Saikia et al. (2013) suggest that much of this gap can be explained by the higher levels of maternal education and wealth in urban areas rather than better provision of health care per se. Thus, development programs aimed at increasing rural standard of living may also work to decrease rural-to-urban early childhood health disparities.

FIGURE 2. Changes in Infant Mortality and Immunization Rates among Selected Developing Countries over Time

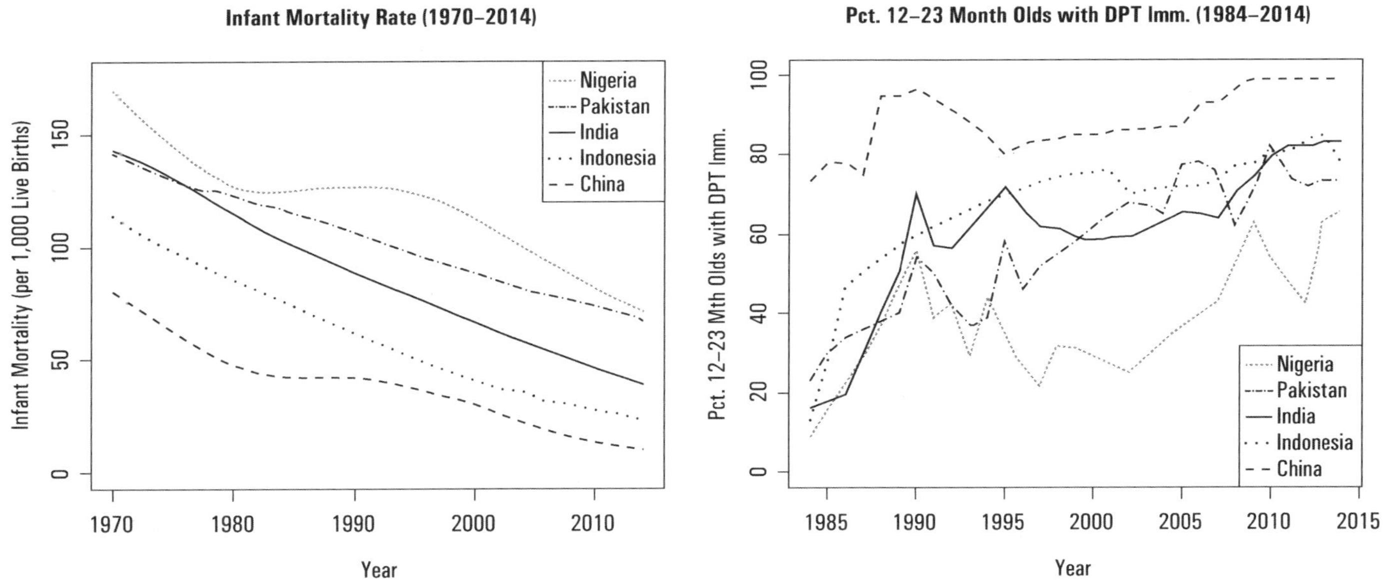

Source: Data on infant mortality and DPT immunization rates from World Bank.

FIGURE 3. Ratio of Rural to Urban Infant Mortality and Immunization Rates by State

Panel A
Ratio of Rural to Urban Infant Mortality Rate

Panel B
Ratio of Rural to Urban Immunization Rates
(% of 12–33 Month Olds with All Immunizations)

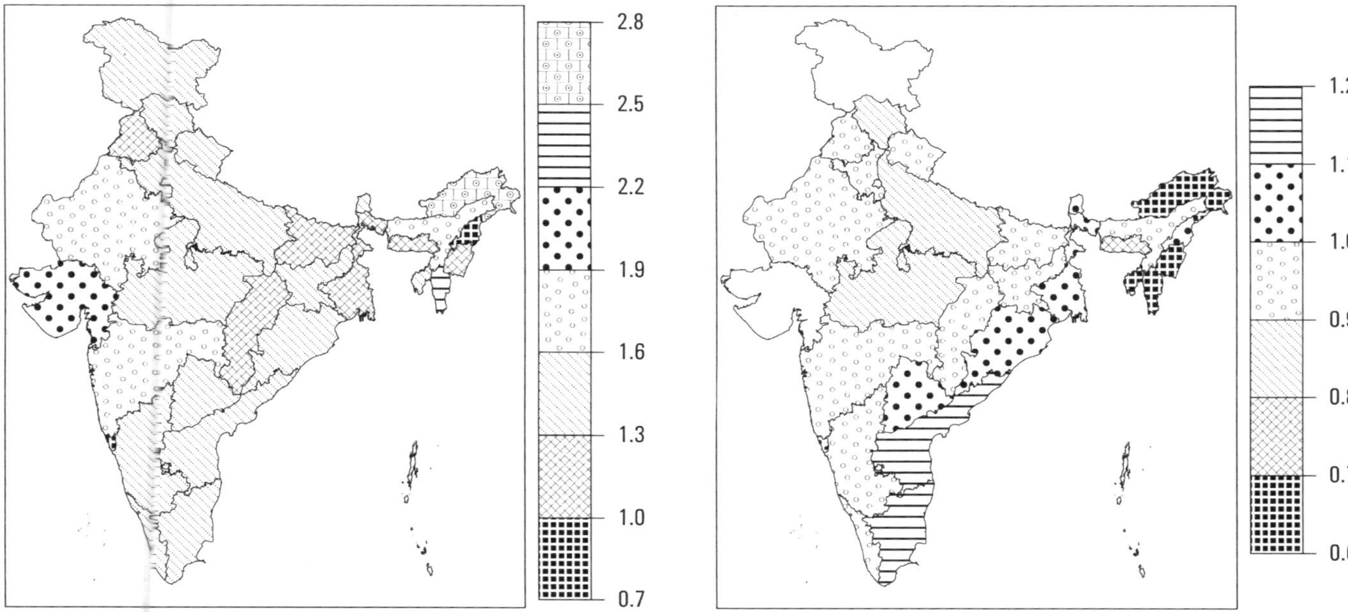

Sources: Infant mortality data from the 2013 Indian Census State Sample Registration Statistical Report and immunization data from the District Level Household and Facility Survey IV (DLHS) and the Annual Health Survey (AHS) 2012–13 state reports.

Notes: In Panel B state reports were not available for Gujarat and Jammu & Kashmir.

These maps are not to scale and may not depict authentic boundaries.

In contrast to infant mortality, rural-to-urban differences in immunization rates, while present, appear smaller.[2] Indeed, in some states, such as Andhra Pradesh, Odisha, and Tamil Nadu, immunization rates in rural areas have reached or surpassed those of urban areas. These results suggest that although Indian government's action has been partially successful in closing the immunization gap between rural and urban regions, they have been less successful in closing the gap in outcomes, at least as proxied through the IMR. Understanding why this is the case is an important area for future research.

Finally, Figure 4 illustrates the ratio of male-versus-female IMRs across states. In most states, male IMRs are 5–10 percent lower than

FIGURE 4. Ratio of Male-to-Female Infant Mortality Rates by State

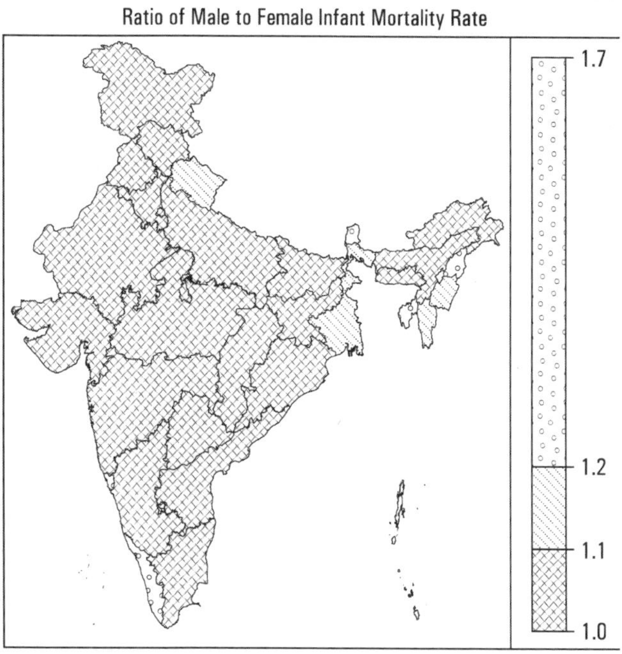

Sources: 2013 Indian Census State Sample Registration Statistical Report.
Note: This map is not to scale and may not depict authentic boundaries.

2. It is important to note that since we create ratios of variables measured on different scales, it is difficult to compare the magnitude of urban–rural disparities across variables. However, the fact that some regions have reached parity between rural and urban areas for immunization rates, while only one state has done so for IMRs, suggests that this larger gap is not simply an artifact of how we chose to display the data. The decline in rural–urban immunization gaps has also been documented in Singh (2013).

female rates.[3] Although these disparities are smaller than the rural–urban gap, unlike the rural–urban disparity, these differences likely cannot be explained by differences in mothers' socioeconomic status or access to health facilities. Understanding the extent to which preference for males leads to higher IMRs for females is an area of highly important ongoing research. Male and female infant immunization rates were only available for a subset of states surveyed in the 2012–13 DLHS, but these data show roughly equivalent immunization rates between boys and girls.

2.3. State-level Variation in Early Childhood Health

India has enormous regional variation in standards of living, culture, language, and gender equality. Thus, it is perhaps unsurprising that there is also substantial state-level heterogeneity in early childhood investments and health outcomes. Figure 5 shows infant mortality and immunization rates at the state level in 2013. In general, the south and northwest of the country have relatively low IMRs while the north and northeast have higher rates. The extent of spatial variation is quite striking: Kerala has approximately the same IMR as Mexico (12 deaths per 1,000 live births), while Madhya Pradesh has a rate similar to Ethiopia (54 deaths per 1,000 live births). There is a similar degree of state-level variation among immunization rates, but much less spatial correlation.[4]

Figure 6 shows state IMRs after adjusting for state GDP per capita. There are two main things to note. First, even after controlling for state GDP, there still exists a large amount of interstate variation in both IMRs and immunization rates. Second, although a number of states under or over-perform their predicted values based on GDP per capita, the rough geographic disparities in infant mortality and immunization rates remain.

3. The ratio between male and female IMRs in Kerala and Goa is particularly low because the overall IMRs are extremely low. In absolute terms, the difference between the Keralan male and female IMRs is only 3 deaths per 1,000 live births.

4. Some of the low immunization rates reported in DHLS IV are surprising, especially those of Tamil Nadu (56 percent). Indeed, the 2009 UNICEF coverage survey recorded immunization rates more than 20 percentage points higher than the DLHS IV estimates. However, early reports from the National Family Health Survey IV (2016) also found relatively low (though still 13 percentage points higher than in the DLHS report) immunization rates and a decrease of similar magnitude since 2005. Thus, although the DLHS reports of immunization rates in Tamil Nadu appear inexplicably low, the directionality of the trend over time appears to agree with other data sources.

FIGURE 5. 2013 Infant Mortality and Immunization Rates by State

Panel A

2013 Infant Mortality Rate (Deaths per 1,000 Live Births)

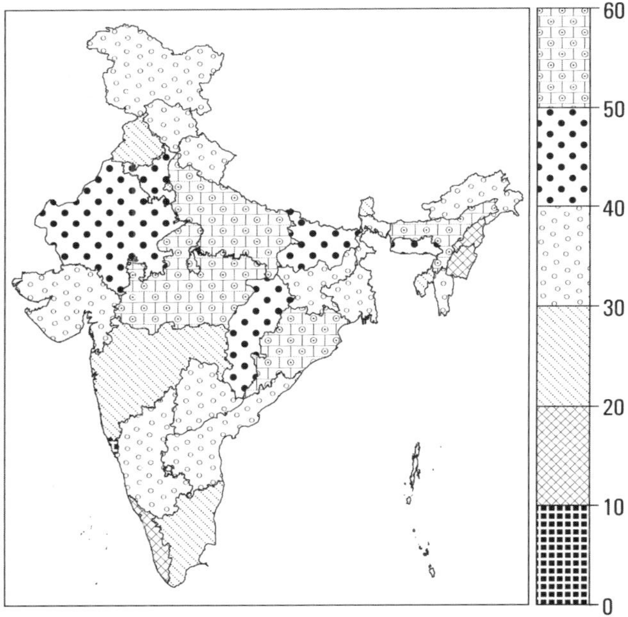

Panel B

2012 Percent 12–23 Month Olds with All Immunizations

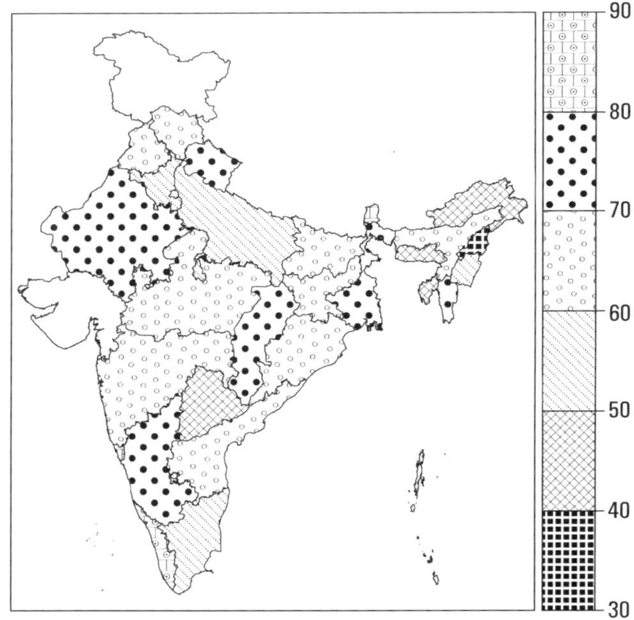

Sources: Infant mortality data from the 2013 Indian Census State Sample Registration Statistical Report and immunization data from the District Level Household and Facility Survey IV (DLHS) and the Annual Health Survey (AHS) 2012–13 state reports.

Notes: In Panel B of the above figure, state reports were not available for Gujarat and Jammu & Kashmir.

These maps are not to scale and may not depict authentic boundaries.

FIGURE 6. 2013 GDP/Capita Adjusted Infant Mortality and Vaccination Rates

Panel A
GDP-Adjusted Infant Mortality Rates
(Relative to Manipur)

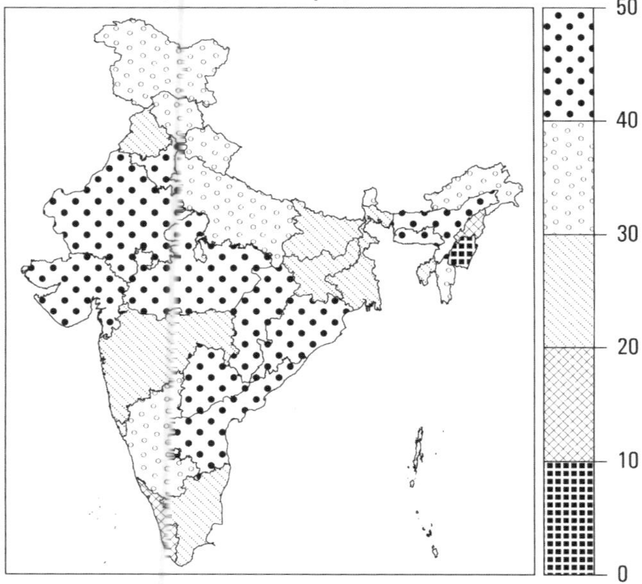

Panel B
GDP-Adjusted Immunization Rates
(Relative to Nagaland)

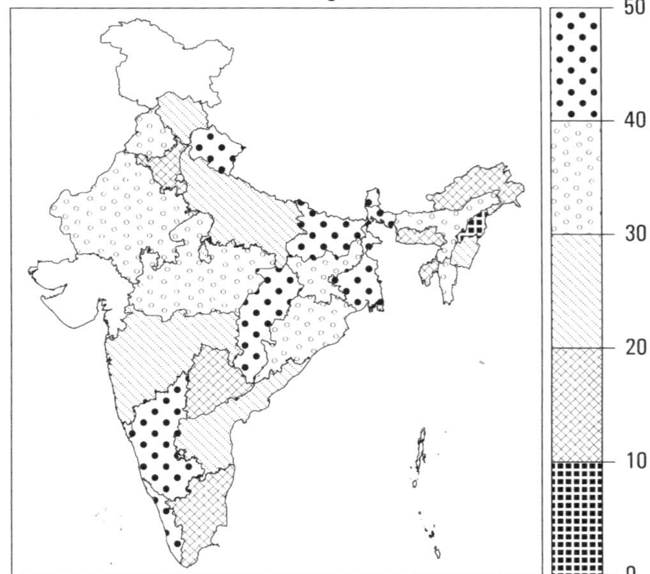

Sources: Infant mortality data from the 2013 Indian Census State Sample Registration Statistical Report and immunization data from the District Level Household and Facility Survey IV (DLHS) and the Annual Health Survey (AHS) 2012–13 state reports.

Notes: The above GDP-adjusted figures show the residuals of an OLS regression of the outcome variable on log GDP/capita. These residuals were then normalized such that the value for the state with the lowest value was set equal to 0.

In Panel B of the above figure, state reports were not available for Gujarat and Jammu & Kashmir.

These maps are not to scale and may not depict authentic boundaries.

Figure 7 shows how infant mortality and vaccination rates have changed at the state level between 1993 and 2013.[5] There are several important takeaways. First, infant mortality fell dramatically in almost all Indian states during this time frame with the exception of Jammu and Kashmir. Second, this decrease was especially prominent in the north and Tamil Nadu, with reductions of 40 to 55 deaths per 1,000 live births—a remarkable public health accomplishment. Third, vaccination rates also increased throughout much of the country, but these gains were particularly pronounced in the north. Indeed, several wealthier states, including Tamil Nadu, Maharashtra, and Haryana, saw only small gains or small falls in immunization rates over this time period.

The relative stagnation of immunization rates in India's higher income states is not well understood. Dasgupta et al. (2014) found in a correlational analysis that the districts experiencing immunization-rate declines in nine higher income states were more likely to be urban and less likely to have a higher proportion of Scheduled Castes/Scheduled Tribes. However, much more research is required to understand why immunization gains may have stopped in India's wealthier states, especially because early data from the 2015–16 DHS suggests that this trend has continued in the years since 2012.

Broad-based gains in both infant mortality and immunization rates, especially in the poorest regions of India, suggest that various factors including economic growth and government initiatives have been relatively successful over the past few decades in improving investments in child health and child health outcomes. However, despite these improvements, large parts of the country still remain plagued by high IMRs and nonuniversal vaccination, reminding us that much work still lies ahead.

Finally, Figure 8 shows the level of inter-district variation in vaccination rates within the same state.[6] Each point on the graph represents a specific district, with the *Y*-axis reflecting the percent of 12 to 23 month olds fully vaccinated in that district and the *X*-axis standing for the state in which the district is located. This figure shows huge intra-state variation in immunization rates; even lower performing states such as Uttar Pradesh and Arunachal Pradesh have some districts with more than 70 percent of children vaccinated, while higher performing states such as Kerala and West Bengal have

5. Changes for the newly formed states were computed by subtracting the full average of the 1993 state from which the new state was formed with the 2013 average of just the new state.

6. Districts with less than 10 children surveyed were not included.

FIGURE 7. Changes in Infant Mortality and Immunization Rates by State between 1993 and 2013 (Percentage)

Panel A
Change in Infant Mortality Rate between 2013 and 1993

Panel B
Change in Percent 12–23 Months Olds with All Immunizations (1993–2012)

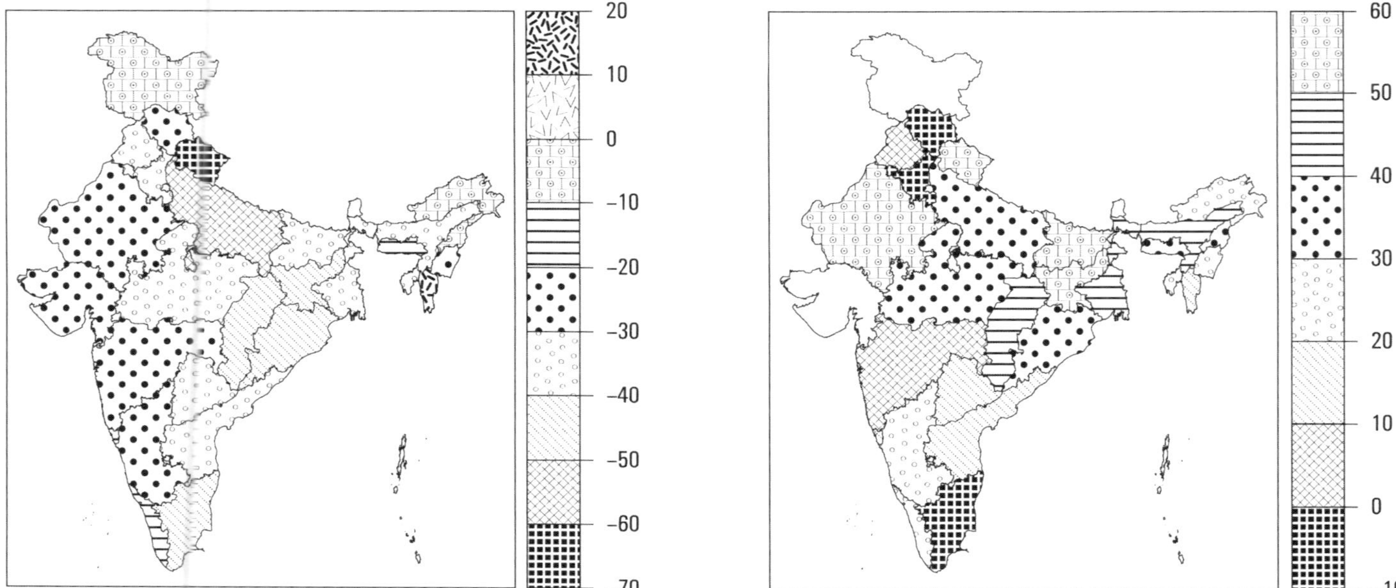

Sources: Infant mortality data from the 2013 Indian Census State Sample Registration Statistical Report and immunization data from the District Level Household and Facility Survey IV (DLHS) and the Annual Health Survey (AHS) 2012–13 state reports. Infant mortality and immunization data for 1993 are from the 1993 Demographic and Health Survey (DHS).

Notes: In Panel B of the above figure, state reports were not available for Gujarat and Jammu & Kashmir.

These maps are not to scale and may not depict authentic boundaries.

FIGURE 8. Intrastate Variation in District-Level Immunization Rates

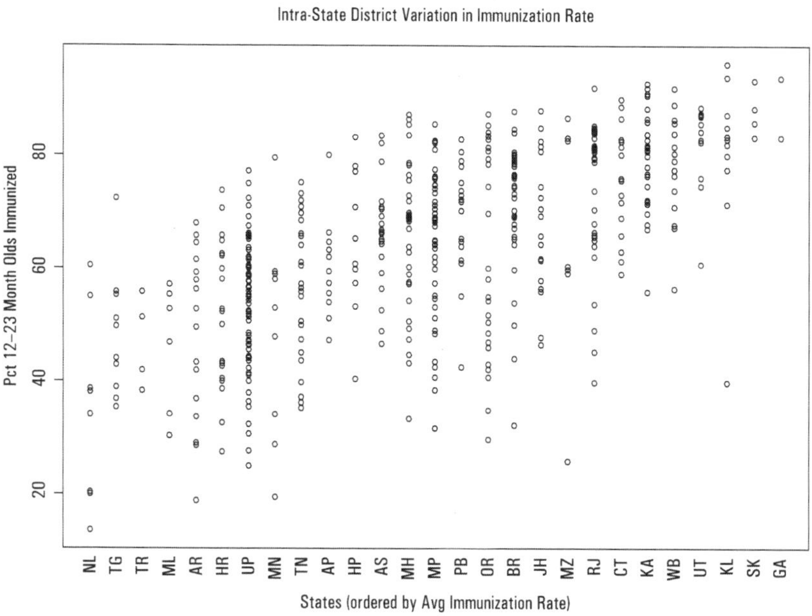

Sources: District-level immunization data from District Level Household and Facility Survey IV (DLHS) and the Annual Health Survey (AHS) 2012–13 state reports.

districts where fewer than 50 percent of 12 to 23 month olds have received full immunization.[7] This high level of variation both between states and between districts within states has been documented by Rammohan and Awofeso (2015). The authors show that district education levels, income per capita, and access to health facilities (for DPT vaccinations only) are highly correlated with district-level differences, but they do not report how much variance is left unexplained after accounting for these factors.

2.4. State-level Variation in Child Cognitive Ability

The earlier sections summarized the current state of physical child health. While decreasing infant mortality, improving child nutrition, and increasing access to medical facilities for children is of first-order policy importance,

7. One concern is that this variation is driven by sampling error (some districts only have 50–100 respondents). We addressed this in two ways. First, for 23 of 27 states, we can reject the null (alpha equal to 0.1) that an interquartile range of that size would arise from chance alone if no true district-level variation existed. Second, we replicated this figure excluding districts with fewer than 80 respondents. The figure remains qualitatively unchanged.

recent research has also emphasized the significance of early childhood cognitive and emotional development for later-life outcomes. However, unlike child physical health, nationally representative data on the state of early childhood cognitive and non-cognitive development in India is lacking.

In this sub-section, we summarize the largest known nationally representative survey of child ability in India.[8] In 2004 and 2012, the NCAER IHDS tested more than 11,000 eight to eleven year olds across India on math, reading, and writing skills. Figure 9 summarizes the 2012 state-level averages[9] in reading and math scores. A respondent is assigned a reading score on a scale of 0 to 4, where 0 means the student does not recognize letters, 1 is for students who recognize letters but not words, 2 means the student can read words but not sentences, 3 signifies the student can read sentences but not paragraphs, and 4 indicates that a student can read paragraphs. Across Indian states, average scores range from just above 3 (can read sentences) to less than 2 (can only read words). Scores are highest in the northwest and Kerala, and lowest in the north and southeast. There also appears to be a high spatial correlation in scores.

We see a largely similar pattern for math scores. In math, a score of 0 means the student cannot recognize numbers, a score of 1 is for students who recognize numbers but who cannot subtract, a score of 2 means the student can subtract but not divide, and a score of 3 indicates that the student can divide. Again, across Indian states, average scores range from around 1 (student can only recognize numbers) to 2 (student can subtract), and state-level variation is high: scores are likewise highest in the northwest and Kerala, and lowest in the north. Andhra Pradesh and Tamil Nadu were found to perform much better on math than reading.

A different (and perhaps more intuitive) way to examine these data is to analyze the percentage of students who have attained the most basic level of proficiency by state. Figure 10 shows the percentage of 8 to 11 year olds who can recognize letters and numbers in most Indian states. Here, the degree of state-level variation in reading and math ability is especially stark: 76 percent of 8 to 11 year olds in Uttar Pradesh can recognize letters compared with 99 percent in Kerala and 96 percent in Andhra Pradesh. Similarly, only 69 percent of students can recognize numbers in Uttar Pradesh, compared with 99 percent in Kerala and 95 percent in Andhra Pradesh. These findings

8. The ASER Centre also provides India-wide testing of 5–14 year olds but only in rural districts.

9. State-level averages were computed for all states with 100 or more observations.

FIGURE 9. Average Math and Reading Scores of 8 to 11 Year Olds by State

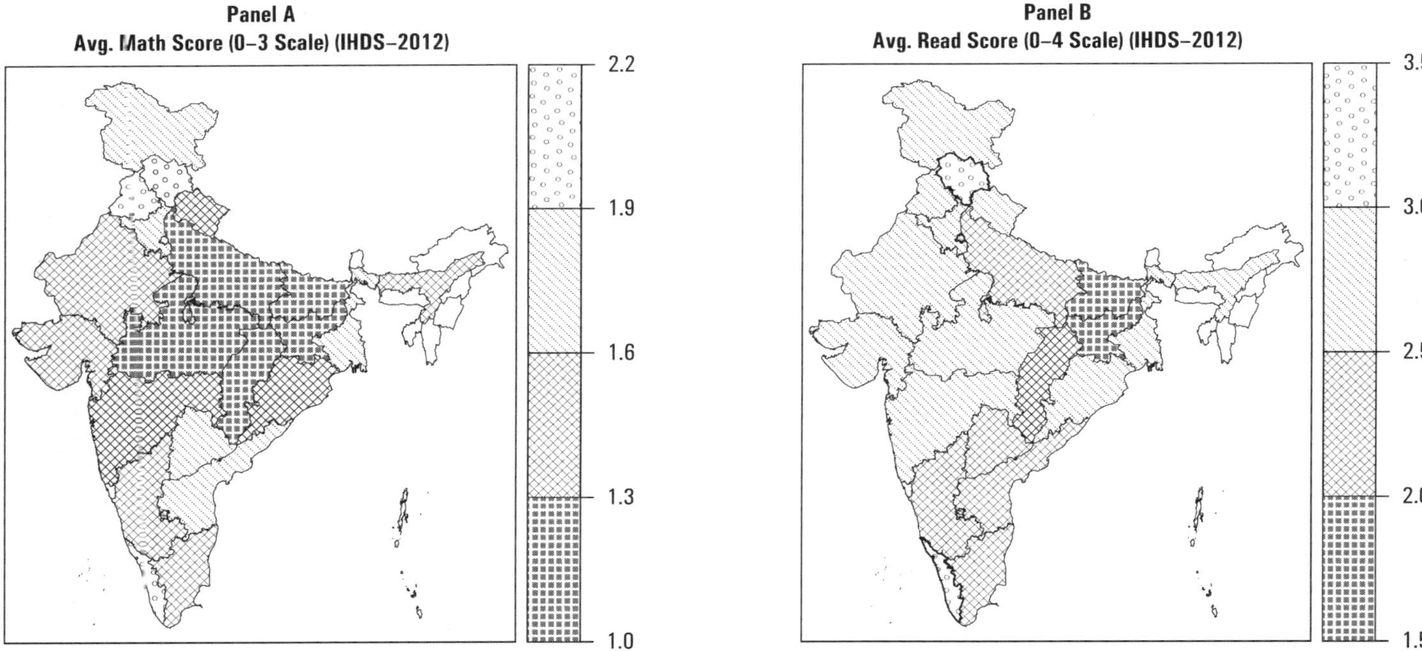

Source: Data on math and reading scores from the 2012 India Human Development Survey (IHDS).

Notes: The scale in the panels of the above figure represents the range of possible scores on the math and reading tests provided to 8–11 year olds in the 2012 IHDS. Students in the math and reading test receive 3 and 4 questions of increasing difficulty, respectively, and their score is the total number of questions they get right. The values on the map are the mean scores for students in each Indian state with at least 100 respondents. All states with fewer than 100 respondents were dropped.

These maps are not to scale and may not depict authentic boundaries.

FIGURE 10. Proportion of 8 to 11 Year Olds by State Who Can Recognize Numbers and Letters

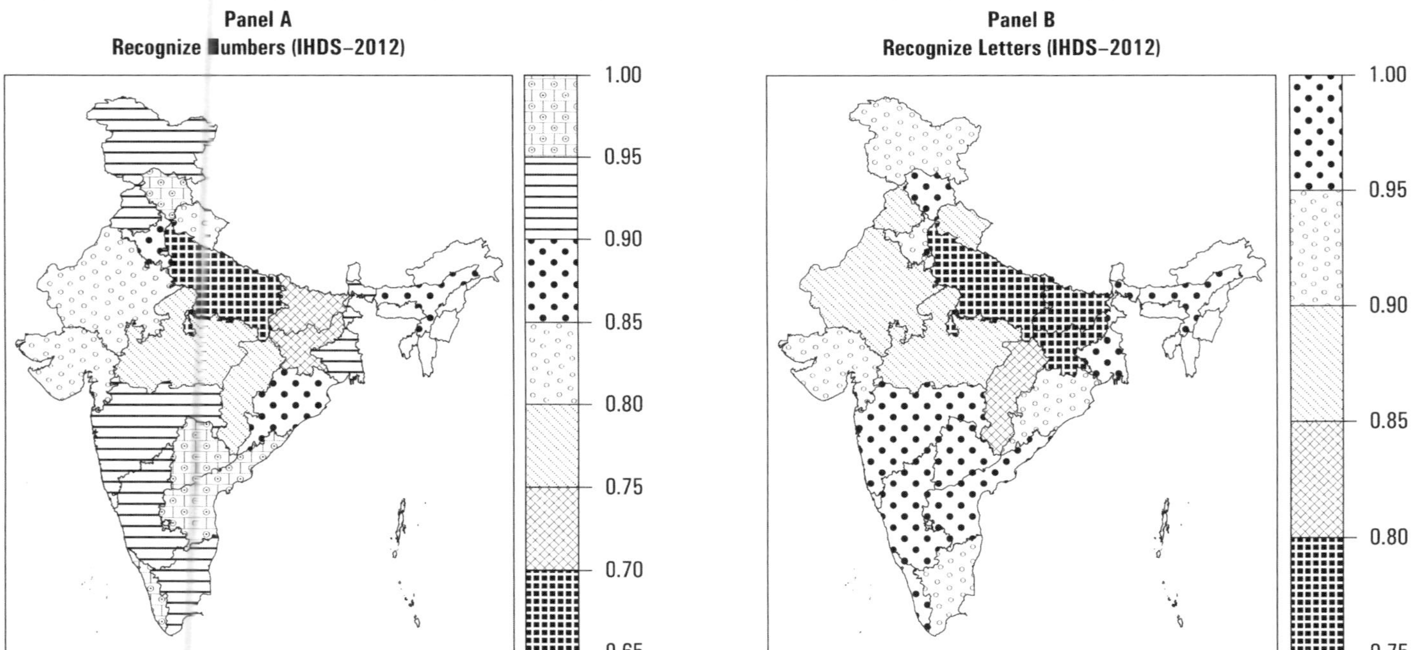

Source: Data on math and reading scores from the 2012 India Human Development Survey (IHDS).

Notes: The scale in the panels of the above figure represents the range of possible scores on the math and reading tests provided to 8–11 year olds in the 2012 IHDS. Students in the math and reading test receive 3 and 4 questions of increasing difficulty, respectively, and their score is the total number of questions they get right. The values on the map are the mean scores for students in each Indian state with at least 100 respondents. All states with fewer than 100 respondents were dropped.

These maps are not to scale and may not depict authentic boundaries.

FIGURE 11. Correlation between 2005 Infant Mortality Rate and 2012 Average Math Score by State

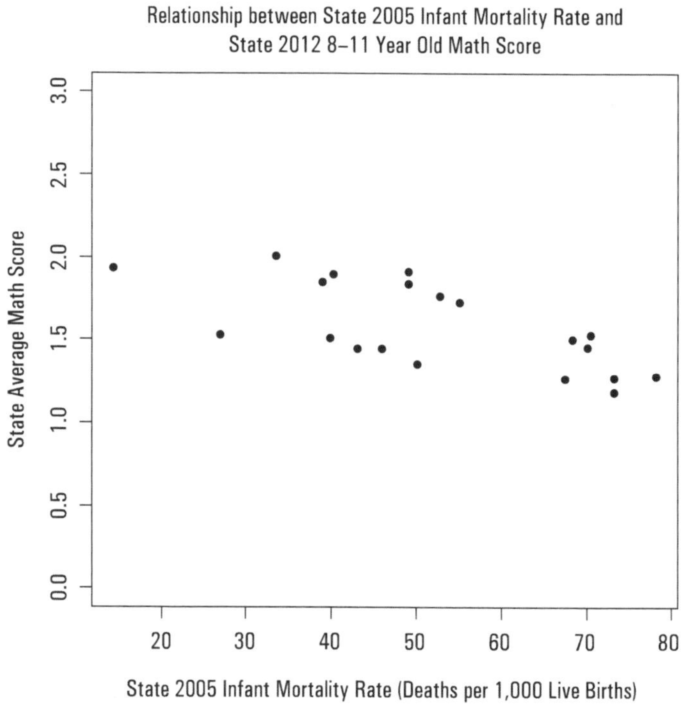

Sources: 2005 Infant mortality data from the National Family and Health Survey-3 (NFHS-3). Data on math scores from the 2012 India Human Development Survey (IHDS).

are especially surprising given that almost all test-taking 8 to 11 year olds in the survey stated that they attended school.

Finally, Figure 11 conveys the relationship between state IMRs in 2005 and state math scores in 2012 (the relationship is nearly identical for reading scores). There is a strong negative relationship: the higher a state's 2005 IMR, the lower its children's math scores (correlation of –0.58). Obviously this relationship is not causal, but the strong correlation does provide evidence that low levels of development may lead to both higher infant mortality and lower scores in school.

2.5. The Need for Better Measurement of Early Childhood Cognitive and Non-cognitive Skills

These data on childhood math and reading ability provide a window into both the absolute and state-level variation in core skills across India, but it is unclear whether these differences are caused by deficiencies in the education system, different levels of income, variability in physical health, gaps in early childhood cognitive/non-cognitive development, or other factors entirely. Therefore, the disparities found here call out for more exploration. Although we have detailed data on many potential contributors to these disparities, one important area where data is almost nonexistent is cognitive and non-cognitive skills among children in early childhood (0 to 3 years).

To amend this information gap, we recommend that the Indian government sponsor a nationally representative survey aimed at providing a comprehensive understanding of the state of early childhood development. One potential survey is the Multiple Indicator Cluster Survey (MICS) developed by UNICEF (Aslam et al. 2014). MICS has been carried out in many developing countries over the past decade and includes modules on child physical health, child developmental ability, parental caretaking activities, and maternal health. MICS only focuses on children under 5, but the study could be adapted for older ages. Implementing this type of survey in India would provide important insight into the types of barriers that lead to large regional disparities in childhood learning and ultimately in long-term labor-market outcomes.

3. Theoretical Considerations and a Framework

The process of health and human capital accumulation throughout childhood is a complex one—a combination of the capabilities that children are born with (so-called "endowments"); investments in children made by parents, caregivers, local communities, and government; and adverse as well as positive experiences that affect child development. Understanding how these elements interact over the course of childhood to determine adult health and skill capabilities (and, in turn, economic outcomes) is crucial to developing sound policies that achieve high returns while remaining cost-effective.

In this section, we review a theoretical framework for health and skill formation in childhood, with an eye toward identifying the key elements of good policy that arise. The basis for this theory has played an important role in academic research for decades (Becker and Lewis 1973; Behrman 1997; Behrman, Pollak, and Taubman 1982; Grossman 1972; Rosenzweig and Schultz 1983), but recent works by Heckman et al. (2010), Cunha and Heckman (2007), Heckman and Mosso (2014), and Heckman, Pinto, and Savelyev (2013) have developed a formal mathematical structure specific to the analysis of early childhood development, which has made strides toward estimating the framework's parameters (Aizer and Cunha 2012; Cunha, Heckman, and Schennach 2010).

3.1. A Framework for Childhood Health and Skill Formation

The process of health and human capital accumulation begins at conception. Even before birth, children are endowed with "stocks" of health and skills. These stocks are multidimensional. For example, health might include pulmonary, cardiovascular, and immune function. Skill generally refers to cognitive function as well as non-cognitive capabilities, such as grit, conscientiousness, and adaptability. These endowments capture the variation in initial states observed in the population. For example, some children have robust immune systems while others are predisposed to illness. Similarly, some children are naturally gifted when it comes to cognitive functions while others have lesser natural ability. These endowments surely have a genetic component, driving a correlation in the characteristics (and corresponding outcomes) of parents and children.

Stocks of health and skills in this model can be thought of in the same way as capital in a standard model of economic growth: they depreciate over time; they can be augmented through investment; and they are prone to exogenous shifters, or "shocks," which are out of the child's control.

Endowments form the initial stocks, which then evolve from period to period, starting at gestation and continuing through birth, early and late infancy, the toddler years, childhood, adolescence, and finally, adulthood. During gestation, prenatal investments (for example, maternal nutrition, decisions regarding smoking and alcohol consumption, prenatal checkups), shocks (for example, illness episodes, traumatic events), and depreciation shift initial stocks. The resulting stocks of health and skills at birth are then taken as inputs into a similar process in the next period, early infancy. Here, the stock continues to evolve as parents devote their material resources and time to the infant.

There are several key features in the model that deserve mention. First, the levels of stocks coming into a given period may impact the effectiveness of investments during that period. For example, an infant with a weak immune system (a low stock of immunity) may benefit greatly from supplementation with Vitamin A, which helps boost the body's natural immune response. An infant with a more robust immune system may still benefit from Vitamin A but less so than the weaker infant. As we highlight below, this interaction between stocks and investments is absolutely critical to elucidate for the purposes of good policy making.

Second, the stocks of health and skills may directly impact each other, and one stock may also affect the productivity of investments in the other. For example, investing time in a child's socio-emotional development may yield the greatest returns for children with the highest stocks of health. In other words, it may be difficult to teach socio-emotional skills to a sick child. Third, as a corollary of the last point, certain investments may affect both health and skill stocks. For example, antimalarial treatment will certainly improve a child's health if she is sick with malaria, but it may also have indirect impacts on cognitive function and other capabilities.

Finally, inherent in the capital-like dynamics of the model is the idea that health and skill stocks are linked over time, and the extent of this linkage depends on the way in which particular stocks and investments interact (and potentially how this interaction changes over the course of childhood). If, for example, investments have the highest returns for children with higher endowments, then children with low initial stocks may find it difficult or impossible to catch up to their better-endowed peers, despite consistent targeted investments. On the other hand, if early remediation of poor endowments is possible, then catch-up should also be possible.

3.2. Policy Implications

The theoretical framework described earlier is important because it gives us a lens through which to evaluate policies for early childhood development in attempting to target the highest impact interventions. Implicit in our discussion is a motivation to reduce inequalities that stem from health and human capital formation in childhood. This entails implementing policies that remediate outcomes for disadvantaged children as well as protect against further disadvantage. Several significant lessons emerge from this framework.

3.3. Timing Matters

The evolution of stocks plays a central role in the model. The fact that one period's "outputs" of health and skills are taken as the next period's "inputs" generates the potential for long-run consequences of temporary investments or one-time shocks. For the purposes of policy making, it is therefore critical to understand how much the timing of investments can matter at different points in time in this model, because their impact determines the long-run returns to the intervention. In particular, we would like to know when children with low stocks of health and skills are most receptive to investments.

While we still have much to learn about these parameters, recent research has made some significant strides, combining detailed data on many dimensions of stocks of health and skills over time with rigorous structural estimation techniques (Cunha, Heckman, and Schennach 2010;

Heckman and Mosso 2014). This research shows that there are substantial differences in the way in which stocks and investments interact at different ages. In particular, very early in life, say from in utero to age 2, investments and stocks of health and human capital are highly substitutable, that is, if a child is disadvantaged at birth, or faces a large shock early in life, it is relatively "easy" to remedy the disadvantage. Later in childhood, however, stocks and investments become less substitutable, or even complementary to each other, within a given time period; that is, beginning at some point in childhood, skill starts to beget skill. However, the exact point at which this change occurs is open to debate. Early work on the importance of the first 1,000 days of life suggested that early life nutritional or health deficits were extremely difficult to overcome (Martorell, Khan, and Schroeder 1994). Yet more recent work has found that growth even up to age 8 can still have beneficial effects on adolescent outcomes (Georgiadis et al. 2016). Although the effects of growth on long-term cognitive achievement for children of different ages remain an ongoing debate, there remains a consensus that early life investments have especially strong effects. Therefore, even if investing in disadvantaged adolescents is ethically desirable, it may be highly inefficient economically.[10]

Perhaps the easiest way to understand this set of results is through an example. An attentive care provider may be able to ameliorate cognitive disadvantage for a very young child by providing intensive time inputs, a specialized curriculum, and material resources such as toys and play activities, while even a very high quality teacher may not have the same effect on a teenager who has done poorly in school throughout her life. Put another way, later in childhood, high-quality inputs might best serve those with high baseline abilities.

This changing extent of substitutability over childhood suggests two crucial lessons related to timing: to remediate disadvantage, the highest return investments are those made very early in life, and investments late in childhood are more productive if the stocks of health and skills are already higher. The latter insight implies a "dynamic complementarity" between early and late investments: the greater the level of early investment (and thus the larger the early stocks of health and skills), the more productive later investments become.

10. It should be noted that the timing of this investment remains in disequilibrium—it is likely that shifting even large quantities of resources to early childhood investments and away from later childhood inputs would not equalize the marginal returns to additional investment, at least in the Indian context.

3.4. Crowding Out and Complementarity in Investments

There are likely many potential policy levers focused on early childhood development at a government's disposal. What sub-set of these is most appropriate for a given population is a question that the theory is largely silent about. But one insight regarding multiple interventions that does come from the model is the potential for both crowding out and complementarity.

Crowding out implies that in a given period, investments that act in very similar ways on the same dimensions of the human capital stock are likely to substitute for one another.

There is some empirical evidence to back up this idea. For example, Rossin-Slater and Wüst (2015) study the long-term impacts of two early life programs in Denmark: high-quality preschool childcare and home visitation by a trained nurse. The researchers find that the two programs, intervening at slightly different times in the child's early life (infancy and around age 3), effectively act as substitutes for one other in terms of generating positive long-term outcomes such as educational attainment and family income. Adhvaryu et al. (2015) and Gunnsteinsson et al. (2014) find strikingly similar results among much poorer populations in Mexico and Bangladesh, respectively.

On the other hand, complementarity suggests that investments that act to augment human capital stocks in different ways may have stronger effects when deployed together than they would have in isolation. There are two remarkable recent examples of this from settings that could not be more disparate: 19th-century Boston and present-day rural India. Alsan and Goldin (2015) examine the impact of water and sewerage infrastructure in historical Boston. They find that changes in clean water and sewerage infrastructure alone had no effect on IMRs (which, in the late 1800s, were comparable to present-day developing countries). But in parts of Boston that happened to get both interventions, there was a marked impact on mortality, suggesting that the two interventions were highly complementary. Duflo et al. (2015) produced similar evidence of improvements in diarrheal disease from an evaluation of an integrated water and sanitation improvement program in rural Odisha, which offered piped water as well as latrines to village households.

3.5. Parental Involvement

Thus far, we have focused on how the stocks of health and human capital evolve over time as they face shocks, depreciate, and are augmented via investments. While the first two factors—shocks and depreciation—may be considered exogenous (out of the control of children and other relevant decision-makers), the last factor, investment, is certainly endogenous: how much parents, communities, and governments invest in children is an active decision, likely governed by preferences, budget constraints, characteristics of the child, local economic opportunities, and prevailing cultural norms (Becker and Lewis 1973; Behrman 1997; Rosenzweig and Schultz 1983).

Parents—mothers in particular—are often the primary caretakers of infants and young children and thus play a pivotal role in children's early lives (Adhvaryu and Nyshadham 2014; Almond and Mazumder 2013). Accordingly, they act both as a source of investment of time and material resources as well as an important mediator of other investments. For example, parents decide how much time to devote each day to their children; how much and what to feed them; how much to spend on preventive and curative health care; whether and how early to enroll them in school; how much after-school tutoring they receive; and a whole host of other decisions, which, when aggregated, determine the level of total investment in the child. In many cases, parents also determine access to, and the effectiveness of, community or government programs aimed at helping children.

With some care, the theoretical framework laid out previously can be expanded to allow for such investment decisions to be analyzed. This extended theory links parental preferences and budget constraints to the amount they choose to invest in their children, and ultimately to the stocks of child health and human capital on which we have focused in this section. The main lesson emerging from this model of parental decision-making and the empirical studies that aim to test its predictions is that, depending on the context, parents can both augment and undo the impacts of interventions targeting children (Almond and Mazumder 2013). Though the evidence is mixed, studies in low-income settings tend to demonstrate a propensity to reinforce interventions with additional parental investment (Adhvaryu and Nyshadham 2014; Adhvaryu, Fenske, and Nyshadham 2014; Datar, Kilburn, and Loughran 2010; Grantham-Mcgregor et al. 1991, 1997), while studies in higher income settings generally reveal the opposite (Bharadwaj, Eberhard, and Nielson 2010). The reinforcing or compensatory effects need to be accounted for to understand the full impacts of policies targeting disadvantaged children in each particular setting.

4. Evidence on Early Childhood Development Programs

This section provides a summary of effective interventions shown to reduce infant mortality, combat malnutrition, and promote child development. The key takeaways from this section are twofold. First, while interventions such as micronutrient supplementation, improving food security, and strengthening public health infrastructure are essential in the continuing fight against childhood mortality and malnutrition, we emphasize the importance of a role for stimulation and home visitation, which have been shown to be effective along with traditional malnutrition-based interventions in improving child development. Second, the delivery of these interventions is crucial. While there is plenty of evidence on what works with regard to improving child health and development, it is important to note that what works in the laboratory or in theory might not work in real life. With that in mind, we can broadly think of problems of take-up or lack of effectiveness of proven theories as coming from demand- or supply-side constraints. In this sense, the problems nations face in improving early childhood health are not entirely different from the challenges in improving education; hence, understanding the role of market failures in terms of supply and demand is crucial for making progress in this arena.

Given our earlier findings on the immense heterogeneity in health outcomes across states and even districts within states, it should be noted that it is inadvisable to impose a "one size fits all" policy when it comes to improving early childhood health. Further, as Section 3 points out, the timing of these interventions is crucial for maximum efficacy. Therefore, if policy makers want the highest return on their investments, it is important to target policies in the most vulnerable places, and for children in specific age groups. Finally, policies are rarely evaluated at scale and those in the early childhood health space are no exception. These are salient issues to keep in mind when considering what policies to create, how and when to implement them, and what the effects of these policies might look like when scaled up in the long run. In this section, we first review the evidence about what works for child physical health and overall child development (cognitive and non-cognitive aspects) before addressing implementation and take-up issues.[11]

4.1. Child Survival and Physical Health

While India has made strides in reducing infant mortality over the last few decades, neighboring countries such as Sri Lanka and China still lose far fewer children in the first year of life. In fact, Sri Lanka and China's IMRs in 2014 (8.4 and 9.2 per 1,000 live births, respectively) were less than the

11. One important caveat to the discussion below is that many aspects of a child's environment matter for child health and development; given space constraints, we cannot review them all thoroughly. For example, our review does not focus on issues such as women's education, empowerment, and domestic violence.

average IMR in high-income, non-OECD countries (10.2). In India, as is true around the world, a significant portion of deaths under the age of 5 is driven by neonatal mortality (death within the first month of life). This is important as the causes of neonatal and infant mortality can be quite variable, leading to different policy prescriptions. For example, recent work by Chen, Oster, and Williams (2016) finds that while the United States lags behind other developed nations in infant mortality, it actually has an advantage in terms of neonatal mortality. Such findings lead to sharper policy prescriptions, which rely on detailed analyses of the causes of neonatal and infant/child mortality.

However, since most deaths in India do not occur at a hospital, obtaining reliable information and representative data on cause of death over time has been challenging. A study published in *The Lancet* in 2010 (Million Death Study Collaborators 2010) provides some of the first analyses of neonatal cause of death by using nationally representative data collected as part of the Sample Registration System, covering about 1.1 million homes in India. According to this study, the top three causes of neonatal mortality in India, explaining about 78 percent of all deaths within the first month of life, were (a) prematurity and low birth weight, (b) neonatal infections, and (c) birth asphyxia and trauma. For deaths occurring after the first month of life and before 60 months, the main causes (explaining about 50 percent of deaths) were pneumonia and diarrheal diseases. Each of these five causes is eminently preventable. As the study concludes, "Our results suggest that almost half of India's neonatal deaths are caused by birth asphyxia and birth trauma, sepsis, pneumonia and tetanus—conditions that can be avoided by increases in delivery care and postnatal care."

Darmstadt et al. (2005) conduct a review of interventions that demonstrate strong evidence for reducing neonatal deaths. Examples of such interventions include folic acid supplementation, clean delivery practices, food supplementation, kangaroo mother care for low birth weight infants (Bera et al. 2014; Samra, Taweel, and Cadwell 2014; Suman Rao, Udani, and Nanavati 2008), and vaccinations. There is ample evidence that these individual interventions work: for example, a meta-analysis of studies that examine the efficacy of the tetanus toxoid immunization (aimed at lowering deaths due to neonatal infections) found that two properly timed doses for pregnant women can reduce neonatal deaths by a staggering 94 percent (Blencowe et al. 2010). In a *Lancet* review, Black et al. (2008) focus on the link between maternal and child nutrition and mortality. They find effective interventions to include promotion of breastfeeding, micronutrient supplementation (including multiple instances of micronutrient supplementation during pregnancy), and food supplementation for populations with insufficient food. Studies suggest that pregnant mothers and young children particularly benefit from increased protein intake (Puentes et al. 2016; Stevens et al. 2015). Supplementary nutrition for women and infants in the United States (the WIC program) has been shown to be effective in decreasing the incidence of low birth weight, especially among vulnerable populations (Bitler and Currie 2005). It is also clear that improving health facilities, and access to facilities, can help with child survival. Access to high-quality medical care such as neonatal intensive care units has been found to reduce neonatal and infant deaths among a subset of extremely vulnerable infants in many countries (Almond et al. 2010; Bharadwaj, Loken, and Neilson 2013).

We next move on to a predominant cause of death during childhood, diarrheal diseases. One of the most effective ways to curb this disease is to provide access to clean water and waste management. In developing countries, the burden of diarrheal disease is often the greatest in urban areas, whereas problems such as food insecurity and lack of antenatal care tend to be more prominent in rural areas. The centerpiece of the fight against diarrheal deaths in the developing world (including India) currently is the use of Oral Rehydration Therapy (ORT) with Oral Rehydration Salt (ORS), along with exclusive breastfeeding and zinc supplementation. While knowledge of ORT with ORS is high in India, effective use is still low (Lakshminarayanan and Jayalakshmy 2015).

However, preventing diarrhea from occurring in the first place should be the underlying policy goal. Infrastructure investments by the government to combat open defecation would likely yield high returns by lowering the burden of this disease. Such investments would not only decrease diarrheal deaths but might also reduce the incidence of stunting (Spears, Ghosh, and Cumming 2013). While the provision of clean water is a major part of the fight against diarrhea (a meta-analysis by Fewtrell et al. [2005] finds water quality interventions to be incredibly important), sewage systems in urban areas can be complementary in reducing infant mortality. A recent study by Alsan and Goldin (2015) concluded that a combination of clean water and sewerage provision dramatically reduced infant mortality in Massachusetts between 1880 and 1915. However, it is important to note that simply increasing investments in public health infrastructure alone cannot be the solution. Building toilets and sewers is obviously crucial, but if children are not informed about the importance of behaviors like washing their hands after using a toilet, the returns to these basic investments will fall short. Thus, developments in infrastructure and access to clean water need to be coupled with campaigns such as the Global Handwashing Day to have the most impact.

While there are undoubtedly short-term benefits to these interventions in terms of child health and reductions in mortality, studies have also considered their long-run effects. Research in economics has looked at the long-term impacts of micronutrient supplementation, strengthening food security, and access to advanced health facilities. Two examples of the long-lasting impacts of micronutrients come from Adhvaryu et al. (2014) and Gunnsteinsson et al. (2014). The first found that exposure to iodine in the form of iodized salt in the 1930s led to increased educational attainment and better labor market outcomes in the United States. The second study discovered that exposure to Vitamin A supplementation for infants in Bangladesh reduced the risk of harm done by exposure to such environmental events as typhoons. This is an important result since developing countries like India tend to also suffer disproportionately from climate- and environment-related shocks. With regard to supplemental feeding programs, Hoynes, Schanzenbach, and Almond (2016) as well as Aizer et al. (2014) found positive impacts of safety net programs such as food stamps and welfare payments in the United States on later-life health and labor market outcomes. Finally, Bharadwaj, Loken, and Neilson (2013) showed that access to neonatal intensive care units in Chile and Norway increased cognitive performance in school many years later.

Conditional on surviving the early years, one of the most pervasive problems facing many developing countries, and India in particular, is the issue of childhood malnutrition often measured by stunting (height for age below 2 SD). Stunting and its correlates (apart from mortality, which we have already mentioned above) are well studied, are associated with lower cognitive abilities (Lewit and Kerrebrock 1997), are a likely driver of later-life obesity and related diseases (Eckhardt 2006), and might increase malaria-related deaths (Shankar 2000). Nearly half of all Indian children under age 5 are estimated to be stunted (UNICEF). Many of the strategies outlined previously such as supplemental and complementary feeding, vitamin supplementation, and lowering the burden of diseases like diarrhea are also thought to be effective in combating stunting (Bhutta et al. 2008).

4.2. Child Development

While micronutrients, supplemental feeding, and investments in public health infrastructure are all important tools in the fight against childhood mortality and malnutrition, it is also essential to focus on overall child development as measured by the inter-related domains of cognitive–language, sensory–motor, and social–emotional skills and capabilities. As Section 2 points out, we know less about where childhood cognitive disparities lie in Indian populations, but they are likely correlated with disparities in mortality. A *Lancet* series on early childhood development identifies four important risk factors among children under age 5 in least developed countries (some of which are also risk factors for mortality): stunting, inadequate cognitive stimulation, iodine deficiency and iron deficiency, and anemia (Grantham-McGregor et al. 2007). Hence, there is considerable overlap between factors that matter for neonatal and child survival and those that affect child development (conditional on survival). Engle et al. (2007) discuss evidence on how interventions that reduce malnutrition, iodine deficiency, and iron deficiency improve behavior, cognitive skills, and motor development. In this subsection, we therefore focus on strategies that have been shown to work for improving a child's cognitive and non-cognitive skills, but are not directly aimed at decreasing malnutrition and micronutrient deficiency.

The best-known example of such studies focused on developing countries is the Jamaica experiment (Grantham-McGregor et al. 1991). The Jamaica intervention randomized 129 stunted Jamaican children between the ages of 9 and 24 months into three treatment arms and a control group. The treatments were: (a) psychosocial stimulation, (b) nutritional supplementation, and (c) both psychosocial and nutritional supplementation. Working with community health workers, the psychosocial component comprised weekly one-hour play sessions at home, which lasted two years. The main idea behind the play sessions was to improve the quality of time that mothers spent with their children. The broad set of results from multiple papers that analyze the short- and long-run consequences of the Jamaica intervention agree that stimulation and stimulation plus nutritional supplementation are most important for realizing long-term gains in cognitive functioning and other adult outcomes (Gertler et al. 2014; Grantham-McGregor et al. 1994, 1997; Walker et al. 2011). Perhaps the most important insight from these studies is that nutritional supplementation alone is not effective in helping children build skills. In fact, a 20-year follow-up of the original program participants by Gertler et al. (2014) found that on average, participants who received the stimulation intervention had 42 percent higher earnings later in life.[12]

The results from the Jamaica intervention align with several other papers, including a review by Baker-Henningham and Boo (2010) of over 25 studies in low-income and middle-income countries that focus on early childhood

12. It must be stressed here that (a) wider replication of stimulation programs is needed in order to fully claim validity in the Indian context and (b) studies have found long-run and intergenerational consequences of macronutrition, underscoring that intervention has potentially high returns. For example, Hoddinott et al. (2013) found evidence of a long-run economic effect for men exposed to nutritional supplementation alone before age 3. Behrman et al. (2009) show that the children of women exposed to this same program are significantly less underweight than the children of women from the control group.

stimulation through parenting interventions. The authors concluded, "Early stimulation interventions are effective in improving child and maternal outcomes and these benefits are likely to be sustained over the long term." This sentiment is again echoed in an excellent review by Schodt et al. (2015) of interventions largely focusing on home visitation programs in Latin America.

While high-quality early childhood interventions have shown promising results in developing countries, some of the best evidence on this front actually comes from the developed world. While these are excellent studies, the different time period and context of these interventions are important to consider while thinking about translating these into the Indian context. The most well-studied intervention shown to have an impact on labor market (and other) outcomes is the Perry Preschool Project (Heckman et al. 2010). The Perry Preschool Project was an early childhood education initiative targeting disadvantaged African–American youth in Ypsilanti, Michigan, in the 1960s. The program—which started with 3-year-old children and lasted for two years—consisted of a two-and-a-half-hour preschool session on weekdays that focused on supporting a child's cognitive and socio-emotional skills. This was supplemented by weekly home visits by teachers. While many studies estimate the rate of return of this program, Heckman et al. (2010) compute the impact using various econometric techniques that account for some of the compromises that occurred in the randomization protocol. Taking these into account, the rate of return is estimated to be between 7 percent and 10 percent. This rate of return includes not just the labor market return, but also the gains from access to this program on better health and reduced involvement in crime much later in life. Other studies of early childhood interventions in developed nations also find large benefits (see the Nurse Family Partnership Program [Olds 2006]; Chicago Child–Parent Study [Reynolds et al. 2001, 2002]; Head Start [Currie and Thomas 1995; Garces, Thomas, and Currie 2002]; and the Abecedarian Program [Barnett and Masse 2007]). While these interventions differ in the target population, the specifics of the interventions, and, importantly, in the age of enrollment and length of intervention, the broad lesson from these studies is that stimulation-based interventions in early childhood have very high returns.

4.3. Delivery of Interventions

While many of the previous interventions have proven powerful in improving child health and development, it is important to keep in mind the challenges of implementing initiatives in the field. This is a salient issue in developing countries in particular, where multiple market failures may pose barriers to the take-up of what could be a very effective intervention.

A telling example of the failure to adopt effective technology due to sub-optimal distribution policy comes from Adhvaryu (2014). Adhvaryu studies the take-up of artemisinin-based combination malaria therapy (ATC; effective in helping children and adults recover faster from malaria) in Tanzania and finds that while adoption is initially high, there is a steep drop-off two years after introduction. One of the major reasons for the decline appears to be misinformation about the effectiveness of ATC, perpetuated by misdiagnosis at the primary health care center. Hence, while effective in combating malaria, ATC was perceived by villagers to be less useful, perhaps since it was prescribed even when children and adults did not have malaria. Another example in the case of malaria is the low take-up of mosquito nets. While bed nets have obvious benefits, adoption has remained problematic. Cohen, Dupas, and Schaner (2015) find that short-run subsidies for bed nets promote long-term adoption, since subsidies allow individuals to learn about the product. A similar study in India by Tarozzi et al. (2014) involves giving microloans to promote the adoption of insecticide-treated bed nets. The research reports increased take-up, though the effects on health are mixed, likely due to low overall usage of the nets.

Further, consider the case of double-fortified salt. While the intervention seems rather simple—to fortify salt with iodine and iron (which directly tackles anemia, a major problem for children and women in India)—fortification alone guarantees neither take-up nor improved health outcomes. Banerjee, Barnhardt, and Duflo (2015) find that promoting the use of double-fortified salt through the use of information and incentives to sellers dramatically increases consumption in Bihar. Yet in a separate paper (Banerjee, Barnhardt, and Duflo 2016), they show that increased consumption of fortified salt does not lead to better health outcomes. Therefore, even improved take-up, resulting from efforts such as providing fortified salt for free, or through seller incentives, may not solve complex problems such as anemia. In contrast, Thomas et al. (2006) notes large positive impacts of direct iron supplementation (iron tablets distributed by a local health worker) and excellent compliance with the supplementation protocol. One of the reasons Banerjee, Barnhardt, and Duflo's (2016) results may differ is due to the lower dosage of iron that is delivered through double fortification. Similar cautionary tales about "effective" health technology confronting take-up problems in the field appear in studies about cooking stoves aimed at reducing indoor air pollution (Hanna, Duflo, and Greenstone 2016; Miller and Mobarak 2014). In short, what works in the laboratory does not necessarily work in the field since the adoption of new technologies is often a matter of learning, preferences, incentives, and costs. Understanding proper delivery of effective technologies is crucial to making progress on these issues.

4.4. Potential in the Indian Context

The examples we have focused on not only show policy makers what works but also why one should care about what works. From a policy perspective, it is useful to think about supply and demand issues for the delivery of effective early childhood investments. One broad approach to increasing the demand for health services is the use of conditional cash transfers. There is ample evidence from various developing countries that conditional cash transfers improve the take-up of preventive health services (Lagarde, Haines, and Palmer 2007) and result in better child health (Gertler 2004). An excellent example of the role of cash transfers comes from Macours, Schady, and Vakis (2008), which studies a large cash transfer program in Nicaragua and finds dramatic improvements in child development among the treated households. The findings suggest that the improvements in cognitive development are not due to the cash aspect of the program alone; the treated children are also more likely to receive stimulation at home. Such behavioral changes can have long-term impacts, even after the cash program ends. Banerjee, Duflo, Glennerster, and Kothari (2010) examine the role of conditional transfers in the take-up of immunization in India. They show that while improving the reliability of immunization camps improves attendance, coupling this reliability with small non-financial incentives nearly doubles the take-up. This is an important finding since it showcases how both demand- and supply-side constraints are extremely important in improving take-up of health services.

India has experimented with many cash transfers. In multiple studies of the Janani Suraksha Yojana (JSY), a large conditional cash transfer program aimed at increasing deliveries in institutions rather than at home, researchers have found increased take-up of institutional deliveries but conflicting evidence on improvements in health measures such as infant mortality and maternal mortality (Das, Rao, and Hagopian 2011; Lim et al. 2010; Powell-Jackson, Mazumdar, and Mills 2015; Randive, Diwan, and De Costa 2013). In fact, the JSY provides a perfect case study for why careful policy evaluation is essential before implementing an intervention at scale. The JSY is one of the largest conditional cash transfer programs in the world given its scope, but its rollout and lack of precise data on outcomes before and after threatens the reliability of results. Studies have to rely on quasi-experimental methods, and while this can be an effective tool, the results can be sensitive to identification assumptions and it is harder to get at mechanisms and deeper issues about implementation under quasi-experimental methods. While cash transfers are popular for other health-related goals in India (especially to promote gender equality through programs such as Apni Beti Apna Dhan, Dhanlakshmi, and Devi Rupak), as the literature suggests, their evaluations often result in mixed findings regarding effectiveness (Anukriti 2014; Sinha and Yoong 2009). Careful implementation and sound evaluation is crucial before implementing these schemes at scale.

On the supply side, Darmstadt et al. (2005) emphasize the delivery of antenatal and postnatal care through family–community interventions. These are interventions wherein components of antenatal and postnatal care, such as home visitation, are provided by trained community health workers. The interventions can be thought of as providing a suite of treatments rather than any one specific treatment. In a follow-up *Cochrane* review, Lassi and Bhutta (2015) analyze 26 randomized and quasi-randomized studies on the effectiveness of such family–community interventions, including studies done in India, cite tremendous promise and recommend scaling up these types of interventions.

An important part of India's community-based approach to health is the ASHA model. ASHAs were formally included under the National Health Mission in 2005 and the current number of ASHAs is around 860,000 (Ministry of Health and Family Welfare [MoHFW] India 2013). Despite the emphasis on ASHAs, there has been little rigorous research done on how best to improve this network. Recent work in economics has emphasized the recruitment of and incentives for government workers (Ashraf, Bandiera, and Lee 2015; Dal Bó, Finan, and Rossi 2013; Das et al. 2015; Muralidharan and Sundararaman 2011) in addition to incentives for communities as a whole (the PNPM Generasi program in Indonesia). For example, Dal Bó, Finan, and Rossi (2013) discovered that offering a higher wage attracts not only more qualified people to the government sector but also the most motivated to engage in public service. An in-depth evaluation of the PNPM Generasi program in Indonesia found that using incentivized block grants was crucial in improving health indicators among young children and pregnant mothers. One of the key features of the Generasi program was the training of community health workers, which could have played an important role in improving health outcomes. In addition, the communities got to choose how they would improve on a pre-selected set of target health indicators. Given the heterogeneity in health outcomes in India highlighted in Section 2, allowing communities to choose how to focus grants might be an important step forward.

Our stance is that research on the recruitment and incentive structures for ASHAs, as well as understanding whether mothers demand and trust information given by ASHAs would be incredibly useful in making policy decisions regarding how best to improve the functioning and service delivery of ASHAs. Improving neonatal and infant mortality requires a multipronged approach, but understanding the demand for and raising the quality and quantity of service delivery seems to be of great importance.

The ICDS is India's flagship program that has the potential to deliver high-quality child health and development services. The front-runner of these services is the *anganwadi* center (AWC). While an entire suite of early childhood services is provided at AWCs, the focus of this institution has largely been on supplemental nutrition, immunization, and other basic health and early preschool education needs. There is also clear potential to use AWCs as delivery centers for high-quality early childhood stimulation programs. However, a report by the Planning Commission on the effectiveness of ICDS on key health outcomes says, "Conclusive evidence of positive impact of ICDS is not available" (Planning Commission 2011). Furthermore, while early childhood care and education (ECCE) received national attention due to the Constitution Act of 2002, how the programs that were established are delivered or monitored is highly variable. While many agencies at the national and state level provide ECCE services, a report by the Ministry of Women and Child Development states, "There is no reliable data available about the actual number of children attending ECCE provisions and their breakup as per delivery of services/type of services." For a program like ICDS that has been in place since 1975 and whose budget in the 2014–15 year was nearly US$2.2 billion, the lack of rigorous evaluations is a serious concern.

Similarly, while having immense potential, another important policy—the RGNCS for the children of working mothers—may not have proper evaluation processes in place. The RGNCS aims to provide precisely the types of services that we know work from other settings, such as early stimulation for children under age 3, supplementary feeding, and growth monitoring. According to the website of the Ministry of Women and Child Development, there are currently more than 21,000 such centers across India, and the program had a total budget allocation of just US$15 million in 2014–15. Considering that the number of births per year in India is around 27 million, even if only a tenth of infants and children needed services, the budget would only include about six cents per child per day. Since services such as stimulation typically last more than a year, the financial allocations for these kinds of services are woefully low. In an excellent review of various child protection and child health programs in India, Das and Kundu (2014) report that only 0.02 percent of the total Union Budget is allocated to services that can be classified as "care and protection" for children—this includes schemes such as the RGNCS, Dhanlakshmi, and Integrated Child Protection Scheme (ICPS).

Perhaps it is not surprising then that a report by the Planning Commission in 2013 finds that these centers have low-quality infrastructure and training of crèche helpers as well as an inadequate flow of funds. The report, however, contains no information about whether the crèche program actually leads to greater child skills, nutrition, and the like. While documenting process is crucial and something that routinely seems to be done for such programs, recording impact is just as important. Multiple examples from the education sector have shown that typical inputs such as infrastructure and teacher pay are not always causally related with improved performance of students (Glewwe and Kremer 2006).

While studies such as the Jamaica intervention detailed previously reveal the incredible promise of investing early in children, these programs have largely not been scaled up in developing countries. Universal pre-K programs contain some of the same services. Several have been successful (Gormley et al. 2005) whereas others have shown mixed results in developed and developing countries (Baker and Milligan 2008; Berlinski, Galiani, and Manacorda 2008; Bernal and Fernandez 2013; Blanden et al. 2016; Rosero and Oosterbeek 2011). Ongoing research is imperative for future policy making in this area. A version of the Jamaica program has been replicated by researchers in Colombia with scale in mind (Attanasio et al. 2015). This was achieved by training local female leaders who were already part of one of the largest welfare programs in the country. In the short term, the study finds impressive gains in cognition and receptive language among children. This program is now being tested in Odisha, relying on trained local women for delivery. While scaled-up interventions sound promising, a recent article by Attanasio, Cattan, and Krutikova (2016) identifies the key challenges in this process: (a) adapting programs to local contexts, (b) ensuring quality of provision, and (c) continued investment at later ages in childhood. The results from the Odisha study will be a good starting point for thinking about bringing high-quality early childhood stimulation programs up to scale in India. In a similar vein, Jed Friedman and co-authors from the World Bank and IFPRI are working on an evaluation of adding one additional *anganwadi* worker to AWCs. Experimental analysis of such programs is essential moving forward.

Budgets for child development in India absolutely need to be increased, but rigorous evaluations of what works in programs such as ICDS and

RGNCS must also be part of the equation. Analysts should also carefully consider the consequences of scaled-up programs and the possibility of overlap with other early childhood development (ECD) or household interventions (such as the Mahatma Gandhi National Rural Employment Guarantee Act [MGNREGA]). For example, does the work of RGNCS crowd out what ASHAs do or affect whether a child goes to an AWC? Are households that get benefits under MGNREGA more or less likely to take advantage of these schemes? It is these kinds of thoughtful questions that could lead to better programs that can have a real impact on Indian children.

5. Conclusion

There is growing consensus among researchers in developmental psychology, economics, epidemiology, nutrition, sociology, and a host of other disciplines that investing in children early in childhood has large, persistent returns to health and economic well-being. India has made significant progress in terms of reducing infant and child mortality and malnutrition in the past three decades. While there is much more to be done in terms of improving these basic measures of child health, we urge policy makers to take seriously the idea that focusing on overall child development, measured by socio-emotional and gross motor skills, is crucial. As we emphasize in this IPF paper, pairing nutritional supplementation with stimulation and cognitive interventions have been shown to be much more effective in raising development measures than nutritional interventions alone.

From a policy perspective, it is extremely important to consider how these interventions are delivered. We note many examples of theoretically sound and field-tested interventions failing when implemented at scale. The delivery of child development interventions is no less complicated than the delivery of basic educational services; yet research is severely lacking on how governments in developing countries can best provide these crucial services. While India has the basic ingredients needed to competently deliver child development services, policy makers ought to consider field-testing and rigorously evaluating the various schemes they implement. For example, the ASHA program, the RGNCS, and other conditional cash transfers aimed at improving child development should be implemented with a view to first evaluate and then scale-up. The *anganwadi* program is another example of an excellent vehicle that can deliver high-quality child development services; yet there is very little by way of empirically sound evaluations available to understand whether these centers are working efficiently.

There are two main takeaways from this article that we urge policy makers to consider. First, focus on further improving basic child health through interventions aimed at reducing malnutrition and infant mortality, but begin to focus as well on stimulation and home visitation programs. Second, while there is immense potential to deliver these interventions through ASHAs, AWCs, and crèche schemes, there is a great need to do rigorous empirical evaluations that inform how best to improve their functioning.

References

Adhvaryu, A., T. Molina, A. Nyshadham, and J. Tamayo. 2015. *Helping Children Catch Up: Early Life Shocks and the Progresa Experiment*. Mimeo.

Adhvaryu, A., 2014. "Learning, Misallocation, and Technology Adoption: Evidence from New Malaria Therapy in Tanzania," *Review of Economic Studies*, 81(4): 1331–1365.

Adhvaryu, A. and A. Nyshadham. 2014. "Endowments at Birth and Parents' Investments in Children," *Economic Journal*, 126(593): 781–820.

Adhvaryu, A., S. Bednar, T. Molina, Q. Nguyen, and A. Nyshadham. 2014. "Salt Iodization and the Enfranchisement of the American Worker," *Discussion Paper*, http://www.sole-jole.org/14193.pdf (accessed May 1, 2017).

Adhvaryu, A., J. Fenske, and A. Nyshadham. 2014. "Early Life Circumstance and Adult Mental Health," *Working Papers 698,* University of Oxford, Department of Economics.

Aizer, A., S. Eli, J.P. Ferrie, and A. Lleras-Muney. 2014. "The Long-term Impact of Cash Transfers to Poor Families," *NBER Working Paper 20103*, Cambridge, MA: National Bureau of Economic Research.

Aizer, A. and F. Cunha, 2012. "The Production of Human Capital: Endowments, Investments and Fertility," *NBER Working Paper 18429*, Cambridge, MA: National Bureau of Economic Research.

Almond, D., J. J. Doyle Jr., A. Kowalski, and H. Williams. 2010. "Estimating Marginal Returns to Medical Care: Evidence from At-Risk Newborns," *The Quarterly Journal of Economics*, 125(2): 591–634.

Almond, D. and J. Currie. 2011. "Killing Me Softly: The Fetal Origins Hypothesis," *The Journal of Economic Perspectives*, 25(3): 153–172.

Almond, D. and B. Mazumder. 2013. "Fetal Origins and Parental Responses," *Annu. Rev. Econ.*, 5(1): 37–56.

Alsan, M. and C. Goldin. 2015. "Watersheds in Infant Mortality: The Role of Effective Water and Sewerage Infrastructure, 1880 to 1915," *NBER Working Paper 21263*, Cambridge, MA: National Bureau of Economic Research.

Anukriti, S. 2014. "The Fertility-Sex Ratio Trade-off: Unintended Consequences of Financial Incentives," *IZA Discussion Paper No. 8044*, SSRN: https://ssrn.com/abstract=2412865 (accessed May 15, 2017).

Ashraf, N., O. Bandiera, and S. S. Lee. 2015. "Do-gooders and Go-Getters: Career Incentives, Selection, and Performance in Public Service Delivery," *STICERD-Economic Organisation and Public Policy Discussion Papers 54,* http://sticerd.lse.ac.uk/dps/eopp/eopp54.pdf (accessed May 1, 2017).

Aslam, A., A. Grojec, C. Little, T. Maloney, and J. Tamagni. 2014. *The State of the World's Children 2014 in Numbers: Every Child Counts. Revealing Disparities, Advancing Children's Rights.* New York: UNICEF Publications.

Attanasio, O., S. Cattan, E. Fitzsimons, C. Meghir, and M. Rubio-Codina. 2015. "Estimating the Production Function for Human Capital: Results from a Randomized Control Trial in Colombia," *NBER Working Paper 20965,* Cambridge, MA: National Bureau of Economic Research.

Attanasio, Orazio, Sarah Cattan, and Sonya Krutikova. 2016. "Early Childhood Development Policies: The Evidence and the Research Agenda," *Working Paper Series*, London: Institute for Fiscal Studies, https://www.ifs.org.uk/publications/8306 (accessed June 1, 2017).

Baker, M. and K. Milligan. 2008. "Maternal Employment, Breastfeeding, and Health: Evidence from Maternity Leave Mandates," *Journal of Health Economics*, 27(4): 871–887.

Baker-Henningham, H. and F. López Bóo. 2010. "Early Childhood Stimulation Interventions in Developing Countries: A Comprehensive Literature Review," *IZA Discussion Paper 5282*, http://ftp.iza.org/dp5282.pdf (accessed May 1, 2017).

Banerjee, A.V., E. Duflo, R. Glennerster, and D. Kothari. 2010. "Improving Immunisation Coverage in Rural India: Clustered Randomised Controlled Evaluation of Immunisation Campaigns with and without Incentives," *BMJ*, 340: c2220, https://doi.org/10.1136/bmj.c2220 (accessed May 1, 2017).

Banerjee, A., S. Barnhardt, and E. Duflo. 2015. "Movies, Margins and Marketing: Encouraging the Adoption of Iron-Fortified Salt," *NBER Working Paper 21616*, Cambridge, MA: National Bureau of Economic Research.

———. 2016. "Can Iron-Fortified Salt Control Anemia? Evidence from Two Experiments in Rural Bihar," http://cepr.org/active/publications/discussion_papers/dp.php?dpno=11193 (accessed May 1, 2017).

Barnett, W. S. and L. N. Masse. 2007. "Comparative Benefit–cost Analysis of the Abecedarian Program and Its Policy Implications," *Economics of Education Review*, 26(1): 113–125.

Becker, G. S. and H. G. Lewis. 1973. "On the Interaction between the Quantity and Quality of Children," *Journal of Political Economy*, 81(2): S279–S288.

Behrman, J. R., M. C. Calderon, S. H. Preston, J. Hoddinott, R. Martorell, and A.D. Stein. 2009. "Nutritional Supplementation in Girls Influences the Growth of Their Children: Prospective Study in Guatemala," *The American Journal of Clinical Nutrition*, 90(5): 1372–1379.

Behrman, J. R., R. A. Pollak, and P. Taubman. 1982. "Parental Preferences and Provision for Progeny," *The Journal of Political Economy*, 90(11): 52–73.

Behrman, J.R. 1997. "Intra-household Distribution and the Family," *Handbook of Population and Family Economics*, 1: 125–187.

Bera, A., J. Ghosh, A. K. Singh, A. Hazra, T. Som, and D. Munian. 2014. "Effect of Kangaroo Mother Care on Vital Physiological Parameters of the Low Birth Weight Newborn," *Indian Journal of Community Medicine,* 39(4): 245.

Berlinski, S., S. Galiani, and M. Manacorda. 2008. "Giving Children a Better Start: Preschool Attendance and School-age Profiles," *Journal of Public Economics,* 92(5): 1416–1440.

Bernal, R. and C. Fernández. 2013. "Subsidized Childcare and Child Development in Colombia: Effects of Hogares Comunitarios de Bienestar as a Function of Timing and Length of Exposure," *Social Science & Medicine,* 97:241–249.

Bharadwaj, P., K. V. Løken, and C. Neilson. 2013. "Early Life Health Interventions and Academic Achievement," *The American Economic Review*, 103(5): 1862–1891.

Bharadwaj, P., J. Eberhard, and C. Neilson. 2010. "Do Initial Endowments Matter Only Initially? The Persistent Effect of Birth Weight on School Achievement," Department of Economics, San Diego: University of California.

Bhutta, Z. A., T. Ahmed, R. E. Black, S. Cousens, K. Dewey, E. Giugliani, B. A. Haider, B. Kirkwood, S. S. Morris, H. P. S. Sachdev, and M. Shekar. 2008. "What WORKS? Interventions for Maternal and Child Undernutrition and Survival," *The Lancet*, 371(9610): 417–440.

Bitler, M. P. and J. Currie. 2005. "Does WIC Work? The Effects of WIC on Pregnancy and Birth Outcomes," *Journal of Policy Analysis and Management*, 24(1): 73–91.

Black, Robert E., L. H. Allen, Z. A. Bhutta, L. E. Caulfield, M. de Onis, M. Ezzati, C. Mathers, and J. Rivera. 2008. "Maternal and Child Undernutrition: Global and Regional Exposures and Health Consequences," *The Lancet*, 371(9608): 243–260.

Black, M. M., S. P. Walker, L. C. Fernald, C. T. Andersen, A. M. DiGirolamo, C. Lu, D. C. McCoy, G. Fink, Y. R. Shawar, J. Shiffman, and A. E. Devercelli. 2016. "Early Childhood Development Coming of Age: Science through the Life Course," *The Lancet*, 389(10064): 77–90.

Blanden, J., E. Del Bono, S. McNally, and B. Rabe. 2016. "Universal Pre-school Education: The Case of Public Funding with Private Provision," *The Economic Journal*, 126(592): 682–723.

Blencowe, H., J. Lawn, J. Vandelaer, M. Roper, and S. Cousens. 2010. "Tetanus Toxoid Immunization to Reduce Mortality from Neonatal Tetanus," *International Journal of Epidemiology*, 39(suppl 1): i102–i109.

Britto, P. R., P. L. Engle, and C. M. Super. 2013. *Handbook of Early Childhood Development Research and Its Impact on Global Policy*. New York: Oxford University Press.

Britto, P. R., S. J. Lye, K. Proulx, A. K. Yousafzai, S. G. Matthews, T. Vaivada, R. Perez-Escamilla, N. Rao, P. Ip, L. C. Fernald, and H. MacMillan. 2016. "Nurturing Care: Promoting Early Childhood Development," *The Lancet*, 389(10064): 91–102.

Chen, A., E. Oster, and H. Williams. 2016. "Why Is Infant Mortality Higher in the United States Than in Europe?, *American Economic Journal: Economic Policy*, 8(2): 89–124.

Cohen, J., P. Dupas, and S. Schaner. 2015. "Price Subsidies, Diagnostic Tests, and Targeting of Malaria Treatment: Evidence from a Randomized Controlled Trial," *The American Economic Review*, 105(2): 609–645.

Conti, G., J. Heckman, and S. Urzua. 2010. "The Education-health Gradient," *American Economic Review*, 100(2): 234–238.

Crookston, B. T., W. Schott, S. Cueto, K. A. Dearden, P. Engle, A. Georgiadis, E. A. Lundeen, M. E. Penny, A. D. Stein, and J. R. Behrman. 2013. "Post-infancy Growth, Schooling, and Cognitive Achievement: Young Lives," *The American Journal of Clinical Nutrition*, 98(6): 1555–1563.

Cunha, F. and J. Heckman. 2007. "The Economics of Human Development: The Technology of Skill Formation," *The American Economic Review*, 97(2): 31–47.

Cunha, F., J. J. Heckman, and S. M. Schennach. 2010. "Estimating the Technology of Cognitive and Non-cognitive Skill Formation," *Econometrica*, 78(3): 883–931.

Currie, J. and D. Thomas. 1995. "Does Head Start Make a Difference?" *The American Economic Review*, 85(3): 341–364.

Currie, J. and T. Vogl. 2013. "Early-Life Health and Adult Circumstance in Developing Countries," *Annu. Rev. Econ*, 5(1): 1–36.

Dal Bó, E.,F. Finan, and M. A. Rossi. 2013. "Strengthening State Capabilities: The Role of Financial Incentives in the Call to Public Service," *Quarterly Journal of Economics*, 128(3): 1169–1218.

Darmstadt, G. L., Z. A. Bhutta, S. Cousens, T. Adam, N. Walker, L. de Bernis, and Lancet Neonatal Survival Steering Team. 2005. "Evidence-based, Cost-effective Interventions: How Many Newborn Babies Can We Save?" *The Lancet*, 365(9463): 977–988.

Das, Ashis, J. Friedman, E. Kandpal, G. N. V. Ramana, R. K. Das Gupta, M. M. Pradhan, and R. Govindaraj. 2015. "Strengthening Malaria Service Delivery through Supportive Supervision and Community Mobilization in an Endemic Indian Setting: An Evaluation of Nested Delivery Models," *Malaria Journal*, 13(6901):482.

Das, S. and P. Kundu. 2014. "Public Investment in Young Children in India," *Working Paper*, http://www.cbgaindia.org/working-paper/public-investment-in-young-children-in-india/ (accessed May 16, 2017).

Das, A., D. Rao, and A. Hagopian. 2011. "India's Janani Suraksha Yojana: Further Review Needed," *The Lancet*, 377(9762): 295–296.

Dasgupta, Rajib, Purnamita Dasgupta, and Ankush Agrawal. 2014. "Decline in Immunization Coverage across Well-performing Districts in India: An Urban Conundrum?" *The Indian Journal of Pediatrics*, 81(9): 847–849.

Datar, A., M. R. Kilburn, and D. S. Loughran. 2010. "Endowments and Parental Investments in Infancy and Early Childhood," *Demography*, 47(1): 145–162.

Duflo, E., M. Greenstone, R. Guiteras, and T. Clasen. 2015. "Toilets Can Work: Short- and Medium-run Health Impacts of Addressing Complementarities and Externalities in Water and Sanitation," *NBER Working Paper 21521*, Cambridge, MA: National Bureau of Economic Research.

Eckhardt, C. L. 2006. "Micronutrient Malnutrition, Obesity, and Chronic Disease in Countries Undergoing the Nutrition Transition: Potential Links and Program/Policy Implications," *FCND Discussion Paper 213*, Washington, D.C.: IFPRI.

Engle, P. L., M. M. Black, J. R. Behrman, M. C. de Mello, P. J. Gertler, L. Kapiriri, R. Martorell, and M. E. Young. 2007. "Child Development in Developing Countries 3: Strategies to Avoid the Loss of Developmental Potential in More Than 200 Million Children in the Developing World," *Lancet*, 369(9557): 229–242.

Fathima, F. N., M. Raju, K. S. Varadharajan, A. Krishnamurthy, S. R. Ananthkumar, and P. K. Mony. 2015. "Assessment of 'Accredited Social Health Activists'—A National Community Health Volunteer Scheme in Karnataka State, India," *Journal of Health, Population, and Nutrition*, 33(1): 137.

Fewtrell, L., R. B. Kaufmann, D. Kay, W. Enanoria, L. Haller, and J. M. Colford. 2005. "Water, Sanitation, and Hygiene Interventions to Reduce Diarrhoea in Less Developed Countries: A Systematic Review and Meta-analysis," *The Lancet Infectious Diseases*, 5(1): 42–52.

Garces, E., D. Thomas, and J. Currie. 2002. "Longer-term Effects of Head Start," *The American Economic Review*, 92(4): 999–1012.

Georgiadis, A., L. Benny, B. T. Crookston, P. Hermida, S. Mani, T. Woldehanna, A. D. Stein, and J. R. Behrman. 2016. "Growth Trajectories from Conception through Middle Childhood and Cognitive Achievement at Age 8 Years: Evidence from Four Low- and Middle-income Countries," *SSM-Population Health*, 2: 43–54.

Gertler, P., 2004. "Do Conditional Cash Transfers Improve Child Health? Evidence from PROGRESA's Control Randomized Experiment," *The American Economic Review*, 94(2): 336–341.

Gertler, P., J. Heckman, R. Pinto, A. Zanolini, C. Vermeerch, S. M. Chang, and S. Grantham-McGregor. 2014. "Labor Market Returns to an Early Childhood Stimulation Intervention in Jamaica," *Science*, 344(6187): 998–1001.

Glewwe, P. and M. Kremer. 2006. "Schools, Teachers, and Education Outcomes in Developing Countries," *Handbook of the Economics of Education*, 2: 945–1017.

Gormley Jr, W. T., T. Gayer, D. Phillips, and B. Dawson. 2005. "The Effects of Universal Pre-K on Cognitive Development," *Developmental Psychology*, 41(6): 872.

Grantham-McGregor, S. M., C. A. Powell, S. P. Walker, and J. H. Himes. 1991. "Nutritional Supplementation, Psychosocial Stimulation, and Mental Development of Stunted Children: The Jamaican Study," *The Lancet*, 338(8758): 1–5.

Grantham-McGregor, S., C. Powell, S. Walker, S. Chang, and P. Fletcher. 1994. "The Long-term Follow-up of Severely Malnourished Children Who Participated in an Intervention Program," *Child Development*, 65(2): 428–439.

Grantham-McGregor, S. M., S. P. Walker, S. M. Chang, and C. A. Powell. 1997. "Effects of Early Childhood Supplementation with and without Stimulation on Later Development in Stunted Jamaican Children," *The American Journal of Clinical Nutrition*, 66(2): 247–253.

Grantham-McGregor, S., Y. B. Cheung, S. Cueto, P. Glewwe, L. Richter, B. Strupp, and International Child Development Steering Group. 2007. "Developmental

Potential in the First 5 Years for Children in Developing Countries," *The Lancet*, 369(9555); 60–70.

Grossman, M. 1972. "On the Concept of Health Capital and the Demand for Health," *Journal of Political Economy*, 80(2): 223–255.

Gunnsteinsson, S., A. Adhvaryu, P. Christian, A. Labrique, J. Sugimoto, A. A. Shamim, and K. P. West Jr. 2014. "Resilience to Early Life Shocks," *Working Paper*, http://sites.bu.edu/neudc/files/2014/10/paper_47.pdf (accessed May 14, 2017)

Hanna, R., E. Duflo, and M. Greenstone. 2016. "Up in Smoke: The Influence of Household Behavior on the Long-run Impact of Improved Cooking Stoves," *American Economic Journal: Economic Policy*, 8(1): 80–114.

Heckman, J. J. 2006. "Skill Formation and the Economics of Investing in Disadvantaged Children," *Science*, 312(5782): 1900–1902.

———. 2007. "The Economics, Technology, and Neuroscience of Human Capability Formation," *Proceedings of the National Academy of Sciences*, 104(33): 13250–13255.

Heckman, J. J., S. H. Moon, R. Pinto, P. A. Savelyev, and A. Yavitz. 2010. "The Rate of Return to the High Scope Perry Preschool Program," *Journal of Public Economics*, 94(1): 114–128.

Heckman, J., R. Pinto, and P. Savelyev. 2013. "Understanding the Mechanisms through Which an Influential Early Childhood Program Boosted Adult Outcomes," *The American Economic Review*, 103(6): 2052–2086.

Heckman, J. J. and S. Mosso. 2014. "The Economics of Human Development and Social Mobility," *Annu. Rev. Econ*, 6: 689–733.

Hoddinott, J., J. A. Maluccio, J. R. Behrman, R. Flores, and R. Martorell. 2008. "Effect of a Nutrition Intervention during Early Childhood on Economic Productivity in Guatemalan Adults," *The Lancet*, 371(9610): 411–416.

Hoynes, H., D. W. Schanzenbach, and D. Almond. 2016. "Long-run Impacts of Childhood Access to the Safety Net," *The American Economic Review*, 106(4): 903–934.

Lagarde, M., A. Haines, and N. Palmer. 2007. "Conditional Cash Transfers for Improving Uptake of Health Interventions in Low- and Middle-income Countries: A Systematic Review," *Jama*, 298(16): 1900–1910.

Lakshminarayanan, S. and R. Jayalakshmy. 2015. "Diarrheal Diseases among Children in India: Current Scenario and Future Perspectives," *Journal of Natural Science, Biology, and Medicine*, 6(1): 24.

Lassi, Z. S. and Z. A. Bhutta. 2015. "Community-based Intervention Packages for Preventing Maternal and Newborn Illness and Death So That Newborn Outcomes Are Improved," Cochrane Database of Systematic Reviews, Issue 3, Art. No. CD007754, *The Cochrane Library*.

Lewit, E. M. and N. Kerrebrock. 1997. "Population-based Growth Stunting," *The Future of Children*, 7: 149–156.

Lim, S. S., L. Dandona, J. A. Hoisington, S. L. James, M. C. Hogan, and E. Gakidou. 2010. "India's Janani Suraksha Yojana, a Conditional Cash Transfer Programme to Increase Births in Health Facilities: An Impact Evaluation," *The Lancet*, 375(9730): 2009–2023.

Macours, K., N. Schady, and R. Vakis. 2008. "Can Conditional Cash Transfer Programs Compensate for Delays in Early Childhood Development?" *Draft Paper,* Washington, D.C.: World Bank.

Martorell, R., L. K. Khan, and D. G. Schroeder. 1994. "Reversibility of Stunting: Epidemiological Findings in Children from Developing Countries," *European Journal of Clinical Nutrition*, 48: S45–S57.

Miller, G. and A. M. Mobarak. 2014. "Learning about New Technologies through Social Networks: Experimental Evidence on Non-traditional Stoves in Bangladesh," *Marketing Science*, 34(4): 480–499.

Million Death Study Collaborators. 2010. "Causes of Neonatal and Child Mortality in India: A Nationally Representative Mortality Survey," *The Lancet*, 376(9755): 1853–1860.

Ministry of Health and Family Welfare [MoHFW]. 2013. "2011–2013: Update(s) on the ASHA Programme," New Delhi: Government of India.

Muralidharan, K. and V. Sundararaman. 2011. "Teacher Performance Pay: Experimental Evidence from India," *The Journal of Political Economy*, 119(1): 39–77.

Olds, D. L. 2006. "The Nurse–Family Partnership: An Evidence-based Preventive Intervention," *Infant Mental Health Journal*, 27(1): 5–25.

Planning Commission. 2011. "Evaluation Report on Integrated Child Development Services," New Delhi: Government of India.

Powell-Jackson, T., S. Mazumdar, and A. Mills. 2015. "Financial Incentives in Health: New Evidence from India's Janani Suraksha Yojana," *Journal of Health Economics*, 43: 154–169.

Puentes, E., F. Wang, J. R. Behrman, F. Cunha, J. Hoddinott, J. A. Maluccio, L. S. Adair, J. B. Borja, R. Martorell, and A. D. Stein. 2016. "Early Life Height and Weight Production Functions with Endogenous Energy and Protein Inputs," *Economics & Human Biology*, 22 (2016): 65–81.

Rammohan, Anu, and Niyi Awofeso. 2015. "District-level Variations in Childhood Immunizations in India: The Role of Socio-economic Factors and Health Infrastructure," *Social Science & Medicine*, 145(2015): 163–172.

Randive, B., V. Diwan, and A. De Costa. 2013. "India's Conditional Cash Transfer Programme (the JSY) to Promote Institutional Birth: Is There an Association between Institutional Birth Proportion and Maternal Mortality?" *PloS One*, 8(6): e67452.

Reynolds, A. J., J. A. Temple, D. L. Robertson, and E. A. Mann. 2001. "Long-term Effects of an Early Childhood Intervention on Educational Achievement and Juvenile Arrest: A 15-year Follow-up of Low-income Children in Public Schools," *Jama*, 285(18): 2339–2346.

Reynolds, A. J., J. A. Temple, D. L. Robertson, and E. A. Mann. 2002. "Age 21 Cost-Benefit Analysis of the Title I Chicago Child-Parent Centers," *Educational Evaluation and Policy Analysis*, 24(4): 267–303.

Richter, L. M., B. Daelmans, J. Lombardi, J. Heymann, F. L. Boo, J.R. Behrman, C. Lu, J. E. Lucas, R. Perez-Escamilla, T. Dua, and Z. A. Bhutta. 2016. "Investing in the Foundation of Sustainable Development: Pathways to Scale up for Early Childhood Development," *The Lancet*, 389(10064): 103–118.

Rosenzweig, M. R. and T. P. Schultz. 1983. "Estimating a Household Production Function: Heterogeneity, the Demand for Health Inputs, and Their Effects on Birth Weight," *The Journal of Political Economy*, 91(5): 723–746.

Rosero, J. and H. Oosterbeek. 2011. "Trade-offs between Different Early Childhood Interventions: Evidence from Ecuador," *Tinbergen Institute Discussion Paper No. TI 2011-102/3*, https://papers.tinbergen.nl/11102.pdf (accessed May 15, 2017).

Rossin-Slater, M. and M. Wüst. 2015. "*Are Different Early Investments Complements or Substitutes? Long-run and Intergenerational Evidence from Denmark*," Mimeo, University of California, Santa Barbara.

Saikia, N., A. Singh, D. Jasilionis, and F. Ram. 2013. "Explaining the Rural-Urban Gap in Infant Mortality in India," *Demographic Research*, 29(2013): 473–506.

Samra, N. M., A. E. Taweel, and K. Cadwell. 2013. "Effect of Intermittent Kangaroo Mother Care on Weight Gain of Low Birth Weight Neonates with Delayed Weight Gain," *The Journal of Perinatal Education*, 22(4): 194–200.

Schodt, S., J. Parr, M.C. Araujo, and M. Rubio-Codina. 2015. "Measuring the Quality of Home-Visiting Services: A Review of the Literature," Inter-American Development Bank, http://www.iadb.org/SocialProtection (accessed May 10, 2017).

Shankar, A. H. 2000. "Nutritional Modulation of Malaria Morbidity and Mortality," *Journal of Infectious Diseases*, 182(Supplement 1): S37–S53.

Singh, P. K. 2013. "Trends in Child Immunization across Geographical Regions in India: Focus on Urban-Rural and Gender Differentials," *PloS One*, 8(9): e73102.

Sinha, N. and Yoong, J. 2009. "Long-term Financial Incentives and Investment in Daughters," Gender and Development Group, *Policy Research Working Paper 4860,* Washington, D.C.: World Bank.

Spears, D., A. Ghosh, and O. Cumming. 2013. "Open Defecation and Childhood Stunting in India: An Ecological Analysis of New Data from 112 Districts," *PLoS One*, 8(9): e73784.

Suman Rao, P. N., R. Udani, and R. Nanavati. 2008. "Kangaroo Mother Care for Low Birth Weight Infants: A Randomized Controlled Trial," *Indian Pediatrics*, 45(1): 17.

Stevens, G. A., J. E. Bennett, Q. Hennocq, Y. Lu, L. M. De-Regil, L. Rogers, G. Danaei, G. Li, R. A. White, S. R. Flaxman, and S. P. Oehrle. 2015. "Trends and Mortality Effects of Vitamin A Deficiency in Children in 138 Low-Income and Middle-Income Countries between 1991 and 2013: A Pooled Analysis of Population-based Surveys," *The Lancet Global Health*, 3(9): e528–e536.

Tarozzi, A., A. Mahajan, B. Blackburn, D. Kopf, L. Krishnan, and J. Yoong. 2014. "Micro-loans, Insecticide-treated Bednets, and Malaria: Evidence from a Randomized Controlled Trial in Orissa, India," *The American Economic Review*, 104(7): 1909–1941.

Thomas, D., E. Frankenberg, J. Friedman, J. P. Habicht, M. Hakimi, N. Ingwersen, N. Jones, C. McKelvey, G. Pelto, B. Sikoki, and T. E. Seeman. 2006. "Causal Effect of Health on Labor Market Outcomes: Experimental Evidence," *California Center for Population Research*, http://people.virginia.edu/~sns5r/microwkshp/dthomas.pdf (accessed May 14, 2017).

Walker, S. P., S. M. Chang, M. Vera-Hernández, and S. Grantham-McGregor. 2011. "Early Childhood Stimulation Benefits Adult Competence and Reduces Violent Behavior," *Pediatrics*, 127(5): 849–857.

Weil, D. N. 2014. "Health and Economic Growth," *Handbook of Economic Growth*, 2: 623–682.

Comments and Discussion*

Rohini Somanathan
Delhi School of Economics

I enjoyed this paper and thanks for the opportunity to comment on it. Early childhood investments in education and health are now widely acknowledged to be important worldwide. We have been learning extensively about their role in the United States and other countries in recent years but know little about their impact in India. The authors do a very good job of summarizing the findings from studies in this field. They also discuss Indian programs in some detail.

Let me try to be usefully critical on the present draft of the paper. I have two main sets of comments. The first is on the data used to describe trends on early childhood outcomes in India. The second relates to the question of how to do rigorous impact evaluation to understand which policies can be effective in improving early childhood outcomes in India.

The paper focuses on three main outcomes: infant mortality rates (IMRs), immunization, and cognitive outcomes for 8 to 11 year olds. The importance given to immunization is a bit puzzling because from 1990 to 2010 there was not much action on immunization while IMRs were steadily declining. Perhaps immunization is easier to track. It is much harder to observe nutrition and parental inputs, or similar determinants of early childhood development. But looking at the Figure 2 on immunization, you are roughly at the same level in 2010 as in 1995, and it seems to me that these are not central to the IMR decline. This reminds me of the important 1975 paper by Samuel Preston in which he shows that if you compare "before" and "after" the introduction of antibiotics, you find effects on longevity, but a longer historical analysis reveals that these mortality declines had been occurring for many decades before the introduction of antibiotics and were probably the result of other factors.

*To preserve the sense of the discussions at the India Policy Forum (IPF), these discussants' comments reflect the views expressed at the IPF and do not necessarily take into account revisions to the conference version of the paper in response to these and other comments in preparing the final, revised version published in this volume. The original conference version of the paper is available on www.ncaer.org.

The rural–urban and interstate disparities in IMRs are well presented. Urban IMRs are about half of the rural rates in many states. Given the rapid increases in urbanization in India, it may be useful to do some back of the envelope calculations to show how much of the overall IMR decline can be explained by a movement of the population from rural to urban areas. This would tell us how much of the decline we observe in the IMRs is simply a result of the urban–rural composition of the population and not attributable to specific policies aimed at improving child health. I also noticed that the rural–urban difference in immunization rates is really pretty small. So once again, it does not seem that immunization is an important part of the IMR story. It would be useful to get a better idea of why urban infant mortality is lower. The paper also shows that male–female infant mortality differences are not large. This is interesting because it suggests that interventions later in childhood could be critical for gender equality.

From infants, you jump to the cognitive abilities of 8 to 11 year olds using National Council of Applied Economic Research's (NCAER) India Human Development Survey (IHDS). I wondered why you did not use more of the IHDS data to look at the ages in between. There is a lot of data on anthropometrics and nutrition intake in the NCAER data, and you could also exploit the IHDS panel to say more about how early childhood outcomes are related to those in later years. You suggest other surveys in the paper, but I think you could use the IHDS much more intensively than you do.

Let me now turn to the question of how we can build evidence on early childhood development to guide policy in India. Existing research in this area says intervene early, stimulate cognitive and non-cognitive, and target the areas with low stocks. The authors emphasize the need for rigorous studies on various policy interventions such as the Accredited Social Health Activist (ASHA) program. So what constitutes rigor in policy evaluation in this field?

There are two aspects of child development that make policies very difficult to evaluate using randomized experiments. First, the returns to any policy are non-linear and depend on the existing stocks of child health and education. Second, there are a number of complementary factors that determine the effectiveness of a policy. To elaborate, suppose I have just one background variable, along which children differ, and one possible policy. The question then is just a "yes" or "no" for that policy. I am in the perfect world for randomized trials. I just need to have a control and treatment group, I need to look at whether they match up on that one right-hand side variable, and since my answer is just whether I should go for this policy or not, I am in very good shape if I get a sizable treatment effect and my cost is reasonable.

What happens if I have two possible policies? I then need a factorial experiment with four treatment arms to estimate policy impact. I need places with both policies in place, only the first policy, only the second, and places with no policy in place. Now, go to three possible policies. The number of treatment arms expands exponentially. Once we allow for non-linearity in response, we also need to ensure that the initial stocks of the outcome we are interested in are the same in all the treatment and control arms. When we are thinking about whether we should spend more on the Integrated Child Development Services scheme, subsidized grains, or putting in more crèches, then all these policies are complementary and expensive, and using only randomized trials for looking at effects is really not going to work. We will probably need a better understanding of child physiology and use this in combination with innovative modeling and experiments.

Bharat Ramaswami

Indian Statistical Institute

Like Rohini Somanathan, I too enjoyed reading the paper. I am a consumer of such research and not a producer of such research. But a happy consumer is not necessarily a satisfied consumer. So here is my wish list of what I would have liked. The first part of the paper is the data, followed by three major sections on the theoretical framework, its implications, the empirical findings, and the Indian context.

The theoretical framework models the outcome that initial and early life experience can have long-lasting and irreversible impacts. Of course, this is an important perspective, and the paper urges us to understand human capital in terms of stocks and investments and the substitutability between the two. I think that is a good point and it is not very hard to understand, and I presume the contribution of theory here is really to permit consistent and rigorous estimation of the extent of substitutability or complementarity at different points of time. Although the paper devotes a substantial discussion to the theoretical framework, I do not find the same amount of discussion in empirical findings. For instance, there is one important point at which I was confused, and here I quote the paper. There is a statement here that says, "… very early in life, say from ages 0 to 2, investments and stocks of health and human capital are highly substitutable." What confused me was the word "say." Does this mean that the empirical findings are not specific enough, and so is there a range of uncertainty here about when that substitutability ends or fades away? If so, what implications does that have for policy? I think again from the point of view of a consumer of such research, I would have certainly liked to know what exactly the research says about this substitutability and what the range of uncertainty is about those findings.

Assuming that there is precise knowledge about substitutability, I found the policy discussions to be a little one-sided. Of course, I grant that the paper makes a solid case for investments in early childhood, but in the Indian context, what do we do about the large stock of children who are undernourished and understimulated? For instance, the research findings seem to imply that investments made at a later age may not make the stocks as productive as those made at an early age. But what about the productivity of the investment itself? What are the payoffs to that? That would be a useful and practical finding, and perhaps the paper does not want to go in that direction, but it is an important trade-off for us because we do have a large stock of children who are in that category. It is important even just to acknowledge the issue, because the whole emphasis in the literature has been on the first 1,000 days, but what happens after that, what happens to those who are already beyond their first 1,000 days, and where are we regarding that with respect to policy?

The second thing that occurred to me is that when we talk about empirical findings, the paper very rightly points out that various investments might be complementary or substitutable. While there is the possibility of crowding out, therefore, I did not understand whether there are some general lessons here that carry forward to policy. If every situation is specific, then of course we are at a very preliminary stage in knowledge generation, and it might be a little premature for us to talk about policy.

Similarly, I found the discussion in the paper about parental behavior, which I assume is the key to most interventions, to be fairly general and not specific enough. The paper says that additional parental investment in low-income settings tends to reinforce and augment interventions targeting children, while studies in higher income settings generally reveal the opposite. I think that is an intriguing statement, but what do we make of it and why does it happen? The question again, is whether our research is at a very preliminary stage or is there something that we can say about policy?

Finally, about the Indian context, I think the authors have very correctly pointed out that we need policy evaluations to be built into interventions at the pilot stage. When we want to scale an intervention, we need feedback mechanisms and monitoring. But, I wonder whether the paper is a little too dismissive of quasi-experimental methods. I say this because many of the programs are already in place, and quasi-experimental methods are pretty much all that we can do. It would have been useful to know from the paper what the best evidence from quasi-experimental methods tells us about interventions relating to early childhood development. If the answer is nothing at all, then the paper should say so and try to explain why. If the answer is that we can learn something, then it would have been nice to know what that something was.

The last paragraph in the paper talks about the two main takeaways. The paper urges policy makers to consider not only interventions aimed at reducing malnutrition and infant mortality but also to focus on stimulus and home visitation programs. Second, the paper urges us to do rigorous empirical evaluations of Indian programs in the Indian context. I would say that these are really important takeaways, but the discussion that leads up to this message is much too slender as compared to the rest of the paper.

To summarize, as a consumer of this research I did learn a lot, but I would have liked the findings to be placed in different buckets for my own convenience, such as (a) what we know well, and what are the implications, (b) what is likely to be true but not fully definitive, and (c) what is perhaps speculative. I think that kind of a categorization would have helped me much more in knowing what to do about these fascinating and interesting findings reported in the paper.

General Discussion

T. N. Srinivasan suggested that the authors should convert their charts showing interstate comparisons into charts that rank states on unit-less measures, such as the percentage deviation for states' rate relative to the all-India average, say on infant mortality. If the states are so ranked, it would turn out that the most morbid states relative to the average are the southern states, namely, Kerala, Tamil Nadu, and Andhra Pradesh, while the least morbid ones are the former BIMARU states (Bihar, Madhya Pradesh, Rajasthan, and Uttar Pradesh). So what was remarkable was the persistence of this situation over a long period of time.

Srinivasan then commented on Rohini Somanathan's observations about the interdependency and nonlinearity of the complex relationships being discussed here. Precisely for this reason, he advocated a three-stage piloting-to-scaling-up process that has seen so much success in the Green Revolution and its aim of raising yields per hectare (Srinivasan and Katkar 2015). We knew that interventions providing increased irrigation and supplementary nitrogen, phosphorous, and potash could interact non-linearly with soil, seed, and climate to produce higher yields. But we did not simply implement one scheme across the country. The intervention was broken up into three stages: first, working on the science at experimental stations to identify alternative combinations that showed the greatest promise; second, an intermediate stage where the farmer did the experimentation under real-life conditions; and third, randomized trials across the country. He suggested that a similar approach to childhood development needs to be adopted that can carefully observe the interaction between technology and public policy under conditions of uncertainty until we are sure of our policy design and can scale up the intervention with much greater confidence.

Adding a footnote to Srinivasan's comment, Pranab Bardhan (Chair) remarked that the National Sample Survey (NSS) data also reveal that richer people are more often ill than poorer people. Hence, morbidity seems to vary systematically not only geographically but also in relation to expenditure groups. Achyuta Adhvaryu noted that the Demographic Health Survey (DHS) also showed the same results and suggested that this had to do with greater health awareness among richer and better educated populations. Bardhan suggested that greater access to health facilities is also likely to produce the same result. Srinivasan suggested that all of this came together in the state of Kerala.

Sandeep Sukhtankar wanted to hear from the authors how India fared on its overall expenditures on these programs in comparison with countries such as the United States, China, or Mexico.

Devesh Kapoor asked if the paper or the authors had explored the links between fertility changes and early childhood outcomes in India. Nirvikar Singh urged the authors to take a look at the World Bank's analysis of Integrated Child Development Services (ICDS) undertaken some 10 years ago, which showed why ICDS was not working and how it could be made to work better.

Rohini Somanathan wondered if we should look at how interventions work or do not depending on whether they are built around visits to homes or to ICDS centers or other places where kids gather, particularly given that we are still not very often dealing with nuclear families in India. This went to the broader point mentioned by Bharat Ramaswami that the paper could reflect more on whether, how, and why the global research on early childhood development can apply to India. On cost-benefit, Somanathan suggested looking at the way states were spending money on such programs in the aggregate, as Sukhtankar had suggested. Also, in looking at complementarities, the paper could look at how the ICDS is run in different states—just as a feeding program despite the inclusion of many other elements, or supplemented by some of these other elements that can then shed light on complementarities. This could be done for other programs and how they are implemented in different states.

Karthik Muralidharan flagged the issue of the enormous variation in outcomes across states, set against the morning's comments by the keynote speaker, Amitabh Kant, who had emphasized the growing importance of policy at the state level. Even if a lot of the variation was due to income, Muralidharan recommended to the authors that they do a variance decomposition exercise for the variation in early childhood outcomes of interest, and after including income, see the residuals and assess how much the residuals could be shrunk by including more proximate observables with a possible impact on the outcomes, variables such as population density, sanitation status, public expenditures, etc. This would not be testing for causality but would still be an important exercise for the paper to do. It would help answer Preston curve type questions about interventions in health and education that could shift the curve upwards. Muralidharan's second point reflected a bit of what Bharat Ramaswami and Rohini Somanathan had said about the disconnect in the paper, that all the data described are from India but the suggestions and policies are mostly from work done abroad. He suggested greater attention in the paper to programs designed and implemented in India, the thinking informing these programs, and their performance. This would be particularly important for the paper to have salience for an Indian policy audience, says the secretary of Women and Child Development in the Government of India.

Shekhar Shah recalled the paper presented by Shikha Jha and Bharat Ramaswami (2012) on food subsidies and the public distribution system (PDS) in India at the 2011 India Policy Forum (IPF) and the paper by Sonalde Desai and Reeve Vanneman (2015) on India's Food Security Act in the 2014 IPF. He suggested that since part of the motivation for these large, expensive, very blunt interventions, such as the PDS and the Food Security Act is child nutrition, it would be useful for the paper to comment on them, perhaps outlining their opportunity costs.

Rohini Somanathan intervened to refer to the paper by Cutler and Miller (2005) on water quality, and its findings on clean water—based on filtration and chlorination—being responsible for nearly half the total mortality and two-thirds of the child mortality reductions in major US cities during the late 19th and early 20th centuries. Filtration and chlorination were jointly important in reducing mortality and were substitute technologies, though major cities had adopted filtration technologies first since they had been developed first, and so it appeared that filtration was more effective than chlorination. Her point was that we need to first look at the scientific evidence before going into complementary and crowding out concerns at the national level. She suggested that the authors could also use the vast clinical evidence available for the Indian context in nutritional journals on, say, anaemia interventions, among other things.

References

Cutler, D. and G. Miller. 2005. "The Role of Public Health Improvements in Health Advances: The Twentieth-century United States," *Demography*, 42(1): 1–22.

Desai, Sonalde and Reeve Vanneman. 2015. "Enhancing Nutrition Security via India's National Food Security Act: Using an Axe instead of a Scalpel?" *India Policy Forum 2014–15*, 11: 67–113.

Jha, Shikha and Bharat Ramaswami. 2012. "The Percolation of Public Expenditure: Food Subsidies and the Poor in India and the Philippines," *India Policy Forum 2011–12*, 8: 95–127.

Srinivasan, T.N. and Pavan Katkar. 2015. "Technology and Public Policy Interaction: The Green Revolution," *Yojana*: 33–45, January.

SHOUMITRO CHATTERJEE*
Princeton University

DEVESH KAPUR†
University of Pennsylvania

Six Puzzles in Indian Agriculture‡

ABSTRACT A quarter century after India's historic shift to a more market-oriented economy, the agriculture sector continues to be racked by severe policy distortions, despite its importance for the livelihoods of the majority of India's population and in addressing major long-term challenges facing the country, from food security to natural resource sustainability. The paper highlights some key empirical realities and data anomalies to raise some fundamental questions about Indian agriculture and anchors the analysis in six major puzzles: prices, procurement, political economy, trade, productivity, and exit. While the list is neither exhaustive nor original in and of itself, these puzzles raise important policy issues. We conclude by arguing that more unified frameworks of analysis are needed for effective policy in a much neglected but crucial sector for securing India's future.

Keywords: *Agriculture, Market Imperfection, International Trade, Agriculture and Environment, India, Land Ownership, Political Processes*
JEL Classification: *D43, D45, O1, Q11, Q12, Q13, Q18*

1. Introduction

A quarter century after India's historic shift to a more market-oriented economy, with industrial delicensing, trade liberalization, and (more limited) reforms in factor markets, one sector continues to be plagued by severely intrusive government regulations in both factor and product markets, an arbitrary policy and regulatory environment, and low public investment. Unfortunately, that sector—agriculture—not only accounts for the livelihoods of the majority of India's population but also is critical to multiple long-term challenges facing the country, from food security to natural resource sustainability, especially soil and water.

* *shoumitrochatterjee@gmail.com*
† *dkapur@upenn.edu*
‡ The authors would like to thank Amarsingh Gawande and Beeban Rai for their excellent research assistance.

The challenges facing Indian agriculture and its tens of millions of farmers have been well recognized, whether by the media attention and hand wringing on farmer suicides, the reports of the National Commission on Farmers (led by M. S. Swaminathan) or official government documents, such as the *Economic Survey, 2016*. Yet academic research has largely not kept pace with the most pressing challenges facing Indian agriculture, barring certain exceptions.[1] Given the increasing availability of computing power, novel geospatial datasets and new quantitative tools in trade, industrial organization, economic geography, and political science, this might be an opportune moment to focus on some old and new puzzles in Indian agriculture—all of which have major welfare implications for the tens of millions of Indian farmers.

The primary purpose of this paper is to raise some fundamental questions about Indian agriculture by highlighting a number of empirical realities and anomalies in the data. We discuss six major puzzles in Indian agriculture related to prices, procurement, political economy, trade, productivity, and the near-absence of exit. Our list is by no means exhaustive. Nor do we claim to be the first ones to identify these issues, but these puzzles raise, we argue, important policy issues, and they are all the more salient when viewed through the lens of a unified framework. We argue that it is often simplistic and naïve to provide isolated answers to these questions. For instance, as we note below, there appears to be little change in the time trends of spatial price variation in agriculture at both the retail as well as the wholesale level, and this is despite substantial investments in rural infrastructure in recent years, especially in rural roads and cell phone connectivity.

More broadly, our goal is to assemble some of the building blocks for an internally consistent framework and, in doing so, also highlight the need for more quantitative macro-research in agriculture. Much recent research on agriculture in developing countries has a micro-focus with limited generalizability. However, for policy, it is essential to be able to build a macro-framework that not only enables the incorporation of key actors and modeling their interaction with each other but also helps analyze meaningful policy counterfactuals with general equilibrium effects. We discuss this in greater detail in the concluding section.

We examine six key puzzles in detail below. First, we highlight high and stable spatial price dispersion (of wholesale prices) in the decade 2005–2014. Others have found the same in retail prices (Li 2016). This observation is

1. Examples include the following: Allen and Atkin 2016; Banerji, Gupta, and Meenakshi (2012); Banerji and Meenakshi (2004, 2008); Fafchamps and Minten (2012); Goyal (2010); Kapur and Krishnamurthy (2014a, 2014b); Krishnamurthy 2011; and Mitra et al. (2015).

at odds with the law of one price, which would predict a decline in price dispersion following massive investments in rural roads and communications (via cell phone penetration) in this period. Second, we show that while in principle the Minimum Support Price (MSP) policy is a national policy meant to protect the incomes of all farmers, there is substantial variation (both across regions and crops) in its implementation. Third, while farmers' incomes have languished, they have been unable to leverage their sheer numbers into pressuring governments to undertake policies and programs that benefit them, as one might expect in a democracy. Why has this been the case?

Fourth, India produces an excess of commodities and then exports them even though they have a high factor content of its scarce natural resources—water and land. This violates one of the central tenets of international trade theory—the Heckscher–Ohlin theorem. What factors might explain this puzzle? Fifth, there are large productivity gaps across geography, that is, the productivity level that can be reached conditional on natural endowments. Why? And why do these productivity gaps persist, that is, what prevents the diffusion of efficiency/efficacy norms across space? Finally, why do farmers not exit agriculture even when agricultural incomes remain abysmally low and highly uncertain, when they could potentially earn a riskless stream of income by selling their land, for instance?

We hope that the cataloguing of these puzzles in a unified manner will help to structure and motivate future research on Indian agricultural markets, policies, and their consequences.

2. The Price Variation Puzzle

Economic theory predicts that spatial price dispersion is a function of trade costs (such as transport costs and information asymmetries) and mark-ups charged by market intermediaries (the law of one price). Since the early 2000s, there have been large public investments in India in constructing highways and rural roads. The Pradhan Mantri Gram Sadak Yojana (PMGSY), launched in end-2000, aimed at providing all-weather road connectivity to every rural habitation with a minimum population of 500 in the plains (250-plus in hill states, tribal districts, and desert areas). Of a total of 178,184 habitations identified, two-thirds were connected by mid-2016 with nearly half a million km of roads. In the case of telecommunications infrastructure, the investments were made by the private sector. According to the Socio-Economic and Caste Census 2011, two out of every three rural Indian households have access to cell phones (from negligible numbers in 2000), and there have been active efforts by the central and state governments to inform farmers of *mandi* prices near them (Tewari 2015). The twin investments in core connectivity infrastructure—roads and cell phones—have resulted in substantial reductions of both transport and information costs in India. Yet we do not see evidence of spatial price convergence in agriculture commodities during this time period. As we show below using high frequency data, the variation in prices of commodities between agricultural markets or *mandis* has been stable over the past decade and is consistent across different crops.

Fafchamps and Minten (2012) found no evidence of the impact of SMS-based information on the prices received by farmers in a field experiment in Maharashtra. Although Goyal (2010) finds mild effects of improvement in farm gate prices for soybean farmers because of the introduction of electronic kiosks in villages of Madhya Pradesh (MP) in early 2000 by Indian Tobacco Company (ITC), the aggregate effects are negligible since the overall price variation has not gone down.

Before we look for possible answers, we examine the data in detail. We focus on average monthly price data for eight, major, non-perishable commodities—paddy, wheat, barley, maize, finger millet, pearl millet, sorghum and soybean—sold in any *mandi* in India between 2005 and 2014. It should be noted that the prices we analyze are wholesale prices observed at Agricultural Produce Market Committee (APMC) *mandis*. It is very likely that these are not prices received by farmers in general, since it is large farmers who sell in *mandis*, whereas small farmers are more likely to sell to local village intermediaries (Table 1). However, our price data has

TABLE 1. Percentage of Cereal Output by Farm Size Sold to Various Buyers

			Paddy		
Farm Size	*Local Private*	*Mandi*	*Government*	*Input Dealers*	*Processors*
0–2 ha	55.44	20.19	11.17	8.72	1.62
2–5 ha	41.89	28.92	5.54	19.44	2.44
5–10 ha	29.58	34.77	6.52	27.46	0.51
> 10 ha	14.15	50.43	3.76	15.38	0.65
			Wheat		
Farm Size	*Local Private*	*Mandi*	*Government*	*Input Dealers*	*Processors*
0–2 ha	41.40	38.71	11.01	8.1	0.14
2–5 ha	25.23	49.97	5.02	19.42	0.24
5–10 ha	16.68	45.68	7.36	29.8	0.3
> 10 ha	6.07	40.45	1.67	51.77	0.08

Source: NSS Situation Assessment Survey of Agricultural Households (2012).

several advantages. They are actual prices recorded at a high frequency and at a crucial stage in the supply chain: *mandis* are key points of aggregation. Other sources of price data are usually recalled estimates of unit values, geographically aggregated and at a very low frequency.

We use log (real) prices (with the consumer price index for agricultural laborers [CPIAL; food] as the deflator) so that the variance of log prices is unit-independent and compatible for pan-country comparisons. The average standard deviation of log (real) prices across *mandis* in a given month is 0.17. For comparative purposes, this is higher than the Philippines: for rice and corn (the country's principal home-grown food commodities), Allen (2014) found the standard deviation to be 0.15, and this in a country comprising a group of over a thousand islands, with high transport and information costs.

As stated earlier, we do not observe any trend in time-series of the standard deviation, which implies that the trade cost during this period does not appear to have had a causal effect on price variation in grains across India (Figure 1). There is some heterogeneity in the price dispersion across

FIGURE 1. Average Spatial Variation in *Mandi* Prices

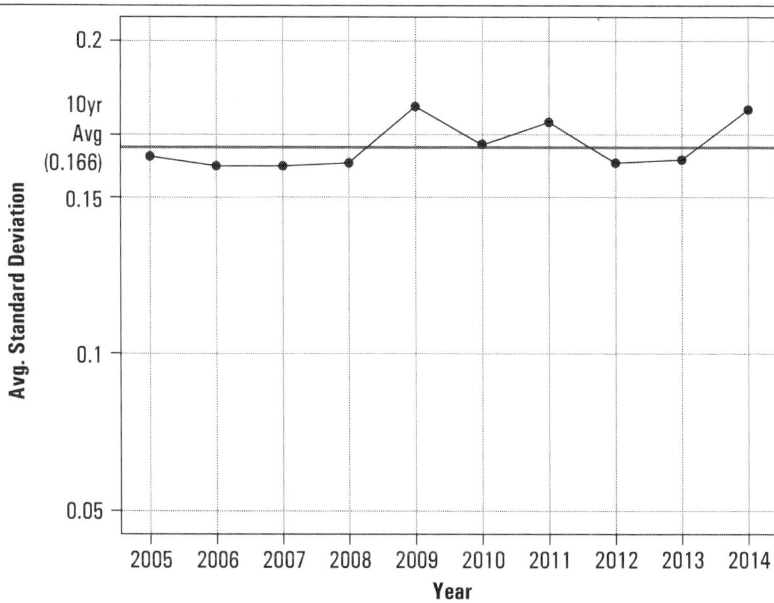

Source: AgMarknet data.

Notes: Standard deviation computed for each month and each crop. The figure plots the yearly averages. Commodities in data: Barley, pearl millet, finger millet, maize, paddy, soybean, sorghum, wheat.

TABLE 2. Price Variation between *Mandis* in Commodities

		Avg Std Dev
Full Sample	All commodities	0.17
	Paddy	0.22
	No Basmati/Superfine	0.21
	Wheat	0.13
	All other	0.17
Trimmed Sample	All commodities	0.16
	Paddy	0.21
	Wheat	0.13
	Soybean	0.07
	Sorghum	0.28
	All other	0.16

Source: Authors' Calculations from AgMarknet data.

Note: The trimmed sample drops the top 5th percentile of the sample in terms of prices. Commodities in data: Barley, pearl millet, finger millet, maize, paddy, soybean, sorghum, and wheat.

commodities. It is lowest for soybean, which is chiefly grown in MP as well as parts of Maharashtra, and higher for other cereals (Table 2).

Some of the variation in price might be due to high-value varieties—for example, basmati rice is more expensive than common rice. To control for that, we drop the top 5 percentile of our data by crop in terms of prices. That brings down the average annual variation only mildly. Most importantly, however, even in the trimmed sample, we do not see any evidence of reduction in spatial price variation over time (Table 3).

The average standard deviation of log (real) prices across *mandis* within states is also high. To the extent that high average standard deviation of log (real) prices across *mandis* in the country might be due to different varieties of wheat and rice grown in agro-ecological zones that vary across different states, this finding attenuates the concern. High within-state variation provides additional evidence that the variation is not entirely due to quality.

TABLE 3. Spatial Price Variation in Commodities over Time

	2005	*2006*	*2007*	*2008*	*2009*	*2010*	*2011*	*2012*	*2013*	*2014*
Barley	0.11	0.14	0.11	0.12	0.16	0.16	0.16	0.11	0.11	0.11
Millets	0.19	0.16	0.17	0.18	0.20	0.17	0.17	0.16	0.18	0.20
Maize	0.17	0.17	0.15	0.14	0.16	0.13	0.14	0.15	0.16	0.16
Paddy	0.18	0.19	0.22	0.23	0.23	0.22	0.19	0.20	0.24	0.21
Soybean	0.06	0.06	0.06	0.06	0.09	0.05	0.06	0.09	0.06	0.09
Sorghum	0.25	0.25	0.27	0.25	0.27	0.31	0.38	0.29	0.24	0.32
Wheat	0.14	0.15	0.14	0.11	0.12	0.13	0.14	0.12	0.13	0.12

Source: Authors' calculations from AgMarknet data.

TABLE 4. Variation in Real Prices Across *Mandis* Within States in 2014

State	*Standard Deviation*
Andhra Pradesh	0.15
Chhattisgarh	0.13
Gujarat	0.14
Haryana	0.13
Jharkhand	0.14
Karnataka	0.18
Kerala	0.17
Madhya Pradesh	0.21
Maharashtra	0.16
Odisha	0.70
Punjab	0.26
Rajasthan	0.14
Tamil Nadu	0.21
Uttar Pradesh	0.11

Source: Authors' calculations from AgMarknet data.

We present the results for 2014 in Table 4. The results for previous years are similar.

What is the relative weight of different factors in the variation in prices? To get at this, we performed a Shapley–Shorrocks decomposition. This procedure considers the various factors that together determine an indicator (such as the overall variation in prices) and assigns to each factor an average marginal contribution. This technique ensures that the decomposition is always exact and that the factors are treated symmetrically. The results from the Shapley–Shorrocks decomposition found that 37 percent of the variation in log (real) prices is due to time-invariant district fixed effects (which in this case could be soil quality effecting yields and hence prices), 20 percent is due to location-invariant aggregate time shocks (like global demand), 4 percent is due to differences in monthly rainfall across districts, and 39 percent remains unexplained. The residual time- and location-varying effects could be due to changes in connectivity, crop choice, or the expansion of welfare schemes—such as the Public Distribution System (PDS) and National Rural Employment Guarantee Act (NREGA)—impacting agriculture.

This analysis is revealing because, if the law of one price is valid, then trade costs alone cannot create the binding constraint. The law of one price states that the difference in prices at two locations is a function of trade costs and market power. There is compelling evidence that the PMGSY has reduced trade costs in rural India (Agarwal 2014), and highways have done so between regions (Allen and Atkin 2016). Therefore, it must be either that the market power of intermediaries has stayed constant over the years and/or that it interacts with trade costs in ways that need better understanding.

In ongoing work, Chatterjee (2017) explores the role of spatial competition in price variation between *mandis*. Using a large dataset on prices in *mandis* and their geo-locations, the paper finds evidence that additional markets create more competition and hence increase the prices received by farmers. A causal border-discontinuity model, which exploits restrictions to inter-state movement of goods to tease out the competition effect, estimates price increases of 4 percent for an additional *mandi* in the neighborhood. The limitation of this approach is that it is unable to capture any within-*mandi* friction that might give rise to market power.[2] While we have a good understanding of how trade costs impact prices, we know much less about the sources of market power within a *mandi*. To that end, understanding the *mandi* as an institution, and its internal political economy that gives market power to traders vis-à-vis farmers, is the logical analytical next step. Then, ideally, economists can model these forces and should be able to quantify their effects on price dispersion.

3. The Procurement Puzzle

Two key government interventions that affect agriculture markets and commodity prices in India are the MSP and procurement by government agencies (mainly, but not solely, at *mandi* sites). The MSP sets a floor price and thereby shapes the investment decisions of farmers. Its rationale is to ensure that farmers are not compelled to sell their produce below the support price due to either exploitation by large market players or a bumper harvest. The MSP is effective mainly for four crops: wheat, paddy, cotton (albeit only to a modest degree), and sugarcane (for which mills are legally obligated to buy cane from farmers at government-fixed prices).

The puzzle is that although in principle the MSP procurement policy is a national policy and should benefit all farmers regardless of their location or crop choice, in practice, it varies (a) across states, (b) across districts within states, and (c) across crops. Although we understand some of this variation, a large part of it is still left unexplained. To highlight this puzzle, we first consider an indirect measure: farmers' awareness about MSP. The reason

2. See Krishnamurthy (2011) for an ethnographic study of the multiple ways in which market power works within a *mandi*.

FIGURE 2. Farmer Awareness about Minimum Support Prices 2012–13

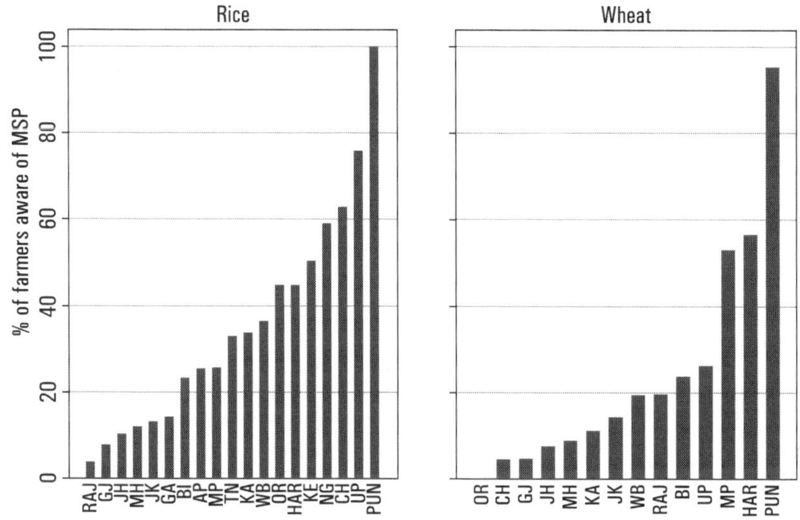

Source: NSS Situation Assessment Survey of Agricultural Households Round 70.

for choosing this measure over actual procurement is that the quantum of procurement is a choice of the farmer. If market prices are above MSP, then even in the presence of efforts by public agencies, farmers may choose not to sell since the MSP acts like an option. However, the farmers' awareness about MSP is more likely to reflect the presence of government agencies in his neighborhood.

Figure 2 shows that most farmers are not even aware of the existence of MSPs, and there is considerable variation across states. Whereas most farmers in Punjab and Haryana are aware of MSP, very few are aware in other states such as Gujarat, Maharashtra, Jharkhand, or West Bengal. This is indicative of the absence of active government procurement efforts by public agencies in many parts of the country.

It follows, therefore, that there are large disparities across states in actual procurement. In Tables 5 and 6, not surprisingly, one observes that the states where awareness of MSP is high are also the states where there is heavy procurement of grains—both in absolute terms and relative to total production. Therefore, awareness is highly correlated to the intensity of procurement in a state (Figure 3). Notice also that as paddy is more intensely procured than wheat (as a percentage of total production), the overall level of awareness is higher for paddy than for wheat.

TABLE 5. Production and Procurement of Rice

State	Production (million tons)		Procurement by FCI and State Agencies (million tons)		% of All India Procurement	Procurement as a % of Total Production
	2013–14	*2014–15*	*2013–14*	*2014–15*	*2013–15*	*2013–15*
Andhra Pradesh	6.97	7.23	3.737	3.596	11.65	51.63
Bihar	5.51	6.36	0.942	1.614	4.06	21.55
Chhattisgarh	6.72	6.32	4.29	3.423	12.26	59.16
Gujarat	1.64	1.83	0	0	0.00	0.00
Haryana	4.00	4.01	2.406	2.015	7.03	55.23
Jharkhand	2.81	3.36	0	0.006	0.01	0.10
Karnataka	3.57	3.54	0	0.088	0.14	1.24
Kerala	0.51	0.56	0.359	0.374	1.16	68.42
Madhya Pradesh	2.84	3.63	1.045	0.807	2.94	28.62
Maharashtra	3.12	2.95	0.161	0.1988	0.57	5.93
Odisha	7.61	8.30	2.801	3.357	9.79	38.70
Punjab	11.27	11.11	8.106	7.786	25.26	71.03
Rajasthan	0.31	0.37	0	0	0.00	0.00
Tamil Nadu	5.35	5.73	0.684	1.051	2.76	15.66
Telangana	5.75	4.44	4.353	3.504	12.49	77.06
Uttar Pradesh	14.64	12.17	1.127	1.698	4.49	10.54
West Bengal	15.37	14.68	1.359	2.032	5.39	11.29

Source: Ministry of Agriculture and Farmers Welfare, Government of India.

TABLE 6. Production and Procurement of Wheat

State	Production (lakh tons)		Procurement by FCI and State Agencies (lakh tons)		% of All India Procurement	Procurement as a Percentage of Total Production
	2013–14	*2014–15*	*2013–14*	*2014–15*	*2013–15*	*2013–15*
Andhra Pradesh	0.04	0	0	0	0.00	0.00
Bihar	47.38	39.87	0	0	0.00	0.00
Chhattisgarh	1.34	1.35	0	0	0.00	0.00
Gujarat	46.94	30.59	0	0	0.00	0.00
Haryana	118.00	103.54	58.73	6.50	23.29	55.8
Jharkhand	3.70	3.30	0	0	0.00	0.00
Karnataka	2.10	2.61	0	0	0.00	0.00
Madhya Pradesh	129.37	171.04	63.55	70.94	25.33	44.8
Maharashtra	16.02	13.08	0	0	0.00	0.00
Odisha	0.01	0.006	0	0	0.00	0.00
Punjab	176.20	150.50	108.97	116.41	42.45	69.0
Rajasthan	86.63	98.24	12.70	21.59	6.46	18.5
Telangana	0	0.07	0	0	0.00	0.00
Uttar Pradesh	298.91	224.17	6.82	6.28	2.47	2.5

Source: Ministry of Agriculture and Farmers Welfare, Government of India.

FIGURE 3. Farmer Awareness versus Procurement

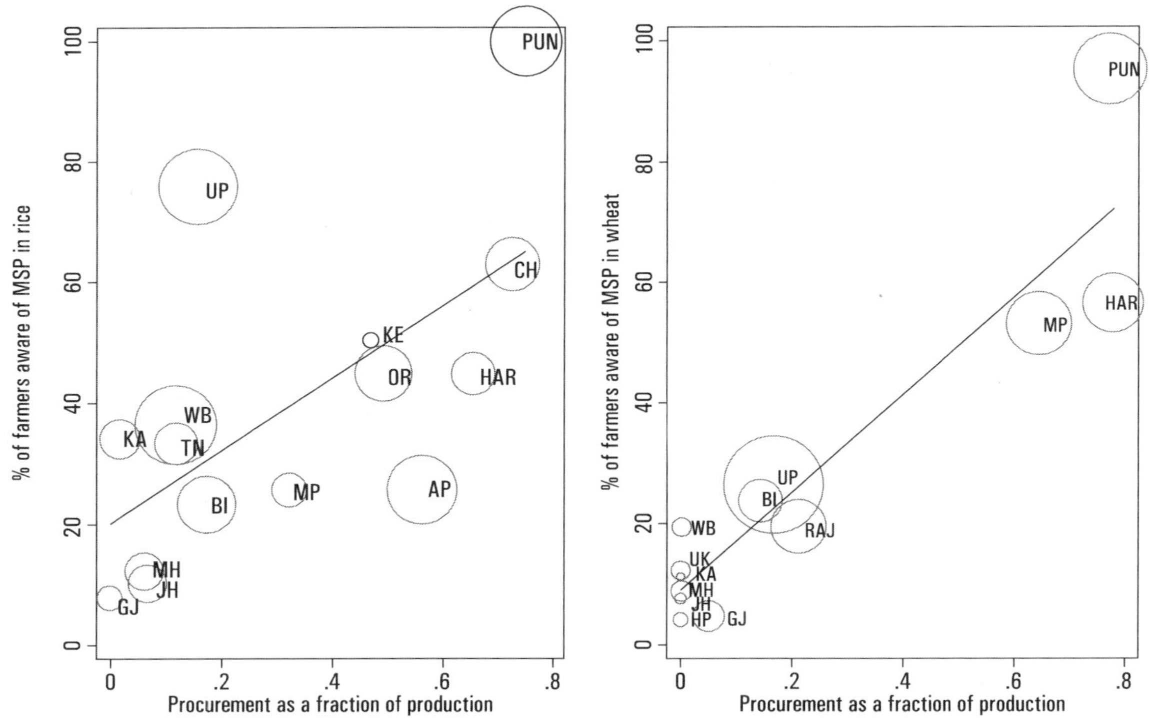

Source: NSS–SAS (2012).

Note: Size of the bubble represents state shares in national output. Acronyms refer to state names.

While there has been considerable discussion on procurement of food grains by public agencies for the PDS, the key point that is often missed is that government procurement is a luxury for most farmers in the country. There are large differences not only across states but within them as well. And this variation in procurement has substantial consequences on the price that farmers receive and the crops they choose to produce.

The disparity in procurement within states can be seen in the maps in Figures 4 and 5. The figures plot, for each district, paddy and wheat procured as a percentage of total production for that district. Although there is

FIGURE 4. Average Fraction of Paddy Production Procured 2005–14

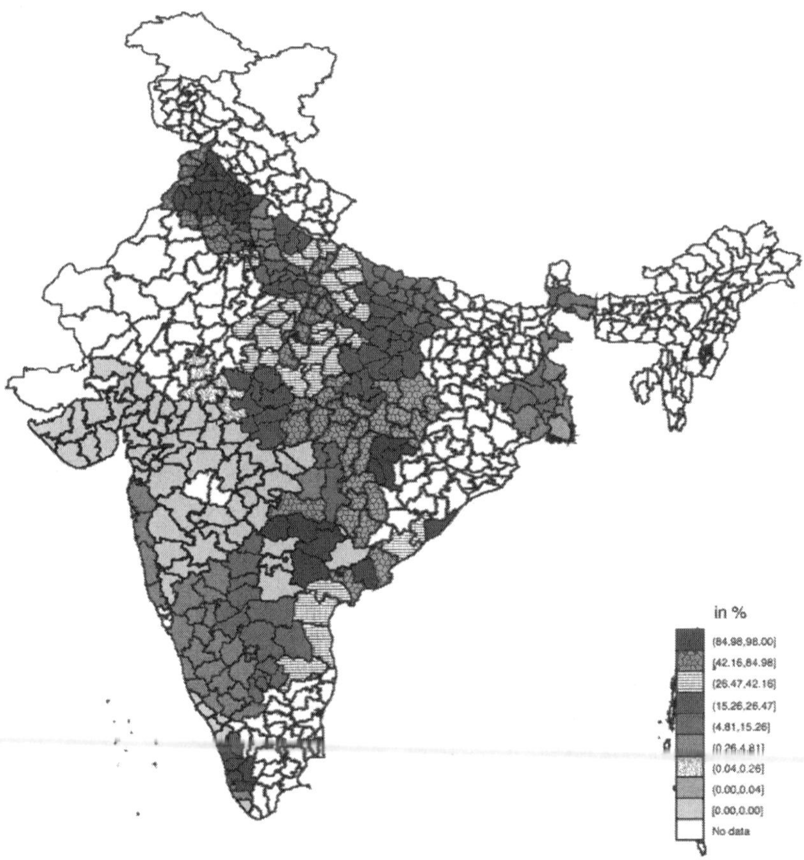

Sources: Food Corporation of India and Ministry of Agriculture and Farmers Welfare, Government of India.
Note: This map is not to scale and may not depict authentic boundaries.

FIGURE 5. Average Fraction of Wheat Production Procured 2005–14

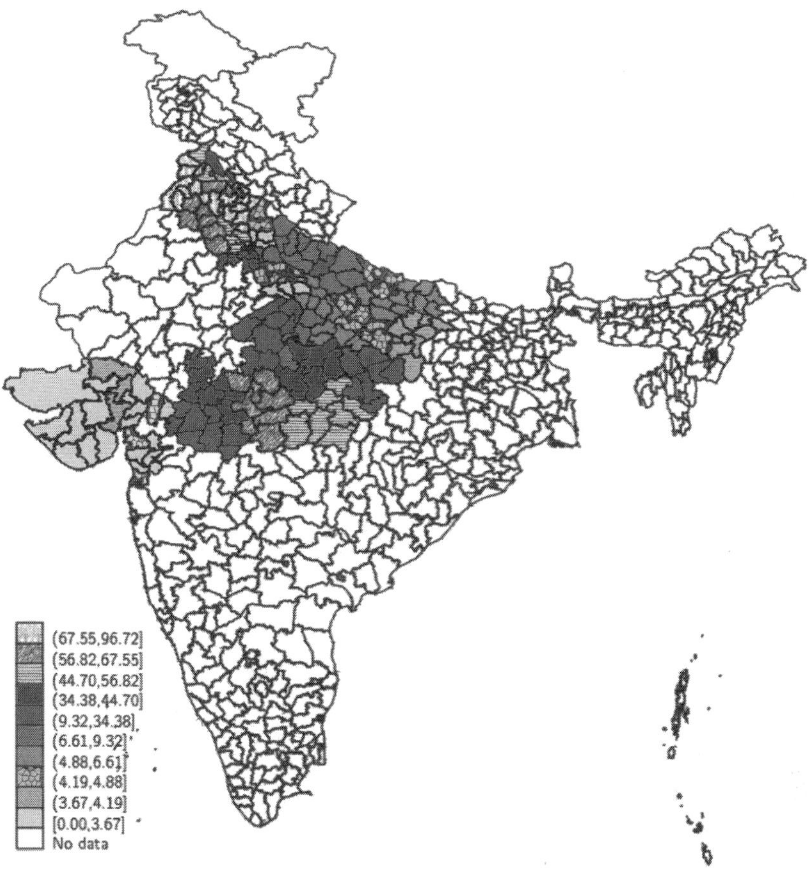

Sources: Food Corporation of India and Ministry of Agriculture and Farmers Welfare, Government of India.
Note: This map is not to scale and may not depict authentic boundaries.

uniformly high procurement across districts in Punjab and Haryana, there is large variation across districts in UP, MP, Maharashtra, and Odisha.

What explains the variation in procurement across districts? Potential explanations (all of which require careful research) include the following:

1. In districts where procurement is low, market prices are above MSP such that it is not in the farmers' interest to sell to the government.
2. Output per person is relatively low in districts where procurement is low, indicating that low procurement reflects low marketable

surplus. In other words, a larger fraction of production is used for self-consumption.

3. Variations in procurement could also reflect variations in the nodal procurement agencies. While the Food Corporation of India (FCI) is the principal storage and distribution agency for food grains, a substantial portion of the actual physical procurement is done by state agencies on behalf of the FCI. All procurement agencies—whether the FCI or state agencies—face resource constraints. However, since they must procure a target amount of grains for the PDS, they are likely to deploy limited resources efficiently by mobilizing them in spatially concentrated, high-productivity districts.
4. Procurement of grains can also be used by politicians to selectively channel resources toward their constituencies (or away from their rivals' constituencies) and thereby reward or penalize sections of the electorate. For instance, if the local politician is from the ruling party at the Center, then he can potentially influence the FCI on the location and number of purchase centers or, if he is from the ruling party in the state, the state procurement agencies.

The first and second explanations are in line with government-mandated policies. The last two, however, can have important welfare and policy implications. If we regress fraction of output procured in each district on log yields and log population, we indeed find support for (2) and (3) (Table 7). Districts with larger populations have relatively lower procurement, and districts with higher productivity have relatively greater procurement. Nonetheless, these regressions can only explain about 30 percent of the cross-sectional variation in procurement, which leaves much scope for future research.

TABLE 7. Regression Table

	Dep var: Fraction of Output Procured	
Log yield	28.40	32.22
	(2.68)***	(5.58)***
Log population	−10.00	20.78
	(1.40)***	(2.76)***
N	445	188
R^2	0.32	0.35
Crop	Rice	Wheat

Source: District population is from 2011 Census of India.

Notes: All observations are district averages between 2011 and 2014. Crops include paddy and wheat. $^{*} p < 0.1$, $^{**} p < 0.05$, $^{***} p < 0.01$.

4. Political Economy Puzzles

Historically, India has been seen as a rural society, with farming the dominant occupation and economic mainstay for the vast majority of the population. In the 1950s, agriculture accounted for more than half of India's gross domestic product (GDP), and cultivators accounted for half of the workforce. From that position, agriculture's share of GDP had declined by two-thirds (to about 16 percent) by 2011, while the percentage of cultivators in the workforce had declined from nearly 50 percent in 1951 to 24 percent in 2011. Nonetheless, the absolute numbers are very large (118.6 million as per the 2011 Census), and if we add agricultural laborers who account for 30 percent of the labor force (144 million in 2011 up from 27.3 million and 19.5 percent of the workforce in 1951), the two still constitute more than half of India's labor force.

Furthermore, as per National Sample Survey (NSS) data from the 70th Round, during the agricultural year July 2012–June 2013, rural India had an estimated total of 90.2 million agricultural households, which constituted about 57.8 percent of all rural households and 37 percent of all households. In a democracy, these massive numbers suggest that farmers should be a potent political force. But their economic travails suggest otherwise. Why have Indian farmers not leveraged their sheer numbers into pressuring governments to undertake policies and programs that benefit them more?

An obvious counter to this question is that farmers do enjoy substantial political influence. Many of India's agriculture policies are in place precisely because of farmers' political clout. Subsidies on inputs—whether electricity, water, fertilizer, or credit—or on outputs (especially price supports) are in place precisely because farmers matter politically. While there are many questions on the incidence and distributional impact of these subsidies, the reality that the vast majority of Indian farmers have low and volatile incomes is not in doubt. And yet, the reality is that famers' movements were much more politically salient in the 1970s and 1980s than in the last two decades.

In the early decades following India's independence, the Indian state enjoyed substantial autonomy from powerful rural interests, which, while they could thwart rural programs (such as land reforms or community development programs), had weak impact on agriculture policies and programs. This changed dramatically after the Green Revolution. Initially there were fears that the Green Revolution would "turn red," based on apprehensions that the gains would accrue disproportionally to large farmers, widening the gap with marginal farmers and landless laborers (Frankel 1978). Instead, as the Green Revolution started empowering the landed peasantry (owner-cultivators—the so-called "bullock capitalists"), the focus shifted to rural farmer-led "demand groups" that became an important political constituency shaping public spending on agriculture subsidies and pitting rural India against urban India (Rudolph and Rudolph 1987). The "Bharat versus India" tension was especially manifest in pressures for higher MSPs, since these benefited producers (farmers) at the expense of consumers (or the public exchequer, if consumer subsidies rose). This drove farmers' movements to demand higher support prices (Varshney 1995), but farmers' incomes continued to be dismal, as we note below. This is even more puzzling since the 1990s saw marked growth in regional parties dominated by farmers. Why have farmers been unable to translate their large numbers into more pro-farmer policies and programs?

An obvious explanation of the failure of collective action by farmers goes back to Olson (1965), who famously argued that large and dispersed groups are hard to organize anywhere. And, given the fragmented nature of Indian society, they are more susceptible to cross-cutting religious, caste, and ethnic/linguistic appeals. But two developments of the 1990s appear to have further weakened collective action by farmers. The sharpening of caste-based political cleavages since the late 1980s (following the implementation of reservations under the Mandal Report in 1990) may have caused the glue of common economic interests to come unstuck. A second possibility is the 73rd Amendment to the Indian Constitution, which made statutory provisions for Panchayati Raj as the third level of administration in villages. This was a much-needed effort at administrative decentralization. But by mandating elections at the base of rural society (villages), it appears to have shifted political energies inward—in the form of electoral competition within villages to capture increasing resources coming to villages—and thereby diluted efforts to project collective farming interests outward and upward.

These factors, however, only explain the demand side of the story. They do not explain why politicians have been willing to spend vast resources and efforts on programs aimed at rural India, for which there was pressure from civil society groups, but little from rural voters (for example, NREGA), while remaining unwilling to commit resources and efforts to improve farmer productivity and incomes, whether through rural markets, agriculture research and extension, or better credit and irrigation systems.

Under the Indian Constitution, agriculture is a state subject. One might, therefore, expect considerable inter-state variation in agriculture policies stemming from differences in the politics and political economies of states. But, in fact, differences in the policy approaches of politicians across states in agriculture—be it taxes, subsidies, or trade laws—are quite limited. Why?

To take one example: reforms to the APMC Act. In 2003, recognizing that the role of the APMCs and the state agriculture marketing boards needed to change from market regulation to market development, which required removing trade barriers and creating a common market, the Central Government formulated a model APMC Act for adoption by the states.

The reality of the reforms carried out by the different states paint a different picture. Maharashtra, for example, went back on the reforms soon after they were announced.[3] UP has not yet adopted any of the main features of the model APMC Act except giving permission to some big players for direct procurement of food grains (primarily wheat), on the condition that their total procurement in a season should be greater than 50,000 tons. Crucially, this notification is issued year to year, and no changes have been made in the legislation, thereby ensuring little private investment (and possibly substantial annual rent seeking). In other states, by putting in large up-front license fees to set up new markets or insisting that traders outside the market still pay market fees, the reforms have been effectively stymied. Even when licenses are awarded, they are for selected crops. For example, in Karnataka, of the 36 licenses awarded at the time of writing, all were either for cotton or fruits and vegetables.[4]

A research agenda on the limited inter-state variation in agriculture policies could investigate two possibilities. First, whether multiple interventions by the Center on different issues have important structural consequences for agriculture that limit what states can do. The National Food Security Act, 2013, for instance, mandated legal entitlements for existing food security programs at a fixed price for specific food grains. Inevitably, this sets certain structural incentives for the states' own procurement efforts and thereby farmers' crop choices, with cascading effects on ecologically sustainable agriculture practices. A second explanation might stem from certain common features of agriculture markets across rural India, namely the layer of intermediaries constituting the trading-cum-moneylending classes. The persistence of interlinked markets in credit and outputs enhances the bargaining power of these intermediaries vis-à-vis farmers, as well as giving them more influence in local politics, thereby making it easier to undermine reform efforts. Research into the political economy of the structure of rents that accrue under the status quo, and whether and why these might affect the incentives of governments to implement reforms, would be valuable.

3. http://tinyurl.com/maharashtra-apmc-reform

4. Data based on interviews with Karnataka state government officials by authors.

FIGURE 6. Per Capita Availability of Renewable Freshwater Resources

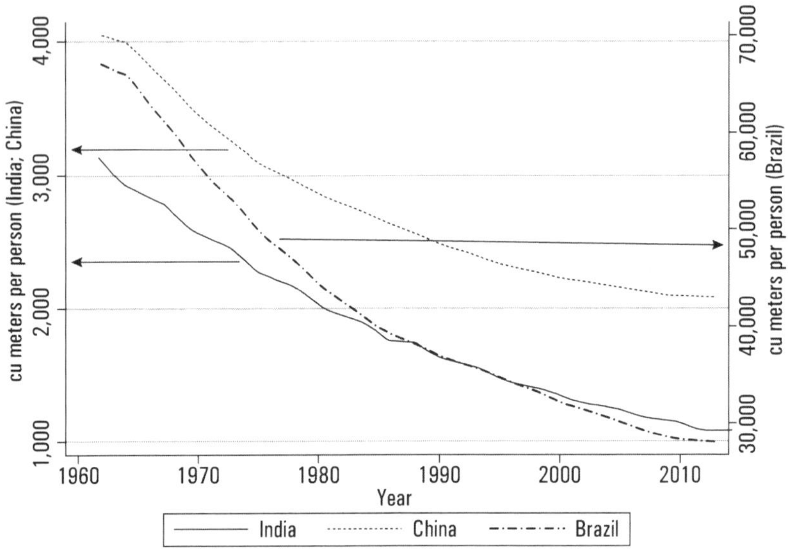

Source: FAOSTAT, http://faostat3.fao.org/

5. The Trade Puzzle: Exporting Scarce Resources

One of India's scarcest natural resources is water. Figure 6 provides an international comparison of availability of fresh water resources. The scarcity of fresh water in India is much worse than even what is depicted in the picture since Brazil and China use only 60 percent of their stock of fresh water availability, while India uses a little over 90 percent. In an era of globalization, as the Hecksher–Ohlin trade model would also predict, India should produce relatively more of the commodities that use its scarce natural resources less intensively and should export them. And it should produce relatively less of commodities whose production requires intense use of its scarce resources and should import them.

In aggregate, India's production patterns are the converse. Hoekstra and Mekonnen (2012) compute the water footprint (amount of water used for production) of crop production around the world from 1996 to 2005. Not only is India's water footprint the highest (followed by those of China and Brazil) but also, at 1,047 cu gm per year, it is thrice that of Brazil (329 cu gm per year), despite India having fewer water resources than other countries to begin with. Furthermore, India's production technology and crop choice amplifies the amount of water it uses for production. This can also be seen in Figure 7. Further, globally among all provinces or states, the water footprint

FIGURE 7. Water Footprint of Agricultural Production

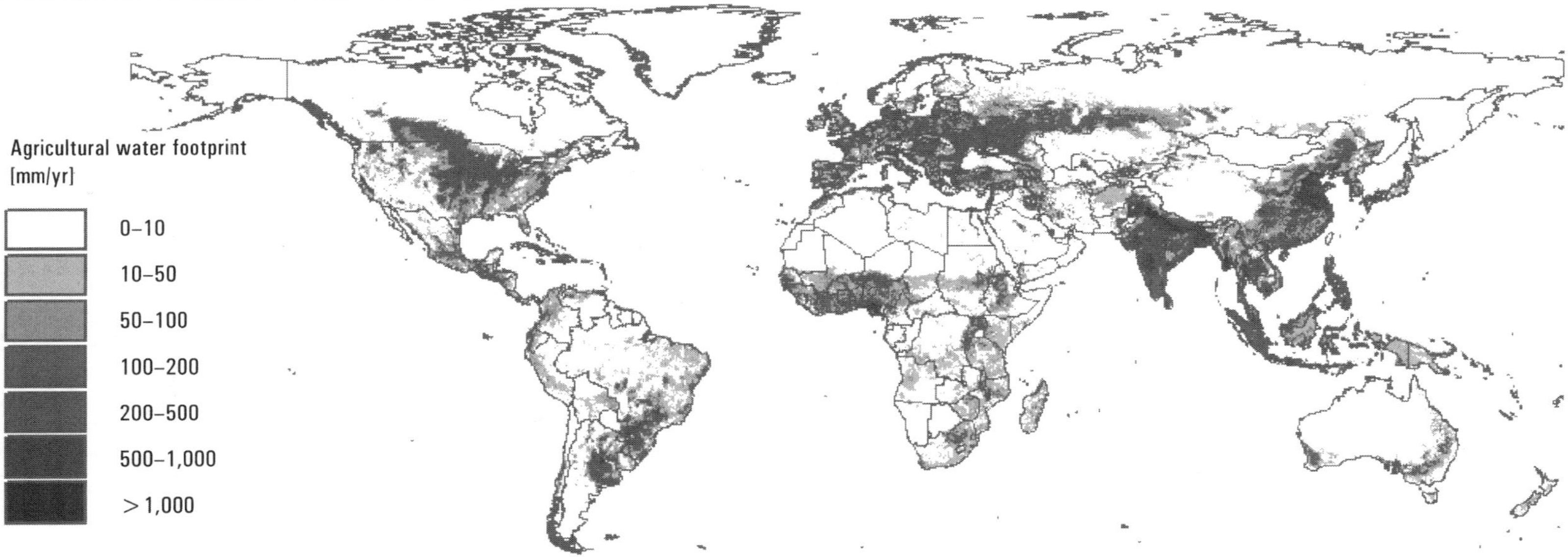

Source: Hoekstra and Mekonnen (2012).

is the highest for UP, Maharashtra, Karnataka, Andhra Pradesh, and MP. This, to some extent, reflects the large size of these provinces. Within India, per 5 arc minute by 5 arc minute grid cell, the water footprint is the highest in the Punjab–Haryana region, as can been seen in Figure 8.

FIGURE 8. Water Footprint of Agricultural Production in India

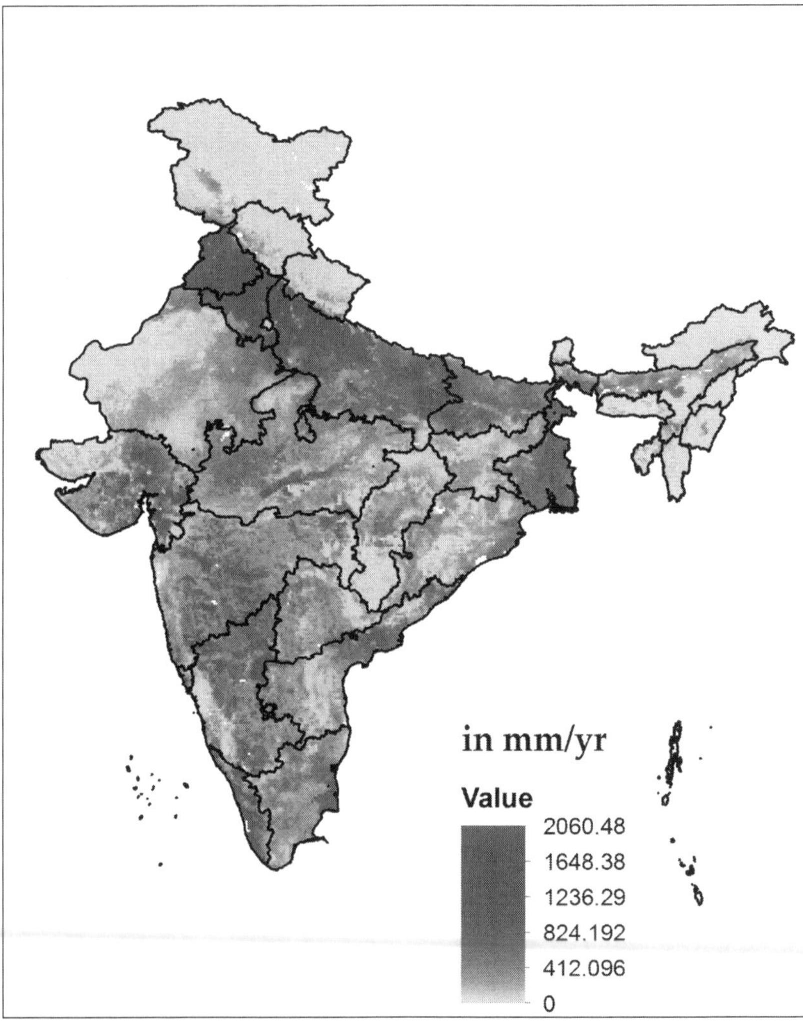

Source: Hoekstra and Mekonnen (2012).

Notes: The map reflects water footprint for every 5 arc minute by 5 arc minute surface of the earth. This is roughly a cell of 100 sq km area.

This map is not to scale and may not depict authentic boundaries.

To understand the trade patterns of water, Goswami and Nishad (2015) estimate water content embedded in crops at the time of trade. This is different from water used in production, which is much higher and partially recoverable. Water "embedded" in crops, on the other hand, is the water content of each crop which, once the crop is exported, cannot be recovered. In 2010, India exported about 25 cu km of water embedded in its agricultural exports. This is equivalent to the demand of nearly 13 million people. India was a net importer of water until the 1980s. With increasing food grain exports, India has now become a net exporter of water—exporting about 1 percent of its total available water every year. The ratio of export to import of virtual water is about 4 for India and 0.1 for China. Thus, China remains a net importer of water.

What might have led to this trading pattern? India's major agriculture exports (by weight or value) are rice and wheat. India exported 11.9 million tons of paddy and 2.9 million tons of wheat in the year 2014–15. In the same year, India's major agriculture import was 4.6 million tons of pulses and 11.5 million tons of edible oils. This pattern has been consistent in the last two decades, ever since the country became self-sufficient in rice and wheat. Since the water content by weight of paddy and wheat is 15 percent whereas that of pulses is 10.5 percent, India's agriculture trade has become a net exporter of water, even as domestic water supplies dwindle.[5]

Thus, India's trade pattern reveals that it is massively over-producing rice and under-producing pulses. The root cause is the distorted relative prices of paddy and pulses, which in this case operates through the MSP. Free (or underpriced) water for irrigation, coupled with a guaranteed MSP for paddy and wheat, incentivizes farmers to overproduce these crops. India's water exports rapidly increased around 1990, coinciding with sharp increases in the MSPs for paddy and wheat (Goswami and Nishad 2015). If prices were to reflect market demand and incorporate the social externalities of water, India's trade pattern in food commodities would reflect the relative scarcities of its natural endowments. If we look at China, for example, which is also a water-scarce country, major imports

5. The water footprint (water required for production) is much higher for pulses (5,354 m^3 per ton) than paddy (~3,000 m^3 per ton). But much of this water is recoverable. In addition, water used for the production of pulses does not use flood irrigation (unlike rice) and comes from closer to the top soil, thereby protecting the water table. The production of pulses also helps fix nitrogen (thereby reducing the consumption of urea). More importantly, the water content in the final grain is 10.5 percent of the weight in pulses, compared to 15 percent in paddy and wheat.

are soybeans, cotton, meat, and cereal grains,[6] and exports are vegetables, fruits, and processed food.

The pernicious consequences of India's MSP policy for water sustainability and availability have been evident for a while, as water tables decline across the country. Analytically, it is important to disentangle the relative roles of MSP and free power and water on declining water tables. In principle, this could be done by comparing regions which have similar water policies but different procurement policies. However, this would require controlling for the underlying bedrock system, which is analytically difficult. Policies meant to help farmers in the short run, such as the MSP for wheat and rice, are having deeply negative long-term consequences for the same farmers, due to the shrinking availability of water. One can argue that both farmers and politicians have high discount rates and are myopic. Hence, they cannot internalize the devastating effects of the MSP in the long run and consequently persist with the current MSP policy. Furthermore, even if this were not the case, high switching costs (from more water-intensive crops to less water-intensive crops) may make them loath to advocate a change in MSP policies. But such an equilibrium persisted for many years in the case of fuel subsidies, and it was eventually addressed by incremental increases in price over a protracted period of time. Under what conditions might something similar be possible in the case of MSP policies is unclear. For instance, what political economy conditions would make it possible to implement annual increases in MSP inversely proportional to the water intensity of the crop, for example, modest increases in MSP for paddy and sugarcane, and more rapid increases in MSP for pulses and oilseeds?

6. The Productivity Gap Puzzle

Geography, availability of natural resources, and endowment of fertile soil make Punjab, Haryana, and the flood plains of the Indo-Gangetic Plain one of the most fertile lands in the world. This can be easily seen in Figures 9 and 10. However, comparing the actual productivity of land in this belt to its own potential raises several important questions.

The Food and Agriculture Organization's (FAO's) Global Agro-Ecological Zones (GAEZ) dataset provides data on actual agricultural

6. See http://www.ers.usda.gov/media/1784488/eib136.pdf and http://www.fao.org/fileadmin/templates/est/meetings/wto_comm/Trade_policy_brief_China_final.pdf

FIGURE 9. Paddy Yields in 2013–14

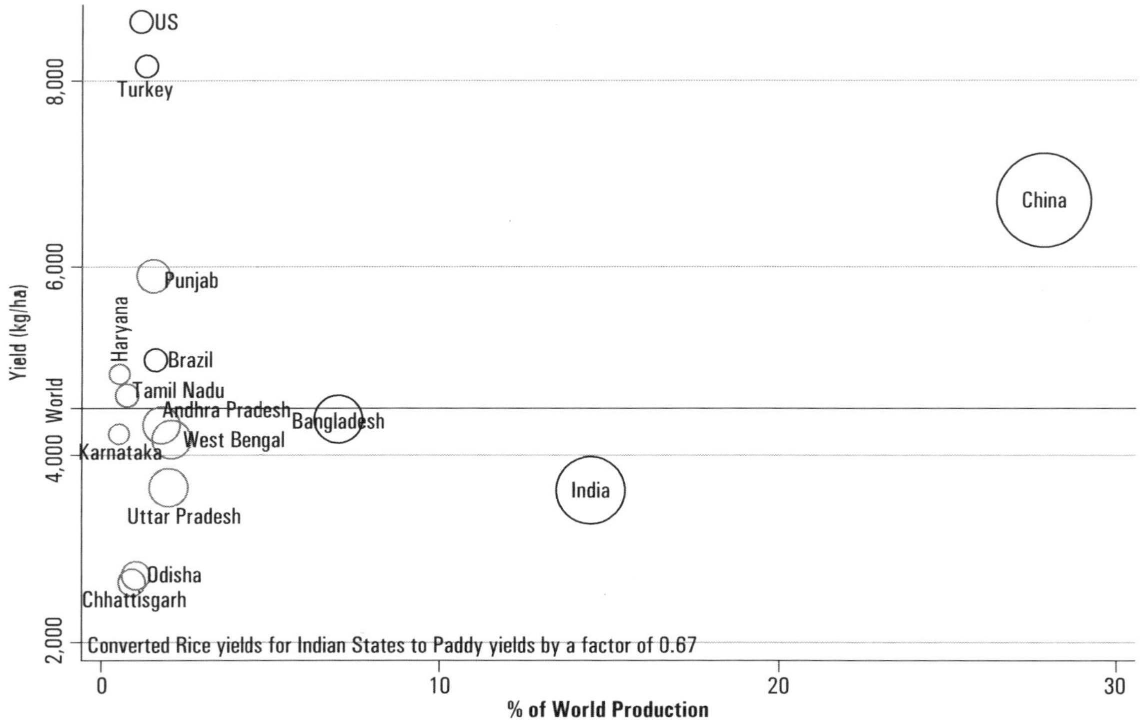

Sources: FAO STAT for the World and Agricultural Statistics at a Glance, 2014, GoI, for India. All estimates for 2014–15.
Note: Size of the bubble is proportional to the quantity of total production in the state/country.

FIGURE 10. Wheat Yields in 2013–14

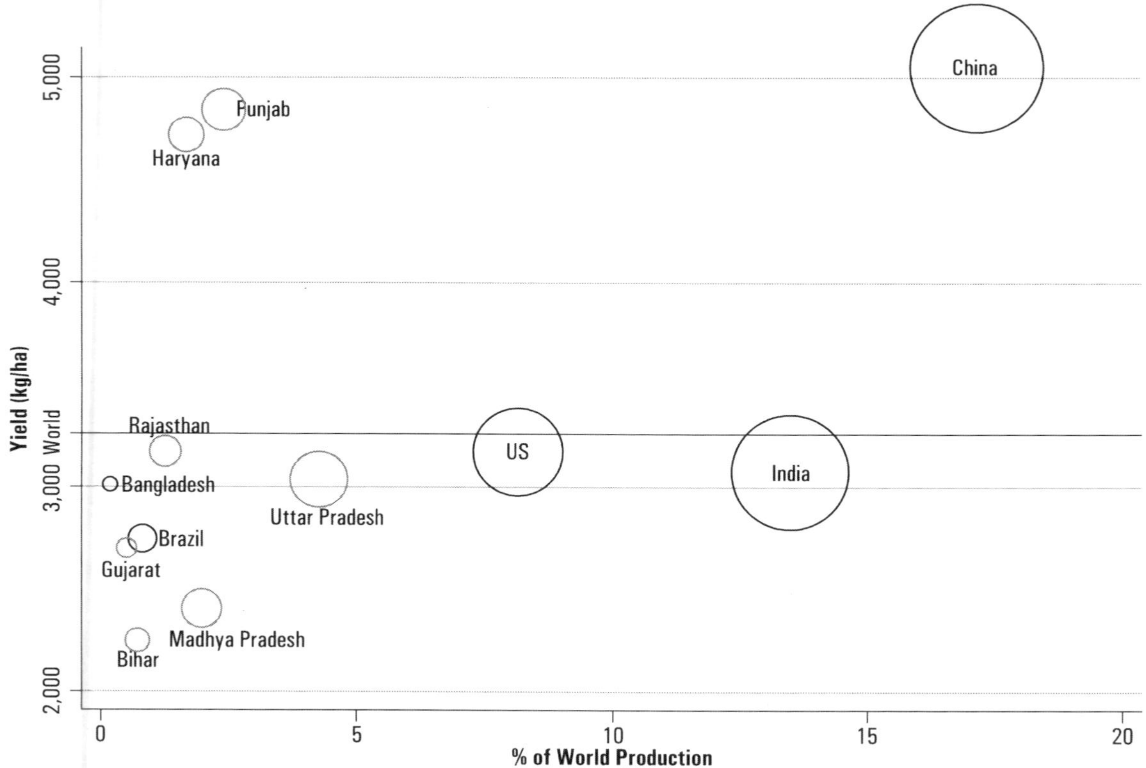

Sources: FAO STAT for the World and Agricultural Statistics at a Glance, 2014, GoI, for India. All estimates for 2014–15.
Note: Size of the bubble is proportional to the quantity of total production in the state/country.

productivity on any piece of land as well as the potential productivity that could be realized if inputs were used optimally, conditional on the crop that is being currently grown there. The data are available for every 5 arc minute by 5 arc minute grid cell of the earth, roughly equal to 10 km by 10 km blocks.

Therefore, if a district in Punjab and another in eastern UP grow paddy, we can estimate their current and potential productivity. Since the potential productivity takes into account the crop choice and local agro-environmental conditions, the gap between actual and potential productivity should only be due to spatially specific distortions. In other words, in the absence of local distortions, all districts should produce at their true potential and there should be no difference between the actual realized and potential productivity.

From the data, however, it is clear that this is not the case. Table 8 notes the fraction of all districts (in percent) whose productivity gap is less than 10 percent, 25 percent, 50 percent, and more than 80 percent for rice, wheat, sorghum, and millet. The productivity gap is calculated as (1 – actual productivity/potential productivity) × 100: if actual productivity was equal to potential productivity, the gap would be zero. The larger the number for the fraction of districts in the < 10 percent productivity gap column, the more India's districts are closer to their true potential for that particular crop.

There are about 27 percent paddy-producing districts and 39 percent wheat-producing districts where the productivity gap is less than 25 percent. Similarly, about 5 percent paddy-producing districts and 6 percent wheat-producing districts have a productivity gap of more than 80 percent. These are the districts with the potential for the largest gains because they are so below their potential. Comparing across crops, whereas in paddy and wheat about 18 percent and 32 percent, respectively, of all districts operate within 10 percent of their potential, this number is starkly low for sorghum (4.2 percent), a dryland crop.

TABLE 8. Distribution of the Agricultural Productivity Gap of Indian Districts

	< 10%	*< 25%*	*< 50%*	*> 80%*
Rice	18.5%	27.3%	62.6%	5.1%
Wheat	31.9%	38.6%	80.9%	5.7%
Sorghum	4.2%	5.0%	6.7%	79.5%
Millet	30.5%	31.5%	34.4%	2.9%

Source: FAO Global Agro-Ecological Zones Database.
Notes: % of districts within × % of their potential.
Productivity gap = (1 – actual productivity/potential productivity) × 100.

What is probably happening is that Punjab, Haryana, and parts of UP are operating close to their potential, and these are the regions that dominate paddy and wheat production and have also been seen to optimize their productivity potential. In other parts of the country, farms are operating far from their productivity potential and there is substantial scope for improvement through better resource allocation alone.

The evidence also strongly suggests that the use of inputs is distorted. Table 9 provides evidence on inter-state variation in the use of nitrogen, phosphorus, and potash per hectare. The proportions in which the fertilizers are used are also skewed. A lower absolute consumption does not necessarily imply that fertilizer use is sub-optimal. The proportions also need to be balanced. While the correct proportions are context-specific, measuring deviations from the accepted rule of thumb of N:P:K in the ratio of 4:2:1 is revealing.

Table 9 also presents deviations from the optimal N:P and N:K ratios (with respect to N). It is clear that fertilizer use is disproportionately tilted toward the use of urea (the principal source of N) as compared to other fertilizers. These distortions—more in N:K than N:P, indicating extremely low application of potash—are significantly higher as compared to those in China, Bangladesh, Vietnam, and Thailand.

Most states use almost twice the amount of nitrogen as compared to phosphorus than they should using the rule of thumb. These include the most productive states such as Punjab, Haryana, UP, and Gujarat. The distortions are less in Maharashtra, Karnataka, and Kerala, which consume close to the optimal ratio, although this could simply be the result of different crop mixes. The overuse of urea as compared to potash is even more perverse. Relative to the accepted rule of thumb, Bangladesh uses only 4 percent more urea than potash, whereas Indian states such as Punjab and Haryana use over 1,300 percent more urea as compared to potash.

Understanding the reason for such large distortions in fertilizer use is important not only because of their impact on current productivity but also because of their impact on future productivity due to their long-term effects on soil health. While the structure of fertilizer subsidies might be the obvious suspect, the fact is that fertilizer subsidies are a national policy, and prices are broadly similar across the country. While variances in fertilizer inputs may be due to varying agricultural production functions, we do not have careful estimates to see if this is the case. It is also important to note that the productivity gap across space is at least in part due to differences in the intensity of use of inputs, but further work is needed to understand why that is the case.

TABLE 9. Fertilizer Consumption and Distortion in Use of Urea (N), Phosphorus (P), and Potash (K), 2014

	Nitrogen (N)(kg/ha)	*Phosphorous (P)(kg/ha)*	*Potash (K) (kg/ha)*	*Total*	*N:P Distortion*	*N:K Distortion*
Delhi	93.33	0	0	93.33		
Nagaland	2.26	1.48	0.72	4.45	-47%	-22%
Mizoram	30.31	2.37	2.99	35.67	1079%	153%
Meghalaya	10.35	3.07	0.8	14.22	137%	223%
Manipur	22.66	3.75	3.18	29.59	404%	78%
Himachal Pradesh	35.03	8.69	9.03	52.74	203%	-3%
Assam	36.24	9.99	19.19	65.41	163%	-53%
Rajasthan	37.97	11.51	0.21	49.69	130%	4420%
Jharkhand	65.72	13.79	2.94	82.45	277%	459%
Thailand	68.4	19.2	22.5	110.2	156%	-24%
Uttarakhand	118.89	19.24	5.67	143.8	418%	424%
Tripura	28.73	21.27	11.73	61.73	-65%	-39%
J&K	57.83	21.87	9.37	89.07	64%	54%
Odisha	63.05	23.71	11.37	98.13	66%	39%
Gujarat	88.52	24.09	6.92	119.52	167%	220%
The United States	74.1	24.8	26.7	125.6	99%	-31%
World	69.5	26.3	17.9	113.7	64%	-3%
Kerala	51.06	26.42	43.55	121.03	-7%	-71%
Bihar	124.88	27.44	12.55	164.87	255%	149%
West Bengal	74.09	28.11	28.97	131.17	64%	-36%
Madhya Pradesh	53.76	28.17	2.5	84.43	-9%	438%
Chhattisgarh	63.08	28.72	8.43	100.22	20%	87%
India	85.79	28.85	10.75	125.39	97%	100%
Uttar Pradesh	115.18	29.63	4.06	148.86	189%	609%
Haryana	146.49	30.58	2.41	179.48	279%	1420%
Tamil Nadu	93.27	33.47	27.03	153.76	79%	-14%
Maharashtra	72.41	35.29	19.37	127.07	5%	-7%
Karnataka	78.37	36.67	21.01	136.06	14%	-7%
Punjab	172.55	41.14	3.04	216.73	219%	1319%
Brazil	42.6	48.8	56.1	147.5	-113%	-81%
Bangladesh	140.7	53.9	33.9	228.5	61%	4%
Andhra Pradesh	153.55	54.32	18.85	226.72	83%	104%
Vietnam	127.5	66.7	43.1	237.3	-9%	-26%
China	267.6	91	41.2	399.8	94%	62%

Source: Agricultural Statistics at a Glance, 2014, Ministry of Agriculture, Government of India.
Note: Distortion is relative to rule of thumb of using N:P:K in the ratios of 4:2:1.

7. The Exit Puzzle

Adamopoulos and Restuccia (2014) document that the typical farm size in the 20 richest countries is 34 times greater than that in the 20 poorest countries. The average farm size in rich countries is 54 hectares, while in poor countries, it is only 1.6 hectares. The median farm size in India is

1.5 hectares, while the mean is much lower. Diego Restuccia, in a series of papers with different co-authors, has estimated the gains of approximately 3 to 4 times in productivity if land is reallocated to the most productive farmers in developing counties such as Malawi, Ethiopia, and China.[7]

A critical reason for the underlying misallocation of land is distortions in land markets. Agricultural land in India is a peculiar asset. Its rental value for farming purposes (a proxy for farming income that may be derived from it) is a fraction of a risk-free stream of income that would accrue from its sale (that is, its capital value), which in turn is a fraction of the price if it is converted to non-agricultural land (for commercial use) if in proximity to an urban area. Yet farmers are reluctant to sell their land. Understanding the effects of these distortions in land markets on agriculture productivity and the reasons why farmers seem reluctant to follow economic logic are two fruitful areas for further research.

There are several potential reasons why agriculturalists may not be exiting farming. First, there might be high opportunity costs of exiting. Figure 11 shows that this is not likely to be the case. Our analysis of NSS data suggests that the average annual income from cultivation of the median farmer (net of production costs) is less than ₹20,000 in 17 states. This includes produce that farmers did not sell valued at local market prices. Given the large wedge between retail and farm gate price, this might underestimate income, but it is still very low. Some farmers who own cattle, for example, might substitute this income with allied-agriculture income. Even then, a vast majority of farmers live very close to the poverty line.

A second—and perhaps key—factor may be the paucity of other livelihood options. India's failure to industrialize has meant that the classic ladder of occupational mobility—from farms to factories, as has been the case with China—has been foreclosed, leaving low-end service jobs in severe urban environments or modest self-employment opportunities as the only options facing someone who exits farming. With 72 percent of India's farms below 1 hectare, the investment required to increase productivity in these tiny farms is unlikely to be readily forthcoming. Exit would allow for land consolidation, and increases in farm size would, in turn, allow for more investments and productivity. But that requires the sort of labor-intensive manufacturing growth that has simply not been taking place. Research on rural–urban linkages in factor and product markets is needed to improve our understanding of its effects on farm productivity.

7. For a comprehensive survey, see Restuccia (2016).

FIGURE 11. Net Annual Income for Indian Farmers in 2012–13

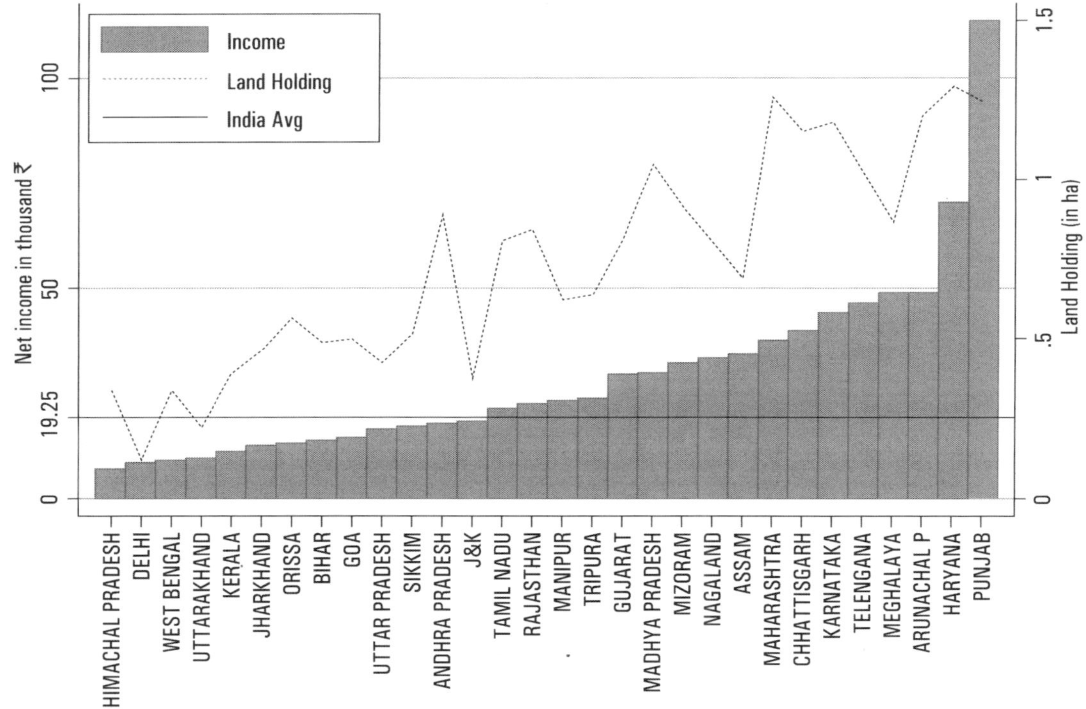

Source: Data frcm NSS SAS Round 70.

Notes: Sample restricted to households surveyed in both Rabi and Kharif. Income only from cultivation net of costs. Unsold produce valued at local market rate.

8. Conclusion and Directions for Future Research

Sectoral policies need to draw on research that is generalizable and offers feasible policy options. Even if the research is micro, it is imperative that we uncover mechanisms that are more general, at least if the goal is to help formulate national level policies. Although the random and quasi-random experimental literature has been insightful, it has its limitations for policy counterfactuals when formulating sector-level policies owing to external validity, general equilibrium effects, and other statistical challenges (Cartwright 2007; Deaton 2010; Deaton and Cartwright 2016; Monte, Redding, and Rossi-Hansberg 2015; Redding and Rossi-Hansberg 2016). Here we illustrate this point with specific examples.

The literature analyzing the effects of information provision has mostly relied on randomization and quasi-randomization techniques and remains inconclusive (Fafchamps and Minten 2012; Goyal 2010; Mitra et al. 2015). First, it is unclear whether the literature suggests traders are already offering competitive prices conditional on trade costs, or whether farmers are unable to utilize this information to improve their bargaining position. Second, the provision of price information seems to "work" in certain regions and not in others, and the literature has not reconciled what underlying factors may explain these differences. Third, we do not know what happens in general equilibrium. For example, once farmers have more information, how do traders respond? Do they exit because their margins shrink? If some traders quit, does that eventually concentrate market power further? Therefore, we do not know the macro-implications of information frictions in the Indian agriculture sector. Consequently, we need studies like Allen (2014) for the Philippines, who, through a more macro-trade approach, found that half of the price dispersion in that country was due to information frictions. This approach, however, requires time series and regionally disaggregated data on (a) cellphone penetration and (b) time series data on efforts made by the government to relay price information to farmers. We tried to obtain this data for India from the Telecom Regulatory Authority of India but were told that this data does not exist.

We know from micro-experiments that traders in some *mandis* of western UP collude (Banerji and Meenakshi 2004, 2008). However, we do not know whether we are likely to find collusion even in other *mandis* and, if so, whether this would necessarily require a similar set of economic factors. This limits generalizability. Furthermore, even when there is collusion within a *mandi*, we do not know if other *mandis* can be a source of competition, and how spatial (distance) or other considerations (for example, transport) would affect the results. The latter channel would be particularly important because that helps us better estimate the welfare effects of new *mandi* construction. Again, this requires studying forces that have been present for some time when the economy is in equilibrium. Introducing random variation in micro-regions could lead us to false conclusions when in reality, the local economy might just be in transition. Moreover, studying spatial competition requires variation of market power in space, which is inherently a macro-problem.

As a final example, consider the policy of making India "one market." This is an important and pivotal policy that the Central Government has been trying to implement through its initiative on the National Agricultural Market. However, the policy has faced severe road blocks from states. Since agriculture is a state subject, implementation requires states to reform their respective APMC Acts. However, for various reasons, states have not been interested and instead appear intent on trying to protect the monopoly power of the *mandis*. There are three points to note here. First, even though this is a critical policy issue with huge potential benefits, there is dearth of academic research (especially in economics).[8] Second, understanding the issue requires unearthing the political economy of the *mandi* structure in the internal politics of the states. Third, general equilibrium counterfactuals that policy makers would be interested in, like changes in economic welfare due to the removal of inter-state trade barriers, require understanding the sources of monopoly power of the *mandis*, how their market power would change once border restrictions are removed and then a model to estimate welfare changes.

A notable exception in the literature is Allen and Atkin (2016). Using four decades of micro-data for the entire country, they find that the creation of highways integrated Indian districts and made farmer revenues more volatile by breaking the negative correlation between local prices and productivity shocks. Increase in farmers' revenue volatility made them switch toward crops with less risky yields. This shift in production amplified the gains from integration for farmers. We can draw many lessons (without having to worry about external validity and missing general equilibrium effects) from such research. For example, greater market integration is likely to negatively impact the production of riskier crops like pulses unless supported with insurance policies. Many more studies of this type are needed to understand the many puzzles and principal challenges facing Indian agriculture.

8. We could only find and cite news articles. As an example, see: http://indianexpress.com/article/business/business-others/farm-marketing-reforms-not-in-name-alone-2884499/ (accessed June 15, 2017).

References

Adamopoulos, T. and D. Restuccia. 2014. "The Size Distribution of Farms and International Productivity Differences," *The American Economic Review*, 104(6): 1667–1697.

Agarwal, S. 2014. "Do Rural Roads Create Pathways out of Poverty? Evidence from India," Unpublished. Santa Cruz: University of California. http://cegadev.org/assets/cega_events/61/3A_Program_Evaluation_in_Developing_Countries.pdf (accessed May 1, 2017).

Allen, T. 2014. "Information Frictions in Trade," *Econometrica*, 82(6): 2041–2083.

Allen, T. and D. Atkin. 2016. "Volatility and the Gains from Trade," *NBER Working Paper 22276*, Cambridge, MA: National Bureau of Economic Research, http://www.nber.org/papers/w22276 (accessed May 1, 2017).

Banerji, A., N. Gupta, and J. V. Meenakshi. 2012. "Auctions in Grain Markets and Farmer Welfare," *Economic and Political Weekly*, 47(52): 65.

Banerji, A. and J. V. Meenakshi. 2004. "Buyer Collusion and Efficiency of Government Intervention in Wheat Markets in Northern India: An Asymmetric Structural Auctions Analysis," *American Journal of Agricultural Economics*, 86(1): 236–253, https://doi.org/10.1111/j.0092-5853.2004.00575.x (accessed May 1, 2017).

———. 2008. "Millers, Commission Agents and Collusion in Grain Markets: Evidence from *Basmati* Auctions in North India," *The BE Journal of Economic Analysis & Policy*, 8(1): 1–25

Cartwright, N. 2007. "Are RCTs the Gold Standard?" *BioSocieties*, 2(1): 11–20.

Chatterjee, S. 2017. "The Tiller's Travails: Borders, Misallocation and Welfare," Princeton University Dissertation (in progress).

Deaton, A. 2010. "Instruments, Randomization, and Learning about Development," *Journal of Economic Literature*, 48(2): 424–455.

Deaton, A. and N. Cartwright. 2016. "Understanding and Misunderstanding Randomized Controlled Trials," *NBER Working Paper 22595*, Cambridge, MA: National Bureau of Economic Research, http://www.princeton.edu/~deaton/downloads/Deaton_Cartwright_RCTs_with_ABSTRACT_August_25.pdf (accessed May 17, 2017).

Fafchamps, M. and B. Minten. 2012. "Impact of SMS-based Agricultural Information on Indian Farmers," *The World Bank Economic Review*, 26(3): 383–414.

Frankel, F. R. 1978. *India's Political Economy, 1947–1977: The Gradual Revolution*. Princeton, NJ: Princeton University Press.

Goswami, P. and S. N. Nishad. 2015. "Virtual Water Trade and Time Scales for Loss of Water Sustainability: A Comparative Regional Analysis," *Scientific Reports*, 5, Article No. 9306.

Goyal, A. 2010. "Information, Direct Access to Farmers, and Rural Market Performance in Central India," *American Economic Journal: Applied Economics*, 2(3): 22–45.

Hoekstra, A. Y. and M. M. Mekonnen. 2012. "The Water Footprint of Humanity," *Proceedings of the National Academy of Sciences*, 109(9): 3232–3237.

Kapur, D. and M. Krishnamurthy. 2014a. "Market Towns and the Dynamics of India's Rural and Urban Transformations," *CASI Working Paper Series 14-02*, http://www.theigc.org/wp-content/uploads/2014/10/Kapur-Krishnamurthy-2014-Working-Paper.pdf (accessed May 1, 2017).

———. 2014b. "Understanding *Mandis*: Market Towns and the Dynamics of India's Rural and Urban Transformations," http://casi.sas.upenn.edu/sites/casi.sas.upenn.edu/files/research/Understanding%20Mandis%20-%20D.%20Kapur,%20M.%20Krishnamurthy.pdf (accessed May 1, 2017).

Krishnamurthy, M. 2011. "Harda Mandi: Experiencing Change in an Agricultural Market in Central India (1980–2010)," PhD Dissertation, University College London, http://discovery.ucl.ac.uk/1333230/ (accessed May 1, 2017).

Li, N. 2016. "Marketization Costs and Household Specialization: Evidence from Indian Farmers," *Macro, Trade, and Finance Seminar Series*, Washington, D.C.: The World Bank.

Mitra, S., D. Mookherjee, M. Torero and S. Visaria. 2015. "Asymmetric Information and Middleman Margins: An Experiment with Indian Potato Farmers," *SSRN Scholarly Paper No. ID 2639972*. Rochester, NY: Social Science Research Network, https://papers.ssrn.com/abstract=2639972 (accessed May 1, 2017).

Monte, F., S. J. Redding, and E. Rossi-Hansberg. 2015. "Commuting, Migration and Local Employment Elasticities," *NBER Working Paper 21706*, Cambridge, MA: National Bureau of Economic Research, http://www.nber.org/papers/w21706 (accessed May 2, 2017).

Olson, M. 1965. *The Logic of Collective Action: Public Goods and the Theory of Groups*. Cambridge, MA: Harvard University Press.

Redding, S. J. and E. Rossi-Hansberg. 2016. "Quantitative Spatial Economics," *NBER Working Paper 22655*, Cambridge, MA: National Bureau of Economic Research, http://www.nber.org/papers/w22655 (accessed May 20, 2017).

Restuccia, D. 2016. "Resource Allocation and Productivity in Agriculture," Mimeo, University of Toronto.

Rudolph, L. I. and S. H. Rudolph. 1987. *In Pursuit of Lakshmi: The Political Economy of the Indian State*. Chicago: University of Chicago Press, http://www.press.uchicago.edu/ucp/books/book/chicago/I/bo5972167.html (accessed May 20, 2017).

Tewari, R. 2015. "Socio Economic & Caste Census 2011: A Mobile in 2 of Every 3 Rural Homes, a Salaried Job in 1 of 10," *The Indian Express*, New Delhi, July 6, http://indianexpress.com/article/india/india-others/socio-economic-caste-census-2011-a-mobile-in-2-of-every-3-rural-homes-a-salaried-job-in-1-of-10/ (accessed May 19, 2017).

Varshney, A. 1995. *Democracy, Development, and the Countryside: Urban-Rural Struggles in India*. New York: Cambridge University Press.

Comments and Discussion*

N. Chandrasekhara Rao
Institute of Economic Growth

Variations in agriculture prices impact the livelihoods of many people in India, as in other countries (Swinnen and Riera 2013). Chatterjee and Kapur employ an innovative methodology to understand these price swings. The existing literature uses structural models that show how prices are determined (see, for example, Gopakumar and Pandit 2014; Gupta 2013). This paper, for the first time, uses high frequency price and quantity data (from the AgMarknet portal of the Government of India), in contrast to the annual data used earlier. This has not been attempted to my knowledge in India, except by Dasgupta, Dubey, and Sathish (2011), and I hope others will follow. The paper tries to develop a general theory of price formation in Indian agriculture and employs advanced econometric tools to control for unobserved heterogeneity. The significance of this paper is in the innovation in the conceptual framework and methodology and the use of high frequency data.

This analysis brings forth some interesting results that can be of immense significance, though some of them can be questioned on the basis of the existing known or stylized facts. There are four key results. First, the variation in prices both within and among states is very high as compared to that in other developing countries. Second, this substantial price variation persists despite the adoption of new information and communication technologies that should have led to price signals converging during the years 2005 to 2014 being studied. This is a cause for concern. The authors have tried to show how much of the variation is due to district-fixed effects and that 39 percent of it is unexplained, which could be attributed to the time- and location-varying factors.

* The paper to which these comments relate was originally presented at the IPF 2016 under the title, "Understanding Price Variation in Agricultural Commodities in India: MSP, Government Procurement, and Agriculture Markets." The version published in the IPF journal is a substantially rewritten paper based on discussant and editorial feedback and hence also the change in title. To preserve the sense of the discussions at the India Policy Forum (IPF), these discussants' comments reflect the views expressed at the IPF and do not take into account the revisions made in preparing the version published in this volume. The original conference version of the paper is available on NCAER's website on http://www.ncaer.org/events/ipf-2016/IPF-2016-Paper-Chatterjee-Kapur.pdf.

Third, a counter-intuitive result is that procurement increases the price of paddy by 4 percent above minimum support price (MSP) while it reduces the price of wheat by 2 percent below MSP. Fourth, the paper finds that lack of marketing infrastructure reduces prices by as much as 5 percent. These could all be important findings against the backdrop of the government's intention to deepen the national agricultural market, but as the authors themselves note, they are also puzzling and difficult to understand. A possible answer might have to do with the much greater international trade after the easing of quantitative restrictions, forcing the Government of India since about 2006 to procure wheat at very high prices in order to build stocks. This was a factor creating a wedge between the MSP, cost of production, and therefore wholesale prices (Chand 2009; Dev and Rao 2010).

I have a wish list of variables that would be useful to consider in the modeling of agricultural price variations and the underlying conceptual framework, not that this would be easy. First, the model could control for the overall growth momentum of the economy, which several studies have argued is percolating to the rural and agriculture sectors (Sharma and Rodgers 2015; World Bank 2014). The NSS data also show the growth of rural non-farm opportunities and the diversification of farm incomes. Second, issues such as lagged incomes, production lags, prices of substitute commodities, productivity differences, may all need to be examined in explaining price formation. As the Economic Surveys have pointed out, variation in taxes across states may also have an important bearing on prices, particularly if they are acting as barriers to free trade.

Third, as soon as agricultural prices rise, the government's first reaction is to ban future markets (Chand 2016). Although the Abhijit Sen Committee found that future markets have no significant impact on agricultural prices, several studies, including Dasgupta, Dubey, and Sathish (2011), suggest that there is a large impact. Fourth, while *mandis* do exist, many offer hardly any physical or marketing facilities. Do price variations have anything to do with this or with the level of regulation? Purohit (2016) recently came up with an index of regulation on which states were ranked. These issues should be looked at in explaining price variations.

States like Chhattisgarh are pursuing a "procurement plus" approach, giving crop-specific bonuses beyond the MSP. What is its impact on price variation and the prices farmers are getting? Market and monopsony power may not merely arise across states but is also seen within states as farmers are not allowed to sell in nearby *mandis* if they are in adjoining states or have to incur a cost even if allowed to sell. As a recent *Economic Survey* of the government points out, there are 2,200 agriculture markets in India; Europe effectively has one market.

Examining the impact of private sector participation and its scaling up on price variation would be very useful for policy. I would also suggest the authors going beyond the exclusive focus on paddy and wheat and considering price formation in other crops, such as vegetables and fruits. Before ending, it is worth mentioning that the geographical concentration of procurement centers is not a puzzle and can be explained by the manner in which the Green Revolution unfolded in India.

References

Chand, Ramesh. 2009. "The Wheat Market: Distortions Caused by Government Interventions," *Economic and Political Weekly,* 44(12): 41–46.

_____. 2016. "e-Platform for National Agricultural Market," *Economic and Political Weekly,* 60(28): 15–18.

Dasgupta, Dipak, R. N. Dubey and R. Sathish. 2011. "Domestic Wheat Price Formation and Food Inflation in India: International Prices, Domestic Drivers (Stocks, Weather, Public Policy), and the Efficacy of Public Policy Interventions in Wheat Markets," *Working Paper 2/2011-DEA*, New Delhi: Department of Economic Affairs, Minister of Finance, Government of India, https://mpra.ub.uni-muenchen.de/31564/1/MPRA_paper_31564.pdf (accessed May 1, 2017).

Dev, S. Mahendra and N. Chandrasekhara Rao. 2010. "Agricultural Price Policy, Farm Profitability and Food Security," *Economic and Political Weekly,* 55 (26 and 27): 174–182.

Gopakumar, K. U. and Vishwanath Pandit. 2014. "Price Movements for Rice and Wheat: A Structuralist Policy Perspective," *Working Paper 240*, New Delhi: Centre for Development Economics, Delhi School of Economics.

Gupta, Neha. 2013. "Government Intervention in Grain Markets in India: Rethinking the Procurement Policy," *Working Paper No. 231*. New Delhi: Centre for Development Economics, Delhi School of Economics.

Purohit, Purnima. 2016. "Measurement of Regulations of the Agricultural Produce Markets," *Economic and Political Weekly,* 60(28): 36–45.

Sharma, Alakh N. and Gerry Rodgers. 2015. "Structural Change in Bihar's Rural Economy: Findings from a Longitudinal Study," *Economic and Political Weekly,* 50(52): 45–53.

Swinnen, J. and O. Riera. 2013. "The Global Bio-economy," *Agricultural Economics,* 44(1s): 1–5.

World Bank. 2014. "Republic of India: Accelerating Agricultural Productivity Growth," *Report No 88093 -IN*, Washington, D. C.: Agriculture, Irrigation and Natural Resources Sustainable Development, South Asia, World Bank, http://hdl.handle.net/10986/18736 (accessed May 1, 2017).

Elumalai Kannan*

Jawaharlal Nehru University

The paper by Shoumitro Chatterjee and Devesh Kapur analyzes the spatial variation in the prices of wholesale rice and wheat at the first point of farmer sale, the primary wholesale markets called *mandis*, and focuses on two important government interventions, the minimum support price (MSP) at which the government procures, and the regulation and physical location of *mandis* and their influence on price formation. The paper uses high frequency data available on the Government of India's AgMarknet portal which provides data on weekly and monthly prices and market arrivals by commodity across all Agricultural Produce Market Committees (APMCs). Since the authors mention that it is work in progress, I will suggest a few important analytical issues to be considered while revising the paper.

Let me start with some data issues and problems in the descriptive analysis of the impact of government procurement on prices and in seeing APMCs that run the *mandis* as local monopsonies.

The authors have selected wholesale rice and wheat markets in 16 major states for their analysis. It is not clear why they have selected these 16 states as not all of them produce rice and wheat, so that in some states there would be limited or no government procurement operations. This could be a factor in the contradictory regression analysis results they get for rice and wheat. Some criteria should have been adopted in selecting states that would adequately capture government interventions in procurement and MSP, and thereafter help in analyzing the impact of market location on wholesale prices. A combination of factors such as the level of production, marketable surplus, and procurement should have been used as the key factors in selecting states.

Why is the selection of states important for addressing the research issues raised in this paper? In the case of rice, 10 states—Andhra Pradesh, Punjab, Chhattisgarh, Odisha, Haryana, West Bengal, Uttar Pradesh, Bihar, Tamil Nadu, and Karnataka—accounted for about 86 percent of India's

* The paper to which these comments relate was originally presented at the IPF 2016 under the title, "Understanding Price Variation in Agricultural Commodities in India: MSP, Government Procurement, and Agriculture Markets". The version published in the IPF journal is a substantially rewritten paper based on discussant and editorial feedback, and hence also the change in title. To preserve the sense of the discussions at the India Policy Forum, these discussants' comments reflect the views expressed at the IPF and do not take into account the revisions made in preparing the version published in this volume. The original conference version of the paper is available on NCAER's website on http://www.ncaer.org/events/ipf-2016/IPF-2016-Paper-Chatterjee-Kapur.pdf.

rice production (Government of India 2016). However, the first five states taken together account for about 80 percent of rice procurement. This will influence the overall results from the sample. Some states in the sample may not even have participated in government rice procurement. Furthermore, even in states where rice procurement takes place, the procurement is not necessarily evenly distributed across all districts and *mandis*. This is because marketable surplus and consumption patterns vary across regions and also within states (Government of India 2016). In the case of wheat, 90 per cent of the production comes from six states—Punjab, Madhya Pradesh, Haryana, Uttar Pradesh, Rajasthan, and Bihar. The first three states account for 91 percent of procurement (Government of India 2016).

These figures imply that procurement taken as a dummy variable in the regression model at the district level will have few ones and many zeroes. This may be the reason why the regression model gives contradictory results for rice and wheat. Local production patterns, marketable surplus, and consumption will affect price formation at the *mandi* level. Production may be high in some places but the entire quantity may not reach the market because local consumption might be very high. For instance, West Bengal is the highest rice-producing state, but its marketable surplus is low (Government of India 2016), and hence the arrival of food grains in the market is an important measure to be considered in thinking about what influences local price formation.

The paper uses an interesting equation to analyze the differential effect of government procurement on market prices. It hypothesizes that procurement operations create a wedge between farm gate, *mandi*, and retail prices. Procurement is a dummy variable, which shows the presence or absence of procurement. Unfortunately, the regression model provides inconsistent results; the coefficient of procurement is positive and significant for rice, while it is negative and significant for wheat. Problems in the data and possible omitted variables may be responsible for this inconsistency. It may be useful to measure the procurement variable in a quantitative form with procurement measured as a ratio of market arrivals, which could have been a better explanatory variable.

The location of *mandis* relative to nearby villages can be important. By design, APMC *mandis* are generally located near *tehsil* (district) headquarters, with jurisdiction over a specific number of villages or a specific geographical area. The AgMarknet portal does not provide complete information about the geographical coverage of *mandis*. So it is not clear how the authors have geocoded villages with *mandis*. It is important to let the readers know this because geocoded villages have been used for the subsequent analysis to understand the degree of competition and the price variation within markets and between markets in neighboring states. Further, it would be useful to provide the number of rice and wheat markets covered across the 16 states in the study. The characteristics of the states and markets selected for analysis will certainly influence the results considerably. In fact, studies have shown that wholesale markets for rice and wheat are integrated to some extent within the states, while integration between regions is not very significant (Acharya et al. 2012; Jha, Bhanu Murthy, and Sharma 2005).

Many studies have analyzed the geographical spread of APMCs, poor infrastructure facilities, problems of marketing inefficiency, and so on (Acharya 2004). I am puzzled to see the paper mention that "the number of *mandis* grew commensurately as the Green Revolution took off, but investments in market infrastructure slackened in more recent decades even as output continued to grow." It is very hard to get investment data on agricultural markets; it is usually not available, and there is no supporting citation in the paper.

The AgMarknet data does provide the stock of infrastructure facilities built across *mandis* and APMCs, and one can build an infrastructure index across the *mandis* and correlate it with market performance indicators such as commodity arrival, number of market participants, timely payment, and so on. Further, the effect of telecommunication technology on spatial variation in price also warrants empirical testing based on field level data.

A major contribution of this paper could be in explaining the factors that contribute to spatial variation in wholesale agricultural prices. However, the decomposition analysis in the paper does not provide many insights and it also needs to be explained in context. There are alternative analytical approaches, such as those followed by Chand (2003) and Liefert (2011), to decompose producer prices with useful results that have a lot of policy relevance.

Figure 8 shows a positive relationship between MSP awareness and procurement, while Figures 9 and 10 show a negative association between procurement and production. As I have noted, procurement need not necessarily be evenly spread across districts and *mandis*. It is quite possible that farmers are aware of the MSP in a few states because of procurement operations taking place in those states. The Food Corporation of India (FCI) has the mandate of procuring a fixed quantity of the grains for buffer stock operations. But when the prices fall below the MSP, some state governments intervene under the market intervention scheme to buy whatever quantity is offered by the farmers. It may be useful to relate procurement to the marketable surplus to understand why some districts have high procurement and others have low procurement. Marketable surplus and market arrivals are highly correlated and tend to influence procurement operations.

There is a strong political economy operating in the food grain procurement. It would be useful to analyze how farmers' lobbies in states such as Punjab and Haryana influence their state governments, who in turn put pressure on the central government to procure whatever quantity and quality the farmers would like to offer in the *mandis*. It would be interesting, for example, to examine quantitatively how the "fair average quality" specifications against which the FCI procures grain has been tweaked periodically under the influence of these state governments. Taking these considerations into account in the analysis would enrich the discussion on the political economy of grains procurement.

The functioning of APMCs has been a subject matter of intense debate in recent years for reasons such as poor service delivery, lack of adequate infrastructure, high transaction cost, and collusion among traders (Acharya 2004). With the implementation of a Model APMC Act in 2003, many states have amended their state agricultural marketing acts to facilitate greater transparency, freedom to sell outside the *mandi*, establishment of private markets, and so on. With the push toward greater liberalization of domestic markets, APMCs can no longer be considered local monopsonies. Despite the introduction of market reforms, collusion among traders continues to exist, which tends to affect the efficient price discovery in the markets (for details of the effects of collusion, see Banerji and Meenakshi 2004).

In the paper, the authors maintain that there is collusive behavior among traders within the *mandis*, but assume the absence of such collusion between the markets. With improvements in telecommunications, it is difficult to assume that the traders do not collude between markets, and a potential problem in the formulation of an econometric model to explain price variations through local market power and distance to the *mandi*. Further, dense markets need not necessarily result in better prices for farmers.

To conclude, this is a very interesting paper. However, there is much that can be done to improve its analytical approach. There is also need to discuss the policy implications of the results for the current debate on shifting away from price support to an income support policy for farmers. It would also be useful to throw light on the unified National Agriculture Market and its likely impact on farmers' income and variation in prices.

References

Acharya, S. S. 2004. *Agricultural Marketing, Volume 17, State of the Indian Farmer: A Millennium Study*, New Delhi: Academic Foundation.

Acharya, S. S., R. Chand., P. S. Birthal, S. Kumar, and D. S. Negi. 2012. "Market Integration and Price Transmission in India: A Case of Rice and Wheat with Special Reference to the World Food Crisis of 2007/08," Rome: Food and Agriculture Organisation.

Banerji, A. and J. V. Meenakshi. 2004. "Buyer Collusion and Efficiency of Government Intervention in Wheat Markets in Northern India: An Asymmetric Structural Auctions Analysis," *American Journal of Agricultural Economics*, 86(1): 236–253.

Chand, R. 2003. "Government Intervention in Food Grain Market in the New Context," *Policy Paper 19*, New Delhi: National Centre for Agricultural Economics and Policy Research.

Government of India. 2016. *Agricultural Statistics at a Glance 2015*, New Delhi: Directorate of Economics and Statistics, Ministry of Agriculture and Farmers Welfare.

Jha, R., K. V. Bhanu Murthy and A. Sharma. 2005. "Market Integration in Wholesale Rice Markets in India," *ASARC Working Paper 2005/03*, Canberra: The Australia South Asia Research Centre, Australian National University.

Liefert, W. M. 2011. "Decomposing Changes in Agricultural Producer Prices," *Journal of Agricultural Economics*, 62(1): 119–136.

General Discussion*

Sandip Sukhtankar asked the authors to explain their finding on variance decomposition that suggested that rainfall shocks contributed only about 4 percent to price variation, since rainfall shocks were used as an instrument for basically all kinds of regressions in India.

Rajnish Mehra asked if the formation of *mandis* was actually not endogenous, since the paper had found that every additional *mandi* led to a higher

* The paper to which these comments relate was originally presented at the IPF 2016 under the title, "Understanding Price Variation in Agricultural Commodities in India: MSP, Government Procurement, and Agriculture Markets". The version published in the IPF journal is a substantially rewritten paper based on discussant and editorial feedback, and hence also the change in title. To preserve the sense of the discussions at the India Policy Forum, these discussants' comments reflect the views expressed at the IPF and do not take into account the revisions made in preparing the version published in this volume. The original conference version of the paper is available on NCAER's website on http://www.ncaer.org/events/ipf-2016/IPF-2016-Paper-Chatterjee-Kapur.pdf.

price: if the prices fell in some region, *mandis* would come up there and raise prices, which would then tend to limit price dispersion. Second, he said that futures markets were among the most efficient in the US, and wondered if they were actually quite efficient in India as well. Mehra pointed to the tight links between storage costs, current prices, spot prices, and futures prices, implying that arbitrage would clear markets whenever an opportunity arose. He felt that what the paper was observing had more to do with regulation and institutional factors. If there was free entry of *mandis*, and well-operating futures markets, one would still get a certain dispersion in prices. Properly anticipated prices do fluctuate randomly, and in stock markets the rule of thumb is a standard deviation in prices of about 20 percent, and a little less in bond markets, mainly to do with the arrival and processing of information.

Dilip Mookherjee first noted that procurement is endogenous, so that the paper's finding that wheat prices go down with higher procurement may simply be procurement kicking in when prices are low. So procurement itself should be a primary topic of analysis. The paper looks at spatial variation in the levels of prices, but the huge list of omitted variables—distance, storage facilities, transport costs, and so on—makes that not very credible. Much better to look at the spatial variation in price *changes* over time. Industrial organization and international finance provide nice methodologies that can help gauge market imperfections by looking at the covariation of prices across locations rather than in the level of prices. Transport costs and storage costs may still move in tandem with other factors such as oil prices, bur the level of omitted variable bias would be much less.

Second, Mookherjee noted that while the paper was focusing on spatial variation between *mandis*, his work on agriculture in West Bengal suggested that there was huge price variation within *mandis*. And if one was interested in the prices farmers got, then his work had revealed that the farm gate price was less than half the *mandi* price, and only about 20 percent of this gap was accounted for by transportation and storage costs. The rest was margins going to traders who buy from farmers and sell in the *mandi*s. When you look at the pass through, *mandi* prices co-vary very closely with retail prices, but farm gate prices do not. Hence, the real imperfections seem to be within the *mandis*, rather than between *mandis*.

Third, while Mookherjee agreed that competition is a key issue for APMCs, going into questions—such as the desirable number of *mandis* and competition between them—raised in the paper entail very complicated cost-benefit analysis since we know so little about the cost of creating markets. What would be much easier to do would be to focus on regulation and competition within *mandis*: for example, who has access to the *mandis*? He cited the very interesting ethnographies that Mekhala Krishnamurthy and Jeffrey Witsoe had done that showed the differences between Madhya Pradesh and Bihar, and the role that politics played in the working of *mandis*. He felt therefore that more work needed to be done on the politics of procurement.

Karthik Muralidharan commented that researchers can write two types of papers: a "dependent variable" paper, where the authors discuss a left-hand-side variable they care about and just document the facts and evidence about outcomes in that variable, without making any causal claims. Or they could write a "right-hand-side variable" paper and pin down the identification of one causal factor, even if it cannot explain much of the variation. Currently, the paper was struggling between the two types, and ending up not doing either satisfactorily. The paper could perhaps be more of the first kind, an agenda-setting paper for research, as opposed to one seeking to answer questions about causality, where it runs into a lot of problems with omitted variables. Since the authors have chosen price variation as a theme, they could concentrate on documenting the facts about this, including variation within states, within districts, and within other tiers for which data exists. The paper could then set out proximate right-hand-side variables that might help explain the price variations at different levels, and provide a road map for future research.

Mekhala Krishnamurthy said that there was no question about private sector buyers entering into the markets since they have been there for a very long time. Everybody in the *mandi* is a private actor, except for the government that is procuring. From her ethnographic work, she reported that it does not help the analysis if we think of the private sector as only corporate commercial entities buying outside *mandis*, because large corporates like ITC or Cargill are wherever they choose to be, buying directly from farmers through commission agents with a license, entering *mandis*, using their own single market yards, and entering the futures market. They employ diversified buying strategies. So thinking of them as suddenly entering a market is a bit of a misunderstanding of these markets.

Again, based on her work in Madhya Pradesh and Chhattisgarh, Krishnamurthy pointed to the interesting temporal and seasonal variation in prices for crops that the government procures, and for others that it doesn't, and how competition between *mandis* comes in. The government bought wheat in Madhya Pradesh and Chhattisgarh only in the immediate post-harvest season, and at topped-up bonus prices. This affected prices in the off-season. In the market procurement season, all the *mandis* bought at about the same price, but in the off season, when there was no procurement effect, prices varied. Competition between *mandis* became much more important in the off season, with *mandis* with greater access to flour mills offering higher prices due to the higher offtake than the other *mandis*. In sharp contrast to wheat, in soybean, where there was no government procurement, farmers staggered their sales across the year, effectively hedging for higher prices. There are also interesting instances of possible natural experiments when *mandis* switch licensing or auctioning procedures that could be used to study how competition works: she cited the example of the Gulbarga *mandi*.

Karthik Muralidharan followed up by noting that this showed how important it was to understand the behavior of intermediaries because most of the farmers were not directly selling to the *mandis*.

Indira Rajaraman asked a question about how the authors had dealt with spatial variation in *mandi* fees and taxes, since these revenues don't accrue to the consolidated fund but are supposed to be used locally for improving market infrastructure.

Rohini Somanathan referred to a 1971 paper by the British historian E. T. Thomson, called "The Moral Economy of the Crowd in the 18th Century", which talks about a period when people were protesting the rapid rise in grain prices in England. This was because not enough grain was coming on to the markets due to the signing of forward contracts for grain exports to America with farmers selling the grain before it was harvested. Thomson's paper talked about people blocking grain wagons and forcing sales in the spot market in protest against the violation of laws that stipulated the bringing of all produce to the market after harvest. All this suggested how important it was to model the choice set of the farmer and the different actors involved. But given how complex that could be, it would be hard to come up with a causal story. Rather than looking for causality, she suggested simpler approaches looking at prices and quantities, so that if both were going down then it was a demand effect, and if only prices were going down then it was a supply effect. Using such simpler approaches would still lead to a very provocative paper, even if it did not address causality.

Rajesh Chadha noted that state governments impose different levies on rice, and asked if this had been taken into consideration in looking at price variations. In recent years, in some states procurement had been decentralized to state agencies, with FCI buying from these agencies. He wondered if this had been taken into account in looking at price variation.

The Chair Ramesh Chand concluded by congratulating both authors for taking the research on agriculture marketing in India to a higher level since most other studies were largely descriptive and not analytical, and they did not use quantitative techniques. However, in light of the points made by discussants and participants he suggested using different data sets since the AgMarknet data may not be entirely appropriate. The key question in the paper, as he saw it, was whether government procurement prevented the market price from falling below MSP, i.e., what was the impact of procurement on price variations. The troubling aspect of the paper was that it seemed not to matter for wheat, but mattered for rice. He suggested looking at surplus markets (with procurement) and deficit markets (with little procurement) separately, with procurement keeping prices at MSP only in surplus areas. Wheat prices in the harvest season in the deficit districts of Maharashtra invariably did not fall below MSP even in the months of April and May but they did fall below MSP in Uttar Pradesh. Therefore, procurement affected prices only in surplus districts and not in deficit districts.

Second, Chand emphasized that procurement mattered for prices only in the harvest season. During the lean season, prices were generally half the MSP; otherwise arbitrage would not take place. If after the harvest grain was bought from Punjab and Haryana, market charges would be 14 percent, plus loading and unloading and transport charges, so that there would be a price spread. He referred to a 2003 study by the National Centre for Agricultural Economics and Policy Research that had nicely calculated the normal price spread between a surplus state and a deficit state over all the 12 months of the year by taking into account transportation costs, marketing costs, and normal profit margins for intermediaries.

Chand suggested the use of the farm harvest price rather than the market price when comparing with MSP. Farm harvest prices were available district-wise for major production areas and referred to a particular period, not all the months of a year. Using market prices could be misleading. The market price spread for wheat could be much higher in Punjab than in a deficit state since lean season prices in the latter would in any case be generally higher.

He pointed to a large number of studies, many by Raghavendra Jha, on India's agriculture markets, and Jha's conclusion that wholesale markets were integrated across India and had developed to a point that precluded the need for government intervention.

Finally, Chand advised extreme caution in the use of NSSO data for situation assessments, rich and reliable as the data was for household consumption expenditures and employment. For instance, the NSSO data quoted in Table 1 in the paper suggested that the highest figures for the percentage of wheat and paddy sold by farmers to government agencies was somewhere between the numbers for small and large agricultural holdings of 11 percent and 4 percent, respectively. But, it is a well-known fact that at least 30 percent of paddy and 35 percent of wheat was procured by the government. This clearly highlighted the serious limitations with NSSO data, which is why he felt the authors needed to utilize data from other sources.

SANDIP SUKHTANKAR*
University of Virginia

India's National Rural Employment Guarantee Scheme: What Do We Really Know about the World's Largest Workfare Program?†

ABSTRACT In the ten years since the rollout of India's National Rural Employment Guarantee Scheme (NREGS), there has been much research on its implementation and impact. This paper attempts to synthesize knowledge from the vast array of studies. I present four key takeaways. First, there is large heterogeneity in implementation, with consequences for not only where impact is seen, but also for interpreting what "the scheme" entails. Second, the "Guarantee" in the title is a misnomer, as access is rationed. Third, NREGS seems to have increased rural private sector wages, but has led to worse educational outcomes for older children, with net positive impacts on income and welfare that are debated. Fourth, key questions pertaining to overall impacts on rural productivity remain unanswered. Although serious research on these questions is badly needed, current standards for causal inference and the availability of data will remain high hurdles for those who wish to take on this challenge.

Keywords: *NREGS, MGNREGA, NREGA, Workfare, India, Rural Employment Guarantee Scheme, Rural Wages*

JEL Classification: *H53, I38, J08, J38, J45, J68, O29*

1. Introduction

It has now been ten years since the first workers were employed in the schemes launched by the Mahatma Gandhi National Rural Employment

* sandip.sukhtankar@virginia.edu

† I thank Clement Imbert, Karthik Muralidharan, and Shekhar Shah for helpful discussions, the discussants, Rinku Murgai and Surjit Bhalla, the session chair, Amarjeet Sinha, as well as the IPF 2016 audience for comments, and Michael Kaiser, Kevin Li, Frances Lu and Katherine McAvoy for excellent research assistance.

Guarantee Act (MGNREGA).[1] MGNREGA entitles every adult member of a rural household the legal right to 100 days of minimum-wage employment per year, to be provided within 15 days of asking for it. The state-level public employment schemes required by MGNREGA—collectively referred to as the National Rural Employment Guarantee Schemes (NREGS)—comprise the largest workfare program in the world. The program has spawned various monikers—"landmark", "flagship"—as well as justifiable attention from policymakers, politicians, and academics in India and abroad.

Yet, despite this attention, and reams of research and opinion on the program, there is still enormous debate over the impact of NREGS. Supporters have hailed the program as a "tremendous success", while opponents have derided it as an "expensive gravy train".[2] While these descriptions were coined in the early years of the program, the debate is still quite active: for example, last year witnessed a vigorous debate played out in the print media between groups of social scientists.

This paper synthesizes knowledge based on serious theoretical and empirical research on NREGS, and presents avenues for future research. What complicates this task is the vast array of studies on NREGS, of varying quality, on almost every imaginable outcome and aspect of the program. This leads to what I facetiously call (with apologies to Newton) the "third law of NREGS": *every result has an equal and opposite result.* While it is heartening to see the attention given to this important program, the volume of work makes it impossible for the casual reader to ascertain which direction the weight of evidence points to; finding a citation to bolster your favored opinion of the program is easy. One of the main goals of this article is hence to guide the reader in weighing the evidence on various aspects of the program. In addition, where results seem to contradict each other, I attempt to reconcile them based on differences in data, sample, or methodology. I aim to be clear about whether the evidence is anecdotal or representative, and whether it is merely correlational or causal.

1. MGNREGA or NREGA or NREGS—which is correct? Technically the National Rural Employment Guarantee Act (NREGA)—ex post renamed the Mahatma Gandhi National Rural Employment Guarantee Act (MGNREGA)— is a piece of legislation that created an entitlement to rural employment, which was to be fulfilled by state-level schemes, collectively referred to as National Rural Employment Guarantee Schemes (NREGS). But so that no one, including myself, is confused about which program is being referred to in this paper, I refer to these acronyms interchangeably. I will attempt to use MGNREGA when referring to the Act and NREGS when referring to the actual implementation of the schemes.

2. These terms were noted in the following 2008 Op-ed in the *Hindu* newspaper by Jean Dreze, http://www.thehindu.com/todays-paper/tp-opinion/Employment-guarantee-beyond-propaganda/article15141615.ece.

Digging through the mound of literature, some clarity emerges. I present four key takeaways:

1. First, almost every single empirical paper points out the large heterogeneity in implementation of NREGS. While this point may seem obvious, there are two nuances that are perhaps not so obvious. The heterogeneity means that much of the impacts are seen only in the better implementing states; even impacts, on average, are driven largely by the "star" implementing states. Even less obvious is the point that with these implementation issues, what exactly one is measuring the impact of is unclear. In other words, the "impact of the program" is not really a logical construct; empirical studies are basically estimating the effects of the program combined with varying implementation quality.
2. Second, there is widespread agreement that despite the legal guarantee, on-demand employment is simply not available. Even in the best implementing states, access is rationed, even for the poorest. To what extent this matters is unclear; for example, if most of the demand would have been during the slack labor season, and this is the season in which NREGS operates, then the harm from rationing may be limited. On the other hand, the poorest states, where the need for the program is the greatest, seem to lack the capacity to implement NREGS.
3. Third, there are at least two outcomes that the bulk of the evidence suggests that NREGS impacts. Rural private sector wages seem to have increased modestly as a result of NREGS. On the other hand, this increase in wages may have led to worse educational outcomes for older children, as the opportunity cost of attending school has now gone up. A number of pieces of evidence indicate that incomes may have increased, but this evidence is not as strong and universal as the previous two outcomes.
4. Fourth, despite the passage of ten years, despite much attention from researchers, and despite access to data and transparency measures that are unprecedented for India, there are still large unanswered questions. Perhaps the most important questions—related to NREGS' effects on productivity—remain contested. This is perhaps why there is still so much debate over the impacts of the program.

Why have researchers not been able to provide definitive answers to the big questions? It is a non-trivial task to identify the effects of a large program, particularly given the non-random rollout and current high standards for causal inference. Complications arise in view of implementation problems and the consequent heterogeneity in implementation, and in particular, identifying mechanisms demands even more from data and empirical methods. Moreover, even though data access reflects a vast improvement over other programs—compare, for example, the tiny handful of papers published on the Public Distribution System (PDS) in top social science journals versus the proliferation of similar quality papers in just ten years of the NREGS—problems still remain. For example, even obtaining consistent data over time on the basic aspects of the program for this paper has proven far more difficult than expected, with conflicting sources that are not easy to reconcile.

Finally, how exactly one measures the standard for the success of a program like NREGS is open to debate. For example, in the case of educational interventions, rupees spent per standard deviation increase in test scores might be one reasonable standard. In the NREGS case, however, there is likely disagreement over outcomes: should income, poverty, welfare, distress migration, insurance be counted? Further, what is the benchmark comparison? A natural benchmark might be cash transfers (Murgai and Ravallion 2005); however, we probably know even less about the government's ability to target and deliver these payments as well as the potential cost-effectiveness of these alternatives.

The roadmap for the rest of the paper is as follows. Before delving into details on the impact of NREGS, I provide some background for the reader who is not well versed with the intricacies of the program. Section 2 begins with salient features of MGNREGA, including the main provisions and guidelines laid down by the Act. This section also includes basic figures and numbers to give the reader a sense of the size of the program, its growth over time, and its reach across space and sectors of the population.

In Section 3, I describe how the program has actually been implemented on the ground or the "schemes" as distinct from the "Act". I begin by highlighting the incredible heterogeneity in implementation across states and districts, a fact that every interpretation of each empirical study of NREGS must take into account. This heterogeneity exists in key features of implementation such as access, the efficiency of payments, corruption, and other dimensions of implementation such as worksite facilities and choice of projects.

Section 4 lays out conceptual frameworks for understanding the impact of NREGS. I begin by presenting the basic theoretical underpinnings for the program, as well as the main theoretical mechanisms for impacts on various outcomes that have been studied by researchers. Following this, I present the main empirical strategies that have been used to identify the impacts of NREGS, laying out the pros and cons of each.

In Section 5, I discuss empirical studies of the impact of NREGS on major outcomes such as wages and employment, income, education, migration, agricultural technology and investment, and conflict. For each outcome, I attempt not only to summarize the existing evidence but also resolve the direction that the best evidence points to. The survey of the literature aims to be comprehensive, but in order to make the task manageable, this paper includes papers based on objective criteria on sample selection, sample size, and identification strategy that are defined below.[3]

Despite the large amount of research on MGNREGA, there are still areas that are under-studied. I highlight these areas about which we still know very little in Section 6. Finally, Section 7 concludes with some speculation about the future of the program.

2. Background

MGNREGA was passed by Parliament and notified in 2005, following up on an electoral promise made by the United Progressive Alliance (UPA, a coalition led by the Congress party) after it came into power in 2004. Schedule I of the Act lays out its basic provisions. The employment guarantee schemes mandated by the Act became operational in the 200 "poorest" districts in the country in February 2006.[4] An additional 130 districts received the program in April and May 2007, while the program became operational in the remaining districts of the country in April 2008. Below I describe the main provisions of the Act, and the following sub-section provides some basic numbers and figures.

2.1. MGNREGA Provisions and Rules

While most readers familiar with MGNREGA know that the Act establishes a legal guarantee of a 100 days of employment, there are many other provisions

3. Papers published in major economics, political science, and development studies journals are automatically included. However, given the long delay in the publication process for these journals, there are numerous excellent pieces of research that exist only as working papers as of now; by using the criteria, I hope to have included as many of these as yet unpublished papers.

4. In Section 4, I describe in greater detail how these districts were chosen.

of the Act as well as official guidelines that are less well-known.[5] The fourth and most recent edition of the MGNREGA operational guidelines produced by the Ministry of Rural Development is a rather detailed 232-page document listing workers' rights and procedures to be followed by the implementing agencies. This comprehensive document does not preclude the production of other ad-hoc documents with procedures.[6]

Logistical challenges and deviations from these guidelines are to be expected given the current level of implementation capacity across India. I discuss these implementation issues in Section 3. The current section is, however, devoted to documenting the provisions of the Act on paper, which I categorize into basics, projects, finances, administration, and monitoring.

2.1.1. Basics

To begin with, the 100-day guarantee established by the Act applies at the household level for rural households in a financial year. Households are required to obtain job cards from local government offices, which list all adult members of the household and have space for recording work done and payments received. Once the job card is obtained, households are supposed to apply for work whenever they need it. The local administration must provide employment within 15 days and within 5 kilometers of the applicant's home, failing which the applicant is to be paid unemployment allowance (for non-provision of work within 15 days) or a travel and subsistence allowance (if work is available only beyond 5 kilometers).

While in general, the work involves doing manual unskilled labor and pays minimum wages, there are provisions for other types of work that can pay slightly higher wages (for example, supervisors at job sites). However, 60 percent of the expenditure incurred on the program must be spent on wages. In addition, 33 percent of the jobs must be reserved for women, and women are guaranteed the same wages as men (which is not de facto true in the private sector, thus making NREGS more valuable for women). Finally, wages are to be paid weekly, and no later than a fortnight of the work being done.

5. For example, a little known feature that may be of interest to researchers is the fact that the Government invites proposals for studies on MGNREGA, and will pay for them! See http://nrega.nic.in/Circular_Archive/archive/Guideliness_Research_Studies_under_MGNREGA.pdf.

6. For example, "Guidelines for Construction of Play Ground in IAP Districts". See http://nrega.nic.in/GUIDELINES_CONST_IAP.pdf for more details.

2.1.2. Projects

Projects taken up under NREGS are typical of public employment schemes, and include the construction of public goods such as roads and irrigation channels. One of the major goals of MGNREGA is related to water management, with both drought-proofing and flood management being priority projects. Projects are meant to be chosen by the Gram Sabha, or the full meeting of the village, in consultation with the block and district administration. This process is supposed to produce a roster of projects in advance of the financial year that can be taken up as demand dictates.

It is also possible for NREGS work to take place on private land, if the land is owned by people belonging to Scheduled Castes/Scheduled Tribes (SC/ST). For example, clearing of land for cultivation is a common such activity in order to provide livelihoods to the most disadvantaged groups. In any type of project, there are also supposed to be provisions for worksite facilities such as drinking water, shade, and a crèche for workers' children.

2.1.3. Finance and Payments

In order to incentivize States to generate employment, the Central Government pays all labor costs fully, but only 75 percent of the material costs. Since wage rates are set by States in order to adjust to local conditions, this feature also incentivizes States to increase wage rates, and has been a bone of contention between the Central and State governments since the inception of the Act. Workers may be paid either a daily wage rate or piece rates depending on the amount of work done.

Initially, payments were made in cash by the same administrative bodies in charge of implementation. However, the most recent guidelines explicitly call for payments to be made to the workers' bank or post office accounts, and also for separation between the implementing and payment officials. Cash payments are still possible, particularly in areas in which bank or post office branches are inaccessible, although according to the rules, administrative bodies must obtain prior permission to make such payments.

2.1.4. Administration

Given that the Act explicitly states that Gram Panchayats (GPs)—the lowest administrative tier of the Indian bureaucracy—must implement at least 50 percent of the works in terms of cost, MGNREGA has advanced the legitimization of GPs as state actors. The GP is in charge not only of implementing works, but also of keeping records (particularly "muster roles" of work attendance and payments) and transmitting them to higher levels of administration. In these tasks, the GP is assisted by a wider array of local officials, some of whose positions were specifically created by the Ministry of Rural Development to assist with MGNREGA. These include the *Gram Rozgar Sahayak* or Employment Guarantee Assistant, Mates or worksite supervisors, Field Assistants, Technical Assistants to measure and monitor the work, Computer Assistants to maintain, update, and transmit records,[7] in addition to the elected officials (for example, *Sarpanch*) and appointed officials (for example, GP Secretary), who are in overall charge of the program.

The Block and District level administrations are meant to support and assist the GP in implementation, as well as implementing some work directly through line departments (for example the irrigation department). These entities are meant to have Program Officers in charge of MGNREGA implementation. These officials approve work plans, and in some cases also budgets, although this provision may be changing.

2.1.5. Monitoring

MGNREGA is unusual among large welfare programs in creating provisions for transparency and monitoring from the outset. The Monitoring and Information System (MIS) gives anyone with an Internet connection unprecedented access to official records of works and payments. It relies on custom-built and sophisticated software—NREGASoft—to document every aspect of the program electronically, with the updated operational guidelines including detailed instructions on how to enter information into the software.

District and state administrations are required to audit the works and expenses of GPs and blocks. In addition, "social audits" are meant to be performed once every six months in order to ensure accountability as per Rule 4 of Audit of Schemes Rules, 2011. These involve public verification of muster rolls and other expenditure in a Gram Sabha, and can involve workers as well as civil society organizations. The audits are also meant to be a platform for workers to air grievances.

2.2. Figures and Numbers

NREGS is a large program by any account. Over 121 million rural job cards had been registered for the program as of 2014 (Figure 1), which would amount to practically all of India's rural population if each household had only one job card, although that is likely not the case.[8] The total number of

7. Every GP does not necessarily have each of these officials; for example, the Technical Assistant and Computer Assistant are generally based at the block level.

8. Calculations by Muralidharan et al. (2016a) suggest 1.9 job cards per NSS-defined household in Andhra Pradesh in 2011–12.

FIGURE 1. NREGS Jobcards

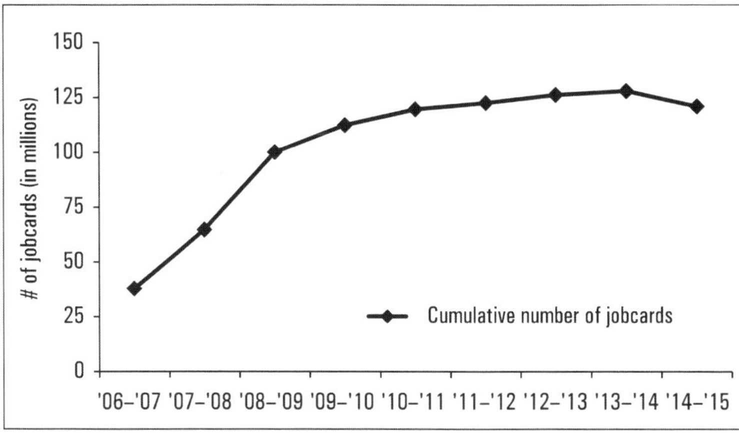

Source: Ministry of Rural Development, Government of India.

person days on the program in 2013–14 was 2.20 billion, which is actually a drop from the peak of 2.83 billion in 2009–10 (Figure 2). Nearly 48 million individuals actually worked on the program in 2013–14, belonging to 24.4 percent of rural households (Desai et al. 2015).

FIGURE 2. Person Days Worked on NREGS

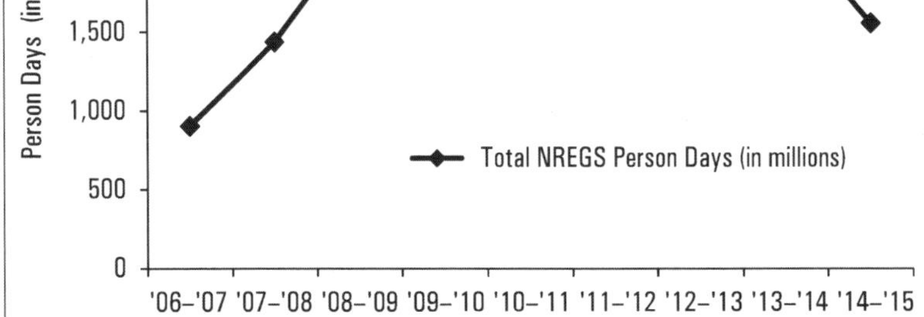

Source: Ministry of Rural Development, Government of India.

FIGURE 3. **Person Days: Women and SC/ST**

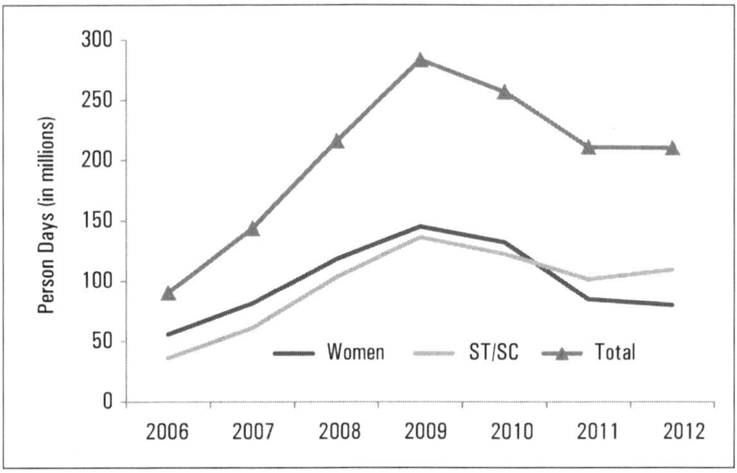

Source: Ministry of Rural Development, Government of India.

A striking feature of the program is participation by women. Since the program pays the same wages for women as men, while women are paid less than men in the private sector, women's participation is high, amounting to an average of 47.5 percent over the years 2006–2012. Participation by marginalized sections of society is also high, with SC/ST accounting for 49.4 percent of person days paid for (Figure 3).

Expenditure on the program amounted to about ₹37,000 crores in 2013–14.[9] This makes it amongst the biggest public programs in India, although not the single largest public expense. In comparison, subsidies for kerosene alone amounted to ₹30,574 crores in 2013–14. Fiscal expenditure on fertilizer subsidies, including consumer and producer subsidies, amounted to ₹73,790 crores in the same year (Ministry of Finance 2014).

Comparisons with programs across the world can be made by calculating expenditure as a percentage of GDP. NREGS expenditure in 2013–14 was 0.33 percent of GDP in India. In comparison, US spending on Medicaid (assistance with medical costs for people with limited resources) was

9. Despite the huge efforts made in ensuring data transparency, it has proven difficult to pin down a precise figure for expenditure in the last two financial years, with various conflicting figures available that are not easy to reconcile. Thankfully, they are all in the same ballpark.

FIGURE 4. Total Expenditure on NREGS

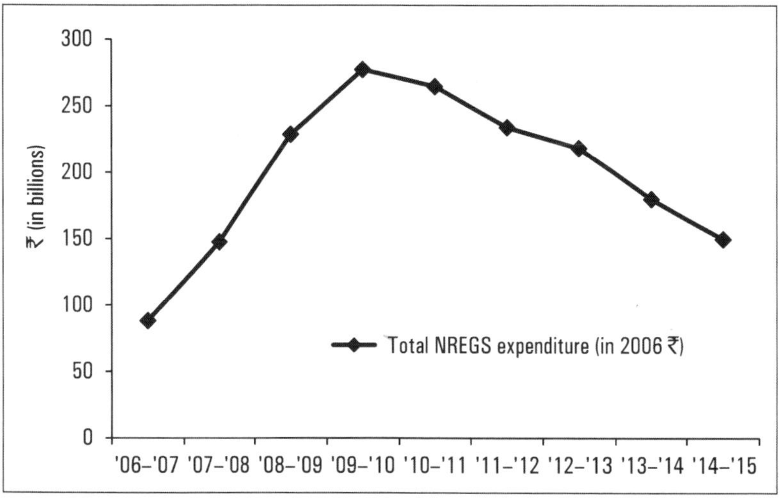

Source: Ministry of Rural Development, Government of India.

2.9 percent of GDP, while spending on the Temporary Assistance for Needy Families TANF program (providing temporary financial assistance for pregnant women and families with one or more dependent children) was 0.19 percent of GDP.[10]

The trend in program statistics so far suggests that expenditure and participation on NREGS rose steadily as the program scaled up from 2006 onwards, but have declined somewhat over the last three to four years (Figure 4). For example, total expenditure on NREGS (in 2006 rupees) dropped to ₹14,982 crore in 2014–15 from ₹27,736 crore, its peak in 2009–10. The number of person days has also dropped, as has the expenditure per person day, although how much of this is due to actual declines as opposed to reduction in corruption (see Section 3) is not known (Figure 5). Meanwhile, the utilization of available funds has increased steadily, and recently state and local governments have been using almost all their budgeted funds (Figure 6).

The almost 50 percent drop in real expenditures on NREGS between 2009–10 and 2014–05 deserves some explanation. A number of factors

10. Sources: Medicaid spending and GDP from www.cms.gov, and TANF spending from www.acf.hhs.gov.

FIGURE 5. Spending per Person Day

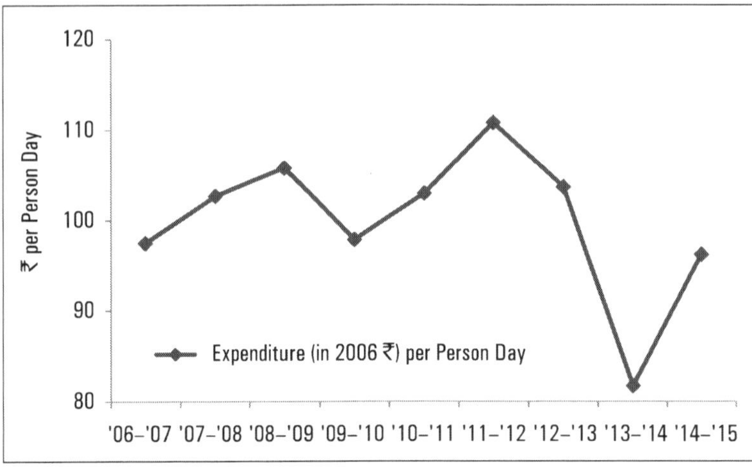

Source: Ministry of Rural Development, Government of India.

FIGURE 6. Proportion of Funds Utilized

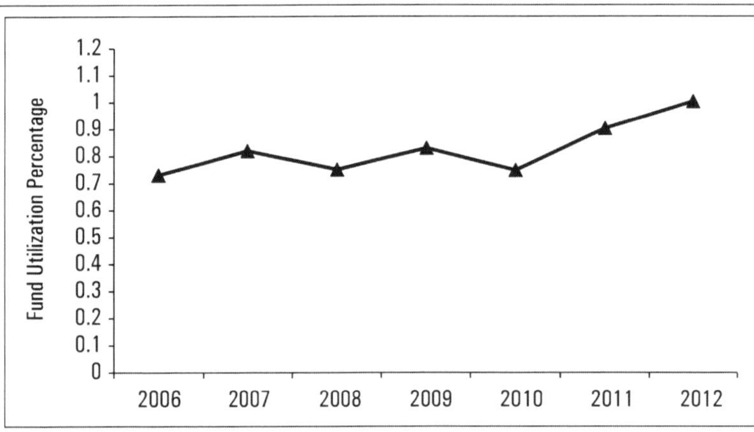

Source: Ministry of Rural Development, Government of India.

contributed to this drop. First and foremost, both the monsoon and annual rainfall in 2008 and 2009 were significantly lower than average, and also significantly lower than in 2013 and 2014, suggesting that greater demand for work had a possible role to play in the earlier period. Second, as discussed below, it is likely that corruption has gone down over time, thereby reducing outlays.

3. Implementing NREGS

It will come as no surprise to anyone that the exhaustive guidelines laid down by the Ministry of Rural Development (MoRD) for MGNREGA implementation are not followed to the letter, and the numbers cited above are not entirely correct. What is important for practical purposes, however, is the extent and nuances of differences between on-the-ground practices and on-paper ideals. In this section, I present the evidence collected on implementation of key features of MGNREGA.

3.1. Heterogeneity in Implementation

The most remarkable characteristic of NREGS is the enormous heterogeneity in implementation quality across states, and even within them. Heterogeneity of implementation across states has been a feature since the very beginning of the program. Dreze and Oldiges (2009), in commenting on performance of the program during the first two years, pointed out that just three states, Rajasthan, Madhya Pradesh, and Chhattisgarh, were responsible for over half of the total employment generated. Imbert and Papp (2015a) coined the term "star states" to describe the seven leading states, where employment on NREGS accounted for over one percent of all working days in rural areas.

This situation has not changed much in recent years; Figures 7 and 8 show the large variation in NREGS employment and expenditure per capita across

FIGURE 7. Person Days by State

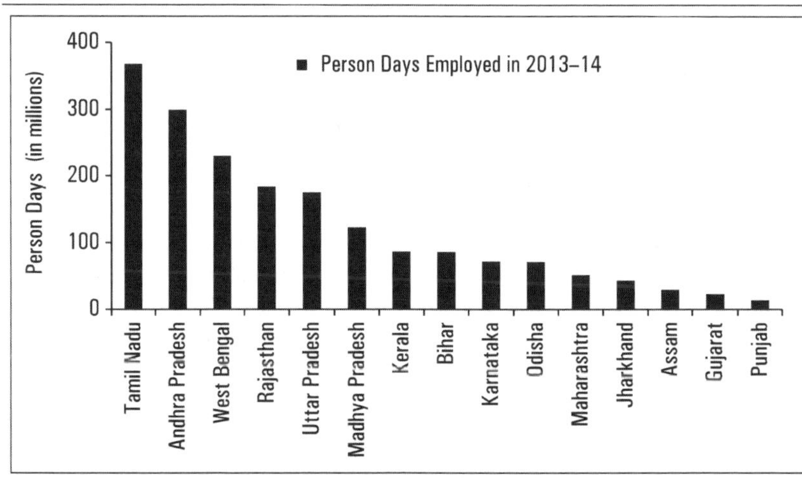

Source: Ministry of Rural Development, Government of India.

FIGURE 8. Expenditure per Capita by State

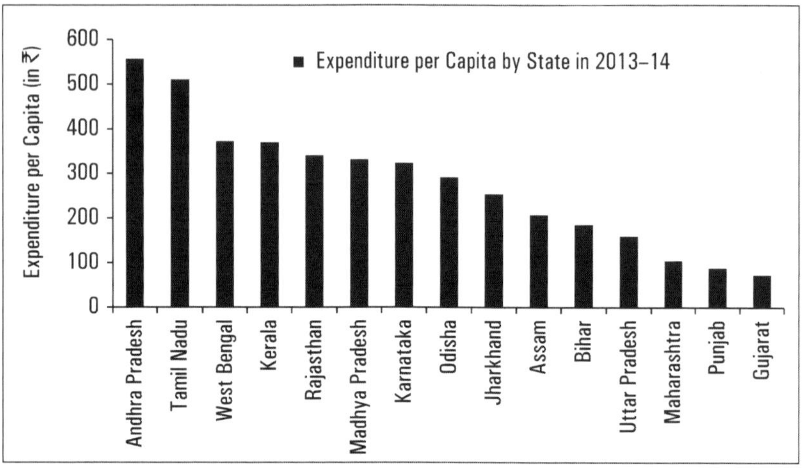

Source: Ministry of Rural Development, Government of India.

the 15 largest states in India in 2013–14. While Andhra Pradesh and Tamil Nadu consistently rank amongst the states with best implementation, poorer states like Bihar and Uttar Pradesh, where one might expect high demand for NREGS, implement with as much intensity as much richer states like Gujarat and Maharashtra (with presumably much lower demand). Overall, there is no relationship between spending per capita or NREGS participation and the rural poverty headcount across states (Dutta et al. 2012).

There are a number of reasons for this heterogeneity. Most obviously, local labor market conditions and the need and demand for employment differ across states. However, as in previous examples of employment guarantee schemes (Ravallion et al. 1993), supply constraints are also extremely important. These supply constraints are related to fiscal capacity, implementation capacity (particularly the way the program is implemented at the local level), as well as political factors.

While the Central Government pays for most expenses under the program, states are still responsible for a share of the costs as explained below, including some of the administrative costs. If state governments have limited fiscal capacity to pay their part, corresponding transfers from the Central Government would be affected, which perhaps explains the apparent regressivity across states noted above.

Administrative capacity in poorer states may also be limited. Witsoe (2014), using detailed anthropological work in one of the worst-performing states, Bihar, documents how the idealized world of MGNREGA is a far cry from the reality of how NREGS is implemented. He notes that "the state government lacks the capacity to run projects as documented. Limitations on state capacity are complex, ranging from inadequate staffing, training and salaries to an inability of officials to navigate panchayat politics and the entrenched opposition of landowners." On the other hand, in Andhra Pradesh the government was able to build on the network of self-help groups to employ women as Customer Service Providers (CSPs) and successfully implement the Smartcards initiative to markedly improve the functioning of NREGS (Muralidharan et al. 2016a).

Finally, the motivation of bureaucrats and politicians to implement NREGS also matters. Gulzar and Pasquale (2015) show that political incentives affect NREGS implementation using a clever empirical strategy to identify the effects of these incentives. Boundaries of political constituencies and administrative units often do not coincide in India; thus administrative units (blocks) can be entirely within political constituencies and answerable to a single politician, or split across constituencies and answerable to multiple politicians. The authors find that person days as well as the number of people employed in NREGS is higher when blocks are entirely within constituencies, as opposed to split across constituencies, even when the comparison is restricted to boundaries of blocks within the same constituencies (where one block is split and the other is not). They argue that politicians are better able to motivate block officials to implement NREGS when blocks are not split, largely because politicians can then more unambiguously claim credit for the improvements. This paper makes clear how implementation quality may differ even within districts.

The heterogeneity observed in NREGS implementation is important not only for the effectiveness of NREGS, but also for two other, less obvious, reasons. First, the interpretation of results and observations that rely on small and selected samples should be done with caution. This is the normal caveat for the extrapolation of results from one area to another. Second, one-size-fits-all solutions must also be viewed with caution.

3.2. Implementing Key Features of MGNREGA

The deviation of the abstract ideal of MGNREGA from the reality of NREGS is best captured by the following quote from Witsoe (2014):

> There are, in fact, three distinct NREGAs. The first is the NREGA enacted through legislation, the vision of which is operationalized through a centrally maintained documentary system. The second is the NREGA practiced by a vast bureaucracy under control

of state governments, whose main task is the production of documentation within the broad parameters of the centrally maintained architecture. Since this documentation is compiled into data and reports, this is the NREGA most visible to academics. And lastly, there is the NREGA as practiced in villages.

Below, I present evidence on the extent of differences in the key dimensions of the Act between the Act on paper and the schemes as practiced in villages, including access to work and payments.

3.2.1. Access

Of all the features of MGNREGA, the most important is simply the access to work on demand. How has NREGS fared in fulfilling this key provision? The most comprehensive work on this suggests that there is still a long way to go to fulfil the ambition of employment when desired. Dutta et al. (2012) use data from the 2009–10 National Sample Survey (NSS), which is representative across India, to find that 44 percent of those who desired work from NREGS did not get it. As suggested by the previous section, there is wide variation across states, with rates varying from 15 percent to 84 percent. Similar results are found in the data from NCAER's India Human Development Survey (IHDS), 2011–12, with 60 percent of the participating households desiring more work but not able to obtain it, and 29 percent of all rural households experiencing rationing of some kind (Desai et al. 2015). Moreover, the IHDS data suggest that employment and spending on NREGS is not strongly correlated with poverty across states, and poorer states have greater unmet demand for NREGS. The lack of capacity described above could be one factor explaining this.

Evidence from our work in Andhra Pradesh suggests that this problem has not gone away. Andhra Pradesh is generally considered one of the better implementing states—it is a "star state" as defined by Imbert and Papp (2015a). However, even here in our end-line survey in 2012, we found that only 4 percent of respondents answered 'yes' to the question, "In general, can anyone in this village who wants work on NREGS get it?" Access looks better when respondents were asked about specific personal experiences, with only 20 percent of respondents answering that they were unable to get work despite asking for it in May (the slack season), while 42 percent of respondents answered that they were unable to get work despite asking for it in January.[11]

11. If more people wanted work in May rather than January, which seems likely—then the weighted average rate would be very similar to the 25 percent reported rate for Andhra Pradesh from the Dutta et al. (2012) data in 2009–10.

The seasonality indicated by these differences in May and January is common across India. As suggested by the fact that a higher number of respondents were unable to get work in January despite asking for it, seasonality is not simply due to variation in demand. It is accepted that no one really "applies" for work; projects generate labor demand when planned for the slack labor season. For example, Witsoe (2014) notes that "contractors are the ones who initiate projects and they are, therefore, the ones who actually generate demand for work." Further evidence from Dutta et al. (2013), based on a randomized experiment in Bihar, suggests that increasing awareness of workers' rights, including the fact that workers can demand work when needed, does not lead to actual increases in employment. This strengthens the argument that supply of jobs, rather than the demand, constrains NREGS employment.

In general, state and local governments seem to plan NREGS projects for the slack labor market months of May and June prior to the monsoons, while such work generally is not planned during the peak harvest months of December and January. There is some suggestion that part of the seasonality may be due to elite pressure. For example, Lakha and Taneja (2009) suggest that "in many parts of rural India, poverty alleviation schemes such as the NREGS face resistance from landlords whose control over labor is threatened by the availability of employment opportunities outside their authority." Similar broad arguments have been made by Anderson et al. (2015), who contend that landlords seek to control local governance in order to dampen wage pressure from schemes like the NREGS. However, more conclusive evidence of widespread collusion between local governments and landlords to smother NREGS implementation is lacking, since such evidence would clearly be difficult to obtain directly.

3.2.2. Targeting

How well does the self-selection aspect of MGNREGA work to target the poor? The poor are more likely to work on NREGS than the non-poor, with 30 percent of poor households participating as compared to 21 percent of non-poor (Desai et al. 2015). Households in which no adult is literate are also much more likely (30 percent) to participate than households where at least one adult is a graduate (13 percent). Again, implementation matters, as 60 percent of poor households participate in NREGS in the better implementing states, as suggested by data from IHDS 2011–12. However, there is also the fact that 70 percent of poor households did not participate in NREGS that year, and mostly because they were not able to access work, not because they did not desire to work.

Other papers corroborate both the targeting and rationing results above (Gaiha et al. 2010). This paper also suggests that increasing statutory wages on NREGS to the point where it is substantially higher than the agricultural wage worsens targeting, since the program then draws in relatively richer workers. Dutta et al. (2014) summarize the situation best: "the rationing process is pro-poor and the scheme is reaching poor families, though richer households also share in the gains."

Qualitative work also supports the 'glass is half-full/half-empty' nature of targeting. For example, Marcesse (2016) points out that in Uttar Pradesh, although the workers actually doing work were often from the poorest section of society, many other workers (from more fortunate castes) also received payments for not doing any work. Moreover, he notes that "variation in the extent to which work benefits were allocated, and whether the work was performed reflected patterns of political allegiance at the village level."

3.2.3. Payments

Operational guidelines clearly state that payment for work must be made within two weeks of the work being done. This is far easier said than done; unless funds are made available in advance to GPs, work must be recorded, and these records uploaded, which triggers disbursal of payments down the hierarchy from states to districts to blocks to GPs. While attempts to circumvent this system are under way (Banerjee et al. 2014), the best available evidence suggests that simply getting payments on time and in a predictable fashion is a recurring problem. Even the operational guidelines state that "Timely payment of wages has emerged as one of the main challenges of Mahatma Gandhi NREGA over the last few years" (Ministry of Rural Development 2013).

Anecdotal evidence on payment delays abounds, with extreme cases such as suicides related to delayed wages capturing media attention (Pai 2013). Representative data at the all-India level are difficult to obtain, with the NSS not asking specific enough questions about the lag between work done and receipt of payment. State-level evidence from our work in Andhra Pradesh suggests that the mean lag is over a month (34 days), easily more than the two weeks allowed on paper (Muralidharan et al. 2016a). Again, Andhra Pradesh is one of the better-performing states.

While delays in payments receive media attention, the banal act of collecting payments does not. The fact that there is no mention of this in extensive operational guidelines suggests the lack of importance given to this by policymakers. However, the time spent on collecting payments can result in significant lost wages. On average, in Andhra Pradesh, workers spent close to two hours collecting their money for every payment. Moving to electronic funds transfer, biometric authentication using Smartcards, and CSPs at the village level considerably reduced both this collection time as well as delays in payments (Muralidharan et al. 2016a).

Perhaps the biggest stick wielded by NREGS critics is that of corruption in the program. For example, Bhalla (2011) contends that programs such as NREGS comprise scams that are annually the size of the famous 2G corruption scandal. While even its most fervent supporters would not deny that some funds are captured by middlemen, putting a precise number on country-wide annual leakage is very difficult.

A good starting point is the estimate by Imbert and Papp (2011), updated in Imbert (2014). They use representative NSS data from 2009–10 and 2011–12, which asks respondents about the number of days they were employed on NREGS, and compares these numbers to official figures on employment provided by MoRD. They find that the NSS household data can only account for 42 to 56 percent of the official MoRD reports in 2009–10. The number improves to about 80 percent in 2011–12. However, these numbers are not a precise estimate of the leakage of NREGS funds since they are in terms of days, not rupees. A major complicating fact is that many states pay piece rates rather than daily wages, and workers often work on NREGS in the mornings while working on their own farms later in the day, biasing the comparison in terms of days.

If we took these figures seriously, we could calculate fiscal losses due to leakages. This would amount to approximately ₹19,000 crores in 2009–10, and ₹7,500 crores in 2011–12. For comparison, leakage rates for the PDS ranged from 44 to 58 percent in the years 2004–05 and 2007–08. The fiscal loss to the government of these leakages in the PDS in 2013–14 amounts to ₹28,500 crores (Ministry of Finance 2014), as compared to the mean value of about ₹36,000 crores and a median value of ₹12,000 crores of the 28 largest Indian scams between 2000 and 2014 that received the greatest media attention as chosen by Sukhtankar and Vaishnav (2015).

The only way to improve on the basic methodology would be to obtain official records of employment and payments and attempt to track these down to the actual beneficiaries. Clearly this is labor intensive and would be difficult to do on a nationwide basis. Moreover, any partial sample would need re-weighting to obtain population estimates, and this is a non-trivial task since for many states, since the number of households in existence does not correspond exactly to the number of job cards in existence. Our level estimates using this methodology in Andhra Pradesh suggest leakage rates of 30.7 percent in 2012 (Muralidharan et al. 2016a). Previous estimates in Odisha using a similar methodology estimated rates of 70–80 percent, but that survey had a much longer recall period of 6–8 months; moreover, they pertained to early years of the program, and to what are regarded as particularly poorly administered districts (Niehaus and Sukhtankar 2013a; 2013b).

In addition to levels of corruption, there is also some limited evidence on the determinants of corruption. The broad takeaway from Niehaus and Sukhtankar (2013a) is that bureaucrats respond acutely to incentives to steal from the NREGS, trading off increased rents today for the ability to stay in the job and steal more tomorrow. In Niehaus and Sukhtankar (2013b), we find that workers' ability to use their voice to tackle corrupt bureaucrats may be limited, unless possibly helped by NGOs.

Finally, the Smartcards experience in Andhra Pradesh suggests that strengthening state capacity to implement the program may reduce corruption in a highly cost-effective manner. Building a new payments infrastructure that relies on electronic transfers to NREGS workers and biometric authentication at the time of payment collection reduced leakage by 40 percent (Muralidharan et al. 2016a). Another technological innovation—this time from the other end of the implementation capacity spectrum, in Bihar—suggests that using an electronic system for fund request and transfer that bypassed the middle layers of districts and blocks also reduced corruption in NREGS (Banerjee et al. 2015). In this case, a reduction in outlays rather than an increase in receipts was the major source of reduced leakage.

4. Conceptual Frameworks for Assessing Impact

In order to understand the impact of NREGS, I present first the theoretical basis for impact, and then the most commonly used empirical strategies for estimating impact.

4.1. Theoretical Frameworks

The basic premise underlying a workfare program like NREGS, as opposed to welfare, involves self-selection (Besley and Coate 1992). Since it is difficult for governments, particularly in developing countries like India, to evaluate household income, adding on a work component helps target funds to those who are poor. In addition, the on-demand nature of NREGS is meant to tackle the information problem that the government may not know exactly when particular households need assistance. The self-selection logic has a long history; apparently it was the rationale for public works programs in India under the British as well as similar programs in the US (Dreze and Sen 1990).

The impacts of NREGS on a number of outcomes can be understood through its primary micro and macro impacts. First, at the micro level, the program affects the household time optimization problem by allowing households to work at a (potentially) higher wage on NREGS. It also provides insurance for household members who may not be able to find employment in the lean season. At the basic macro level, it channels additional funds into rural areas. In addition, the program also creates public goods that may improve productivity.

For households that choose to work on NREGS, the time that is now allocated to NREGS work in the household time-allocation decision might come from leisure or other non- or less productive activity, or it might come from other market work. The extent to which it comes from the former versus the latter is an important factor in determining the efficiency impact of NREGS on the economy. How households re-optimize given the new budget constraint determines the impact on various other outcomes, including potential general equilibrium impacts that change factor prices in the economy.

For example, much attention has been given to the impact of NREGS on labor markets, particularly on private sector wages and employment. It is straightforward to show that in the case of perfectly competitive markets, the introduction of NREGS with a wage above the market wage will lead to increases in the private sector wage and declines in private sector employment (Imbert and Papp 2015a). Under non-competitive markets, such programs may actually increase both wages and employment (Basu et al. 2009). Whether these labor market impacts lead to increases in average household annual income depends on labor supply and demand elasticities in both cases, although income increases are clearly more likely in the latter case with non-competitive markets.

To this standard framework, Basu et al. (2009) add important twists related to access and credibility. As already highlighted, the implementation of NREGS is uneven and access imperfect; even with an on-paper guarantee, discretion over access is afforded to local agents. Under this scenario, the government must choose both the wage and access; Basu et al. (2009) show theoretically that the government could target aggregate employment and achieve the right mix of private and government employment. However, in order to be able to do so, its commitment to provide the set wage and access targets must be credible.

A variant of the household optimization decision is related to the insurance channel. If NREGS is able to protect households against shocks and improve insurance, this may, for example, lead farmers to invest in higher variance but higher average yield crops. At the macro level, the first channel relates to public goods or assets created through NREGS. If these public goods lead to an increase in productivity—for example, irrigation canals could increase agricultural productivity—this may lead to increased employment and household income.

Finally, it is worth mentioning channels that work simply through additional funds flowing into rural areas, and hence are not necessarily extra channels as compared to standard welfare schemes. The first channel is the aggregate demand/multiplier channel: the additional flow of funds could increase local economic activity if there are local scale economies or internal trade frictions (Krugman 1991). A second channel could be that the additional money helps reduce credit constraints more generally in areas receiving NREGS.

The impact of NREGS on other outcomes derives chiefly from the primary channels described above. For example, one might see an impact on education related to changing labor market opportunities for child versus adult labor, or to simple income effects. Similarly, changes in labor market opportunities, as well as income, might affect migration, civil conflict, or health.

4.2. Choice of Papers for This Review

Given the vast proliferation of studies attempting to examine the impact of NREGS, it is difficult to parse the results of every single study. The difficulty is magnified since many are still in working paper stage—given long publication processes—making it harder to judge quality. To be as inclusive as possible, I used a variety of academic search platforms, including Google Scholar, EconLit, and JSTOR, with various combinations of search terms including India, national rural employment guarantee, and every acronym used for the Act and schemes. From this large list, papers that were published in the main economics, political science, and development journals were automatically included. The remaining unpublished papers were subjected to the following inclusion criteria:

1. *Sample selection and representativeness.* The first criterion is that samples selected must be representative, i.e., randomly drawn from a larger universal sample, particularly at the level of the unit of analysis: generally households and villages. Some arbitrariness in selection of larger units of aggregation—for example, states and districts—is inevitable given logistical challenges, as well as simply that some

studies intentionally plan to study a particular state.[12] However, the unit that is analyzed must not suffer from selection bias.

2. *Plausible identification strategy*. The second criterion, and the hurdle that most empirical studies of NREGS impact stumble upon, is that papers must aim to separate out causation from correlation. For reasons described below, this hurdle is particularly challenging in the case of NREGS, but papers must at least attempt to deal with the problem head-on, and describe the threats and challenges clearly.
3. *Sample size and effective sample size.* This criterion applies in the following cases that were excluded: i) a study attempts to show no effect, but does not adequately discuss whether it has the statistical power and sample size to detect an effect, and ii) a study attempts to show an effect, but does not adequately cluster standard errors for intra-cluster correlation.

4.3. Empirical Strategies: Advantages and Pitfalls

In this section, I discuss the main empirical strategies used to identify the effects of the program. At the outset, it is important to figure out what the strategies are identifying the impact of. This is not as obvious as it seems. Given the wide deviations from the ideal world of MGNREGA discussed in Section 3, in fact there is no single logical construct pertaining to the effects of "the program". Any empirical study claiming to study the impact of NREGS is thus simply estimating the effects of varying implementation quality. One could conceptualize a scale from 0 to 100, with zero being no program and 100 being a perfectly implemented program; every paper that identifies the "impact of the program" actually identifies the effect of moving along the scale. For example, studies that use the rollout of the program for identification might be identifying the impact of going from 0 to 20 on this scale; our paper on the Andhra Pradesh Smartcards experiment might be identifying the impact of moving from 50 to 70 (all numbers are arbitrary).

In order to avoid repetition when discussing individual papers, I describe below the main empirical strategies used in assessing impact, and discuss their advantages and pitfalls as they relate to the particulars of NREGS.

1. *Experiments*. The gold standard for causal inference is a randomized control trial (RCT) experiment. In the most famous case of evidence from an RCT used to determine public policy, the initial rollout

12. Of course, most large states in India are larger than most countries in the world.

of Mexico's PROGRESA was randomly assigned, and provided incontrovertible evidence in favor of its impact, thus leading to both scale-up as well as the ability to withstand political pressure after a change in government. In the MGNREGA case, the initial rollout was obviously not randomized. However, given difficulties in implementation, there is scope for experimentation via interventions that improve functioning, as in the Muralidharan et al. (2016a) case. Nonetheless, there are at least two difficulties in conducting RCTs on NREGS; first, getting governments to agree to randomize, and second, doing so at a large enough scale. The latter, in particular, is an under-appreciated issue: given the size of NREGS, it is bound to have general equilibrium effects, and in order to capture these effects, the size of units randomized, not just the number of units randomized, must be large (Muralidharan et al. 2016b). The common criticism of experiments is that while they have strong internal validity, they may lack external validity as they may be done on smaller samples. Of course, the same issue applies to many non-experimental studies as well, for example, those that only focus on one state.

2. *Difference-in-differences.* Given the non-experimental but staggered rollout, the obvious and commonly used strategy is a difference-in-differences approach. This strategy allows for level differences between districts in various phases of rollout, as long as the trend in outcomes prior to implementation of MGNREGA was the same. Unfortunately, the major problem with this strategy is that trends were not actually parallel for the vast majority of outcomes studied. For example, wages in Phase 1 and 2 districts seemed to be converging to wages in Phase 3 districts, as seen in Figure 2 in Berg et al. (2012). Figure 6 in Imbert and Papp (2015a) also confirms that pre-trends in wages were not parallel using NSS data. Given that rural wage series were not parallel, the likelihood is that other outcomes also do not exhibit parallel trends. A second, possibly under-appreciated issue with this strategy is related to the implementation issues highlighted in Section 3: it is difficult to interpret impacts from the rollout. Given these difficulties, the estimated impacts may be of limited value when extrapolating to steady-state NREGS implementation. Moreover, since NREGS mainly works in the summer months, one year of difference between Phase 1 and Phase 2 implementation may not correspond to a large difference in intensity of treatment.

3. *Regression discontinuity*. Given the lack of parallel trends in difference-in-differences designs, some researchers have used regression discontinuity designs to estimate the causal impact of NREGS implementation. This idea is based on the assumption that MGNREGA phases were assigned by an algorithm based on an underlying continuous variable that measured backwardness, with an arbitrary cutoff determining the 200 districts assigned to Phase 1. Thus districts just above and below the cutoff value are quasi-randomly allocated to receive NREGS treatment early or late. The problem with this strategy is that the selection of districts for phases was not fully based on a technocratic algorithm. There are at least two known deviations, with states and districts facing Naxalite issues prioritized, and also each state had to have at least one district in Phase 1. Other political considerations, particularly at the state level, are also possible (Chowdhury 2014; Gupta 2006). Thus, the discontinuity is not very sharp, and the controls used for the underlying forcing variable assume importance. Moreover, since the actual algorithm is not known, there is also a lack of transparency when compared to the difference-in-differences approach, in which one can easily evaluate whether pre-trends are parallel. This strategy also faces the issue highlighted above, which is related to limited implementation in early years.
4. *Other*. While the second and third approaches represent the main empirical strategies, other strategies including those based on using household panels and those based on using instrumental variables have also been used by researchers examining the impact of NREGS. For these strategies, the standard issues remain: panels do not account for selection in and out of NREGS, and instrument variable strategies must not have weak instruments and must satisfy the exclusion restriction. Moreover, studies based on comparing participants to non-participants may be biased if the program also affects non-participants, for example via general equilibrium effects.

5. The Impact of NREGS

In this section, I discuss the impact of NREGS on six main categories of outcomes: labor markets, income and consumption, education and health, migration, agricultural choices, and conflict. In each case, I attempt to distil the key takeaways from the current literature, and also highlight areas of conflicting research or missing knowledge.

5.1. Impact on Labor Markets

Not surprisingly, the impact of NREGS on labor markets has been studied intensely. At least four papers study the impact using nationwide data and the phased-in rollout of NREGS for identification, with another paper relying on experimental variation in Andhra Pradesh. The main outcomes studied are private sector wages and employment.

The only published paper (Imbert and Papp 2015a) uses the difference-in-differences approach (empirical strategy 2 above) and NSS data for the periods 2004–05 (pre-MGNREGA) and 2007–08 (post-MGNREGA) to find that private sector wages for casual labor (temporary, informal contracts as defined by the NSS) rose by 4.7 percent as a result of NREGS. This strategy basically compares trends in Phase 1 and 2 districts ("early phase") with those in Phase 3 districts ("late phase"). They further find that the wage effect is concentrated in the "star states", the label given to the states that implemented NREGS well. They attempt to control for the fact that wages in the early-phase districts were already converging to wages in the late-phase districts prior to MGNREGA by using district-level pre-program controls for caste composition, agricultural wages, and agricultural output per worker, as well as time-varying controls capturing rainfall and the election cycle (separately for the early and late phase districts. Worker level controls attempt to control for selection into the labor force. The paper also finds that NREGS employment crowds out private sector employment (defined here as including casual labor, salaried work, domestic work, and self-employment) almost one-for-one—a 1.17 percent increase in public sector employment to a 1.46 percent decline in private sector work.

Using a similar approach and the same data, Azam (2012) finds broadly similar results. He finds an increase in public employment resulting from NREGS, as well as an increase in labor force participation, particularly for women. The results on wages are strikingly similar, with a 5 percent overall increase in real wages due to NREGS. This paper also presents the increase in wages separately for men and women, and finds that the increase for women (8 percent) is higher than the increase for men (3.8 percent).

Using a similar approach and *different* data, Berg et al. (2012) also find extremely similar overall wage results as the previous two papers. This paper uses the Agricultural Wages in India series, which provides wage rates at the month-district level, separating out wages for unskilled labor and skilled labor, and even including various sub-categories such as field labor, including ploughing, sowing, weeding, and reaping. The headline result is that real agricultural wages increased by 4.8 percent per year as a result of NREGS, with the effects concentrated in the main agricultural season (i.e., the non-NREGS season). The authors find no difference in impact on men's versus women's wages.

A change in empirical approach, however, leads to somewhat more substantial differences in results. Zimmermann (2015) uses a regression discontinuity approach—empirical strategy 3 discussed above—and the same NSS data to argue that NREGS did not lead to increases in public employment or private sector wages. The advantage of the regression discontinuity approach is that it does not need the parallel trends assumption. On the other hand, it requires other assumptions on assignment to treatment and control groups, which are difficult to evaluate since the "algorithm values are not directly publicly available"; and is also most meaningful for the districts closest to the cutoff between Phases 2 and 3. In addition, it is important to note that the comparisons are between different samples: Zimmermann (2015) compares Phase 2 to Phase 3 districts, while all the other papers compare both Phase 1 and Phase 2 districts to Phase 3 districts. Since Phase 2 started in April and May 2007, whereas the NSS data collection started on July 1, 2007, some of these Phase 2 districts would have barely had any experience with NREGS. As the author notes, given implementation issues and the time taken to scale up the program, many Phase 3 districts did not actually receive the program until after July 2008 even though officially the program started in April 2008. So the non-results in this paper are not incompatible with the positive wage effects found in the other papers, particularly given the large standard error bounds.

Although the results from the different approaches are reconcilable, it would be ideal if there were a way to positively adjudicate using an empirical strategy that relies on less strong assumptions. While experimental evidence at the all-India level is not available, our experiment examining Smartcards which improved the functioning of NREGS in Andhra Pradesh provides a benchmark (Muralidharan et al. 2016b). We find that private sector wages for unskilled labor increased by 6.2 percent in the month of June as a result of improvements in NREGS, consistent with the results in Imbert and Papp (2015a); Azam (2012); Berg et al. (2012). It is interesting to note that the impact on wages of *improving* NREGS is of the same magnitude or even slightly higher than that of the *introduction* of NREGS, which again highlights the importance of implementation, and the fact that all papers are basically identifying the impact of a shift on a scale of implementation. Moreover, this magnitude may, in fact, be biased downward due to spillover effects onto control areas, for which we find strong evidence.

In addition to the wage results, we find no statistically significant effects on private sector employment, again for the month of June. However, these are not incompatible with the results in Imbert and Papp (2015a), since their measure of private sector employment includes domestic work and self-employment. Since we ran our own survey and are able to separate the types of work, we run separate regressions and find no effect on working for others but a decline in self-employment and idle time. This is thus compatible with the explanation provided in their paper, which suggests that "the fall in private sector work may in part represent a fall in disguised unemployment or private sector work with close to zero productivity."[13]

So what should the discerning reader take away from these results about the impact of NREGS on the labor market? It seems very reasonable to conclude that the program had a modest positive effect on wages for agricultural/unskilled labor. However, questions remain about the precise seasonality of the effects. While it is most likely that wage effects happened during times when NREGS was most active, it is also possible—particularly given nominal wage rigidities (Kaur 2015)—that these effects persist throughout the year. Moreover, the effect of this "crowding-out" on productivity is still uncertain. Finally, the channels through which wages increased are yet to be positively identified; while Imbert and Papp (2015a) and Azam (2012) both seem to rule out an increase in labor productivity as a result of NREGS assets, there is no actual evidence on this. Indirect evidence from Muralidharan et al. (2016b) suggests that perhaps there is a productivity effect; total employment in treated areas—which saw a rise in work done on NREGS—increased (although not statistically significantly), while total employment in control areas, which only saw wages increase as a result of labor market competition, declined, suggesting perhaps that there was a productivity increase.

5.2. Impact on Income and Consumption

How did the changes in labor markets affect the income and consumption of poor households? Given the uncertainty over private sector employment effects, it is not clear that an increase in wages would unambiguously lead to

13. Zimmermann (2015) makes explicit in her paper the choice between working in the private sector for someone else, working for yourself, and working on NREGS, and points out that the former two may be substitutes. In this model, if NREGS provides an insurance benefit, then one might choose to work for oneself rather than work in the stable private sector. While this is a helpful model in distinguishing between labor choices, the predicted results are the opposite of what we find in Andhra Pradesh.

increases in income and consumption. The additional channel of insurance, which may lead to different agricultural choices (as discussed below), might also lead to changes in income.

At the all-India level, Klonner and Oldiges (2013) use NSS data and a combination of strategies to attempt to tease out the effect of NREGS on consumption and poverty. They use a fuzzy regression discontinuity design that recognizes the fact that there was political interference in the assignment of districts to phases, combined with a difference-in-differences approach. They find no overall effect of the program on consumption and poverty. While they claim to find a reduction in poverty amongst SC/ST, this result is not robust, and the specification with the most straightforward application of the fuzzy regression discontinuity design does not show any significant effects on consumption and poverty.

More unambiguous and robustly identified results come from Andhra Pradesh. The Smartcards experiment mentioned above led to a substantial improvement in the functioning of NREGS, including higher payments to households, and also led to higher private sector wages. The paper finds that the net effect of this improvement is a significant and robust increase in household income, verified not only in the survey data, but also by the entirely independent Socio-Economic and Caste Census (SECC) that was conducted by the Government concurrently (Muralidharan et al. 2016b). The survey data consist of a representative sample of job card holders and pensioners (close to 70 percent of rural households) for whom the paper shows an increase of ₹8,761 (12.7 percent) in annual income. The SECC by definition tracks every single rural household, and here they find that the highest income earner in the household was 24.7 percent more likely to move out of the lowest income category (less than ₹5,000 monthly income) in treatment areas.

Interestingly, the bulk of the increase in income is due to effects through private sector earnings rather than directly through NREGS. Increases in NREGS income accounted for only one-ninth of the income gains for NREGS beneficiaries, with the remaining coming from increases in private sector earnings, suggesting that the general equilibrium effects of NREGS are important. While we do not find statistically significant effects on consumption, our standard errors are large, given the difficulty in precisely measuring consumption in a survey that mainly focused on NREGS functioning. We also do not find evidence of distortions from NREGS on allocation of land or labor, although absence of evidence is not, of course, evidence of absence. A dispositive identification of precise channels is not possible given our data.

Our experimental evidence from Andhra Pradesh is corroborated by other evidence from the same state. Ravi and Engler (2015) use panel data and the fact that some households were denied employment in order to identify effects, comparing households that applied for work and received it to households that also applied for work but did not receive it. They find increases in consumption and food security as a result of work on NREGS. Although the sample is somewhat restrictive—it consists of 1,000 ultra-poor households from 200 villages in one district—the results are robust. Deininger and Liu (2013) also use panel data from the same state, with a slightly larger sample (4,000 households in 480 villages and five districts) and a difference-in-differences approach. They find increased consumption, particularly nutrition, for program participants compared to non-participants. The results, however, must be viewed with some caution given the possibility of selection bias affecting the findings; also, given the fact that private wage effects obviously affect non-participants as well, households may not be the right unit for comparison.

The key takeaway from this section is that it is likely that in places that implemented the program well—like Andhra Pradesh—there were indeed increases in income. Moreover, since NREGS income comprises a small part of overall income, any significant increases in income must come from the impact on private sector labor markets. Nonetheless, the precise channels for any increase remain unclear, as does the evidence for median implementing state.

5.3. Impact on Education and Health

Readers who have not followed the literature will perhaps be surprised to note that the impact of NREGS on education has been more heavily studied than either the impact on labor outcomes or income. Perhaps this is an artefact of data availability, or perhaps it is the fact that the theoretical impact on education is ambiguous. The ambiguity results from the potential of NREGS to have both income and substitution effects. If NREGS increases incomes, then educational outcomes are likely to be positively affected. However, NREGS also increases the opportunity cost of time, particularly for older kids who may be able to work on NREGS themselves (despite adult-only rules), or be close substitutes for adult labor, and hence do more work in households or farms. These children may hence drop out of school, reducing enrolment and eventually test scores.

Consistent with the ambiguous theoretical impact, the empirical literature finds a variety of seemingly conflicting results. However, a closer examination of the breakdown of results and data sources actually reveals a number of consistent stories, which I highlight below.

Perhaps the most comprehensive and clearest paper uses data from Pratham's Annual Status of Education Report (ASER) as well as the NSS, combined with a difference-in-differences strategy, to examine effects on test scores, enrolment, and child labor (Shah and Steinberg 2015). The key advantage of ASER is that it tests children both in and out of school, with a consistent methodology and a large (500,000), representative, repeated cross section. This paper finds that NREGS leads to lower math and reading test scores for all children, with the effects concentrated on older children (13–16 years). In addition, they find that enrolment drops by two percentage points for 13–16 year olds with each additional year of exposure to NREGS. These results are corroborated by data from the NSS, which suggests that children aged 13–17 are 3 percentage points more likely to work, with girls doing more domestic work and boys doing more productive work.

Consistent with the opportunity-cost-of-time hypothesis, there are no or limited effects for younger children (5–12 years). Meanwhile, the youngest children (2–4 years) benefit as a result of the income effect, with increased test scores and higher enrolment at age 5. Shah and Steinberg (2015) are able to show, using NSS data, that trends in educational outcomes were most likely parallel, and also include phase-specific linear time trends to assuage concerns regarding the violation of the parallel trends assumption.

Islam and Sivasankaran (2015) also use NSS data and a difference-in-differences strategy to unsurprisingly find similar results. They find that older children (15–17 years) spend 18 percent more time working outside the household as a result of NREGS, while younger children (6–9 years) spend 3 percent more time in school. They corroborate these results with panel data from three states collected by the NSS, although it is not clear how the identification strategy in the latter case is any different.

Using a different dataset—the District Information System for Education (DISE), based on school level data—Li and Sekhri (2013) examine the impact of NREGS on school enrolment and pass rates. Like the previous papers, this one also finds declines in primary school enrolment, on the order of 1 percentage point. A slight difference is that the results here are driven mainly by primary schools (grades 1 through 5, or roughly ages 6–10) rather than upper primary school (ages 11–13), but this could be explained by differences in the types of schools that only offer upper primary schooling, and the paper does not have data on the older kids in secondary school that might be most affected by NREGS. Li and Sekhri (2013) also find declines in educational attainment, with pass rates declining and repeat rates rising in private schools. The authors are able to include school and year fixed effects, and can also show that differences in trends were not apparent in outcomes prior to the rollout of NREGS.

A paper that also uses the ASER data but a regression discontinuity based empirical strategy seems to find contradictory results to the papers cited above (Thomas 2015). This paper suggests that educational outcomes, including enrolment and test scores, actually improved as a result of NREGS. However, the same paper shows strongly significant pre-program differences in educational outcomes; and while it claims to show parallel trends in educational outcomes pre-program, this is simply not possible as the ASER data only starts in 2005–06, providing only one year of pre-program data. These results must thus be discounted. The same paper uses the District Level Household and Facility Survey data (DLHS–3 and DLHS–2) for 2007–08 and 2002–04, and seems to find improvements in child and maternal health outcomes. These results would be consistent with the improvements in schooling outcomes for younger children that the other papers find.

Another two studies which seemingly contradict the negative education results above are both based on data from only one state—Andhra Pradesh. The first uses data from the Young Lives Panel Study, which covers six districts in Andhra Pradesh with 757 children residing in rural areas (Mani et al. 2014). Given this small sample of districts, four of which were in the early phases of NREGS and two in the later phases, the effective variation in the sample is limited. The second paper uses sub-district level rainfall to instrument for female participation in NREGS, and finds that this led to increased time by girls spent in school, grade progression, and female bargaining power (Afridi et al. 2012).

While the specifics may vary, and reading only the titles and abstracts of the papers may give one a misleading impression, closer examination of all the other papers on the impact of NREGS on education reveals that the set of results in Shah and Steinberg (2015) are mostly corroborated. Educational enrolment and attainment worsened for older children, while these outcomes, and possibly health outcomes, improved for the youngest children.

5.4. Impact on Migration

As compared to education, papers examining the impact of NREGS on migration are few and far between. Preventing short-term, distress migration was one of the goals of NREGS as a safety net (Khera 2011). Moreover, the impact of NREGS on migration is ambiguous—while distress migration might decrease, longer term rural–urban migration might increase as a result of increased income, which may help mitigate risky migration (Bryan et al. 2014). But the lack of data on migration is a binding constraint.

The study by Imbert and Papp (2015b) is the notable exception. They use original survey data from three states as well as NSS data to show that short-term migration is lower as a result of NREGS. In their survey, eight percent of adults report not having migrated as a result of NREGS. In addition, places that provide more government work exhibit less short-term migration. Finally, data from the NSS in 2007–08 shows a lower incidence of short-term migration in early-phase districts as compared to late-phase districts.

Our results from Andhra Pradesh are not exactly consistent with the above results (Muralidharan et al. 2016b). We find no significant results on migration, with the coefficient being small and positive on both the extensive and intensive margins. However, these results are based on slightly different questions related to migration, which ask how many days respondents spent working outside their village. Moreover, the results relate to only one state; thus, they do not necessarily contradict Imbert and Papp (2015b).

Overall, while it is likely that NREGS reduced short-term distress migration, more research on this topic, particularly on impacts related to long-term structural transformation, would be welcome.

5.5. Impact on Agricultural Choices

Given the impacts on labor markets, and the potential insurance provided by the scheme, potential impacts on agricultural choices may be expected. First, for example, if wages increase, landlords may switch to more capital-intensive technologies. Second, if households are confident about the insurance value of NREGS, they may invest in higher-yield, higher-variance crops. Bhargava (2014) examines the first possibility, focusing on technology adoption decisions by landlords. The paper uses data from the Indian Agricultural Census Input Survey (ACIS), collected in 2007 and a regression discontinuity approach, comparing districts just around the Phase 1 and Phase 2 cutoff. It finds that NREGS reduces the proportion of farms using labor-intensive technologies, while increasing the proportion of farms using animal-intensive technologies, both by approximately 20 percentage points. These results are consistent with farmers moving to labor-saving methods in response to higher wages.

Gehrke (2015) examines the second possibility, focusing on crop choices by farmers. The paper uses panel data from the Young Lives Panel Study in six districts in Andhra Pradesh, four of which were part of Phase 1, and the remaining two, part of Phases 2 and 3. The results suggest that households in the Phase 1 districts were more likely to increase the risk profile of their crop mix. However, as in the Mani et al. (2014) paper that uses the same data above, the variation in treatment is limited, and the results must be viewed with caution.

This is another topic on which further research would be welcome. While the result on labor-saving technologies appears reasonable, there is not much else that can be said on this very important issue of what impact NREGS has on agricultural choices.

5.6. Impact on Conflict

Another area which has received substantial attention—to the extent that an entire panel for a broad development conference in the United States was titled "Impact of NREGS on Conflict"—is civil violence. Perhaps this topic particularly interests researchers since an explicit goal of MGNREGA was to assist areas afflicted by the Maoist insurgency, or perhaps it is interesting since theoretically effects could go in either direction. For example, the competition-over-resources theory of conflict would suggest that the greater financial resources that NREGS brings in would lead to increased conflict, while the opportunity-cost-of-time theory of conflict would predict reduced violence given that the higher wages would result in an increased opportunity cost of participating in violence.

Dasgupta et al. (2015) use an originally constructed panel dataset on Maoist conflict violence combined with a difference-in-differences approach to examine the impact of NREGS on both violent incidents and deaths. The dataset is based on local language press sources, allowing for a more comprehensive cataloguing of violence, from 144 districts in six states in the Maoist affected "red belt." The paper finds that NREGS leads to reduced violence, with a large, 50 percent drop in violent incidents, which is larger in districts experiencing negative rainfall shocks. Importantly, the results are entirely driven by Andhra Pradesh and Chhattisgarh, two high capacity states, as the authors state that there is no effect of NREGS in the "non-star" states.

Given that NREGS was targeted to Maoist-affected districts, this paper faces an increased burden of convincing readers that the parallel trends assumption holds. It attempts to do so by including as controls a "backwardness Index", which strongly predicts NREGS assignment to phases, as well as an indicator for "left-wing extremist" district interacted by year. With both district and year fixed effects in addition to the latter control, however, it is not clear how much variation remains to identify the effects.

Fetzer (2014) focuses not on the overall impact of NREGS rollout on violence, but rather on the impact of NREGS on the link between rainfall and violence. The paper points out that rainfall shocks increase civil violence, and also affect agricultural output in wages. The author also collects his own data on violence, using a semi-automatic technique based on Natural Language Processing Tools. The paper uses an interaction of rainfall variation with NREGS rollout, and shows basically that NREGS attenuates violence related to rainfall, possibly by providing insurance. While the results seem plausible, how the precise timing of rainfall shocks interacts with violence and NREGS rollout is a bit unclear.

Khanna and Zimmerman (2015) use a regression discontinuity design, with both cutoffs (between Phase 1 and Phase 2 as well as between Phase 2 and Phase 3), and data from the South Asian Terrorism Portal (SATP), to examine impacts on civil violence. They find that violence increases in the very short run, with increases seen in police-insurgent violence as well as in attacks on civilians by insurgents. However, the results are not apparent from the discontinuity graphs. Moreover, the paper again must deal with the issue of violations of regression discontinuity design specifically related to Maoist insurgency, which it attempts to do by dropping districts.

Finally, Amaral et al. (2015) examine the impact of NREGS on domestic, rather than civil violence. They use data from the National Crime Record Bureau focusing on violence against women, combined with a difference-in-differences approach that compares Phase 1 to Phase 3 districts. The idea is that increased female labor force participation—induced by NREGS—could lead to women's empowerment, but also increase domestic conflict. They find that NREGS actually increases reports of domestic violence, but reduces cases of dowry deaths. The paper uses controls to attempt to control for trends, but does not show the basic parallel trends graph that would be helpful to gauge the assumption. Moreover, given the massive under-reporting of domestic violence incidents (Iyer et al. 2011), it is difficult to know whether the impacts relate to actual violence or merely to reports of such violence.

Given the differing data sources, results, and issues with identification, it is difficult to conclude much about the impact of NREGS on civil insurgency or domestic violence.

6. Outstanding Questions

As the previous section makes clear, while there is much to be learned from the existing studies of NREGS impact, there are still large holes in our knowledge that need to be filled. In addition to the specific issues highlighted in each sub-section above, the following three broad areas represent important open questions to be explored further to help our understanding of NREGS:

1. *Labor efficiency impact.* While we know that NREGS raised rural private sector wages, and at the very least crowded out self-employment labor, we don't know the net impact on efficiency. This is very important for settling the debate over whether NREGS is drawing away labor from productive uses in order to dig holes and fill them up, whether it is providing employment to under-employed labor, or possibly even breaking up non-competitive rural labor markets and enhancing efficiency. Given data and identification constraints, it seems as though it will be difficult to answer this question for the roll-out of the program. However, intensive margin changes as well as improvements in implementation may allow us to make some progress on this subject.
2. *Public goods creation.* There are a large number of papers that study the assets created by NREGS. However, a large-scale, representative study that actually measures return on investment is lacking. Moreover, whether these assets actually raise labor productivity is a question that no reasonable study has been able to answer. This is disappointing because we are currently stuck with the extreme (and likely extremely inaccurate) views of supporters and detractors. Unlike other questions, the answers to which rely on (difficult to find) exogenous variation, simply documenting the existence and value of these assets is eminently doable. For example, Ranaware et al. (2015) survey assets and households in 20 of the 33 districts in Maharashtra, documenting existence, type, and villager perceptions of usefulness. While in principle this study could have been informative, sample selection is flawed: the study selects the five best performing GPs in the best performing block in each district. This severely limits the interpretation of a statistic like 87 percent of completed works were found to be in existence a year and a half after completion.
3. *Longer-term effects.* Finally, many of the impact studies use the rollout of NREGS for identification. As pointed out earlier, given implementation problems at the outset, these studies only capture a small part of the impact of a steady state NREGS. Steady state, long-run impacts on major outcomes such as rural labor supply, rural labor demand, migration, and technology adoption are nowhere to be found. Perhaps we will never be able to identify these impacts, given that NREGS is universal and the gap between phases is too small, long-run impacts are not detectable. But at the very least, an attempt at capturing these impacts would be welcome.

7. Conclusion

I conclude not with a summary of findings, but rather with lessons for the future from the experience of doing research on NREGS, as well as prospects for the near- and middle-term future of the program.

Perhaps the abiding lesson is to build in evaluation prior to the rollout of any large programs. Early evaluation might help in answering the big questions, and quell pointless debate. This is not to criticize the original proponents of MGNREGA: I appreciate that doing public policy and getting Acts passed through Parliament is difficult, and what precious political momentum is available has to be seized. Moreover, the pressure to implement is enormous; everyone wants to do, not necessarily do right. Nonetheless, since knowledge and learning are public goods and individual bureaucrats may not have the incentive to provide them, future programs may do well to build in incentives to learn. The research environment of today, in which large and rigorous experimentation is not unheard of, makes such learning possible.

Another lesson is to think harder about how mandates to capture data will actually be implemented, and also plan for easy data dissemination from the outset. For example, Witsoe (2014) notes, "The actors who create and maintain NREGASoft in Delhi have almost no control over the documentary practices of the officials who produce the paper documentation that is entered into the software platform." Figuring out incentives for these local actors to provide accurate data is, of course, far easier said than done, but must be attempted.

What about the future of the program itself? Does the evidence suggest that it is a well-designed program that might perhaps be badly implemented, but has scope for improvement, or a fundamentally faulty program that should not be expected to alleviate poverty? This question is particularly important in light of the recent advances in payments infrastructure, via which a cash transfer program might be implemented. For example, calculations by Dutta et al. (2014) suggest that a (hypothetical) crude cash transfer scheme would dominate the NREGS in poverty reduction in Bihar.

Given that specific evidence is not available at the moment to answer the above questions, I must step now into the realms of conjecture. I have two thoughts, deriving from my own experience in conducting research on NREGS and on Direct Benefit Transfer (DBT) initiatives, as well as from reading the literature. The first is that at the moment, the state of infrastructure and implementation capacity does not support a large-scale shift to pure cash transfers (the Bihar hypothetical situation cited above notwithstanding—most states have better NREGS implementation). While this may change in the future—the demonetization policy just introduced might push electronic payments further—purely based on anticipated problems with logistics and targeting, such a shift does not seem to be currently warranted.

Second, NREGS has two features that are not shared by cash transfers: the creation of public assets and changes in bargaining power for recipients, which may impact non-participants through general equilibrium effects on wages. Both these features may increase output in the rural economy beyond what might be possible via simple cash transfers (the latter via effects on potential monopsonistic labor markets). To date, evidence that these features of NREGS may be influential is limited to the Muralidharan et al. (2016b) study in Andhra Pradesh; however, if these results extrapolate to other states, this would indicate that the asset creation and bargaining power design features of NREGS are truly important and worth persevering.

Ultimately, as Amarjeet Sinha (Secretary, Ministry of Rural Development, at the time of this writing) has pointed out, the NREGS is not meant to be seen as a program in eternity: "No developed country has a pool of 5 crore households wanting to do unskilled wage labor." In the interim, the NREGS is likely to remain a key policy for protecting rural households.

I end on a hopeful note. The fact that heterogeneity is enormous has been repeated ad nauseam. The implications for policy, however, are that a balance is needed between Central schemes and rules, allowing states to experiment to find local solutions. The Andhra Pradesh experience with Smartcards suggests both that continued tinkering with NREGS implementation may have large benefits, and also that these modular changes to the program may allow for careful and rigorous evaluation. Down this path lies the likeliest probability of success for large public programs such as NREGS.

References

Afridi, Farzana, Abhiroop Mukhopadhyay, and Soham Sahoo. 2012. "Female Labor Force Participation and Child Education in India: The Effect of the National Rural Employment Guarantee Scheme," *Working Paper 6593*, IZA Discussion Papers, http://econpapers.repec.org/paper/izaizadps/dp6593.htm (accessed May 1, 2017).

Amaral, Sofia, Siddhartha Bandyopadhyay, and Rudra Sensarma. 2015. "Public Works Programs and Gender-based Violence: The Case of NREGA in India," *Discussion Papers*, Birmingham: Department of Economics, University of Birmingham, http://econpapers.repec.org/paper/birbirmec/15-09.htm (accessed May 1, 2017).

Anderson, Siwan, Patrick Francois, and Ashok Kotwal. 2015. "Clientelism in Indian Villages," *American Economic Review*, 105(6): 1780–1816.

Azam, Mehtabul. 2012. "The Impact of Indian Job Guarantee Scheme on Labor Market Outcomes: Evidence from a Natural Experiment," *Working Paper 6548*, IZA Discussion Papers, http://econpapers.repec.org/paper/izaizadps/dp6548.htm (accessed May 1, 2017).

Banerjee, Abhijit, Esther Duflo, Clement Imbert, Santosh Mathew, and Rohini Pande. 2014. "Can E-Governance Reduce Capture of Public Programs? Experimental Evidence from a Financial Reform of India's Employment Guarantee," *Working Paper*, https://economics.mit.edu/files/10565 (accessed May 1, 2017).

Basu, Arnab K., Nancy H. Chau, and Ravi Kanbur. 2009. "A Theory of Employment Guarantees: Contestability, Credibility and Distributional Concerns," *Journal of Public Economics*, April, 93(3–4): 482–497.

Berg, Erlend, Sambit Bhattacharyya, Rajasekhar Durgam, and Manjula Ramachandra. 2012. "Can Rural Public Works Affect Agricultural Wages? Evidence from India," *CSAE Working Paper Series 2012–05*, Centre for the Study of African Economies, University of Oxford, http://conference.iza.org/conference_files/worldb2012/bhattacharyya_s8177.pdf (accessed May 1, 2017).

Besley, Timothy and Stephen Coate. 1992. "Workfare versus Welfare: Incentive Arguments for Work Requirements in Poverty-Alleviation Programs," *The American Economic Review*, 82(1): 249–261.

Bhalla, Surjit. 2011. "In the Name of the Poor," *The Indian Express*, February 17.

Bhargava, Anil. 2014. "The Impact of India's Rural Employment Guarantee on Demand for Agricultural Technology," *IFPRI Discussion Paper 01381*, Washington, D.C.: International Food Policy Research Institute, http://www.indiaenvironmentportal.org.in/files/file/Impact%20of%20India's%20Rural%20Employment%20Guarantee%20on%20Demand%20for%20Agricultural%20Technology.pdf (accessed May 1, 2017).

Bryan, Gharad, Shyamal Chowdhury, and Ahmed Mushfiq Mobarak. 2014. "Underinvestment in a Profitable Technology: The Case of Seasonal Migration in Bangladesh," *Econometrica*, 82(5): 1671–1748.

Chowdhury, Anirvan. 2014. "Poverty Alleviation or Political Calculation? Implementing India's Rural Employment Guarantee Scheme," *Working Paper*, Washington, D.C.: Georgetown University, http://sites.bu.edu/neudc/files/2014/10/paper_444.pdf (accessed May 1, 2017).

Dasgupta, Aditya, Kishore Gawande, and Devesh Kapur. 2015. "(When) Do Anti-poverty Programs Reduce Violence? India's Rural Employment Guarantee and Maoist Conflict," *Working Paper*, Cambridge, MA: Harvard University, https://papers.ssrn.com/sol3/papers.cfm?abstract_id=2495803 (accessed May 19, 2017).

Deininger, Klaus and Yanyan Liu. 2013. "Welfare and Poverty Impacts of India's National Rural Employment Guarantee Scheme Evidence from Andhra Pradesh," *Policy Research Working Paper Series 6543*, Washington, D.C.: World Bank, https://openknowledge.worldbank.org/handle/10986/15903 (accessed May 1, 2017).

Desai, Sonalde, Prem Vashishtha, and Omkar Joshi. 2015. *Mahatma Gandhi National Rural Employment Guarantee Act: A Catalyst for Rural Transformation*, New Delhi: National Council of Applied Economic Research.

Dreze, Jean and Amartya Sen. 1990. *Hunger: Economics and Policy*, Oxford: Oxford University Press.

Dreze, Jean and Christian Oldiges. 2009. "Work in Progress," *Frontline*, 26(4): 101–105.

Dutta, Puja, Rinku Murgai, Martin Ravallion, and Dominique van de Walle. 2012. "Does India's Employment Guarantee Scheme Guarantee Employment?" *Policy Research Working Paper Series 6003*, Washington, D.C.: World Bank, http://documents.worldbank.org/curated/en/464991468051015810/Does-Indias-employment-guarantee-scheme-guarantee-employment (accessed May 1, 2017).

———. 2013. "Testing Information Constraints on India's Largest Antipoverty Program," *Policy Research Working Paper Series 6598*, Washington, D.C.: World Bank, https://openknowledge.worldbank.org/handle/10986/15834 (accessed May 1, 2017).

———. 2014. *Right to Work? Assessing India's Employment Guarantee Scheme in Bihar*, Washington D.C.: World Bank, https://openknowledge.worldbank.org/handle/10986/17195 (accessed May 1, 2017).

Fetzer, Thiemo. 2014. "Social Insurance and Conflict: Evidence from India," *Job Market Paper*, November 14, https://barcelonaipeg.files.wordpress.com/2013/09/fetzerpaper.pdf (accessed May 1, 2017).

Gaiha, Raghav, Shylashri Shankar, and Raghbendra Jha. 2010. "Targeting Accuracy of the NREG: Evidence from Rajasthan, Andhra Pradesh and Maharashtra," *ASARC Working Paper 2010/03*, Canberra: Australian National University, https://crawford.anu.edu.au/acde/asarc/pdf/papers/2010/WP2010_03.pdf (accessed May 1, 2017).

Gehrke, Esther. 2015. "An Employment Guarantee as Risk Insurance? Assessing the Effects of the NREGS on Agricultural Production Decisions," *BGPE Discussion Paper 152*, Bonn: German Development Institute, http://www.bgpe.de/texte/DP/152_Gehrke.pdf (accessed May 1, 2017).

Gulzar, Saad and Benjamin Pasquale. 2015. "Politicians, Bureaucrats, and Development: Evidence from India," *American Political Science Review*, 111(1): 162–183.

Gupta, S. 2006. "Were District Choices for NFFWP Appropriate?" *Journal of Indian School of Political Economy,* 18(4): 641–648.

Imbert, Clement. 2014. "MGNREGS Labor Markets and Poverty," *Background Paper for the India Social Protection and Labor Team*, Washington, D.C.: World Bank.

Imbert, Clement and John Papp. 2011. "Estimating Leakages in India's Employment Guarantee," in Reetika Khera (ed.), *The Battle for Employment Guarantee*, New Delhi: Oxford University Press.

———. 2015a. "Labor Market Effects of Social Programs: Evidence from India's Employment Guarantee," *American Economic Journal: Applied Economics*, 7(2): 233–263.

———. 2015b. "Short-term Migration, Rural Workfare Programs and Urban Labor Markets: Evidence from India," *Working Paper*, Oxford: University of Oxford.

Islam, Mahnaz and Anita Sivasankaran. 2015. "How does Child Labor Respond to Changes in Adult Work Opportunities? Evidence from NREGA," *Working Paper*, Cambridge, MA: Harvard University, https://scholar.harvard.edu/files/mahnazislam/files/nrega_mahnaz_anitha_1.pdf (accessed May 1, 2017).

Iyer, Lakshmi, Anandi Mani, Prachi Mishra, and Petia Topalova. 2011. "The Power of Political Voice: Women's Political Representation and Crime in India," *American Economic Journal: Applied Economics*, 4(4): 165–193.

Kaur, Supreet. 2015. "Nominal Wage Rigidity in Village Labor Markets," *NBER Working Paper 20770*, Cambridge, MA: National Bureau of Economic Research, http://www.nber.org/papers/w20770 (accessed May 1, 2017).

Khanna, Gaurav and Laura Zimmerman. 2015. "Guns *and* Butter? Fighting Violence with the Promise of Development," *Discussion Paper 9160*, IZA Discussion Papers, http://ftp.iza.org/dp9160.pdf (accessed May 1, 2017).

Khera, Reetika. 2011. *The Battle for Employment Guarantee*, New Delhi: Oxford University Press.

Klonner, Stefan and Christian Oldiges. 2013. "Can an Employment Guarantee Alleviate Poverty? Evidence from India's National Rural Employment Guarantee Act," *Working Paper*, Heidelberg: University of Heidelberg, http://www.uniheidelberg.de/md/sai/wiw/team/oldiges/klonner_oldiges_2013_employment_guarantee_india_poverty_impact.pdf (accessed May 1, 2017).

Krugman, Paul. 1991. "Increasing Returns and Economic Geography," *Journal of Political Economy*, 99(3): 483–499.

Lakha, Salim and Pradeep Taneja. 2009. "Balancing Democracy and Globalisation: The Role of the State in Poverty Alleviation in India," *South Asia: Journal of South Asian Studies*, 32(3): 408–424.

Li, Tianshu and Sheetal Sekhri. 2013. "The Unintended Consequences of Employment Based Safety Net Programs," *Working Paper*, Charlottesville: University of Virginia, http://people.virginia.edu/~ss5mj/unintendedeffects_safetynets.pdf (accessed May 1, 2017).

Mani, Subha, Jere Behrman, Shaikh Galab, and Prudhvikar Reddy. 2014. "Impact of the NREGS on Schooling and Intellectual Human Capital," *Working Paper*, Philadelphia: University of Pennsylvania, http://repository.upenn.edu/gcc_economic_returns/10/ (accessed May 1, 2017).

Marcesse, Thibaud. 2016. "Public Policy Reform and Informal Institutions: A Moral Economy of Poverty Alleviation in Rural India," *Working Paper*, Ithaca, NY: Cornell University.

Ministry of Finance. 2014. *Economic Survey of India*, New Delhi: Government of India.

Ministry of Rural Development. 2013. *The National Rural Employment Guarantee Act 2005: Operation Guidelines*, 4th edition, New Delhi: Government of India.

Muralidharan, Karthik, Paul Niehaus, and Sandip Sukhtankar. 2016a. "Building State Capacity: Evidence from Biometric Smartcards in India," *American Economic Review*, 106(10): 2895–2929.

———. 2016b. "General Equilibrium Effects of (Improving) Public Employment Programs: Experimental Evidence from India," *Working Paper*, San Diego:

University of California, http://econweb.ucsd.edu/~pniehaus/papers/GE.pdf (accessed May 1, 2017).

Murgai, Rinku and Martin Ravallion. 2005. "Is a Guaranteed Living Wage a Good Anti-poverty Policy?" *Policy Research Working Paper Series 3640*, Washington, D.C.: The World Bank, https://openknowledge.worldbank.org/handle/10986/8188 (accessed May 1, 2017).

Niehaus, Paul and Sandip Sukhtankar. 2013a. "Corruption Dynamics: The Golden Goose Effect," *American Economic Journal: Economic Policy*, 5(4): 230–269.

———. 2013b. "The Marginal Rate of Corruption in Public Programs: Evidence from India," *Journal of Public Economics*, 104: 52–64.

Pai, Sandeep. 2013. "Delayed NREGA Payments Drive Workers to Suicide," *Hindustan Times*, December 29.

Ranaware, Krushna, Upasak Das, Ashwini Kulkarni, and Sudha Narayanan. 2015. "MGNREGA Works and Their Impacts," *Economic and Political Weekly*, 50(13): 53–61.

Ravallion, Martin, Gaurav Datt, and Shubham Chaudhuri. 1993. "Does Maharashtra's Employment Guarantee Scheme Guarantee Employment? Effects of the 1988 Wage Increase," *Economic Development and Cultural Change*, 41(2): 251–275.

Ravi, Shamika and Monika Engler. 2015. "Workfare as an Effective Way to Fight Poverty: The Case of India's NREGS," *World Development*, 67: 57–71.

Shah, Manisha and Bryce Millett Steinberg. 2015. "Workfare and Human Capital Investment: Evidence from India," *NBER Working Paper 21543*, Cambridge, MA: National Bureau of Economic Research, http://www.nber.org/papers/w21543 (accessed May 1, 2017).

Sukhtankar, Sandip and Milan Vaishnav. 2015. "Corruption in India: Bridging Research Evidence and Policy Options," *India Policy Forum,* 11: 193–276, New Delhi: National Council of Applied Economic Research, http://testnew.ncaer.org/image/userfiles/file/IPF%202015/Corruption%20in%20India%20Bridging%20Research%20by%20Sandip%20Sukhtankar.pdf (accessed May 1, 2017).

Thomas, Megan. 2015. "Guaranteeing Children a Better Life? The Impact of the Mahatma Gandhi National Rural Employment Guarantee Act on Child Health and Learning in Rural India," *Working Paper*, Austin: University of Texas.

Witsoe, Jeffrey. 2014. "The Practice of Development: An Ethnographic Examination of the National Rural Employment Guarantee Act in Bihar," Mimeo, New York: Union College.

Zimmermann, Laura. 2015. "Why Guarantee Employment? Evidence from a Large Indian Public Works Program," *Working Paper*, Athens, GA: University of Georgia.

Comments and Discussion*

Rinku Murgai
The World Bank

I want to first thank Shekhar Shah for asking me to comment on the paper. NREGS is a program that I have done some research on, but there are so many papers that have been produced on it that it is difficult to keep track of the literature. So, I think what Sandip has done, by summarizing the lessons emerging across papers, is marvelous. I know about half the papers well, I agree with his read of all the ones that I know well, and I trust his judgment on the others. He has done a service to the development community by sorting through these papers. For the reasons that he has mentioned, it is incredibly difficult to come to a judgment on what we have learned so far about the program. The methods are different, the samples are different, and questionnaire designs are different. We have learnt that questionnaire design can make a huge difference, in the same context, in the same time, on what you can conclude about the program. We get very different estimates even on leakage, on take-up rates, things that should be relatively simple, even setting aside questions of impact.

Also inherent to the design of the program is the fact that we should *expect* to see a lot of heterogeneity. Local government plays a big role, so you should see heterogeneity in different states, you should see heterogeneity in different districts. Implementation capacity varies across states, so we should see heterogeneity as a result of that, and the nature of bottlenecks has continued to evolve over time. Therefore, it is not surprising that we see a very diverse set of results across the studies that have been done. Sandip's work is incredibly useful because keeping in mind the heterogeneity that may arise due to differences in methods across studies, he is able to ask what can be safely concluded from the set of studies currently available on NREGS.

* To preserve the sense of the discussions at the India Policy Forum, these discussants' comments reflect the views expressed at the IPF and do not necessarily take into account revisions to the conference version of the paper in response to these and other comments in preparing the final, revised version published in this volume. The original conference version of the paper is available on www.ncaer.org.

My main quibble with the paper is that it shies away from any reflections on what the wealth of analysis done so far implies for the *future* of the program. It is much too coy here. Let me caricaturize this to be provocative.

There is a large set of papers that focus on challenges of program implementation. There are advocates who focus on building awareness, on employing tools of e-governance, community-based monitoring, strengthening local capacity, improving the productivity of assets, and so on, with the premise that the program design itself is sound, but does not work well in practice. The key questions these papers address are how the program's implementation could be strengthened.

Then there is a set of papers and views, at the other extreme, that are asking the following question: Aren't there simpler alternatives to achieve the poverty reduction objectives within the same budget, in particular, an unconditional cash transfer? This isn't just a hypothetical discussion because the architecture for moving towards cash transfers is being put into place with the emphasis on the so called JAM (*Jan-Dhan* accounts, *Aadhaar* ID, and ubiquitous mobile payments). It is also not hypothetical because India does implement social pension schemes that are unconditional cash transfers, and which work better, at least on some of the issues that NREGA is faulted for. For example, on leakage, on the time taken to deliver payments, on the difficulties that people incur when they are trying to collect payments, the pension schemes actually work reasonably well. So, it is not the case that moving to cash transfers is entirely hypothetical.

Given these two extreme sets of views about the future evolution of the program, I would pose a few questions and suggestions for extending the paper further, and for Sandip to speculate which way the program should go. The first question that we should ask is: Is MGNREGA cost-effective? How does it compare to other schemes, what alternatives should it be evaluated against?

My work with my co-authors, based on panel survey data that we collected for about 3,000 households, about 6,000 workers, in Bihar, compares the performance of NREGS to a hypothetical cash transfer scheme that was totally untargeted, and to one that was targeted based on the current distribution of BPL cards. If we compare the status quo in NREGS and compare it in Bihar with the hypothetical ones, making similar assumptions for example on leakage, we find that MGNREGA would be dominated by this very crude cash transfer program. Why is that? We think that it comes from the fact that there are relatively high levels of foregone income, because people give up income to work on the scheme and that reduces by itself the net impact of the program for a given budget.

But also, in our analysis, we don't take into account any potential spillover impacts of asset creation. So, one of the conclusions I draw from this is that for NREGS to succeed fully, the emphasis on asset creation is incredibly important. This draws me to the point that Amarjeet Sinha made in his comments, immediately following the paper presentation, that we have simply not focused much on the assets being created by NREGS, and that this remains quite an under-studied subject, especially if we were to apply the standards of evidence that Sandip poses in his paper.

The second question that we are not thinking about enough, but is important given the direction in which the Ministry has been moving, and how often it seems to come up in policy discussions, is: Is there mission creep in the NREGS program, and what does that imply for its effectiveness? Partly, it may be mission creep that is what is making it difficult to evaluate. If you say NREGS is not doing well on employment generation, then people say that it is not about employment, the objective is empowerment and asset creation. If somebody faults the program on asset creation, well, then it is not about assets, but it is about preventing distress migration. The direction NREGS is moving in is towards further over-burdening the program on the grounds of 'convergence' with other schemes. Policymakers are pushing not for just vertical performance but also coordination horizontally. As a research community, how can one evaluate these movements?

The third suggestion is to extend and deepen the discussion of implementation challenges. The paper notes these challenges, but they deserve more attention, precisely because the devil really is in the implementation details. Given that the program is already nationwide, as researchers there is room to work with government to understand how the program can work better and think about different modalities of implementation. Even if not at the gold-standard, the Muralidharan, Niehaus, Sukhtankar (2016) paper clearly shows that we can even do RCTs on specific implementation aspects as a worthwhile strategy to address implementation challenges.

Finally, I will not go into my own views on what the key directions for NREGS reform are, but I think Sandip should, having read all the literature. It would be worth having an IPF paper on this.

Reference

Muralidharan, Karthik, Paul Niehaus, and Sandip Sukhtankar. 2016. "Building State Capacity: Evidence from Biometric Smartcards in India," *American Economic Review*, 106(10): 2895–2929.

Surjit S. Bhalla
Oxus Research & Investments and NCAER

Sandip Sukhtankar's paper on NREGS is a comprehensive survey of the issues related to the operation of the world's largest employment program. While informative and rigorous, I find that the literature surveyed reaches some questionable conclusions about the efficacy, or "performance" of the NREGS scheme.

While MGNREGA became law in 2005, the first nation-wide implementation of the NREGS took place in 2009–10. Many of the studies Sukhtankar surveys are for years *prior* to 2009, i.e., they are partial in coverage, and hence in the scope and validity of their conclusions.

The efficacy of NREGS has been discussed ever since its inception. As the evidence has accumulated, the NREGS debate today, and for the last several years, looks to be no different than the evergreen debate about absolute poverty and poverty levels. All conclusions are "valid", i.e., poverty has gone up, gone down, and everything in between. In this circumstance, it is incumbent on economists to point the way towards the most reliable of conclusions.

The conclusions that do *not* appear from Sukhtankar's survey is that NREGS provides much less employment to the poor than popularly believed, that it cannot possibly have increased real wages for non-NREGS workers, its record on targeting is very poor (less than 16 percent of the NREGS expenditure reached the poor), and it is one of the most expensive (corrupt?) programs in terms of government expenditure—₹24,000 were spent to bring one person out of poverty in 2009–10 (see Table 2 and below). Let me elaborate.

What Does the Evidence Say about NREGS?

Before presenting the results on performance, following is a brief summary of the claims made in favor of both the introduction, and continuation, of the NREGS program (Bhalla 2016):

1. It is a self-selecting program and so targeting of beneficiaries is not a problem.
2. The program is *large* in scale, and by mandating and providing minimum wages, it helps raise rural wages.
3. It helps reduce poverty by large amounts and, therefore, may be the most efficacious poverty program not only in India, but in the entire developing world.

4. It also costs very little: less than 0.45 percent of GDP in 2009–10, the first full year of implementation, and also a drought year, so one can attest to its importance.

An important reason for the extraordinary debate on the efficacy of NREGS is that there are two data sources, including on rural employment and wages. The official NREGS source is the data provided by Ministry of Rural Development, the "owner" of the program. The other source is household surveys (the most comprehensive being those of the NSS), which asks individuals about their participation in the program.

In 2009–10, the NSS tagged two or three questions about NREGS onto their five-yearly survey on employment, unemployment, wages, days worked, etc. The survey contained a headline question asked of all 1.25 lakh households: did any member of the household participate in NREGS work, and if they did, how many days were worked, and at what wage rate? In the same NSS survey in 2011–12, the NSS authorities repeated all the questions, including how much salt and toddy was consumed, but the aggregate question on NREGS employment was not asked. Thus, NSS 2009–10 is the best (and only) cross-check on the data provided by the Ministry of Rural Development (MoRD). It is the only data to test the claims of the advocates, and critics, of the NREGS program.

What Does the NSS 2009–10 Data Show?

The political economy of NREGS is indicated by the fact that the data put out by the MoRD (a ministry that has been keen to fund research on NREGS) does *not* match data on NREGS not published by the MoRD.

First, the MoRD data vastly overstates the employment provided by NREGS. The MoRD website claims that in 2009–10, 2,840 million man-days of work were provided to 52.9 million households. The NSS survey indicates that 36.2 million households worked on NREGS for 1,360 million workdays. The overstatement by MoRD is more than double the (actual?) NSS estimate (Table 1).

Second, the total number of days worked in the rural areas in 2009–10 according to the NSS was 90.9 billion (Table 2). The largest employment program in the world provided 1.36 billion workdays, or 1.5 percent of the total. This has to be the smallest tail wagging the biggest dog in the world.

NREGS and Impact on Wage Levels and Wage Growth

In theory, NREGS workers are the poorest of poor, doing back-bending work. So conceptually, we need to ask: what theory suggests that the poorest

TABLE 1. NREGS: Comparing NSS & Ministry of Rural Development Data

Variable *All figures in millions; unless stated otherwise*	2009–10	2011–12	Growth(%)
National Sample Survey Statistics			
Households with NREGS work	36.2		
Work-days of NREGS work	1,360		
Average rural wage (₹/day)	156	244	56.0
NREGS worker wages (₹/day)	89	106	19.1
Ploughman wages (₹/day)	82	123	50.0
Ministry of Rural Development Statistics			
Households with NREGS work	52.9		
Work-days of NREGS work	2,840		
Average NREGS wage (₹/day)	89	115	29.2
Ploughman wages (₹/day)*	126	177	40.5

Sources: As stated, except for ploughman wages marked*, which are from the *Labour Bureau, Government of India*.

segment of the population can cause the average wage to move upwards? Those who claim that 1.5 percent of the poorest workers in the economy, and doing unskilled wage work, lifted the average real wages of the remaining richer 98.5 percent of the population, by as much as 5 percent (as reported by Sukhtankar), have to provide some explanation other than the contention that they did a randomized control experiment (RCT). Even RCTs have to pass a smell test.

As documented in Table 1, the NSS estimate of the wages of NREGS workers and that reported by MoRD are identical at ₹89 per day. However, the rate of growth of NREGS wages differs substantially; NSS estimates this growth to be 19 percent between 2009–10 and 2011–12, while MoRD estimates the growth to be much larger, i.e., 29 percent.

When NREGS went national in 2009–10, the wages it paid were slightly above those of a ploughman according to the NSS. Two years later, the ploughman was making almost half as much again, while the NREGS worker had a wage increase below the rate of inflation. The key point is that *nominal* rural wages did indeed rise after the introduction of NREGS. If NREGS wages were pushing up other rural wages, they would probably be growing faster, not slower, than non-NREGS wages.

Also reported is the average wage per day in the rural economy: ₹156/day in 2009–10 increasing to ₹244 in 2011–12, a 56 percent increase. Given that

NREGS workers account for only 1.5 percent of workers in rural India, and given that the rural wage rate is nearly half of the average, it is a bit inconceivable (and worrisome) that researchers conclude that NREGS made possible a 5 percent real wage increase in the aggregate rural economy.

Poverty Reduction—The Influence of NREGS

The other claim of NREGS advocates is that the NREGS expenditure was well spent because it helped reduce absolute poverty. This is a testable proposition (Table 2).

Less than one-third of poor households received NREGS payments. The average payment received per household in 2009–10 was ₹284/month; per individual, an average of ₹2 per day or ₹61 a month. The impact on poverty was consequently quite limited, while the costs of the program have been substantial.

The NREGS program involved an expenditure of ₹38,900 crores and, in its absence, rural poverty incidence would have increased from 38.3 percent poor to 40.5 percent. In other words, NREGS allowed 2.2 percent of the rural population, or 16.5 million individuals to become non-poor in 2009–10. The cost of this policy: about ₹24,000 to make one individual not poor.

The total subsidy transfer to the poor amounted to an average per capita monthly payment of ₹61; for twelve months, this is equal to a transfer level of ₹732 per person. A total of 89.4 million individuals received this benefit

TABLE 2. NREGS Poverty Reduction: How Successful?

	Rural			*NREGS*		
Variable	*Total*	*Poor*	*Non-poor*	*Total*	*Poor*	*Non-poor*
Workers (*in million*)	282	97	185	78	34	44
Total workdays in the year (*in billion*)	90.9	30.8	59.6	1.36	0.53	0.83
Population (*in million*)	742	284	458	183.7	89.4	94.3
as % of total	100	38.3	61.7	100	48.7	51.3
If no NREGS program:						
Population (*in million*)	742	300.5	441.5			
as % of total	100	40.5	59.5			
Reduction in Poverty due to NREGS						
Population (*in millions*)	16.51					
Population (*in percent*)	2.2					

Sources: NSS Survey, 2009–10; Author's calculations.

for a total transfer amount of ₹6,544 crores. Hence, with a total NREGS expenditure level of ₹38,900 crores, the government was able to transfer 16.8 percent.

Prime Minister Rajiv Gandhi famously said in 1985 that only 15 percent of the money spent on the poor (he was mainly talking about PDS—the public distribution system for food grains) actually reached the poor. This conclusion has, in 2017, also been accepted by the Supreme Court. In their hearings on *Aadhaar*, a bench of justices A. K. Sikri and Ashok Bhushan said:

> A former prime minister of this country has gone on record to say that out of one rupee spent by the government for welfare of the downtrodden, only 15 paisa thereof actually reaches those persons for whom it is meant. It cannot be doubted that with UID/Aadhaar much of the malaise in this field can be taken care of... (*Indian Express*, June 9, 2017).

Both PDS and NREGS are very close to Rajiv Gandhi's assessment made 30 years ago. I want to conclude by stating that the data suggests that India has three of the four most corrupt institutions in the world. Though hard numbers are difficult to obtain, I would guess that FIFA, by universal agreement, would be allegedly the most corrupt institution in the world; that BCCI, allegedly, would be number 2; PDS wins the race and edges past NREGS to be number 3 (less than 15 percent of the expenditure reaches the poor), and NREGS is placed at 4th with 16.8 percent of the expenditures actually reaching the poor.

Reference

Bhalla, Surjit S. 2016. "Food, Hunger and Nutrition in India: A Case of Redistributive Failure", Report prepared for the Brookings Institution, December, https://assets.contentful.com/5faekfvmlu40/3CYusTxjKE0O82sSQeKaOe/0b7ec7141027d770acecd4b69103e88f/Frontier_Issues_Bhalla.pdf (accessed June 1, 2017).

General Discussion

R. Nagaraj asked for a more detailed explanation of the paper's results on household participation in NREGS and education. Govinda Rao urged the author to examine the design of the program in greater depth. Though the conceptual design stipulates that resources be allocated to states based on the incidence of rural poverty, the actual funds following the Act are released based on utilization certificates, and therefore spending capacity. A basic design flaw is that MoRD has no incentive to return any unused funds to the Ministry of Finance, so the entire unused NREGS budget at the end of the fiscal year is reallocated to the states that have utilized the money. As a result, there is little incentive to improve state implementation capacity of the poorest states where such capacity is likely to be the worst, and therefore no assurance that states with the largest concentration of rural poverty will get the most money.

Indira Rajaraman said that in the initial phase NREGS was confined to a small set of districts because there was evidence pointing to the clustering of rural poverty in these districts. The eventual inclusion of all districts in the later phase meant that less and less deserving districts were brought under its ambit. She asked if the author had looked into the question of access to NREGS in the initial, most deserving districts versus access in the final, least deserving districts, to examine whether there was any inter-phase inequality in access.

Pranab Bardhan recalled the days when the NREGA Bill was still under political and popular discussion and had not become an Act, when it was being considered as a safety net and not as a big anti-poverty program. He asked the author that if we took its safety net goal—the last fallback option for workers in the lean season—as the main objective, how far had NREGS fulfilled that goal? Second, Bardhan asked if the literature suggested what the estimates of foregone earnings might be if we looked only at foregone income in the lean season, and not on an annual basis (again, seeing NREGS only as a seasonal relief program and a fallback option during the lean season). Third, he noted in the context of rural labor markets that female participation in NREGS, particularly in recent years, had grown substantially, driven by an identical NREGS wage rate for men and women. Does the literature have any evidence to show that NREGS has had a significant impact on rural male–female wage disparity?

Robert Lawrence was concerned that the paper did not critically evaluate the supply and demand frameworks being used in the literature that it had reviewed. What is the counterfactual that is being considered in the literature? What are the opportunity costs for NREGS workers at a given point in time? The question is not whether labor markets are competitive or not, but what would the workers accepting NREGS work have done in the absence of such work? What if the relevant counterfactual is that people would have been idle, and the impact of NREGS has been to shift the labor supply curve out? Or what if they were doing something already but at lower wages, and have now been drawn into the program? So, there would be different expectations under different counterfactuals. The relevant criterion is not if the market is competitive or not, but rather if the author can explain what the program is trying to do, whether it is emergency work for the idle or it is attracting people earning lower wages into the labor market. What are the counterfactuals?

Dilip Mookherjee turned to Rinku Murgai's comments on her Bihar work comparing NREGS with targeted cash transfers and pointed out that Bihar was particularly poor in implementing NREGS, that the results were sensitive to the poverty measure used, and new work attempting to extend these results to all states and using alternative poverty measures would be useful to review, particularly given the heterogeneity of program implementation. He also noted that the work assumed that the average leakage rate was the same for cash transfers and NREGS. At least in West Bengal, his observation was that many cannot access cash transfers into their accounts, and commissions have to be paid to an intermediary to help with the process of withdrawal. This underscores the need for a lot more work with careful data collection on leakages related even to cash transfers, whether into accounts, through mobile transactions, or through other means, in comparing with NREGS leakages.

Rajnish Mehra suggested that we could view NREGS from an asset pricing perspective as a form of insurance, as a safety net. Insurance on average has a negative rate of return, but is nonetheless important because if pays off in periods of extremely high marginal utility. So it is possible to have a low or negative rate of return for an asset that is being used for consumption smoothening, but which pays off in bad times with very high marginal utilities for society.

Karthik Muralidharan felt that the two positions on NREGS that emerged from the paper framed the debate exactly right: one said that the program is well designed but poorly implemented, and the other said that the program design itself was fundamentally flawed, i.e., NREGS may be implemented efficiently, but its design may be weak, the weakness being one of the fundamental misallocation of resources. For example, if the core driver of economic development is urbanization and structural transformation, and if NREGS holds back the relocation of labor and other resources from migrating to urban areas, that would be the deep design concern about NREGS.

He went on to say that Imbert and Papp (2015) had found wage effects, but no one before the Andhra Pradesh (AP) work of Muralidharan, Niehaus, and Sukhtankar (2016a and 2016b) had found reliable income effects. The SECC data, which was independent of the experiment they ran, showed a significant reduction in poverty. Their work showed the mechanism by which this may have happened: that NREGS not only caused an increase in wages but also an increase in the reservation wage. As basic minimum wage theory would tell us, it was not the number of days worked under NREGS that would affect the market, but it was also the credibility of the outside option, the impact on the reservation wage, that would affect what the market had to pay. In the AP case, smartcards were not just reducing leakage, but also improving the payments process, allowing beneficiaries to get their money faster without paying commissions, and enabling an increase in access. These were improvements in implementation with regard to every metric of what NREGS was supposed to do. So all this was amplifying the general equilibrium (GE) impact of NREGS on the market.

Muralidharan said in responding to Surjit Bhalla's discussant's comment that this was the reason, through the GE effects of NREGS, that the tail could wag the dog. It was difficult to parse the positive impact on incomes in terms of worker productivity effects or the impact on local monopsonies for employment. He did agree with Bhalla that these results came from AP, where the government had made a political decision to invest in the implementation of NREGS. Their AP results show that a well-implemented NREGS is clearly redistributive as landlords were worse off because the wages and bargaining power of landless labor had gone up, signifying that improving NREGS implementation was a conscious political decision. The evidence thus suggests that if the program is well implemented, it has not only GE effects but also direct poverty effects, and in the case of NREGS, the GE effects can be much bigger than just the impact of the cash transfer.

Martin Rama asked a question about whether we could tie NREGS impact to distress land sales during times of drought. Kirit Parikh noted that adverse selection was the basis of the self-targeting approach of NREGS, given the difficulty of identifying the poor, or ensuring that there are no significant leakages to the rich. But if the wage rate was set too high, that advantage would of course be lost.

Prem Vashishtha noted that the problem of low allocations to the poorer states has its roots in the fundamental problem of low capacity at the Gram Sabha level. It is here that communities are supposed to come up with an annual labor budget, and it is not surprising that the results are not very good because capacity at this level varies tremendously. He recalled his own experience in Tripura, where even in a forest village he found a very active Gram Sabha, and contrasted that with his experience in parts of Bihar or UP where there was no such capacity or interest.

Amarjeet Sinha (Chair) concluded the discussion by applauding the paper and the incisive comments of the discussants and other participants. He agreed with the author that for programs like NREGS to succeed, they had to be led by the states, as seen in the case of NREGS from the examples of Andhra Pradesh and Tripura. He noted that levels of corruption have come down in NREGS over the years, thanks to payment mechanisms promoting transparency and greater efficiency in getting the transfers to reach beneficiaries. The Ministry of Rural Development was working with the Department of Financial Services to help deal with these last mile problems.

He noted that self-help groups (SHGs) were vital to success because they led to community ownership and greater accountability, as the example of AP again showed. Women SHGs have been particularly important here. Even Bihar, with not a great record of NREGS implementation, had one of the most vibrant SHGs in its *Jeevika* program. Corruption levels have come down wherever the *Jeevika* SHGs ran the PDS. Thus, MGNREGA has to be seen in the larger framework of the political economy rather than as a standalone program. This is also important from the perspective of the Act's emphasis on livelihood security that can only come from integration with SHGs and with individual beneficiary schemes. It is not the case that all poor households are landless, but assets are required to increase the productivity of the land for a safe one crop, or for multiple crops, or to promote animal husbandry, poultry, and horticulture, among other things.

Sinha agreed that the Act may need changes, especially in the context of its stipulation that work has to be provided wherever it is demanded. That meant that while we may use poverty criteria for allocation of resources to states, those can't be formally promulgated because they would not align with the Act. The labor budget, while it is provided, is a completely tentative figure because if the state ends up using or providing more work, money has to be made available for it according to the Act. There are thus issues with the Act about the allocation of resources to states that need to be resolved. He also touched upon the legal stipulation of maintaining a 60:40 wage and materials ratio under NREGA, and said that the Government was tweaking this rule where possible to augment employment opportunities and improvements in the assets created under NREGS at the Gram Panchayat level.

Sinha noted that in the lean season there clearly are states where there is an element of rationing due to the gap between demand and supply. For instance, a recent, national level study found that even the articulation of the demand for work under NREGS could be conveyed to people responsible for initiating employment works in only 45 percent of designated villages. He suggested that the paper should carefully look at the feminization of labor in NREGS, particularly in states like Tamil Nadu. On wage rates, he mentioned that NREGS exhibits a mixed picture, with 17 states with a minimum wage for agricultural laborers higher than the NREGA wage, and 17 other states and UTs with minimum wages lower than the NREGS wage.

Other measures that should have a positive impact for the beneficiaries of NREGS include universalization of *Aadhaar*-linked bank accounts for payments, geotagging of all assets, periodic outcome-based performance assessments, and the promotion of more independent research studies, all of which should enable the program to improve.

Sinha concluded his comments by noting that NREGS also needs to embrace a skilled workforce since India cannot continue to nurture a pool of 50 million rural households engaging only in unskilled wage labor. He mentioned that the Government had introduced the Livelihood in Full Employment (LIFE) program in 2015 catering to NREGS workers who had done 100 days of work and could then acquire skills for wage employment, self-employment, or livelihood augmentation.

References

Imbert, Clement and John Papp. 2015. "Labor Market Effects of Social Programs: Evidence from India's Employment Guarantee," *American Economic Journal: Applied Economics*, 7(2): 233–263.

Muralidharan, Karthik, Paul Niehaus, and Sandip Sukhtankar. 2016a. "Building State Capacity: Evidence from Biometric Smartcards in India," *American Economic Review*, 106(10): 2895–2929.

———. 2016b. "General Equilibrium Effects of (Improving) Public Employment Programs: Experimental Evidence from India," *Working Paper*, San Diego: University of California, http://econweb.ucsd.edu/~pniehaus/papers/GE.pdf (accessed May 1, 2017).